# Step Out on Nothing

# Step Out on Nothing

## How Faith and Family Helped Me Conquer Life's Challenges

BYRON PITTS

ST. MARTIN'S PRESS NEW YORK

 Printed in the United States of America. For information, address St. Martin's Press, 175 Fifth Avenue, New York, N.Y. 10010.



www.stmartins.com

Book design by Phil Mazzone

Library of Congress Cataloging-in-Publication Data

Pitts, Byron.
Step out on nothing : how faith and family helped me conquer life's challenges / Byron Pitts.—1st ed.
p. cm.
ISBN 978-0-312-57766-7
1. Pitts, Byron. 2. Baptists—United States—Biography. 3. Television journalists—United States—Biography. I. Title.
BX6455.P38A3 2009
277.3'082092—dc22
[B]

2009019891

First Edition: October 2009

10 9 8 7 6 5 4 3 2 1

This is a true story, though a few names
and details have been changed.

*To my mother, Clarice Pitts;*
*my sister, Saundra Judd;*
*and my brother, William M. Pitts.*
*God's brought us a mighty long way.*

# Contents

# Step Out on Nothing

# Introduction

New York City

"In five, four, three, two . . ." This wasn't the first time a floor director had ever counted me down, but it was the first time I ever choked back tears. It was August 25, 2006, my first on-camera studio open for the CBS News broadcast *60 Minutes*. Moments earlier I'd been in makeup with famed artist Riccie Johnson. She'd done up the likes of Mike Wallace, Harry Reasoner, Morley Safer, Dan Rather, Ed Bradley, Lesley Stahl, Steve Kroft, and every other big-name correspondent who ever worked for *60 Minutes*. And the Beatles. And now she was putting powder on *me*.

Executive Producer Jeff Fager poked his head in the dressing room, "Good luck, Brotha! You've come a long way to get here. You've earned it." I think Jeff was talking about my ten years of covering hurricanes, tornadoes, politics, the September 11 disaster, wars in Afghanistan and Iraq, and every other sort of story for *CBS News* during those years.

If he only knew. My mind flashed back to elementary school, when a therapist had informed my mother, "I'm sorry, Mrs. Pitts, your son is functionally illiterate. He cannot read."

Months earlier, another so-called expert had suggested I was mentally retarded. Perhaps there was a "special needs" program right for me. Here I was some three decades later sitting in the "special" chair of the most revered show in the history of broadcast news. Musicians dream of playing Carnegie Hall, astronauts work a lifetime to take their first mission in space, and every broadcast journalist worth his or her salt dreams of *60 Minutes*.

Engineers generally keep television studios icy cold to prevent the equipment from overheating. The *60 Minutes* studio is no different. But in this age of high-tech sets with massive video walls and graphic trickery, Studio 33, where *60 Minutes* is taped, looks more like a throwback. You can almost smell the cigar smoke from decades past. Black-covered walls. Bright lights hanging from the ceiling. There's one camera and one chair. As a correspondent, you sit in the chair, cross your legs, look into the camera, and tell a story.

"Take two. In three, two, one!"

Seven takes later I finally recorded one that everybody liked. It took a while—not so much to settle my nerves as to get everyone settled in that one chair. Sitting with me were my mother, Clarice Pitts; my grandmother, Roberta Mae Walden; my sister, Saundra; and my brother, Mac. We had made the journey as a family, with the help of a few friends and even a few strangers.

What an overwhelming feeling it was and the symbolism was not lost on me.

That afternoon, to all who could see, I was seated alone. But I knew better. Some thirty-seven years before I would ever hear the phrase "Step Out on Nothing," God was writing those words to cover my life. How many times has each of us been in a difficult place and thought we were alone? Standing on nothing. Perhaps it is only in the empty space of those moments we can truly feel God's breath at our necks. His hands beneath our feet. Step out on nothing? Yes. Step out on faith.

So where did I get the title for this book? *Step Out on Nothing*. What does it mean and how does it fit into my life? Most important, how do you find the courage to try it?

I first heard those fateful words on a Sunday in March of 2007, Women's Day at St. Paul Baptist Church in Montclair, New Jersey. My wife was excited. She'd helped with the weekend program. Me, not so much. As usual I was running late for service and she was getting annoyed. We arrived at church in time. The place was packed. Women all dressed in white and black. The guest preacher that morning was Reverend Benita Lewis. She began her sermon by talking about the pain women will endure to be beautiful. She talked about pedicures, high-heeled shoes, and women's sore feet. I thought to myself, *This is going to be a long service*. Nothing here for me. And it got worse. She moved from pedicures to massages and spa treatments. Body wraps to skin treatments. At that point I was drifting away. It felt as if we'd been in church for hours. But Reverend Lewis was just warming up, and I soon discovered that she wasn't speaking only to the women in the congregation. She was telling all of us about overcoming pain and obstacles in our paths. She was talking about a belief in God, a faith so strong that anything is possible. Then Reverend Lewis uttered four words that took my breath away. "Step out on nothing." She encouraged the congregation to "step out on faith" in this journey we call life. To put your life and its challenges in God's hands. To believe in a power greater than yourself.

Step out . . . on nothing . . .

In the time it takes to say those four words, a lifetime flashed before me. She was speaking about my life. How had I overcome my childhood inability to read when I was nearly a teenager? It was my mother stepping out on nothing, despite the doubts she must have had during the nights around the kitchen table when I "just wasn't getting it."

And how do you explain an inner-city kid who stuttered until he was twenty years old becoming a network television news correspondent? Let's start with a college professor who didn't even know my name. She stepped out on nothing and believed in a young man who didn't believe in himself.

Then there's Peter Holthe: a stranger. A college classmate from Minnetonka, Minnesota. "Why's your vocabulary so limited?" he asked. He stayed around to find out why and helped expand it.

Those Franciscan Friars at Archbishop Curley High School in Baltimore, Maryland, who heard I was in a gospel choir at a church across town. These were white men who'd never ventured into a black neighborhood or set foot in a Baptist church. They too stepped out on nothing, figuring that being supportive of one of their students after hours might actually make a difference in his life.

We all have those defining moments in our lives. Moments of great joy. Moments of unspeakable sadness and fear. We usually think we're alone. But if we look into the corners of our memories, we'll find them—those people who had faith in us. Those times when a grace beyond earthly understanding touches us.

This is a story of those times. Those people. And the lessons they taught me. We've all had such people in our lives. If not, it's time to find them.

And for me, this story is my "step out on nothing," revealing a childhood shame that I've hidden from all but those who are closest to me, in hopes that my leap of faith will inspire some young child, or even an adult, who is living with a secret. It took me years to discover my shame was actually a source of strength.

ONE

# Mustard Seed Faith—With It You Can Move Mountains

Because you have so little faith, I tell you the truth, if you have faith as small as a mustard seed, you can say to this mountain, "Move from here to there," and it will move. Nothing will be impossible for you.

—Matthew 17:20

## 1969 Baltimore

At age nine I was a fourth-grader in a Catholic school, and the only whore I had ever heard of was the lady in the Bible. That was until one day when, dressed in my school uniform of blue pants, white shirt, and gray and blue striped tie, my mom picked me up and we set out on one of the defining adventures of my young life.

"Get in the car! We're going to that whore's house!"

It couldn't have been more than a ten-minute ride. My mother, who loves to talk, never said a word. We drove up on a busy street lined with row houses, each tipped with Baltimore's famed three-marble steps. I've never considered my mom an athlete, but that day she pushed at the driver's side door like a sprinter leaping off the starting block and quickly made her way to a house with a narrow door and a small diamond-shaped window. She rang the doorbell several times. A pretty woman with long curly brown hair finally answered the door. I was struck by how much she resembled my mother.

"Tell my husband to come out here," my mother yelled.

The woman answered, "I don't know what you're talking about" and slammed the door.

I could see the rage building in my mother's fists and across her face. She backed off the steps and screamed toward a window on the second floor,

"William Pitts! You son of a bitch! Bring your ass outside right now!"

There was dead silence. So she said it again. Louder. If no one inside that house could hear her, the neighbors did. People on the street stopped moving; others started coming out of their homes. My mom had an audience. I stood near the car, paralyzed by shame. Figuring it was her message and not her volume, my mother came up with a new line.

"William Pitts! You son of a bitch! You come outside right now or I will set your car on fire!"

He apparently heard her that time. Much to my surprise, my father, dressed only in his pants and undershirt, dashed out of that house as my mother made her way to his car. She ordered me to move away from her car and get into my father's car. I did. My father was barefoot, and he slipped as he approached my mother. She picked up a brick and took dead aim at my father's head. She missed. He ran to the other side of his car. She retrieved the brick and tried again. She missed. He ran. My parents repeated their version of domestic dodge ball at least a half dozen times. It must have seemed like a game to the gallery of people who watched and laughed. I never said a word. In the front passenger seat of my father's car, I kept my eyes straight ahead. I didn't want to watch, though I couldn't help but hear. My parents were fighting again, and this time in public.

Eventually, my father saw an opening and jumped into the driver's seat of his car. Fumbling for his keys, he failed to close the door. My mother jumped on top of him. Cursing and scratching at his eyes and face, she seemed determined to kill him. I could see her fingers inside his mouth. Somehow my father's head ended up in my lap. The scratches on his face began to bleed onto my white shirt. For the first time since my mother picked me up from school, I spoke. Terrified, I actually screamed.

"Why! What did I do? Wha-wa-wa-wa-wut!"

I'm sure I had more to say, but I got stuck on the word *what*. Almost from the time I could speak, I stuttered. It seemed to get worse when I was frightened or nervous. Sitting in my dad's car with my parents' weight and their problems pressed against me, I stuttered and cried. It seemed odd to me at that moment, but as quickly and violently as my parents began fighting, they stopped. I guess it was my mother who first noticed the blood splattered across my face and soaked through my shirt. She thought I was bleeding. In that instant, the temperature cooled in the car. It had been so hot. My parents' body heat had caused the three of us to sweat. Fearing they had injured me, my parents tried to console me. But once they stopped fighting, I did what I always seemed to do. I put on my mask. I closed my mouth and pretended everything was all right.

I was used to this—there had been a lot of secrets in our house. My father had been hiding his infidelity. Both parents were putting a good face on marital strife for their family and friends. You see, almost from the time Clarice and William Pitts met, he was unfaithful. Women on our street, in church, those he'd meet driving a cab, and the woman who would eventually bear him a child out of wedlock. I have only known her as Miss Donna. Clarice may have despised the woman, but if ever her name came up in front of the children, she was Miss Donna. The car ride was a tortured awakening for me, but it was just the beginning. The picture our family showed the outside world was beginning to unravel, and when all our secrets began to spill into the open, on the street, in the classroom, and in our church, none of our lives would ever be the same.

My mother was accustomed to hard times. Clarice Pitts was a handsome woman, with thick strong hands, a square jaw, cold gray eyes, and a love for her children bordering on obsession. Her philosophy was always: "If you work hard and pray hard and treat people right, good things will happen." That was her philosophy. Unfortunately, that was not her life.

Clarice was the second of seven children born in a shotgun house in the segregated South of Apex, North Carolina, on January 1, 1934. By mistake, the doctor wrote Clarence Walden on her birth certificate, and until the age of twelve, when she went for her Social Security card, the world thought my mother was a man. Truth be told, for three-quarters of a century, she's been tougher than most men you'd meet. Her father, Luther Walden, was by all accounts a good provider and a bad drinker. He'd work the farm weekdays, work the bottle weekends. Her mother, Roberta Mae, was both sweet and strong. Friends nicknamed her Señorita because she was always the life of the party, even after back-breaking work. All the kids adored their mother and feared their father. On more than a few occasions, after he'd been drinking all day, her father would beat his wife and chase the children into the woods.

At sixteen, Clarice thought marriage would be better than living at home, where she was afraid to go to sleep at night when her father had been drinking. So she married a man nearly twice her age (he was twenty-nine), and they had one child, my sister, Saundra Jeannette Austin. People thought that since Clarice married a man so much older she would have a ton of babies. But she was never one to conform to others' expectations. She promised herself never to have more children than she could care for, or a husband that she couldn't tolerate. He never raised his hand to her. He did, however, have a habit of raising a liquor bottle to his mouth. She divorced him three years later, and by the mid-1950s she and my sister had started a new life in Baltimore, Maryland, which held the promise of a better education and a better job than was available to her in the South.

She finally thought life had given her a break when she met William Archie Pitts. They met in night school. "He was a real flirt, but smart," she said. In 1958 William A. Pitts could have been Nat King Cole's taller younger brother. He was jet black with broad shoulders; his uniform of choice a dark suit, dark tie, crisp white shirt, a white cotton pocket-square, and polished shoes. He dressed like a preacher, spoke like a hustler, and worked as a butcher. Clarice looked good on his arm and liked being there even more. He was ebony. She was ivory, or as Southerners said back then, she was "high yellow." My father had been married once before as well. His first wife died in childbirth, and he was raising their son on his own.

After a whirlwind romance of steamed crabs on paper tablecloths and dances at the local Mason lodge, the two married. A short time later, I was born on October 21, 1960. There was no great family heritage or biblical attachment associated with my name. They chose my name out of a baby book. My mother simply liked the sound of it. One of the few indulgences of her life in the early 1960s was dressing her baby boy like John F. Kennedy Jr. She kept me in short pants as long as she could. She finally relented when I started high school. Just kidding. But to me it certainly felt as if she held on until the last possible moment.

Life held great promise for William and Clarice Pitts in the 1960s. The year after I was born, Clarice finished high school and later graduated college the year before my sister earned her first of several degrees. She worked in a few different sewing factories in Baltimore. She took on side jobs making hats for women at church and around the city. Both of my parents believed God had given them a second chance. Almost instantly William and Clarice Pitts had a family: two boys and a daughter. My parents bought their first and only home together at 2702 East Federal Street.

Outsiders knew my hometown as just Baltimore, but if you grew up there, there were actually two Baltimores; East Baltimore and West Baltimore. And the side of the city you lived on said as much about you as your last name or your parents' income. East Baltimore was predominantly blue collar, made up mostly of cement, ethnic neighborhoods, and tough-minded people. Most people I knew worked with their hands and worked hard for their money. You loved family, your faith, the Colts, and the Orioles. In 1969 my world centered on the 2700 block of East Federal Street. Ten blocks of red brick row houses, trimmed with aluminum siding. Decent people kept their furniture covered in plastic. Each house had a patch of grass out front. To call it a lawn would be too generous. The yards on East Federal were narrow and long, like the hood of the Buick Electric 225 my father drove. Those in the know called that model car a Deuce and a Quarter. Ours was a neighborhood on the shy side of working class. Like I said, my father was a meat cutter at the local meat plant. My mother was a seamstress at the London Fog coat factory. My sister was about to graduate from high school. Big hair. Bigger personality. I idolized her. My brother was sixteen. We had the typical big brother–little brother relationship: we hated each other. Born William MacLauren, we've always called him Mac as in MacLauren, but it could have stood for Mack truck. Not surprisingly, he grew up and became a truck driver. Even as a boy, he was built like a man, stronger than most, with a quiet demeanor that shouted "Fool with me at your own risk." He and Clarice Pitts were not blood relatives; however, they'd always shared a fighter's heart and a silent understanding that the world had somehow abandoned them. They would always have each other.

My nickname in the neighborhood was Pickle. I despised that name, but it seemed to fit. You know the big kid in the neighborhood? That wasn't me. I was thin as a coatrack, my head shaped like a rump roast covered in freckles. We were a Pepsi family, but my glasses resembled Coke bottles. I was shy out of necessity. But whatever my life lacked in 1969, football filled the void. I loved Johnny Unitas, John Mackey, and the Baltimore Colts. I never actually went to a game. I guess we couldn't afford it. But no kid in the stands ever adored that team more than I did.

On Federal Street, the Pitts kids had a reputation: God-fearing, hard-working, and polite. Next to perhaps breathing, few things have meant more to my mother than good manners. She'd often remark, when I was very young, and with great conviction and innocence, "If you never learn to read and write, you *will* be polite and work hard." Most days, that was enough. Back in North Carolina, the only reading materials around my grandmother's home were the Bible and *Ebony* magazine. My parents did one better with the Bible, *Ebony*, and *Jet*. My father read the newspaper. My mother had her schoolbooks, but reading and pleasure rarely shared the same space in our house. Neither one of my parents ever read to me, as best I can recall. We had a roof over our heads, food on the table, and church every Sunday. When my mother compared our lives to her childhood—in which she and some of her siblings actually slept in the woods on more than a few nights, terrified that their father would come home in a drunken rage and beat them—she felt that her children had it good.

Around the house, my mother was the enforcer, dishing out the discipline in our family. My father was the fun-loving life of the party and primary breadwinner. As long as I can remember, relatives from across the country (mostly the South) would call our home, seeking my mother's counsel. When there was trouble, people called Clarice. My dad loved cooking, telling stories, and occasionally, if encouraged, he would sing songs. The same relatives who often called my mom for advice would flock to our house annually to enjoy those times when my dad would cook their favorite foods, retell their favorite stories, and pour their favorite drinks. At some point in the evening, my mother would end up in my dad's lap, and neighbors could hear the laughter from our home pouring out onto the sidewalk. Those were the good days.

For better or worse, there was structure or, at the very least, a routine in the first years of my life. My mother made my brother and me get haircuts every Saturday. We enjoyed one style: The number one. The skinny. And my mother's favorite, "Cut it close." Food was part of the ritual too. We'd have pot roast for Sunday dinner. Leftovers on Monday, fried chicken on Tuesday, pork chops Wednesday, liver on Thursday (I hated liver, so I got salisbury steak), fish sticks on Friday, and "Go for yourself" on Saturday. But mealtime was often the flashpoint for the anger and bitterness that began to consume my parents' marriage. Their fight scene on the street was a rarity, but Fight Night at the Dinner Table, as the kids called it, was a regular feature. Meals always started with a prayer, "Heavenly Father, thank you for the food we're about to receive . . . ," and often ended early.

The fight usually started with very little warning, either my mother's sudden silence or my father's sarcasm. One night we were having fried pork chops (so it had to have been a

Wednesday). Pork chops were my favorite, with mashed potatoes and cabbage on the side, and blue Kool-Aid (that's grape to the uninitiated). The sounds of silverware against plates and light conversation filled the air. Then came the look. We all caught it at different times. My mother was staring a hole through my father's head. It sounded like she dropped her fork from the ceiling, but it actually fell no more than three inches from her hand to her plate. My dad gave his usual response soaked in innocence: "What?"

He didn't realize my mother had been listening on the phone in our kitchen when he had called Miss Donna from an upstairs phone to see how their son, Myron, was doing. Yes, I said their *son*. I think my mother was actually willing to forgive his child by another woman several years after my birth. But his name being so close to mine (Byron/Myron) was what seemed to break her heart and sometimes her spirit. At this point during dinner, however, she wasn't just broken—she was angry. First went her plate. Aimed at his head. And then her coffee cup. Then my plate. Followed rapid-fire by Mac's and Saundra's dinner plates.

"Calm down, Momma!" Saundra, the ring announcer, screamed.

Mac, always the referee, stood up to make sure no one went for a knife or scissors. Me? I just sat there. You ever notice at a prizefight, the people with the best seats don't move a lot? They're spellbound by the action in the ring. That was me at the kitchen table: left side, center seat between my parents, my brother and sister on the other side. That night my mother was determined, if not accurate. Four feet away, four tries, but my mother never hit my father once. Granted he was bobbing and weaving the whole time, like Cassius Clay dodging a Sonny Liston jab. As my father dodged plates and coffee cups, he would call my mother Sweetie. Her name of choice for him was Son of a Bitch. Except for a few potatoes in his hair, he got away without a scratch. The plates and the wallpaper didn't fare as well. With coffee-stained walls and cabinets full of chipped plates and broken utensils, I presumed every family had some variation on the same theme. And as quickly as it started, the fight was over. My father backpedaled to another room. My mother retreated to the comfort of her sewing machine. I cleared the table. My sister washed dishes. My brother dried them. We finished our homework. I was in bed by 8:30 P.M.

For all their bickering, Clarice and William Pitts always worked hard. They always believed in the power of prayer, the goodness of God's grace, and the importance of faith. That partially explains why my mother stayed married as long as she did. For as long as I can remember, she's worn a tiny mustard seed encased in a small plastic ball on a chain around her neck. The story of the mustard seed in the Bible has always given her great comfort.

> Matthew 17:20: "Because you have so little faith, I tell you the truth, if you have faith as small as a mustard seed, you can say to this mountain, 'Move from here to there,' and it will move. Nothing will be impossible for you."

It's a belief that anything's possible if one's willing to work hard enough, if one's faith runs deep enough. I think she still believed in her marriage long after it was over. Her first answer to every difficult situation was always the same: "Did you pray yet?" In the midst of any crisis, whether at the beginning, the middle, or the end, my mother always turned to prayer. That night—after my parents fought on the street and my father bled inside his car on my lap, outside his girlfriend's house, where strangers looked on and laughed, in a neighborhood I'd never seen before but have never forgotten—my mother drove me home and we prayed.

We never said a word in the car on the way home. My mother had climbed off my father, held my hand, and scooted me into her car first. We went home in silence. I ate dinner in those same bloody clothes. I washed my hands but not my face. No one seemed to notice. The tension that evening had exhausted everyone. We all headed for bed early.

"Go take off those clothes and leave them outside your door," my mother told me. "Call me when you've got your pajamas on."

I did. I could hear her walking up the stairs. Slow and deliberate, as if she was carrying a heavy load. Earlier, back in my father's car, when I glanced into my mother's gray eyes, they were narrow and mean. Now at home, in my room, her eyes were soft around the edges and sad. My mother was not the crying type. She wasn't crying then. But she was sad. I could see it in the slump of her shoulders. It was written across her face.

"You okay?" she asked me. Her tone now was 180 degrees lighter than a few hours ago, when she had picked me up from school.

"What happened between me and your father had nothing to do with you," she said. "I wish we could wash away memories as easily as we can wash clothes," she added. Then she took my hands, closed her eyes, and touched her head to mine and started to pray. It's the way I've prayed ever since.

"Dear wise and almighty God, we come to you as humbly as we know how, just to say thank you, Lord. Thank you for blessings seen and unseen. Thank you, Lord, for our family, our friends, and even our enemies. Thank you, Lord, for the bad days, for they help us to better appreciate the good ones. Please, Lord, mend us where we are broken. Make us strong where we are weak. Give us, Lord, the faith to believe our tomorrow will be brighter than our yesterday. Hold us, Lord. Keep us in the palms of Your hands. Give us faith to keep holding on. These and all other blessings we ask in Jesus' name. Amen."

I opened my eyes to her familiar smile. We're not a teeth-smiling family—more grinners. But her grin promised better days were ahead. She hugged me. Tucked me in. Said good night. I remember expecting an apology before she left the room. After the day I'd had? Please! But *sorry* is not a word my mother used very often. The suggestion was, *sorry* indicated regret. With faith, why have regrets? Everything happens for a reason, for the good. Perhaps understanding would come by and by. As I listened to my mother's footsteps beyond my door, I suddenly felt a peace. The clanking of our old electric fan in the window even had a pleasant melody to it. On the surface, not a damn thing good had happened to me that day. But at that moment, after my mother's prayers, all I could think about was rejoicing in the notion that I was now on the other side of a difficult moment.

TWO

# Keep Your Head Up

No good *thing* will be withheld from them that walk uprightly.

—**Psalm 84:11**

KEEP YOUR HEAD UP no matter what. I heard that line so often as a child that I still hear it in my sleep. I've repeated it to colleagues, new acquaintances, even strangers. It was one of my mother's favorite expressions. It was a saying to motivate if needed and redirect if necessary. Keep your head up was never meant as a statement of false pride or arrogance. It was always one of Clarice's go-to phrases in difficult moments, meant to reverse whatever circumstance was pulling us down.

But honestly it was hard for me to keep my head up with so much weighing me down. While I was loved and spoiled, like the youngest child in many families, all that attention could not smooth over the deep flaws that I was hiding. Only my closest relatives, a few friends, and a teacher or two even knew I stuttered. But the big secret: *I couldn't read.* That was top secret. I was a phony, faking it, mouthing words in books that I did not really understand. Hiding my secret from my teachers and my parents. One of my favorite songs of the late 1960s was "Secret Agent Man." That was me carrying what seemed to me one of the great secrets in the world. I could not read, yet no one seemed to notice. It was a distressful combination for a boy who had big dreams. Illiterate *and* barely able to speak. I could read my name and a few simple words that I saw every day. It wasn't much, but for the time being it was enough. I was also unfailingly polite. In public school simply being polite all but guaranteed at least a passing grade in most classes. I was quiet and a good athlete. (I was never first pick as a class project partner, but if it was stick ball, football, or tag, Byron Pitts was a first-round draft pick.) All reasons enough for most teachers to leave me alone and for my peers to give me space. Most of my classes at Fort Worthington Elementary School, known simply as P.S. 85, were overcrowded. It's the same school my brother attended, and so in part I lived off his reputation. My brother was quiet, hard-working, and an average student. My mother was an active participant in parent activities. I was in a sense a legacy student, surviving at P.S. 85 on the family name. It was assumed I was learning, just as Mac had. For a quiet child falling further and further behind, it was a good place to not get noticed.

But I was performing well below average. In first and second grades, there was not a single A or B on my report card. My highest marks were always in behavior. My mother finally decided that the public school system was getting too big and impersonal for me. Because the discipline and attention offered in a parochial school was much more appealing to her, in September of 1968, for the third grade, she moved me to a Catholic school called St. Katharine's.

It didn't matter where I went, school was work, difficult work. And so, walking into St. Katharine's every morning felt like a job I wasn't good at and didn't enjoy. The school was a nondescript three-story cement building surrounded by a cast-iron fence on what appeared to be more like an alley than a street. There were row houses on three sides of the St. Katharine's Church building, which was later converted into a Baptist church, as the neighborhood continued to change. Most of the teachers were nuns. They treated me well. The strict discipline only seemed like an extension of Clarice's rules. It was actually comforting being in a school where nearly everyone was afraid of breaking the rules. There were never any more than twelve to fifteen kids in a class. Hardwood floors were polished to such a high sheen that you could see a reflection. The place had a clean, antiseptic smell. Giant windows were perfect for daydreaming about matters other than school. The boys wore uniform shirts, pants, and ties. The girls wore blue, gray, and white checked dresses. There was great emphasis on prayer and discipline. Reading, writing, and arithmetic seemed like second-tier priorities. Most of my classmates came from working-class homes, and many were raised by single parents. Despite our age, most of us seemed well aware that someone was sacrificing to send us to Catholic school. As usual, I became one of the less visible boys in class.

My third-grade teacher was Sister Clarice. I admit, I had a crush on her. She was the prettiest nun in our school. But that was just about the highlight of my school experience. In this new environment, being polite was no longer enough to get by. I could not read and understand sentences. Even simple ones. And the more difficult the work, the less I tried, the more easily I was distracted. We were required to read aloud at least once a week, and it was torture. Between the stammering and stuttering and mispronounced words, I was hard-pressed to do anything but hang my head in shame.

The only relief I had was that I was bright enough to memorize just about anything read to me. At night during homework time I would torture my family into helping me. A few tears every now and then would seal it. Since my sister was soon to be away at college, these after-dinner study sessions usually fell to my brother. Though our family lived in a three-bedroom home with a living room, dining room, kitchen, and almost-finished basement, we spent most of our time in the kitchen. That's where homework was done. (Perhaps that is why, to this day, I do my best thinking near food.) And it was one of the early front lines in my secret battle to hide my reading problems.

The two of us at the dinner table built for six. We'd sit across from each other. Table covered with our books, two glasses of milk, buttered toast or peanut butter sandwiches. Why buttered toast as an after-dinner homework snack? I have no clue, but it was what it was.

"Mac, help me please. Pretty please," I'd beg.

I was never sure if it was because my brother loved me so much, hated my whining more, or simply feared my mother's reaction if he didn't help, but whatever his motivation he'd suffer patiently.

"Okay! I'll read it to you one more time. Pay attention," he said, frustration wrinkling his forehead. Our study sessions could go on for three hours. Arithmetic, reading, spelling, history—it didn't matter the subject. Before the night was over, my brother would end up finishing my assignment and I'd have sections memorized for class.

In school the next day, when it came time to read aloud, I would have my section memorized. Sister Clarice took great pride in student involvement.

"Today we'll read chapter three."

Hands would shoot up. The smartest student would always go first. That was usually Pauline Tobias. I may have had a crush on her, too, but I know I always marveled at how she could read anything and seemed to know everything. She could read like a church elder. I'd wait around for the hands to thin out. Wait for the reading to get closer to the paragraph I'd memorized.

"Sister, sister, please, please call me," I'd plead. It usually worked. Passage read. My mind was now free to wander. There would be a price to pay later, of course, but why suffer today what could be put off until tomorrow. As long as no one found out, I thought I was safe. At the time the word *illiterate* wasn't known to me. I thought I was just stupid. Who could I tell? I adored my mother but couldn't disappoint her. My siblings already thought I was both spoiled and a geek. Better to find new ways to hide.

I felt out of place almost everywhere except in church. Church had always been my sanctuary, a place to escape the tension between my parents and forget about my own shortcomings. Through some combination of good fortune and

God's grace, I grew up in one of Baltimore's grand chapels. It was affectionately known on the black preacher circuit as the big house.

"We're marching to Zion! Beautiful, beautiful Zion! We're marching upward to Zion, the beautiful city of God!" That was the song that opened every Sunday service at New Shiloh Baptist Church. The old gothic building was originally built as a Lutheran church. In the age before mega-churches, New Shiloh was considered a big church in Baltimore. About a thousand people showed up for two Sunday morning services. A massive stained-glass window framed the pulpit. Scriptures etched in the high ceilings. And long wooden pews laced with soft cushions stood like soldiers in three rows, at least thirty rows deep. In the Baltimore of my childhood there were just a few certainties in every black neighborhood: a black-owned barbershop, beauty parlor, liquor store, funeral home, and the church.

For most of my childhood and adolescence, New Shiloh Baptist Church was the most sacred place on earth to me. I felt safe. I felt loved. I would have slept there if my mother had allowed it. No matter what had occurred in the days prior in the outside world, the songs, the prayers, the sermon, even the smell of the place, seemed to heal all that ailed me. The music spoke to me: "I'm sometimes up! I'm sometimes down! Almost leveled to the ground, but I'll keep on holding on!" Lots of people go to the beach for joy and peace, having the ocean waves wash over their toes and bodies. Who needed the sounds of the Pacific or the Atlantic? I had the New Shiloh Baptist Church mass choir and young adult choir twice on most Sundays.

My mom called church the poor man's therapy session. Ninety minutes of music and song and prayer and a sermon that sent you on your way encouraged and hopeful. There's no co-pay, just the offering plate. My childhood pastor once described church to me this way: "A warm spiritual bath."

New Shiloh was just one of a large number of churches sprinkled across the country with a reputation for drawing grand orators. Preaching at Shiloh was like playing at Carnegie Hall. Through the years, the voices of Reverends Martin Luther King Sr., Ralph Abernathy, and Andrew Young echoed in the sanctuary. The pastor, Reverend Harold A. Carter, a former associate minister to Martin Luther King Jr. in Alabama, was a preacher's preacher. He could hoot with the best of them. Sweat profusely on the coldest days. Draw out the name Jesus the length of the Great Wall of China. I could listen to that man read the words on a can of paint. Churches like New Shiloh have always taken great pride in honoring the oral history of the black church. There's great emphasis given to the spoken word. All my life I've known people who could quote the Bible but couldn't read it. Even in choir rehearsal, we learned most songs from a cassette recorder or at the director's instruction. "You can't learn the song by staring at paper," a choir director once told me. Amid all that joyous noise, it was seemingly a perfect hiding place for a poor reader.

Since no one in my family yet understood my inability to read, it didn't strike anyone as odd or alarming that I would volunteer to work for the radio ministry at church. Every Sunday night listeners could hear Reverend Dr. Harold A. Carter deliver one of his best Bible-thumping, scream-the-Scriptures, make-the-faithful-stand-up-and-shout kind of sermons. There was a small army of volunteers who served as engineers. During the morning service, one person a week would sit at the foot of the pulpit, a big bulky headset covering his ears and a reel-to-reel recorder the size of a suitcase at his fingertips, with several microphones strategically set up around the church. I wanted desperately to try; finally someone picked me. How hard could it be? I would soon find out.

After several weeks of training, I was set to record my first live Sunday morning service. The chief engineer promised he would be with me. That morning the phone rang. "Hey, Byron, I won't make it to church today. But you can do it. All the equipment's labeled. The instructions are all written out for you." A fire alarm should have gone off in my head. It didn't. I went to church figuring I'd memorized enough to get by.

The service was rocking. The spirit was high, and the choir sounded like angels from heaven. By accident I hit STOP on the recorder. The tape stopped. I panicked. I wasn't trained to cue up the tape and record again. Now sweating like the preacher winding down his sermon, I looked at the manual for direction. It might as well have been written in Braille. I couldn't read it. I couldn't fix the problem. And soon everyone would know I was stupid. For the remainder of the service I buried my head in my hands. Most people assumed I was praying. I wished I was dead. For the first time in my life, reading really meant something. And suddenly my safe place in church was no longer so safe.

That night my family gathered around the radio to listen to the service, but rather than Reverend Carter's rousing sermon from that morning, the city got to hear one of Reverend Carter's oldies-but-goodies. "What happened to today's service?" my mother asked. "Must have been technical difficulty," I replied, with my chin buried in my chest.

"Hold your head up. I'm sure it'll be perfect next time," was my mother's response. There would be no next time. I was never asked to record the service again, even though in my aching heart I believed I could have gotten it right. And I've never entered New Shiloh since without feeling the sting of that day. My family assumed I got nervous or lost interest. I knew better.

It was at about this age that I developed a reputation for being quiet and sensitive. I would go almost an entire weekend without speaking. Easier still, I could avoid stuttering. Little did I know then that a lot of children struggle with stuttering when they're first learning to speak. But from my childish perspective, I was simply a freak: The strange one, the one who couldn't get the words out, couldn't do a simple thing like speak clearly. For me, it was like living as a prisoner inside a cell. Oh, the things my heart wanted to say, the times I wanted to yell at my parents to stop fighting, stand up to a bully who taunted me, and the times I just wanted lemonade in the school cafeteria but could only say the word *soda*. I've never liked soda. Would never drink it if I had the choice. We stutterers often think we have few choices in life, so during my silent weekends I'd play baseball or football all day Saturday with my friends. Funny thing: I've never stuttered, never felt out of place or insecure on any ball field. At the time *self-esteem* was a term with little meaning in the world of a child, but it's clear to me now I had very little self-esteem back then. That may explain why harsh words from a teacher would leave me in tears.

As frustrating as it was, my stuttering never kept me from singing. Like a lot of stutterers, my words flowed smoothly when accompanied by music. So I was excited to hear an announcement about a new community choir. Word went out at St. Katharine's elementary school that the archdiocese was putting together a mass choir for a highly publicized winter concert, and I wanted in. "Hey, Momma, can I join the Catholic chorus?" While school was rarely my favorite place, I loved to sing and loved being part of my church choir. I figured that enthusiasm would translate to this event. Since it was winter and I wasn't playing football, I knew I needed something to occupy my time and avoid schoolwork. Rehearsal was at St. Francis Catholic Church, a building just as old and just as breathtaking as my beloved New Shiloh. We rehearsed every Tuesday and Thursday night. Though I'd never become a radio engineer at church, I could stand in the back row of a choir and sing. That first rehearsal in the church basement was packed. Kids from at least a half dozen schools and several adults showed up. Many of them were really gifted singers.

I had wanted to participate because of my love for the New Shiloh Baptist Church choir. But the Catholic chorus was nothing like Shiloh. At Shiloh, rehearsal usually followed a routine: we would tell a few jokes, stand up and sing for about an hour, then pray and go home. Not the Catholic chorus. There were breathing exercises, stretching exercises, and vocal warmups. This wasn't choir rehearsal. This was boot camp.

At Shiloh, tenors stood in the back row. In this chorus, we were positioned by both size and section. God, why couldn't I be any taller? There I was, front row between a woman my grandmother's age and a teenage boy who sang like an angel and never once spoke to me. Maybe he knew I was stupid, not worthy of being acknowledged. And, oh yeah, we all had sheet music. This torture went on for weeks, and without a logical excuse it was too late to quit.

The choir director was a priest from Chicago who was as colorful as he was demanding.

"You can't sing pretty," the director announced. "Open your mouth wide! Enunciate! Sing UGLY, people! Articulate the words, people!"

I already thought I was odd and ugly without someone insisting I sing ugly. And to articulate words I could not read on paper was also a request beyond my abilities. Suddenly even one of my favorite activities, singing, was now threatened by demands I was unprepared to meet. My hiding places were disappearing. It was late February, the coldest days of winter, and my spirit was as chilled as the weather.

Despite the frigid temperature on the night of the performance, I couldn't stop sweating. And then there was the crowd. Not the familiar faces of my home church but hundreds of strangers. I just knew they were all looking and laughing at me. I was ten. I felt like one hundred.

"Good evening, ladies and gentlemen! Welcome," said the director.

Momma had bought me a new blue suit, white shirt, and brown shoes. Extra money spent, so this had to be a big occasion. My brother and I only got new suits for Easter. The shirt still had that new shirt stiffness. The shoes were still smooth at the bottom so I almost fell as we marched in. Each member of the chorus had a beautiful burgundy folder with our sheet music. It was useless to me. The church was full. People lined the walls. When the director cleared his throat, raised his hand, and cued the pianist, it was time. I was ready. Or so I thought. Through each anthem, hymn, and gospel tune, I mumbled or sang one word: *watermelon.* Whether we were singing at the top of our voices or in a whisper, slow cadence or at a deliberate pace, "watermelon, watermelon, watermelon" were the only lyrics to come out of my mouth, because someone in rehearsal had once told me, "If you're struggling with a song, just mouth the word *watermelon.*"

That's what I sang for two hours. No one seemed to notice my strange enunciation, except Momma. I caught a glimpse of those piercing gray eyes. There was both displeasure and curiosity in those eyes.

"What were you doing?" she asked on the ride home. "It didn't look like you knew a single song," she said with disappointment. Once again, my poor performance was dismissed as nerves. But steadily the world was closing in.

The tension level around the house over my academic performance was starting to rise. I was a D student, struggling in a remedial reading class. I would bring home progress reports from school, hand them to my mother, and listen as she read them aloud. Unlike many of my friends, I never tried to steam open the notes from school before my mother read them. Why bother? The notes never made much sense to me anyway. One week, the note home was followed up with a phone call from school.

"Byron's failing math." The Ds were turning into Fs.

My mother had long believed any of life's difficulties could be wrestled to the ground with prayer, faith, humility, hard work, and the more than occasional use of harsh words. So Mom tried that same remedy for bad grades: "Got dammit, boy, you can do this!" That soon progressed to punishment. No television. No going outside, and sometimes I wasn't even allowed to go to choir rehearsal. It didn't make a difference. My math scores stayed rock bottom. Discussions at school were now about keeping me behind a year. And the biggest sin in my house—I was becoming a discipline problem. I never talked back to an adult, but I began to mouth off plenty with classmates. You see, around the playground, the word *stupid* was starting to follow my first name. Being polite and quiet was no longer enough to get by.

"Let's get Byron tested."

Despite the distractions of her own life, my mother was now fully engaged in finding out why I was struggling so with math. Could the school measure my capacity to do math? The archdiocese finally arranged to have me tested. The test took place somewhere in downtown Baltimore. My parents led me to believe we were going to a school. So why did it look like a hospital?

"Momma, are we in the right place?" I asked.

"Yes, honey!" Her answer lacked conviction. She put her hand at the nape of my neck as we walked up the stairs. The scene inside was no more reassuring. There were no children walking the halls. No artwork on the walls. It even smelled like a hospital. That wretched clean smell. As we sat in the waiting area, my father read a newspaper. My mother and I played that child's hand game. She always let met win. My small hands resting on top of her thick strong hands, but I had speed on my side.

"You're too good," she'd taunt me. For a moment I forgot where we were.

"Pitts family," yelled a man wearing a sports coat. He had a kind face. He ushered me into a room.

"Here's a pencil. Please take your time and answer each question."

The room resembled the set from the television show *Romper Room*. Nothing about it felt natural. I was a kid. I knew my way around a classroom. This place was foreign.

"Please focus and take your time" one of many gentle reminders from the man with the kind face. He sat behind a plain wooden desk, flipping pages on a clipboard and tapping a pencil holder crammed with pencils. I was through the test in twenty minutes, but it felt like two days. Some answers I thought I knew. Others I was not certain of, and the vast majority I simply made up. I treated much of the test like an art project. Coloring in the answer boxes in order to form a pattern on the page, instead of actually seeking the right answer to the question. When the test was over, I was sent back to the waiting area. My mom and dad were brought into a private room. Their discussion with some other adult seemed to go on much longer than the actual test. My father walked out first. He looked ashen and embarrassed. My mother looked as if someone had just punched her in the stomach.

"Son, let's go home." That's all she said. "We have to come back tomorrow for more tests." There was no further discussion that night. Two days out of school? I knew that wasn't a good sign.

That next day more tests and more closed-door meetings with my parents. Eventually we were all in the same room. Mom, Dad, me, and a woman they repeatedly referred to as Doctor. She was pleasant and spoke slowly and deliberately with a foreign accent. She asked me a series of questions.

"Do you like school? . . . Do you have many friends? . . . Do you get along with the members of your family?"

What's any of this have to do with math? I wondered. Then, to my parents' amazement, the therapist took a tape measure out of her pocket, leaned toward me, and measured my head. She wrapped the tape around my head as if she were sizing me up for a ball cap. She even touched my head just like my mother would touch melons at the grocery store.

My father yelled, "What the hell are you doing?"

With a straight face, the therapist asked my parents if I'd ever been tested for mental illness. My mother burst into tears. It was the first time I had ever seen my mother cry or even appear vulnerable in public. Mental illness? Does that mean I'm crazy? I'd never felt sadder. Why can't I hide? Why won't Momma stop crying? Why does Daddy look so angry? My father challenged the doctor's competence. Momma grabbed my hand, as if the room was on fire, and whisked me away with my father still yelling at the doctor. My head was throbbing, not from pain but from confusion. Wasn't this just a math test? Someone had neglected to tell my parents I'd failed every test they'd given me.

But that was the case: I'd failed so dramatically that there was concern my problems might go beyond reading and comprehension to mental illness. My parents were told that the archdiocese was going to seek funding to continue having me tested. And that's what happened. Weeks later we were sent to yet another testing facility for another tiresome day-long session, this time with psychologists and psychiatrists. I was interviewed by myself, with my mother, and separately with my father; then they were interviewed together. I was asked to draw pictures of my family. I drew a picture of my father in a suit and a picture of my mother as a queen with a halo. My picture of Saundra was of a teenager on a swing, and I depicted my older brother as a small man with no hands. It was left to the psychiatrists to figure out what all of the drawings meant. But they did conclude that I was not mentally ill. In fact, I demonstrated above-average intelligence.

They could not, however, answer the fundamental question of why I could not read. Their conclusion in a report to my parents: bring him back when he's thirteen. My mother's reaction: "Damn doc, we can't wait that long. He'll either be dead or in jail."

My parents took me home with overwhelming sadness and frustration and no more answers than when we started the testing process. My mother soon asked for a meeting at St. Katharine's and asked the teaching staff for some direction. In response, a staff member came to our house, bringing more test results and finally put a label on my problem. The diagnosis would set my young life on a new course.

The St. Katharine's staff member and I, along with my parents, were all sitting in our living room. He asked to speak to my parents privately, but Mother assured him that whatever he had to say was fine to say in front of me. He had actually brought the results of some tests my parents had not yet seen. His words will always ring in my ears.

"I'm sorry, Mr. and Mrs. Pitts. Byron is functionally illiterate."

My father frowned, my mother raised her hand to her mouth, and I looked puzzled. What does "functionally illiterate" mean? My parents were finding out that in all the years in school I hadn't learned to read. I'd faked and finagled. It wasn't that I couldn't do the math: I could not read the directions. All these years and no one had noticed. Sweet, polite, quiet Byron could not read. I could recognize some words, identify names of certain locations, remember the words I'd memorized at the kitchen table, the name of my school on the side of the building, and the names of my siblings attached to magnets on the refrigerator. I could function, but I could not read. My mother would say years later that it was one of the few nights she cried herself to sleep. Usually knowing is better than not knowing, but initial shock has a pain all its own. She's been asked on more than a few occasions, why didn't you know sooner that Byron couldn't read? The short answer: When did she have time? Two jobs, three kids, night school, and a cheating husband usually made for a very full day.

The anger and tension that often curled through our house like smoke up a chimney was suddenly replaced by sadness. Everyone felt it. Everyone dealt with it in different ways. My brother treated me like his best friend. My mother, whom I used to follow around the house, was now following me. This went on for weeks. As we searched for some resource, some long-term solution, my mother set out the short-term course.

"Okay, honey, if we've spent two hours on homework, we'll try four hours. We will pray when we start. We'll pray when we get tired. And we'll pray when we're done."

Just the idea of working longer hours seemed to make her happy. As sad as I was at the time, I remember the joy I felt in anticipating the journey. I had no control over how poorly I read at the time, but I did have control over how hard I worked. That's what you do if you're Clarice Pitts's child. You work hard.

"Smart people can think their troubles to the ground, honey," she'd say. "We have to wrestle ours."

Soon my father seemed disengaged from the process. He worked more overtime, or at least that's what he told my mother, and stayed away from the house for longer hours. I don't recall a single conversation we ever had after my diagnosis. Maybe he really was embarrassed. Relatives had long teased me, "You're a Momma's boy." From that moment and every day since, I've been proud to be a Momma's boy.

These were the darkest days of my life. It wasn't simply the shame of not knowing how to read: it was not knowing where to start. Unsure where the bottom was, it felt as if I was falling. My mother was holding my hand, but we were both just falling. How easy it would have been for her to give up. Give up on me, give up on her abilities or responsibilities as a parent. This was a vulnerable time for both of us. A working-class family, we lacked the resources to do much more than pray and look to others for help. There wasn't much help around, but the power of prayer was immeasurable. It created comfort where none existed. It revealed a path when earthly avenues seemed closed. And it provided strength that could be explained in no other way.

As my family prayed and looked for answers, a decision was made in school. I was removed from a regular classroom and placed in all remedial classes. I was about to spend fifth grade as one of "the basement boys." Smart kids were taught aboveground; children like me were sent to the basement.

When I had taken classes aboveground, there were those giant glass windows to look through to the street below. The kids in the basement looked up at a window and saw only the feet of people passing by. Deep in my heart, I knew I didn't belong there, or at the very least I had to escape. But I didn't know how. The classroom size was smaller, and these were kids with whom I had rarely spent time. Many often seemed angry, some were violent, and none seemed hopeful. In my regular class, my friends talked and dreamed of becoming teachers, doctors, lawyers, or sports stars. In my new class, the answer was almost always "I 'ont know." I don't know. It's the slogan for those without dreams or a path to follow.

For all the gloom of being a basement boy, this time also proved to be one of life's great teachable moments. I truly believe that it is possible to find good in every moment, especially the difficult ones. Until this point, my academic life was mostly one failure after another. Each day the new challenge had been to find a way to hide. Once I was assigned to the basement, the days of hiding were finally just about over. I can still remember the glance from classmates in the morning. The bright kids, or at the very least, the normal kids walked upstairs, and my kind headed to the basement. I could feel the looks of disdain at the back of my head. Worse still, I could sometimes hear the whispers of pity or contempt. "There go the dummies, fresh off the short bus."

No one at St. Katharine's in the late 1960s and early 1970s took the bus to school, but the reference to the short bus was a reference to kids with learning, physical, or emotional disabilities who went to special schools or were taught in different classrooms. I once overheard two adults in the basement chatting in the hallway. "Today the basement, tomorrow prison." It was clear the basement wasn't a place you went to learn. It's where you were warehoused until fate or the legal system had a place for you.

Many of those in the basement doubted their future, and so did many of those who were paid to be there to help us. Hopelessness breeds more hopelessness. It was the same for many of us in the basement. We tried covering up our academic deficiencies with attitude and bravado. At about five feet four and 90 pounds, thank God I was never able to pull off the tough guy act. My grandmother always said, "The good Lord gives us what we need." I guess He knew I needed to remain skinny and sheepish until He got me through middle school.

There was a whole new look, language, and protocol in the basement. The classrooms were mostly bare. Not a lot of decorative and inspirational learning tools attached to the walls. The desks were older. Supplies and books were more scarce. Basement teachers spoke harshly. Class often started with "Sit down and shut up!" Much more time was devoted to discipline than to education. Almost all of my classmates were boys. An early morning shoving match meant we might spend much of the day in silence in a darkened classroom. I saw the principal and other administrators many times in the hallways upstairs. The janitors' supply room was in the basement. Other than the teachers, the janitor was usually the only other adult down there. And there was a different approach to learning. We seemed to spend a great deal of time in group learning in the basement. We rarely had homework; assignments were completed in the classroom as a group. We still read aloud, but here the teacher would read first, then the entire class would repeat after her or him. Even blackboard assignments were done as a group. Upstairs, I always dreaded going to the blackboard alone, whether for math, reading, or history. Now we would go up two or three at a time.

Unlike many of my classmates, I still had an optimistic spirit. I still believed that, with hard work, success was possible. Upstairs, my optimism was met with skepticism and the clear sense I was naive or even stupid, but oddly, in the basement, at least some of my new friends welcomed me. Though shy and frequently bullied, I was mostly cheerful and could keep people entertained with humor or encouragement. As they did in sports, classmates often chose to work with me because I could make them laugh or lift their spirits. A favorite line from childhood on a ball field or in the classroom was always "We got this." In other words, we can win. Upstairs, I was always alone and afraid at the blackboard, but here I could be the encourager.

"If John went to the store with three dollars and bought

cereal for a dollar forty and gum for fifty cents, how much money would he have left?" the teacher would ask. We were to write out her question and answer it at the blackboard.

"We got this," I'd say through a ragged smile.

One boy would write; the other two would repeat the teacher's sentence and help with spelling. I treated those exercises like a sporting event. We were a team. The question was the opponent. It was easier to rally the group around a sports challenge than an academic problem. We often got the answer wrong, but I took joy in the effort. Upstairs, success was almost always measured by achievement (getting the right answer, passing the test), but here, at least in my heart, success could be measured by effort. No one can always know the right answer, but you can always give your best effort.

Those days in the basement were an early lesson on how to redefine success. Take life in small bites, until you can take on more. Find our own pace and stick to it. In a regular classroom, I was a kid on a tricycle trying to keep pace with cars on a highway. In the basement, some of us had tricycles and some had even less. Admittedly, I had one major advantage over most of my classmates. I had Clarice Pitts. Life has taught me there is a fast-moving river that separates success from failure. It's called giving up. Too many people drown in that river. As a boy in the basement, I was often caught in its undertow, but my mother was always nearby, screaming, encouraging, threatening, praying, and on occasion she'd even dive in to pull me out.

During my years in the basement at St. Katharine's, I always felt embarrassment entering and leaving the basement, but the feeling would subside once I was settled in my seat. I resigned myself to the idea that maybe it was where I needed to be for the moment. But it would not be my destiny—God had something greater in store. But, without question, this was the least optimistic time of my life. And my parents' fights were growing in frequency and intensity.

By sixth grade, I still hadn't learned to read well. And I was feeling a greater separation from the so-called normal world, wondering if I would ever return to it. Often alone at home, I had few reliable friends. They included Butch, the family dog; Wilson (long before Tom Hanks in *Castaway*), the name on my favorite football; and my constant after-school companion: television. Every weekday afternoon and as much of the evening as possible was spent watching television. It was my window to the world and a good escape from my troubles. One afternoon while watching *Captain 46*, the local cartoon show, I saw (and heard) an ad for a reading program for adults who couldn't read. I jotted down the number and told my mother. "Momma, if they can teach adults to read, then maybe it's not too late for me." We were both desperate by this time. She called the number and they agreed to try their program on me.

Days later, a man came to our house with a case that looked like it might have a small television set inside, which made me smile. But it wasn't a TV. It was a microfiche machine along with a box of slides. There was never any clear-cut diagnosis as to why I couldn't read, but we worked from the assumption that I missed the basics early on in grade school, fell behind, and either lost interest or couldn't keep up. The machine was meant to take me back to the beginning. Both my parents and my brother were trained in how to operate the equipment.

Every day after school and after finishing my homework, I was to spend at least one hour with my reading machine, going through the slides reflected on the TV-like screen. It was repetition, rote, memorization. The first lesson was on the alphabet. Learning to recognize and sound out letters. What I should have learned at age four, I was finally getting at age eleven. The session was occasionally interrupted by my uncontrollable tears. I cried in hysterics. "I'm almost in high school, and I'm studying the alphabet? I really am a moron. People will laugh at me. I'll never catch up."

My mother reassured me. "You're not a moron. Son, it doesn't matter how you start, only how you finish. You can do this. We can do this." So we did it, every single day, until the letters and then the words began to come more easily. I practiced until it became second nature.

One of the many great discoveries that came out of my illiteracy is the joy that can exist on the other side of heartache. It can be like the relief you feel after a good cry or the day after you get over the flu. It's often easier to appreciate good health in the immediate days after an illness. When the pain is gone. Such was the case months after I began working with the reading machine. As I've mentioned, until this point any notes from the teacher were delivered home unopened to my mother. The words on the paper read like Braille to me. I never waited around to see my mother's reaction because I could hear it soon enough. It was often "Byron! What the hell is this?" Rarely did teachers criticize my effort. It was always the outcome that fell short. But one day all that changed. Like a newborn to breast milk, I clung to my reading machine and quickly moved from the alphabet to simple sentences. Noun, verb, object. I was, in fact, reading. Well below grade average but reading nonetheless.

By the end of sixth grade there came another note from school. I remember running home with the note in my hand. The news was too big to fit in my bookbag. I bounced around the house like a ball in a pinball machine until my mother came home. In fact, I called to see if she could come home immediately.

"What's wrong, son, why should I come home early?" Years earlier I'd actually set the kitchen on fire. Something about experimenting with a toaster. Anyway, my pleas for her to come home early were always met with some apprehension after that.

"No, Momma, it's good news. Just get home early. I can't tell you over the phone."

"Okay, honey, I'll be there as soon as I can," she replied with an uneasy sigh.

Hours later I met her at the door. "I got a note from the teacher. Can I read it to you?" Those words had never come out of my mouth before. My eyes met my mother's. We were both smiling. I cleared my throat.

"Mrs. Pitts, Byron is doing better in school. He is showing real pro . . . pro . . . progress."

I looked up to see my mother with a big smile on her face and tears rolling down her cheeks. It would be the first and last time my mother and I cried together. They were tears of joy. Something so small remains one of the great highlights of my life. I believe she baked me a chocolate cake to celebrate.

Regardless of the obstacles in your way, one of the great wedges to get you past an obstacle is hard work. There's almost a renewable fuel you get from working hard. The harder you push, the further you realize you can go. As I see it, success is just your work made public. Through the years I've come to enjoy the hard work on the way to success more than the actual achievement. It's the joy of being in the midst of it. It's like a great glass of ice water. Water's good for the body almost any day, but after you've worked hard in the sun, is there anything better than a cold glass of ice water?

Hard work never lies. It may not always reward you in the ways and in the time you'd like, but it's always honest. When you've worked hard, you know where you stand. You know what you've given. I've always believed that someone else could outthink me or outmaneuver me, but I only feared the person who could outwork me. Fortunately, I haven't come across that person too often. It's actually a pretty small fraternity: hard workers. Look at almost any successful person in any field, and you'll find at least this one trait: an ability and willingness to work hard. It's the great equalizer. It's the one gift we can give to ourselves, too often overlooked as we "trade up" for a sexier approach. It's not a shortcut; rather, it's the straightest line to success. It's also a great building block for acquiring other important life skills.

Every door that's ever opened for me in life started by my knocking hard and sometimes even kicking, putting my shoulder against it, and if not patiently, then prayerfully, waiting for it to open or fall off its hinges. Even as a kid who couldn't read, I knew I was fortunate. I had the gift. I knew how to work hard because my mother taught me.

And so it began. The first steps to overcoming my childhood shame of illiteracy. Pure, raw, uncomplicated hard work. Except for a few school administrators and teachers, no one outside my immediate family ever knew I couldn't read. Most days I was deathly afraid of failure, but I refused to let the outside world see it. The mask was coming off . . . but ever so slowly.

Years after that horrible day in the doctor's office, I can still remember my mother's words as we walked to her car: "Keep your head up, son. When we get home, we'll pray about it. Work our way through it." She rubbed the top of my head, pulled at my chin, and then took my hand. I've never walked with my head down since that day.

THREE

# Quiet Discipline

And say unto him, Take heed, and be quiet; fear not, neither be fainthearted. . . .

—Isaiah 7:4

SUMMER WAS ALWAYS A welcome relief from the stress and strain of my school life. And summers meant time with my grandma, Roberta Mae Walden. If it was my mother who taught me the power of passion, it was my mother's mother who taught me the strength that exists in calmness. For my mother it was discipline by force, but for my grandma it was quiet discipline. Both had the same goal: to be tough enough to survive any obstacle. But my grandmother wasn't much of a talker. She was a doer. She'd show her love by making your favorite dessert from scratch. Each grandchild had a favorite. Mine was her chocolate cake with buttermilk. She wouldn't say she loved you very often. She'd always just show you with a hug, a smile, or a laugh at a grandchild's lame jokes. She wasn't big on lecturing, and I never heard her raise her voice. I learned by her example.

As a boy, I spent most summers in Apex, North Carolina. My parents would always drop me off at the end of the school year. After an eight-hour drive from Baltimore, with R&B music and a bucket of Kentucky Fried Chicken in the car, they'd stay a day or two and then head back north. Grandma's home address said Apex, but she lived in the community of Friendship, a spit of a town with two churches, no more than five hundred houses, and not a single traffic light. The Friendship of my youth was a place of dirt roads, open overgrown fields, and weekend barbecues after the local adult league baseball game. Tobacco was still king. Eventually, the tobacco fields would be replaced by subdivisions. So today the sweat-stained overalls of tobacco growers and vegetable farmers have been replaced by salivating developers in khaki pants and blue blazers. Raleigh is twelve miles from Friendship, and as the state capital has spread its boundaries, with Northerners and people from other parts of the country pouring into the South, towns like Apex and Friendship have blossomed into bedroom communities.

In the 1960s my grandmother owned about thirty acres of wooded property. It remains a place where the air is clean and where deer, rabbits, and all kinds of creatures have always found a safe watering hole. There was a shed out back that contained all of her yard tools, including a saw and an ax. It might seem like a dangerous space for a small child, but no one ever worried about the grandkids playing in that shed because it was also a favorite resting place for snakes. My earliest memories include the outhouse and a deep well with one single metal bucket, a chain, and a hook. It was almost too heavy for me to carry, but I would slosh water, along with a cousin, into the house a few times a week.

Every summer vacation would begin the same way. I'd walk through the door of her shotgun house, and she'd greet me with a broad smile, a strong hug, a kiss on the cheek, and the same words in a whisper: "You're the one." Each night as she sent me off to bed, another hug and kiss and those same words uttered in a whisper: "You're the one."

Honestly, I never really knew what she meant. Just that I never wanted to let her down. And no matter what I thought of myself and my shortcomings, this old woman, with thinning hair, penciled-in eyebrows, and one crooked finger, believed in me and loved me unconditionally.

With my parents back in Baltimore, summers at my grandmother's house meant freedom. Cousins lived in nearly every other house. My grandmother, her sister, and her brother had married two brothers and one sister from the same family, so almost everyone in Friendship was (and is) either a Walden or a Womble. I spent my days eating Grandma's home cooking, kicking stones down dusty country roads, playing pickup baseball games, chasing skinny dogs, catching black snakes, spying on giant black ants, and washing down the day's adventures with a moonpie and a sweet tea. North Carolina may be the Tar Heel state, but for many of us who love it, it's also the pork barbecue and sweet tea capital of the universe. It's a place where locals eat hush puppies and most everyone has a nickname. In my family there's a Preacher, an uncle named Feel, a Piggly Wiggly, a Honey Bun, a Chief, a Señorita, Sonny, Hambone, and Poss . . . the short version of my mother's childhood nickname, Possum. There is a story behind every one, and each nickname was meant as a term of endearment. At the center of it all was Momma, as all her children and grandchildren called her. She was Señorita to her closest friends and Miss Roberta to the rest of the world. Her mother, my great grandmother, was born a slave. But there was nothing remotely subservient about Miss Roberta.

Looking back, I realize that one of the reasons I loved those summers in Apex so much was that all the fears of my life washed away. It was a simple existence, not complicated by the subterfuge it took to get homework done or the torment of feeling like the stupid kid in the neighborhood. Friendship was a great place to hide out for a kid who couldn't read or speak clearly. My aunts, uncles, cousins, and my grandmother's friends would always say, "Byron is such a good boy. He's so quiet and polite." My grandmother's longtime boyfriend would always add, "You give that boy a glass of milk and a TV, you'd never know he was in the house." That was high praise for a kid in my position.

I never did a stitch of homework in Apex, but I gained an invaluable education. It was a lesson taught without books or pencils or pens but with a stare, a raised finger, or a simple instruction. My grandmother wanted me to learn that an adversary can be beaten without harsh words or raised fists. That fear can be overcome with a calm resolve. That even an enemy can be treated with respect. It was her lesson in quiet discipline, and it all started with my insatiable sweet tooth.

A Zero candy bar was like a Milky Way bar, except it was white chocolate on the outside. It looked funny, but it was the best thing I had ever tasted. I don't even know if they make them anymore, but at age seven it was my absolute favorite. For some reason, I ate them only when I went to North Carolina in the summer to visit my grandmother. Never even looked for them in Baltimore. (Side note: after someone told me I was a Zero just like that candy bar, I stopped eating them altogether.) My burning desire for a Zero led me to a neighborhood grocery store one summer's day and, ultimately, the wrath of my grandmother.

In those days there were two stores within a mile of my grandmother's house. Segregated stores. My grandmother had brought me with her to do some shopping at the colored store. It was about the size of a trailer, with a dusty hardwood floor and a musty smell. It housed a big red cooler with a Pepsi Cola sign, lots of what I called "man" cigarettes (Kools and Marlboros), smoked meats, and the BC Powder that the women in the family used to treat all their pain, from monthly cramps to migraines. I loved to hear the musical tones of the manual cash register when the numbers would pop up and the drawer would close. My grandmother was taking her time, mulling over the fruit and vegetable stands out front and socializing with her friends. I was seven years old, and I had enough money in my pocket to buy a grape soda, a Zero candy bar, and a moonpie, and to have some change left over. But this store didn't have a Zero. So, without asking my grandmother, I wandered out the door and across the street to what looked to me like a better option.

The whites-only grocery store was fully stocked, refrigerated, and so well lit that from a distance I could see a box of Zeros just fingertips away from the cash register and a few inches away from the man at the register. He was big and a sunburned reddish color, wearing overalls, and I could smell an odor of chewing tobacco. There were other men and a few women in the store, but it was his stare that locked on me as I walked toward the front counter.

I was steps away from my precious Zero candy bar, and not aware of how much trouble I was in until I turned around and my eyes met my grandmother's eyes as she stood in the doorway. She hadn't even said my name, but somehow I had known she was there. She was afraid to walk in. But she knew she had to get me out, with her brand of quiet discipline. She didn't make a sound. In fact, she looked at me and smiled. The urgency was in her eyes. She tilted her chin down, raised one hand toward the middle of her chest, and with that arthritic finger twisted by age and hard work, she gestured for me to walk toward her. She didn't blink. She didn't glance away, and she kept that smile on her face. I turned my shoes in the opposite direction and moved toward her with my arms hanging at my sides.

Before I could reach her, the store clerk shouted, "Miss Roberta, what you doing here?"

"Just tending to my grandson," she said. "We'll be on our way." Her tone was gentle yet firm. Her voice did not betray her, and she never took her eyes off me. I left without my Zero candy bar. As we walked briskly to her car, she squeezed my hand tighter than she ever had before. "We'll talk in the car," she said under her breath.

My grandmother had never spanked me, but that day she came close. I was snuggled next to her in her old Chevy, and my grandmother said, "Don't you ever scare me like that again. There are people in this world who will hurt you just because of the color of your skin. So always be careful. Never be afraid or at least never show it. God won't call you home till your time. But in case He's not watching, you guard yourself." Then she smiled. It was a crash course in how to maneuver in the midst of segregation. We would not discuss it again until I was almost an adult. Then she told me, "I wasn't sure if I should scream or cry first. I didn't think anyone would hurt you, but in those times most anything was possible."

I never wandered in that store again either. Well after segregation ended, I still refused to go in. Fortunately, it was one of the few reminders in my life of what America was and how far we've come.

Whether it's a segregated grocery store or a schoolyard bully, I've remembered the lesson my grandmother taught me that day: Always know where you are and always carry yourself appropriately and respectfully. She wanted me to know that if I was afraid, it should never overwhelm me, and if I was angered by ignorance, I could remain calm and not confrontational. Because I was better than that. But it's one thing to know the lesson. It's another to live it, especially when she wasn't there to hold my hand on the playground or the street back in Baltimore, where I was often afraid for one reason or another. It was the fear of being exposed. The gnawing fear of not being good enough. Fear that my parents' angry words would lead to a split in my family. The fear of letting people down. The truth is, I didn't want to learn to read so that I could actually read. I wanted to learn to read so my mother wouldn't be ashamed, and I wanted to learn to read so people would stop making fun of me.

Small in stature, I was a frequent target of bullies, and the experience has haunted me for decades. Yes, I said decades. I've had nightmares about things I experienced as a child. I've awakened to night sweats and a clenched fist, angry and afraid. They'd take my lunch money and any shred of confidence I might have had. Simple things like going to the bathroom during school horrified me. Alone in the boys' room, kids like me were frequently targeted by bullies. Eventually, even my siblings became my tormentors. Our conversations would usually end with me crying and running to my mother. It became an endless cycle.

There was the group of boys who regularly chased me home from school calling me a sissy. I told my mother I didn't want to go to school anymore because I was afraid. (Actually, it was just another on a growing list of reasons why I didn't want to go.) Her solution was to have my older brother leave his friends and serve as my bodyguard. No wonder he hated me until we were in our twenties.

Then there was the sandwich-stealer. I never knew his name, his age, or where he went to school or lived. But he's lived inside my head since grade school. As best I can recall, we had one encounter. It was rare in our family that there was ever enough extra money around for things like lunch, beyond what was provided in the cafeteria or inside my metal lunch pail. I almost always took a bologna sandwich on white bread with mustard, a piece of fruit, and a Thermos filled with my favorite flavored Kool-Aid. Perhaps once or twice a year, my mom would give me lunch money to eat off-campus with my classmates. What a treat. A chance to buy my own food. It was one of life's simple pleasures that came to an abrupt end.

With three dollars in my pocket and a smile on my face, I walked out of St. Katharine's elementary school, crossed the street, and walked the half block with a few of my classmates to the corner sub shop. The sub shops and Chinese restaurants in the Baltimore of my youth all pretty much looked the same. They had high counters, bulletproof glass, and a menu written out by hand near the ceiling. I would later learn that the high counter and bulletproof glass were meant to discourage thieves. It would be hard to stick-up a sub shop or Chinese restaurant if you had to hold the gun above your head and stand on your tiptoes to threaten the clerk. There were no such safety measures for customers.

From early that morning, when my mom gave me money for lunch, I rehearsed over and over again what I would order. There was no chance I'd try and order off the menu. Someone might detect I could not read it, so I would order what I always ordered when I'd been in a sub shop with my family: a cheeseburger with lettuce, tomato, onions, with hot peppers. All morning in class my mind wandered to that moment. I watched the clock and could almost hear the seconds tick away. Finally the moment had come. I tilted my head up to see the clerk as I gave my order. No worries about reading the menu or stuttering. I'd practiced every word. I was ready. The sandwich was a dollar and seventy-five cents, one small order of fries for seventy-five cents, and one grape soda for a quarter. I was set. The smell of French fries and onions frying, the sizzle of a beef patty on the grill—it was all so intoxicating. My friends all ordered their favorites, from pizza slices to chicken parmesan and steak sub sandwiches. We were happy and laughing as we headed back to school. No one seemed to notice the teenager standing just outside the door. Who was he? Why wasn't he in school? All questions I would ask myself later, and over and over again for years.

"What's in the bags?" he asked.

My friends took one look, heard a threat, and ran. I was still trying to figure out why this big kid wasn't in school. With my friends gone, there we stood. This jerk didn't know my story. Didn't know I couldn't read or that I lived inside my shell. But he could apparently smell something on me besides a free meal. Pickle Pitts and this boy at least three years older and a good bit larger. He was smiling: not a friendly smile but as menacing as you could imagine. It was at that moment I caught a glimpse of his gold tooth. A gold tooth was a popular symbol of something back in the late 1960s and early 1970s. Symbol of what I was never certain. A plain gold tooth or one with a diamond shape in the middle or a champagne glass. Weird, I know. This guy had a champagne glass in his. He smelled like cigarettes.

"What's in the damn bag?" he growled. The smile was gone.

"My lunch," I answered.

"No, bitch, that's my lunch." That sickening smile was back.

I was frozen, gripped by fear and anger and shame. I couldn't move my legs. He grabbed for the bag, but I wouldn't let it go. It was a tug of war over my lunch and my boyish manhood. The bag ripped, the French fries scattered across the cement. The cheeseburger wrapped in aluminum foil rolled on the ground. My eyes welled up with tears. The French fries were wasted, and so was my mother's hard-earned money. This bully with thick stumpy arms bent over and picked up the sandwich, unwrapped it and took a bite. I watched as the gold tooth pierced the bun, his mouth covered with mustard and mayonnaise. Without knowing it, I guess my eyes narrowed and I clenched my fist.

"Oh, sissy boy wants to fight?" the bully asked in a mocking tone. He took his free hand and pushed my face.

"Get out of here before I hurt you." Then he kicked at me and pushed me away.

I stumbled, regained my footing, and backpedaled a few steps.

*Why won't you fight back?* I asked myself. Not only was I a moron; now I was a coward. My parents' money and I was too much of a coward to fight for it! Worse than losing a few dollars, it was the loss of dignity and self-respect that were most costly. I walked back to school in a daze, my eyes still burning, my head down. My pockets and my stomach were empty.

My classmates were waiting in front of the school. "What happened? Why didn't you run with us?" they asked.

I never opened my mouth. Like that moment in the car with my parents, outside my father's girlfriend's house, there were no words. My expression was blank. I shut down. The bell sounded and we proceeded back to class. From my desk I could look out the window and see the corner of the sub shop. The bastard who took my food was still standing there. I knew he couldn't see me, but I've always thought he was staring and laughing at me. I've had nightmares about him. That evening when my mom asked me to tell her about the events of my day, I never mentioned the incident. It still causes a pang of anger and shame. It's probably one reason I have such contempt to this day for bullies. I can still remember what that bully looks like. How much I wanted that cheeseburger. The sense of violation. Eventually, I would learn to stop being a victim. It was an important step on my journey. I have always used my grandmother's tactic of quiet discipline. I do not shout. I do not curse. I do not show fear. But I guard myself with self-respect against the bullies of the world.

On days of victory and days of defeat, my grandmother's words have always brought me great comfort. A peace. A reason to believe I never had to be the victim. My faith teaches me that there are no mistakes in life, just opportunities to learn.

FOUR

# Who's Got Your Back?

*F*OR TWENTY YEARS THE *old man went outside every day and a dug a hole looking for gold. Each morning he'd look out his window, and as far as he could see, there were holes in the ground. One moment he'd smile because those holes were testimony to his discipline. And the next moment he'd frown because he could hear voices laughing from deep inside the holes: What a fool he'd been, wasting his life digging holes looking for gold! Finally, the day came when he stopped digging and just stayed home. The next day he heard a great commotion coming from the center of town. He went to investigate. And there to his great disappointment was a young man with a chest full of gold. He told the masses gathered around him that he followed a trail of holes that went on for as far as the eye could see. Right where the holes stopped, he* *decided to dig. He found a chest full of gold. Now he was rich. All his dreams would come true.*

If I had a piece of gold for every time Clarice Pitts told that story, I would be a rich man. It was her favorite story when she wanted to make a point about the value of staying on course. We are all reminded at times in our lives, how difficult it is to stay on course. Getting off course is a four-letter word: *easy.* Lord knows, at different moments, easy is fun, exciting, and even a bit dangerous. I learned at an early age that staying on course requires a long line of people, like a team sport. But sometimes, I discovered, I had to be at the front of the line and play the game alone.

"The first team to ten wins." That was the one basic rule to street basketball in my neighborhood. Fouling was encouraged, but complaining about a foul was not. Timmy Johnson was the best athlete around. Given the choice, every kid wanted to be on Timmy's team. Not only was he gifted, he was gracious. He might score 9 of 10 points, but he always shared the credit with his teammates. It was a Saturday night, and luck was on my side. Timmy picked me for his team, and we were up, 8–5. There was plenty of time to finish off our opponent and get home before dark. One of Clarice's many rules, "Be home before dark or else." Rarely did any child in our family dare test "or else."

While I was imagining my mother's delight when I walked in the door before she had to yell *BYYYY-RUUUN!*—the kid guarding me stole the ball. Suddenly it was 8–6, then 8–7, and a moment later, 8–8. How awful. We were now in a tight game. Worse still, there was a chance I might not make it home before dark. Damn. Thank goodness Timmy Johnson had a jump shot. We won 10–8. No time for the customary hand slap and trash talk. I had to run. And run I did for about three blocks. It was already dark, so no chance I'd make it. Momma would be waiting, and she'd be angry. What was my excuse? Didn't have one. So run faster. I cut across Mr. Frog's yard (you never walk on anyone's grass, but this was an emergency), jumped over the bush on the right corner of our porch, and slid all the way to the front door.

"Okay. Catch your breath, walk in quietly," I whispered to myself. What did it matter? My mother could be in a room without windows, and she'd still know when the sun went down. It must be some microchip God places in all good mothers. What excuse could I use? That wouldn't matter. It was dark and that meant "or else." Well, at least we won the game. Going to bed early ain't so bad. Getting a whooping, how long could that last? I was resigned to my fate, when much to my surprise, I entered the house and my mother was *not* waiting. Instead, I could hear her and my father arguing in their room. Profanity and anger. First, I felt great relief. Then I was overcome by a sense of loneliness. My parents had no idea whether I was at home or in the street. There was no "or else." I listened to them fight for quite a while, and then I surprised myself. I went back outside and down the street. Slowly at first, assuming my mother would notice my absence and yell for me to come back. She never did. And soon I was beyond earshot or sight of home.

I'd never been out past dark. The street looked different. People I'd never seen before were on the street. My friends were the jock crowd. All we needed was daylight and a ball. But Timmy Johnson was nowhere in sight. These people were standing around. Men and a few women with bottles, beer cans, and bad attitudes inhabited the basketball court. "Hey, shorty, what are you doing?" Who was this stranger speaking to me? "Come here for a second. Come do me a favor." Too scared to run, I walked closer. The guy reached in a pocket. Is this how my life ends? Boy shot, stabbed, hit in the head with a blackjack? My imagination had gotten the best of me. "Shorty, go to the store for me." He'd pulled out a roll of cash thick as his fist. "So-so-so-sorry, sir. I sh-sh-sh-should be-be-be home."

"What! Talk like you got some sense. You stupid or something?" I couldn't move. I couldn't speak. And I was angry. How dare this fool with liquor on his breath insult me?

He and his group laughed and turned back to their conversation. It was clear, at that moment, that this man was no better than I and I no better than he. He was, however, a cautionary tale. His world was not my world. Even as a boy, it was clear to me what his tomorrows might hold for him.

As for me, I returned home. I presumed my parents were still yelling, no one would be looking for me, but I at least had the choice of returning to my home. When I got to Federal Street, my parents were now silent and segregated in different parts of the house. That night, no one noticed I'd just come home after 10:00 P.M. I was a boy, but I felt like a thirty-year-old man. I'd just learned I was as much responsible for my own well-being as the adults in my life. I had to watch my own back.

It's one of the phrases you hear growing up in an urban

environment. Almost every city kid from eighteen to eighty-one has either used it or heard it: "Who's got your back?" It's part of the free education on the street, for which Ivy League schools require large sums of money. In a lot of ways, my neighborhood was just like corporate America. Take, for example, what the business world calls networking. You can't move up in a corporation without a network of mentors and supporters. In the world of my youth, these were called Homeys or Uncle So and So or Auntie So and So. (The key is to make sure the people who've got your back are positive role models and not losers.)

Who had my back when I was growing up? Like any kid who loved sports, I adored my coaches, and they looked after me. There was George Cook, my first Pee Wee football coach. Mr. Cook worked a part-time job with my father and loved teaching kids the fine art of tackling and blocking. At first glance, this small knotty man of Irish German descent, who did shift work at Bethlehem Steel and tossed back Budweiser with his buddies at a watering hole in East Point, Maryland, would seem to have very little in common with a black kid from East Baltimore. Mr. Cook was my first hero who didn't look like me. He was also a testament to something my mother always said: "Everyone your color is not your kind. There are some good white folk in this world."

For four seasons (1969 to 1972), Mr. Cook helped shuttle me back and forth from home to football practice and games, and we got to know each other pretty well. I'm certain he never knew my struggles with literacy, but I'm convinced that if he had, he would have done his level best to help. For all that escaped me in the form of words, much of my early learning came in examples shown by people like Mr. Cook who set an example with actions and his words.

"Pitts, you like tacos?" Mr. Cook asked me once. He'd stuffed me and several of my teammates in his car after a game and wanted to treat us after a win.

"What's a taco?" I asked him. At this point, my taste didn't go much beyond my parent's home cooking and an occasional cheeseburger. My teammates (all white) got a big laugh out of my ignorance.

"Shut up laughing," Mr. Cook barked. "There's no shame in asking what you don't know, son."

Coach Cook, besides my mother, was the first adult who encouraged me to push beyond familiar boundaries. It was enough that he took interest in ways my father never did or for which my father could never make time. In fact, it was during my last Pee Wee football season that my parents' marriage finally came to a merciful end. As my father would explain several years later, "We grew apart. Clarice was no longer the woman I fell in love with."

That statement is absolutely true. William Pitts was a full-time meat cutter and a part-time cab driver on the day he met my mother. He was a full-time meat cutter and a part-time cab driver on the day they separated. Clarice was a girl from the country with a tenth-grade education on their wedding day. When the marriage ended, she was a college graduate with a degree in sociology and a respected social worker, mostly helping single mothers find their way. My parents had indeed grown their separate ways. While William ultimately walked away from both his marriage and his children, Clarice swore, "When I leave, everything that eats goes with me." That meant her stepson, Mac (my sister was away at college), me, and Butch, the mangy dog a stranger left in my father's cab one night.

Clarice left William on Christmas Eve morning in 1972. He left for work and before his key could hit the ignition, his wife was up peeping through the curtains. When his car rounded the corner, she woke all of us up and called her brother. "He's gone. Let's go." By sunset we had a new address, 4817 Truesdale Lane.

While the marriage was falling apart, there were no funds or inclination for babysitters, so I usually tagged along most places my mother would go: church, occasionally to work, night school, even bars. "Anywhere I can go, my children can go" was her motto. I met some really neat people playing Foosball and drinking a grape soda while my mother sat at the bar and had drinks with her friends. That's also how I first met James Mack, barking instructions at my mother and others taking a swimming class at the Morgan State College swimming pool. He seemed rather impatient at the time. "I hope you people study better than you swim," he crowed.

"What are you doing in my class" he snapped at me as I sat in the bleachers.

"Sir," was my sheepish response. With a stern look, he approached me.

"Why are you sitting in my class? You a freshman?"

"No, sir" was my only response.

The frown melted from his face, and with a smile he said, "You look like a freshman. What's your name, champ?"

"My name is By . . . By . . . By . . . ron Pitts, sir. My mu . . . mu . . . mother is in your class."

"Claricc Pitts is your mother? I hope she's a better mother than she is a swimmer." With that, he laughed and returned to yelling at his class.

James Mack coached the men's swim team at Morgan State in the 1970s, as well as a recreational league wrestling team (so everyone called him Coach). By coincidence, he was also a revered deacon and taught Sunday school at my New Shiloh Baptist Church. There were deacons at church who could bring the congregation to tears and shouting. They spoke with such clarity and force it seemed even God would have to stop what He was doing and listen to their prayers.

For all his talents, praying was not Mr. Mack's gift. I never saw a grown man so nervous or sweat so much in church as the rare occasion when Mr. Mack was called to pray. Once he got past "Dear Heavenly Father . . ." it was often downhill. But ask any young man whose life was touched by Mr. Mack, and you would know God uses all kinds of folks in many ways. There were countless boys, myself included, who wished we had a father like Coach Mack. Perhaps because he only had daughters, he was more than willing to step in when he saw a boy who needed a man's influence.

Coach was a bulldog on stilts: a thick jawbone connected to a barrel chest stopping at the waist. If Coach weighed 200 pounds, he was 190 from the waist up, atop 10 pounds of bowlegged twisted steel. The only thing funnier than watching Coach Mack pray was watching him teach swim class in trunks and flip-flops (Adonis he was not). He always addressed me and every other kid as champ. ("Either you're a champ or a chump, and you look like a champ to me," he'd say.) He quickly joined the short list of adults I lived to please.

I don't believe in luck or chance. It was God's grace that brought Coach Mack into my life. I would never be the same. Over the years, Coach taught me to believe that there are no quick fixes. "Lottery tickets are for people looking for shortcuts," he would say. "Shortcuts are for cowards. Cowards don't know God." To this day I have never purchased a lottery ticket, to honor the sentiments of Coach Mack. Success, he often reminded me, was an investment. That's what I loved about Coach Mack. Big lessons in short definitive sentences. I'm sure he was wrong plenty of times, but he was never in doubt. There are probably dozens of cops, lawyers, teachers, counselors, probation officers, coaches, and at least one journalist from East Baltimore now living across the country who owe many of their core values and beliefs to Coach Mack. He helped to keep us all on the right side of trouble. In the neighborhood where I grew up, there was a line that must never be crossed. On one side was education and opportunity, on the other side was incarceration. It was all too easy to cross that line. It was why my mother fought so hard, and what Coach Mack understood so well. One misstep could change the course of a life forever. Coach Mack almost certainly changed that course one day when I was walking to school.

"Hey, champ, what's in the bag?" The night before, I had purchased a pocketknife from the corner store and was on my way to school the next morning when I bumped into Coach Mack. He's never told me how he knew, or maybe it was fate, but this was the one and only time I ever ran into Coach

Mack on my way to school and he asked to see inside my book-bag. Respectfully, I pulled out my books, my lunch, my pencils, even the bubble gum I'd planned on chewing later.

"Anything else," he asked. No, sir! I obviously answered too quickly.

"You sure?"

Perhaps it was the perspiration that gave me away? "Just this." I raised the pocketknife to Coach, as if it was an eighty-pound bag of shame.

"What's the knife for?"

Using the best reasoning available to an eleven-year-old on short notice, I explained to Coach that there was a bully at school who had tormented me for weeks. He'd taken my lunch, and on those rare occasions I had lunch money, he'd taken that too. Since I felt I had no options, the pocketknife would be the equalizer.

"So are you going to stab him or just scare him?" Coach asked. Coach was a real man. He understood my dilemma instinctively.

"Only if I have to, Coach."

"Why don't you practice on me?"

"No sir, Coach. I love you like a father."

"Son, it's not about loving me. It's about loving yourself enough not to do something you know in your heart is wrong." He did not ask. I handed him that brand-new knife. As best I know, he never told my mother and we never discussed it again.

"Love yourself enough," he said. No one had ever told me that before. No one needed to tell me again. Once from Coach was enough.

I shudder to think where I might be without Coach Mack's intervention. Where that knife might have landed, and landed me. He continued to be a part of my life well past college. He supported me in any way he could. Pocket money, on occasion, when I had a date. A sounding board on those frequent occasions my mother's strict rules were enough to drive an adolescent crazy.

What motivates men like Coach Mack? Where does that desire to help come from? I never had the chance to ask him. The last time I saw him at a college basketball tournament, he was in the early stages of Alzheimer's disease, and he barely recognized me. The man who'd guided so many young boys to manhood was now being escorted around by a group of men, some his contemporaries and a few of them guys my age who likely have their own Coach Mack stories. The things he had taught me, all he meant to me, were my memories alone. That same smile was there, but this time it was me saying, "Hey, Champ, good to see you."

At this point in my early teens, most of those watching my back had come from the ranks of my family, my parents' friends, or my community. And with the exception of Coach Cook, they had all been African American, like me. But a culture shock awaited me when I stepped through the doors of my new high school in September of 1974.

Baltimore's Archbishop Curley High School is where blue-collar kids could dream white-collar dreams, as a teacher once described my alma mater. Founded in 1962, it was one of the last all-boys Catholic high schools built in Baltimore, a modest three-story brick building run by Franciscan priests. Their parsonage was attached to one end of the building, next to the school chapel. The population was more than nine hundred boys, most of them Catholic, all but four of them white. So being black and Baptist made me stand out. It was a place that valued discipline, education, service, and physical fitness equally. Curley was, among other things, a jock school. We won championships in football, soccer, cross country, basketball, wrestling, baseball, lacrosse, and track. There was a dean of discipline, Mr. Murphy. His sole purpose in life, it seemed, was to scare teenage boys straight. It was a badge of honor to graduate from Curley without a single scare from Mr. Murphy.

There were a handful of lay teachers, but mostly there were Franciscans in their black robes, dark shoes or sandals, with a white rope around their waist. The three knots in the rope symbolized their vows of poverty, chastity, and obedience. Just seeing those men each day in their black robes with the three white knots changed my perspective on life. Till this time I'd seen sacrifice only as one of the shackles of a modest upbringing. People did without because they had to. But these Franciscans did without by choice, a commitment to service to others. I found the whole concept liberating. It lifted a burden I often felt as the son of a single parent, who was forced to sacrifice so much in order to provide for her children. Now I saw nobility in sacrifice. At the same time, their lifestyle fit perfectly with my mother's notion of hard work or building toward some greater goal. These men were sacrificing to serve God, and their reward would come in heaven. Perhaps if I sacrificed the sinful lures of adolescent life, like drugs and alcohol, then my reward would also come later. So, every day as I walked down the hallway, that concept beat in my brain and heart like a drum. Sacrifice was good. Sacrifice was honorable. I was no longer some poor kid with problems trying to do better. I was a child of God sacrificing now for rewards later, hopefully long before heaven.

By the time I got to Curley, I was no longer functionally illiterate, but I still read well below grade level and was placed in a remedial reading class. Based purely on grades, I probably shouldn't have even gotten into Curley. My admission was more a testament to the power of prayer and the force of my mother's personality. For years teachers talked about my admissions interview. Not about *my* interview but about *my mother's* interview. She pleaded, cajoled, and convinced. Thank God. I've often said those were the four best years of my life. I've never learned, laughed, or cried more in any four-year stretch since. Oddly enough, many people in my life thought Curley was a bad idea. A number of my mother's friends, and even a few relatives, questioned the environment and the expense. (Tuition was nine hundred dollars per year, a steep sum on a social worker's modest salary.)

"Why you send Byron to school with those white people?" one co-worker asked her.

Her answer was always the same. "When it comes to my children, I don't have to justify my actions to anyone. I will do what I think is best for them, *period*." There was rarely any follow-up comment.

She did explain her reasoning to me. "You need to see how white people think and work if you're going to work and succeed in a predominantly white world." That's why Clarice sent me to Curley. "I want you to get the best education available, and Curley is a good school. Plus, they will whoop your ass as quickly as I will if you get out of line." Regardless of the situation, discipline was never far from Clarice Pitts's mind.

My first real teachable moment at Curley had nothing to do with the classroom. And the first ass whooping did not come from a teacher. In 1974, America's racial divide seemed far away from Archbishop Curley. I was never targeted because of my color, though on one occasion it was as good a reason as any for a group of upperclassmen to push me around. The first week of high school I spoke to no one and no one spoke to me. I walked to school alone. It was about a two-mile walk through my racially mixed neighborhood, past a predominantly black housing project, a white blue-collar neighborhood, and finally the homestretch through the school parking lot, which had its own diverse hood: some obnoxious upperclassmen who had cars and angry boys who didn't have cars. Needless to say, I always viewed the school parking lot and the housing project with equal trepidation.

I soon discovered that Joseph Stumbroski shared the same anxiety. Joe was about five feet four inches tall, with dirty blond hair, an edgy Baltimore accent, and a sophisticated (for his age) sense of style, which seemed odd for a child of working-class parents (a Polish father and an Italian mother). Every day on our trips to and from school, Joe and I would eyeball each other suspiciously, but we never spoke. Until one day, through fate or friction, we bonded or, more accurately, bled together. That day, heading home, I was almost clear of the school parking lot (in those days I thought it was at least a mile long, but on a recent trip there, I was astonished to realize how small it actually was) when several upperclassmen approached.

"We hate niggers," yelled one of them. The others nodded in agreement. Just about then, Joe Stumbroski walked past, and for some reason he stopped. "And we hate nigger lovers almost as much as we hate niggers."

Joe looked as stunned as I felt. Didn't these jerks realize that Joe and I were freshmen and that we weren't friends? Before the upperclassmen could jump us, Joe and I took off. We ran as hard as we could all the way to the bridge. A small bridge over a narrow creek, it was the border that separated the safety of our neighborhood from the segregated communities surrounding it. Joe and I had no idea we lived just a few blocks from each other. And why should we? He had gone to an all-white Catholic elementary school and I to a predominantly black one. We were so overjoyed to reach the safety of the bridge, we stopped to celebrate.

"I'm Joe. What's your name?" Joe extended his hand, accompanied by a toothy grin.

I returned the gesture. "I'm Byron." But before we could seal our lifelong bond with a handshake, we were approached by several "project boys." How could we be so stupid? In our sprint from danger, we drew the attention of several teenagers from the housing project. What an odd sight in East Baltimore in 1974: a black boy and a white boy running together. "What do we have here? A cracker boy and an Oreo."

Joe was the cracker, and I was the Oreo (black on the outside, white on the inside). There was no escaping this confrontation. Joe and I fought valiantly. Back to back, we fought like warriors against a barrage of racial slurs and fists. When it was over, Joe and I were tossed in the creek with our books. Bloodied and wet, we looked at each other and started to laugh.

"You fight pretty good for a white boy," I said through a bloodied lip.

Joe returned the compliment. "But why didn't you float like a butterfly," he added with a chuckle. From that moment on, we became friends and remain so to this day, and Joe's parents became like my second parents. I can't imagine that Mr. or Mrs. Stumbroski had any black friends, but they treated me and fed me like family. When my mother underwent surgery and was hospitalized for more than a week, Mrs. Stumbroski made dinner for my brother and me every day. She made sure we ate before her own family ate. And every morning during high school, the neighbors on my block could hear her blowing the horn of her car. "I have to make sure my boys get to high school on time," she'd often say. The Stumbroskis always had my back.

Many of my Curley classmates were like brothers, and the priests were more like older brothers and uncles than teachers. The faculty, staff, and administration took an interest in the whole student. It was always an odd and joyous sight every February at all-black New Shiloh Baptist Church to see a half dozen or more white faces in the audience for our annual young adult choir concert. They came all dressed in black, with trench coats covering their robes, just to see me perform. The first year that a handful of priests from Curley came to my church, it caused a minor crisis. As my choir mates and I were lining up in the back of the church to march in that Sunday evening of the concert, someone yelled "What are the police doing here? Black folk can't have anything without white people messing it up."

Several people in the choir and congregation assumed the white guys in the black trench coats were police officers. It was a great lesson about cultural assumptions on both sides. After a few years, my pastor would even acknowledge the priests in the crowd. It was a great source of pride for my entire family that a group of white priests from Archbishop Curley would drive across Baltimore City to attend my concert. For many of the priests, it also became one of the highlights of their yearly social calendar. Some of my friends would joke: "Those priests aren't here for the gospel; all they want is the soul food afterward."

I was lucky to have them there. At an age when many adolescents were challenging authority, I cherished and needed the uncompromising support of these priests. They weren't simply friars or fathers, they had replaced my real father, who by this time had all but slipped out of sight. At least one time that I know of, my mother had asked him to help with a tuition payment, and he never returned the call. While my mother attended every single one of my football and wrestling competitions in high school, I never saw my father's face in the crowd. I always missed his presence and missed the things a father would teach a son. How to tie a tie, polish a pair of shoes, or ask a girl out on a date. I would learn these things from a collection of men.

John Lattimore taught me that a man could be both rugged and well groomed. Mr. Lattimore was the first man I knew who wore a suit and tie to work. He was my mother's co-worker and longtime friend, part of her drinking and gossiping crowd. Her friends would often gather at our house after work, or my mother would meet them at their favorite bar. Mr. Lattimore's brother was a college football coach. He knew how much I adored football, so sports was always an easy topic. He was on the short list of my mother's colleagues who praised her for sending me to Curley and remaining so demanding. I think she always valued his counsel and support. He was well educated and the only person I knew who had a master's degree and had traveled overseas. He set an example for me of the value of a good education. He and my mom were never romantically involved, but I'm certain he chipped in a time or two to make my tuition payments. My senior year in high school he volunteered to let me drive his Cadillac to the prom. A two-door, blue 1977 Cadillac with a temperature-controlled air-conditioning system (that was fancy stuff in 1978) and white-wall tires. I washed it twice, used Armor All on the tires and interior. I almost slipped out of the seat as I drove to pick up my girlfriend. His kindness always stuck with me. It was one of the first rewards I had ever received for simply being a good kid. It made an impression on me. Do right and eventually people will notice.

Coach Cook, Coach Mack, Mr. Lattimore, Joe Stumbroski, Mr. and Mrs. Stumbroski, they all had my back. Despite the economic circumstances and academic deficiencies of my youth, I never felt deprived or shortchanged. God had blessed me with the priceless gift of family and a rainbow of friends. People who in their own ways looked beyond my limitations or the circumstances of the time and gave freely of themselves without any expectation of return on their investment, and they did so time after time. Where would I be without each and every one of them? Some were Baptist, some were Catholic, some professed no religion of any sort, to the best of my knowledge, but there's no doubt they were sent by God. Who's got your back? Do they know how much you value them? Don't wait too long. How I wish I'd shown Coach Mack how much I value him.

FIVE

# The Hands That Pull You Up

You can't climb a mountain without some rough spots to hold on to.

—**Roberta Mae Walden**

ALL THOSE HELPING HANDS could smooth the path, but none could do the work for me. Soon I would discover the difference between those who loved and supported me just the way I was and those who could lead me to who I needed to become. To this point, my coaches and friends and the like had taught me valuable life lessons. They were encouraging and kept my spirits up, never allowing me to dwell in self-pity. But I reached an age when I needed to learn specific skills. In many ways, I was still a very young child trapped in an adolescent's body. What I needed now was structure and academic discipline, because it was still a struggle for me to keep up in school, especially when it came to reading.

Think of all the books you had read by the time you were fourteen or fifteen. Perhaps an adventure series like Tolkien's *Lord of the Rings* or a classic like *To Kill a Mockingbird* or one of Michael Crichton's great science-fiction thrillers. Poetry by Langston Hughes or the sweeping romance of Zora Neale Hurston. Then imagine if you had never read for enjoyment until you were nearly fourteen or fifteen. It would stunt your reading experience and deny you the rich experiences that all those books would have brought you.

That was me. Playing catch-up. Not a natural reader, but with the years I had invested in my reading machine, I was now a careful and deliberate but slow reader. I could quote Scripture, but I was unfamiliar with the flow of the written word. Not only did it take me longer to read, but since I hadn't read as much, I didn't have the same starting point as my classmates. I read a book for the first time cover to cover, simply for pleasure, when I was about fourteen. It was Ernest Hemingway's *Old Man and the Sea*. Can't be certain why I chose it. It might simply have been because I liked Hemingway's beard. Nonetheless, when I told my mother of my plans, she advised me against it.

"Son, why don't you read a simpler book first," she said. Here was the woman who had been my number-one champion showing some doubt.

"What's wrong ?" I asked her.

"I don't want you to get discouraged if the book gets too hard. Why don't you read something else and work your way up to Hemingway."

More than disappointed, I was startled by her reaction. Fortunately for us both, another one of my core qualities kicked in: stubbornness. "I'll read this book because I can read anything," I proclaimed.

Right away I could relate to the old man's struggles

against the marlin and the predatory sharks, as well as the expectations of others. But I would eventually learn there is a dramatic difference between reading and comprehension. I read Hemingway's words at fourteen, but it would actually take years for me to grasp his meaning. Santiago's triumph over adversity, and his struggle with his pride, has certainly resonated with me and my life.

My struggle, along with the shame and embarrassment, has made me angry most of my life. In fact, seething with anger. Jealous, competitive, and sensitive to the slightest insult, I hated anyone who was smarter than I was, which, by the time I got to Archbishop Curley High School, meant almost everybody. Freshman year at Curley I was ranked 310 out of 330 students. More than making me feel inferior to most of my classmates, it made them the enemy. When I wasn't working to improve my grades to please my mother, I was working harder to prove something to the kids around me. Besides Joe Stumbroski, I had very few friends for the first couple of years of high school. Perhaps Joe and I were close because we were never in the same classes. He was never an adversary. I chose to dislike most of my classmates. In an odd way, it made it easier to function. If a classmate got an A and I got a C, it meant that he was better than me, smarter than me, probably laughed at me and therefore could not be trusted. I avoided study groups. I never wanted anyone to know how slowly I read and how slow I was to comprehend. The same whispers and looks of pity or disgust that followed me into the basement at St. Katherine's tagged along in high school. I was in remedial reading. The class for dummies was how it was commonly referred to. Another familiar insult. A class full of adolescent boys, working through their learning disabilities, while, outside, the cool boys preened and teased.

But I managed to keep all my rage inside (or express it on the football field). The best way for me to cope and live within my mother's rules was to "kill them with kindness." It became my motto. A bad student. *A good kid.* A poor reader. *The most polite boy in class.* Slow to comprehend. *He's the hardest worker we've ever seen.* It's been the same approach most of my professional life. Always the underdog, but unfailingly polite and disciplined. One of the coaches at Curley described our football team this way: agile, mobile, and hostile. That was the attitude I took into class. Every slight was noted. I kept score on everything, ready to settle up in due time. Unlike many of the classmates in remedial reading who displayed their anger by becoming discipline problems or mentally punching out of class, mine forced me to emphasize my strengths as I built on my weaknesses.

However, hard work did not guarantee success. I got a D in reading first term and was placed on academic probation. My mother's finesse may have gotten me into Curley, but in order to stay, I'd have to improve my grades. I was ordered to stay after school to work with a reading specialist and meet with my guidance counselor. Once again, disappointment created an opportunity.

Father Bartholomew was a sturdy-looking man, who wore glasses and had thinning blond hair. Though he rarely smiled, he had a pleasant expression on his face. He was my image of what Christ might look like, not his color but his character and gait. He walked with a purpose. He wasn't athletic, but

This is the earliest photo of me. Looks like I was practicing to hold a microphone even then.

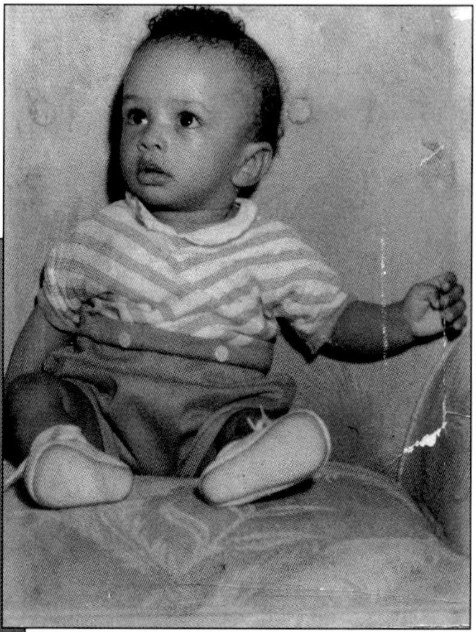

I love this picture of my mother. She looks so glamorous and happy, dressed up to attend a cabaret on board a ship docked at Baltimore's harbor.

My father always dressed well. He was a butcher, but he dressed like a banker.

*Photographs courtesy of the author except where noted.*

This is me on the front porch of our house on Federal Street. My mother, brother, and I moved out on Christmas morning, 1972.

This is the only photo ever taken of my father and me. I was thirteen years old. He had come by to say hello during the Christmas holiday.

My cousin Kim Walden and me loading up a bucket from my grandmother's well. It was one of my chores during the summers I spent in Apex, North Carolina.

An elementary school photo. Is it any wonder my nickname was Pickle? That's the biggest forehead I have ever seen.

My siblings, Mac and Saundra, and me at age eleven. We were dressed for church.

I took my girlfriend Kim Taylor to the junior prom at Archbishop Curley.

That's Father Bart on the left, with the blond hair. The priests from Archbishop Curley were regular attendees at a gospel concert at my family's Baptist church.

Gene and Gustava Stumbroski, Joe's parents. (*Courtesy of the Stumbroskis*)

A suave James Mack. Everyone called him Coach Mack because he coached swimming and wrestling. (*Courtesy of the Mack family*)

Joe Stumbroski's high school graduation photo. (*Courtesy of Archbishop Curley High School*)

I met Dr. Ülle Lewes on the day I decided to drop out of Ohio Wesleyan (*circa 1980*). (*Courtesy of Dr. Ülle Lewes*)

At Ohio Wesleyan, Peter Holthe gave tours of the Botany Department to local elementary school students. (*Courtesy of Peter Holthe*)

I played defense for the Ohio Wesleyan Bishops for three years. During my senior year, I broke a bone in my hand and sat out the entire season.

The three most important women in my life: my mother, Clarice (*left*), Dr. Ülle Lewes (*center*), and my grandmother, Roberta Mae Walden (*right*), seen on my graduation day, 1982.

My family grows up. Mac lives in Missouri and works as a long-haul truck driver. Saundra got her master's in criminal justice and works for child protective services in North Carolina. Mom was a social worker until her retirement in 1996.

My first reporting job in Greenville, North Carolina. The small paycheck was the best diet plan I've ever known. (*Courtesy of WNCT-TV, Greenville, NC*)

As a great cameraman once said to me: "Don't stand when you can sit and don't sit when you can lie down." I have learned how to sleep anywhere, including on the floor of an airport.

November 2001 in Afghanistan. In the front from left to right: reporter Phil Ittner from CBS Radio, producer Larry Doyle, and cameraman Mark Laganga. Next to me in the back is Bob Martin, a reporter from KRQE in Albuquerque.

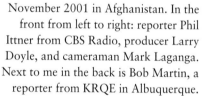

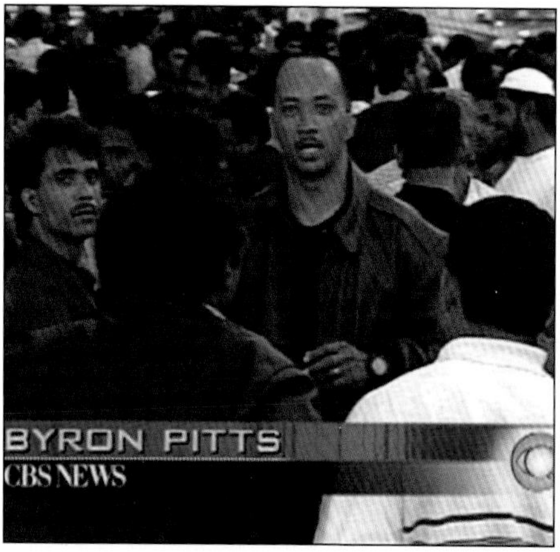


From January 2004 until the war with Iraq started in March, I reported from Kuwait. (*Courtesy of CBS News*)

Covering a firefight in downtown Baghdad on the day Saddam's statue fell. (*Courtesy of CBS News*)

I returned to OWU as commencement speaker in May 2006. Helping me are a very proud Ülle Lewes and Provost David Robbins. (*Courtesy of Ohio Wesleyan University*)

In Washington, D.C., for President Obama's inauguration, I'm joined by producer Daniel Sieberg, soundman Craig Anderson, and producer Rodney Comrie. (*Courtesy of Benson Ginsburg*)

he always looked fit. He wore sandals almost year-round. Father Bart was both practical and encouraging.

He asked a life-changing question: "What's your plan?"

"I want to play pro football," I said with a smile.

He laughed. "That's a nice dream, but what is your plan? What about college? How do you plan on getting there? Your current grades won't get you there. Trade school or community college but not a four-year college." He could see from my expression that this news was saddening to me, so he added, "That's not good news or bad news. That's just where you are."

It was a powerful reality check. It's nice to dream, but you need a way to get there. Father Bart and I first mapped out my four-year plan for high school, and then he said, "Now let's make the plan within the plan. Planning your education, like planning your life, is like building a house one brick at a time. So let's talk about what you have to do today to prepare for college."

That first forty-five-minute session lasted a few hours. Since Father Bart lived only a hallway away in the rectory and I would walk home to an empty house, neither of us was in a hurry. Like an architect at his drafting table, Father Bart laid out everything I'd need to build a "plan within the plan." From his shelf, he pulled out a college directory, which detailed all the entrance requirements. He opened it and pointed at random to the first college he came across and said, "These are the requirements to get in.

"You see," he said, "based on your current schedule, you can't get into this school. We could keep going, but we'd find the same thing almost everywhere." My shoulders rounded with disappointment. "Chin up," he said with confidence, "we've got four years to get you ready."

For the remainder of the session, we pored over my current schedule and coordinated it with the classes I'd need to get into college. It's worth noting he never set boundaries on what kind of college. So at fourteen, still reading below grade level, I was allowed to hold on to the notion of endless possibilities. We went over my syllabus for the remedial reading and math classes, and he described how I would have to progress to get into a so-called good school. Then he went deeper, explaining the kind of time I'd have to put in studying. There were formulas he said for how long good students study.

"You'll have to study even longer and harder," he said. By this point, his tone was more like a football coach. He wasn't quite yelling with excitement, but he was forceful.

We made a schedule for every half hour of my day, from the time I woke up in the morning until bedtime. He arranged for a tutor. He also got me a job mopping the halls after school so that I'd have a reason to be on campus, other than the extra academic help I needed. It remained unspoken, but Father Bart was aware how sensitive I was to being seen as different. The job after school gave me great cover when friends asked, "Why are you hanging around?" Added to that was the fact that my family could use the extra money. I wasn't the only kid whose parent(s) scraped to send their son to Curley. The school had its own work/study program of sorts. After school, boys worked mopping the halls and cleaning classrooms.

The routine suited my mother just fine. Clarice Pitts made

sure I did every extra-credit activity and kept to a strict regimen of school, work, sports practice, homework, and church. My mother didn't allow friends in the house unless she was home. I wasn't allowed to go to anyone else's house other than the Stumbroskis'. House parties were forbidden. I could go to a dance at school or to a church event, but teenage hangouts and the mall were not allowed. I was permitted to go out on Friday nights and was always home by 11:00 P.M. Later in life, my own children and their peers have always found such boundaries barbaric. "Nothing good ever happens after midnight," Clarice often said when I would plead for an extended curfew. Once I gave a well-thought-out rebuttal, "Is that when you and Daddy got married, after midnight?" I thought it was brilliant. She playfully but with an edge punched me in the shoulder. "Don't say that again."

Despite where I was academically, Father Bart never discouraged me. He taught me to know where you are and where you want to go. I wanted to go to college, and Father Bart assured me he would help me get there. In many ways he helped put my reading deficiencies in perspective. I was in remedial reading, but I didn't have to stay there. I could go farther with a plan. It also helped that we always started and finished our meetings with prayer. How wonderful it was for me to be in an environment where prayer was not simply encouraged but expected. All the distance I had traveled to this point came on whispered prayers. Now I was in an environment that affirmed that prayer can take you as far in life as you're willing to plan and work. Who knew Franciscans also believed in the African proverb: When you pray, move your feet.

Gradually I began to improve. There was growing comprehension. I was gaining confidence, though I was still very quiet because of the snickers over my speaking deficiencies. By my sophomore year I had moved out of remedial math and reading. Although I was still closer to the basement than the top of the academic curriculum at Curley, my spirits were buoyed by a sense of accomplishment. Because teachers knew that I was a hard worker, they were willing to spend extra time with me after class. Most were encouraging and supportive. Sports remained the center of my universe, but I was no longer simply surviving in class. I was beginning to thrive. I eventually found a subject I loved—history. From the American Revolution to the Civil War, the stories of conflict and courage appealed to me. I could relate to figures like Crispus Attucks, the first black man reported to have died in the American Revolution. The people around him underestimated his talents, but when the time came, he proved his worth. History had a beginning, middle, and end. That's how I began to see my life. I enjoyed it without prodding from my mother. The more I learned about a given topic, the more I wanted to learn. I was finally reading. And there was a reward. History was the first class in which I ever received an A.

Until this time I was still very much a loner and was afraid to engage in an academic conversation with a classmate or really speak up in a class discussion. But by junior year, especially in history class, there was a gradual recognition by my peers that I excelled in this subject, and they sought my opinion and even my help. This was a new experience for me. I was not accustomed to having a reputation as one of the "smart" students. Around the same time, my other grades began to improve, and I liked being recognized for something other than athletics.

It was also in my junior year that Curley started a school newspaper and I signed up to be a sports writer. I loved sports, and I was beginning to love words. It seemed like a natural fit. It was the first time someone other than a teacher or relative would read my work. I would sit in the cafeteria and watch classmates read an article I had written. It would make me think back to the days when people thought I was stupid. Now people were reading my stories. Sometimes they would laugh, sometimes they would look surprised, and sometimes they would look pleased or at the very least interested. The fact that I could provide people with critical information gave me the sense that I mattered. I served a purpose.

Along with the academic improvements, I was gradually gaining ground on a normal teenage life. Pickle was growing up. I still stuttered, but I was more comfortable, and confident enough to speak up when I had to and didn't even mind friends who finished my sentences. By senior year, I experienced a respite from my struggles. I was a solid B student, ranked 30 out of a class of 240. Four years earlier I'd been ranked 20 from the bottom. My body had finally caught up with the size of my head. I had a steady girlfriend. Kim Taylor lived at home with her parents and three sisters in a suburban neighborhood. Kim was the perfect high school girlfriend. We had known each other since junior high school, when we sang in the church choir together. We shared similar values, neither of us drank or did drugs, and we could dream aloud about college. In my world outside of Curley, there were not many people who had such dreams.

And getting into college was a priority. For years my mother had warned me, actually threatened me, about what life would be like without an education. I learned exactly what she meant after graduation, when I spent the summer working on a maintenance crew for the Maryland State Department of Transportation. At the time, the law required all summer employees to be at least eighteen years old. It was a good paying job, and our family needed the income, so I lied about my age. I got a job cutting grass along Interstate 95 near the Baltimore Harbor tunnel and cleaning the tollbooths and inside the tunnel tube. It was dirty and somewhat dangerous work. The large self-propelled lawn mowers could cut a three-foot-wide swath of grass, a pile of garbage, or a person's leg. I loved the work. Walking up and down the grassy median of the interstate behind my industrial-strength lawn mower, often under the hot sun, was almost therapeutic. The walking would strengthen my legs for football, and pushing around the lawn mower and lifting debris was as good as lifting weights. It may have been the most instructive job I've ever had.

Every day, twice a day, employees would punch a clock. We could arrive early if we wanted to, but the paycheck would only reflect a change (a deduction) if we were late. I don't remember the names of any of the men I worked with, but I can still see their faces. The foreman was a small, tightly wound white man in his midfifties. His dark pants and orange work shirt were always neatly pressed. Even his black work boots had a nice shine. If not the orange shirt, then the white socks always gave him away. One of the workers in our crew was always responsible for keeping his government-issued white pickup truck clean and the tire rims polished. He had an awful habit of calling all the black crew members Skip. The first time he called me Skip, I walked past him. He pulled my arm and said, "Didn't you hear me, boy?"

"You said Skip, sir. My name is Byron Pitts," I answered.

He looked confused and walked away in a huff. From then on I'd always respond appropriately if he yelled Skip. I took it to mean whichever one of you colored boys is close, come do such and such. There were three other men assigned to our crew full-time (there were several other crews). Two of my crew mates were black and one was white. The white guy had a distinct accent, pure Dundalk (only people from Baltimore have heard it or at least would recognize it), a beer belly, and a perpetual three o'clock shadow. He was always pleasant and, for the most part, minded his own business.

Whenever our day was interrupted by rain and the boss would pick us up, the white guys rode up-front and the brothers back in the flat. There was a constant barrage of harsh language, lots of cigarettes without filter tips, and the frequent liquid lunch if the boss man wasn't around. Since they thought I was older, I had talked about my plans to go to college soon. One payday the white member of our crew yelled at me, "Why are you going to college? You oughta just get a job. I gotta job. And every two weeks my paycheck speaks to me."

Before I could answer, the eldest and quietest member of our crew did something he rarely did when we were in a group; he spoke up. "Leave the boy alone," he said in my defense. He went on to say, "Son, stay in school. Someday your paycheck is gonna scream at you."

We all chuckled. I had a smile on my face the remainder of our shift. I wish I could remember his name. I would work with him for three summers of my life; he was more like a favorite uncle than a co-worker. I never knew if he could read. On those rare occasions when we had to read instructions on a piece of equipment, he'd always ask me to read for him, explaining he'd forgotten his reading glasses. There's no doubt the fourth member of our crew could not read. He had a stutter far worse than mine, and the boss often treated him more like an animal than a man. He never objected. He and I would exchange greetings only in the morning and at the end of the day.

We may have been an odd collection of men, but five days a week, eight and half hours per day, we were together. Thirty minutes for lunch was usually spent under a bridge or on the side of the truck. Ten minutes to eat (I usually carried my familiar bologna sandwich with mustard on white bread) and twenty minutes to nap, either in the shade beneath the bridge or on the ground beneath the truck. Learning to sleep on the side of Interstate 95 (with your back to traffic, of course) would be great training for one of the vital skills of being an international journalist: the ability to sleep anywhere at any time.

There were also tremendous role models for the value of hard, honest work. For some of the men I toiled with that summer, cutting grass on the interstate was the pinnacle of their working lives. It's what they were good at and where they found satisfaction. They maximized the talents God gave them. That may be hard for many people to understand. My mother was clear about such things. Do your very best at whatever God has given you to do. Push past what you think is possible. If that's a perfect shrub in landscaping, so be it. She saw a different potential in me. Today I work in a profession with people who are well compensated and well respected for what they do. Yet many complain about being overworked, underpaid, and underappreciated. Many of those men in orange shirts whom I had the honor to work beside never complained about jobs that paid barely north of minimum wage. They were decent men who saw dignity in their work. They didn't make excuses.

I don't look back on those days through rose-colored glasses. At the end of the workday, my hands and limbs were sore. I smelled. I was sweaty for hours. Yet there was structure and simplicity to the tasks. Gas the mowers in the morning. Walk north or south behind the mower until it ran out of gas or it was lunchtime. Fill the tank, and then walk until the workday was done. In a few days or a few weeks, we'd reach the end of our section of highway, then we'd simply turn around and head the other way. It was the Forrest Gump approach to work. On bad weather days we'd get to clear trash near the toll plaza, and at least once per summer paint the booths.

For me, that summer was like a year at prep school. It crystallized the reasons why I wanted to go to college and what the alternative would be if I failed. Earlier that spring, I had been accepted to a few schools—I received average SAT scores, but I had strong extracurricular activities, which included football, and glowing recommendations. All those who wrote letters said pretty much the same thing, "Give this kid a chance."

My mother and I had decided on Ohio Wesleyan University for some of the same reasons she chose Curley, a small school with good academics in a safe, supportive environment. And by safe, I mean middle of nowhere. Delaware, Ohio, is about as far from East Baltimore as one can imagine. One is overwhelmingly black. The other is overwhelmingly white. My mother and I flew to Columbus and took a shuttle van to campus. I wondered to myself, "Am I going to college or a farm?" Nothing looked familiar. East Baltimore is a world of row houses, parked cars, blacktop streets, mixed-breed dogs, and lots of black people. That first day in Ohio I saw more cows than people who looked like me. It took about ten minutes to drive the entire length of the town. The college campus is compact, easy to walk from end to end, with a population of about 2,400 students. About 500 were brand-new, just like me.

My brief taste of college life had been when I was a high school senior on a recruiting trip (not to Ohio). The football players took me to a fraternity party. During the course of the evening, they began to pass a marijuana-filled bong around the room. When my turn came, never having seen a bong before, I did what I thought all the others had done. I blew as hard as I could. Pot sprayed everywhere. All over the floor, the walls, books, even on one of my hosts. To say the least, I made a poor impression. I think the guys would have jumped on me if not for having to explain why a fight broke out on a recruiting trip. Needless to say, I bypassed that school and was never tempted to try pot again, or any other drug, for that matter. I had never heard the term *recreational drug use* until I got to college. In my world back in Baltimore, junkies did drugs and drunks drank alcohol. Their shocked reaction always surprised me when classmates found out I didn't do either.

Since my mother and I arrived before my roommate and his family, I got to stake out the best spot for my belongings. The time alone in the room also helped calm my nerves a bit about meeting him and about living with a stranger for the very first time in my life. I was a football recruit, a full-fledged jock. Usually, those are the most confident characters on campus. I, on the other hand, was a bit of a geek. Not a book-smart geek. But an unworldly young man who thought church choir rehearsal was a great night out.

I had spent weeks thinking about whether or not I would fit in at Ohio Wesleyan University, facing the academic challenges I anticipated and the social pressure I dreaded. I was relieved that Mother had made the trip with me. She helped me unpack. It didn't take long: I had one suitcase and one box. Inside the box was the same stereo my sister had taken to college ten years earlier and my mother's childhood pencil holder. It was just a tin can wrapped in brown paper, but as far as I was concerned, it was a family heirloom. My sister had taken it to college. It was mine now. God willing, someday I'd pass it on to my children. The only other item of value was my Bible. Actually, it was my grandmother's pocket Bible. Most of the pages were dog-eared and worn.

Mom and I said a prayer before she sent me off to football practice that afternoon. Eventually I walked back to my dorm room, where my mother would be waiting, so we could go to dinner and talk about my first day of college. Much to my surprise, Mom was gone. In her place, a letter and a single dollar bill.

Dated August 21, 1978, it read:

*Dear Son,*

*I pray your first team meeting went well. I know how excited and nervous you are to be playing college football. I wish I could have been there. My heart reflects back to your days in Little League in East Point. I was so proud of you then. I am even prouder of you now. Please know I'm sorry I couldn't be here when you returned to your dormitory.*

*I didn't want you to worry or lose your focus, but I only had enough money for us and your stuff to get to Ohio Wesleyan and then get my butt back to the airport (smile). As you see, I've left you a dollar. I wish I had more to give, but I only have two dollars left in my purse. Like we always have done, we share. So I gave you half of what I had and kept the other half. I know a dollar won't get you much, but God has always met our needs. So know that God will meet your needs today, tonight, and in the years to come.*

*Byron, you've always been a good boy. Please continue to be that. Be the polite young man I raised you to be. Work hard. Pray hard. Study hard. This is a good school. You will do great things here.*

*Son, always remember I love you, your sister Saundra loves you, your brother Mac loves you, your grandmother loves you, all your aunts and uncles love you. Not a day will pass when we won't be praying for you and believing in you.*

*Do your best and God will do the rest.*

*Love,*
*Momma*

Mom headed home with a buck . . . and I started college with my sister's old stereo, my mom's pencil holder, my grandmother's pocket Bible, a dollar, and a tractor-trailer full of love and prayers. I would need all of it because college was about to kick my behind in new and unfamiliar ways. In all honesty, my freshman year in college was the scariest year of my life. My course load included freshman English, geology (which I hated), philosophy, introduction to journalism, and Spanish. Each class required more reading than all of my classes in high school combined. Nothing unnerved me more than the daily torture of that pile of books I faced every day. And there was the realization that my mother was not there to schedule my day and yell threats or encouragement in my ear. It was up to me.

But it wasn't just the academic pressure. I was beginning to feel alone and isolated, in part because of the economic gap between me and many of my classmates. Even when I had issues at Curley, we were all blue-collar kids. At OWU I had a classmate with a BMW. I had never seen one before. A few messy students whined about missing their housekeepers. I couldn't tell anyone that my grandmother was a housekeeper. I had classmates who had traveled the world, spent semesters abroad. At Curley we considered Ocean City, Maryland, a big excursion. I began to feel resentful, deficient, and overwhelmed. The loner was returning.

But out of the agony of this experience came a friendship forged in battle. For every person who's ever told me, "No, you can't, you're not ready, you're not good enough," God has always brought people like Peter Holthe into my life. Pete lived down the hall from me in our dormitory. Our floor was divided into social groups: the farm boys, the frat boys, and the others. Pete wasn't associated with any group, and as a committed bookworm, he often found himself eating alone in the cafeteria. I was usually alone too. We "others" gradually found our way together. Pete is one of the smartest people I have ever known. He arrived at OWU intent on majoring in the sciences. His parents had hoped he would go to an Ivy league school or one of the nation's top business schools. Pete's dad was a partner in a major accounting firm back in their hometown of Minnetonka, Minnesota. Pete decided to study business and zoology, with advanced degrees in decency and friendship.

"My dad may have thought I was rebelling by going to OWU, and perhaps I was. But I was determined to go my own way. I barely paid attention my senior year in high school but aced my SATs, and that's what got me into OWU."

I remember when Pete told me about his journey to college. I was struck by the notion that his attending Ohio Wesleyan was seen as disappointing by his parents, whereas, for my mom, getting me to OWU was a miracle.

I've always described Pete as the whitest white guy I've ever met. Not just pale white (Nordic white), with reddish hair, but he wore thick glasses and had a formality to him that made him seem more like thirty-eight than eighteen. We hit it off right away. Pete thought I was equally weird.

"Why do you play football?" he asked me one day. "You're not going to play professionally, and you must not be very good at it because every time I see you, you're limping or have a limb in a sling. It doesn't make sense why you'd punish your body for no good reason."

That was Pete—everything needed to make sense to him. He's always been analytical. There's an answer to every problem if only one takes the time and puts in the effort to figure it out. He became a dominant voice in the nightly discussions about politics and world affairs that would take place in our dorm, often in his room. Pete and the other guys would exchange ideas, but I rarely said a word. My verbal contribution would be laughter, a grunt, or an occasional one word assent. Mostly, I just listened. Pete knew I had a problem and had the courage to point it out. Actually, at the time, I thought he was incredibly rude.

"Byron, your vocabulary sucks. Sometimes you talk like you're in grade school. And sometimes you use big words that make no sense. What's your problem?"

By then, I thought I was pretty good at masking my remaining shortcomings. I was an incredibly slow reader, but I studied alone so no one really knew how long it took me to read and comprehend my schoolwork. In a new environment, without the comfort of people who knew me well, I slipped back into my pattern of silence to avoid the shame of stammering and stuttering. I generally limited myself to one- or two-word answers. I was never comfortable speaking outside my very limited range. Hiding my deficiencies was a very comfortable state for me. And now, in a matter of weeks, this wise guy from Minnetonka had penetrated my carefully crafted façade.

When Pete was done verbally undressing me, I wanted to punch him in the mouth.

"Who the hell do you think you're talking to?" I barked.

Pete's reply. "I'm talking to you, my friend. Clearly you have a problem communicating, and I want to help."

I was embarrassed and angry. "What gives you the right to t-t-talk down to me?" I sputtered again.

"I'm not talking down to you. I'm sitting, you're standing, so I can't be talking down to you," Pete said with a smile and the clipped laugh I came to appreciate. "Look," he went on, "I'm your friend, and if I didn't care about you, I wouldn't say anything. I know you're not stupid, though sometimes you sound like it. Be honest, what's wrong? You can trust me."

I had spent so many years hiding behind a curtain of lies and secrecy, it wasn't easy for me to tell the truth. But I did. I confided in Pete, told him how long it had taken me to learn to read, told him about the fear I faced every day in class. How overwhelmed I felt before the mountain of reading that was required. Any freshman year in college is tough, but I felt as if I was starting a race and everyone else had already run the first few laps. Being a slow reader was not my only issue. My inability to communicate in class and speak with my professors in a meaningful way was really slowing me down. I rarely spoke in my classes because I didn't have the confidence to express myself.

Pete was not judgmental; nor did he express any shock or

surprise. His response was simple. "If I can help, I will. If I can't, I'll help you find someone who will." And he did help. "Here's what we'll do," Pete said with confidence. "Every day I will give you a new word from the dictionary. I want you to study it. Then, the next day, say it, spell it, define it, and use it in a sentence—deal?"

"What do you want in return?" I asked.

"Nothing. You'll be my first great college experiment. Let's see how we do." That's pure Pete. He was helping me but wanted it to seem as if I was helping him (though I convinced myself that being friends with a football player probably wasn't the worst thing for Pete's social life). That was our secret. We kept the arrangement to ourselves through a few years of different roommates and a few different girlfriends.

Before long, I was coming up with words, and that always made Pete laugh. Like so many of the wonderful people God brought into my life, Pete taught me more by his actions than he did by his words.

When I struggled in a class, Pete devised a study routine for me. It was his idea for me to take all my notes from class and type them out at night in a separate notebook. "Redundancy is good for you," he said. "Plus, your handwriting sucks."

For the remainder of college, I kept two notebooks for every class. One I took with me to the classroom; the other I kept with its neatly typed pages in my dorm room over my desk, and that's the one I would use for studying. As hard as I worked, though, I couldn't match his ferocious and disciplined study habits. Pete studied every night except Fridays. That was his drinking night. Pete knew his way around a chemistry lab and a beer bottle. It was the one area I could keep him in check.

"Pete, what's our limit on beer tonight?" As a nondrinker, by "our" I actually meant "his." Always loyal and always honest, whatever number of beers we'd agree to, that's how many Pete would drink. By Saturday he was back to his books, and on Sundays he read the Sunday *New York Times* from cover to cover. (The only time I ever saw Pete angry was when someone touched the *Times* before he got through reading it.) I just marveled at this guy, my age, taking such enjoyment out of reading everything from textbooks to magazines and newspapers. Not to mention the effort. Since *The New York Times* wasn't delivered on campus, Pete had to walk at least a mile to the store and buy it. Though he was never a fan of exercise, Pete's devotion to making that walk in rain, sleet, or snow on Sundays was impressive. I was never able to convince him to go with me to church on Sunday, and he never got me to read the Sunday *New York Times* either.

Our freshman year in college he was already talking about graduate school and his career, and not in broad terms. He already knew the best schools in the country for his particular discipline, the grades required to get in, and the names of the department heads. Grad school was still three or more years away, but Pete already had a plan. Perhaps Pete was actually Catholic and had a Father Bart back in Minnesota, I often thought to myself. I was already considering my career, too—journalism, believe it or not. Having written for my high school newspaper, I somehow had fooled myself into thinking I might be a pretty good writer. Despite my limited vocabulary, I enjoyed words and expressing myself. So much had been bottled up inside me for the years I couldn't read that I welcomed any chance to read and write. My English teacher in freshman year was Dr. Paul Lucas, who had been at OWU for decades. He was both a brilliant English professor and an unforgiving taskmaster. A tall, thin, balding, pipe smoker, who seemed fond of sweater vests in and out of season, he carried himself like a man who got lost on his way to teach class at Harvard. I had heard Dr. Lucas was tough. I was on a first-name basis with tough, but I still wasn't ready for him. Perhaps he had his favorites, but I seemed to play the role of his whipping post.

He kept his classroom as he carried himself, neat and orderly. He had us working out of small blue notebooks. He didn't want black or gray or brown. He wanted blue. He was meticulous about grammar and proper punctuation. My classmates and I were told early on how he wanted assignments written; the details included which side of the page for our names and the date. No exceptions. I was used to order. Many of my teachers back at Curley insisted a student stand up before giving an answer. We walked on the right side of the hallway and the staircase. I understood order. College was far different from high school. More reading. More freedom. More was expected. I got all that. Dr. Lucas I never got.

"Fine work, Mr. Pitts," he'd say as he handed me an assignment in class marked with a D, if I was lucky, or an F, quite often. Visits to his office were humiliating and often painful. Dr. Lucas pulling on his pipe, puffing smoke as he critiqued my work: lousy grammar, terrible spelling, poor sentence structure, and poor composition. I was befuddled by little things. Because I didn't know how to type and couldn't afford to pay anyone to type my papers, it would take a painstaking amount of time to finish my work. That sometimes meant the essays were not well thought out or corrected. Sometimes papers were simply turned in late. There was no extra credit, and unlike high school, there was no acknowledgment for effort. The sessions went quickly. Dr. Lucas never offered suggestions on how to improve, only criticism. It was clear that he expected my baseline of understanding to be higher than it was. Because I wasn't very verbal, I wasn't equipped to say what I needed. My only response was that "I'm doing the best I can." It got so bad Clarice tried to intervene, eight hundred miles away, from back in Baltimore. Tired of my tearful phone calls home, she called Dr. Lucas directly. I don't think he was accustomed to getting phone calls from parents. Certainly not someone like Clarice Pitts. Her counsel to me, just keep praying and working hard, didn't seem to work. Despite my mother's encouraging words and prayers and Pete's study tips, I failed Dr. Lucas's class and did poorly in several others.

At the end of my first semester in college, I was on academic probation. Another poor showing next semester and I might be kicked out of school. Perhaps as testament to my stubbornness or stupidity, I signed up for Dr. Lucas again. I thought if I was more disciplined with my time and worked harder, I could pass the class. There was no guarantee that another professor was going to be any easier. I believed that the problem was my effort, not his teaching.

After a wonderful Christmas break of home-cooked meals, visits to my church, and time with Kim Taylor, I came back to OWU refueled and ready to conquer the world. I had been down before, but Dr. Lucas seemed to be waiting to take me down another notch every day. So I prayed harder, typed longer, and studied more notes.

When a crucial midterm exam was approaching, Pete worked with me, and my mother made more than her routine phone calls. More nerve-wracking than the actual exam was the day when Dr. Lucas would pass out the results. Nervously waiting near the back of class, my palms sweating, my academic future on the line, I watched and listened as Dr. Lucas passed out papers and puffed on his pipe. Finally, he came to me. Instead of continuing on with the rhythm of passing out papers and moving along, Dr. Lucas stopped at my desk. With a big smile, he placed my test results on my desk and announced to the class, "Congratulations, Mr. Pitts, your best work thus far. D plus. Bravo!"

He proceeded to pass out the remaining few papers to my other classmates. As for me, I was back in my father's car: silent, warm, staring straight ahead, expressionless. I put my hands under my chin and refused to cry or get angry. I never heard another sound the rest of the class. I didn't even realize class was over until my classmates started to leave.

On my way out, Dr. Lucas asked me to follow him to his office. Raised to always respect authority, I gave the only response I knew to give, "Yes, sir." Once I was in his office, Dr. Lucas said what he had to say quickly. At the time it seemed almost kind.

"Mr. Pitts, I'll make this quick. No need to sit down." Rarely did Dr. Lucas ever look directly at me when he spoke, but this time he made an exception. "Mr. Pitts, you are wasting my time and the government's money. You are not Ohio Wesleyan University material. I think you should leave." I had no reaction. He continued. "You're excused. Nothing further. Please tell your mother what I said. Good luck to both of you. Now excuse me."

That's it. Game over. I was done. Hard work and prayer had taken me as far as it could. This professor in a position to know had declared my fate.

What did he mean by "the government's money"? I had received a few grants and scholarships, but he made it sound as if I was on some college welfare program. More than anything else, I wanted to simply be able to walk out of his office with my head still up. I wouldn't give him the satisfaction of seeing me cry. But, at that moment, in the mind of an eighteen-year-old kid, my pursuit of a college education was over. My dreams, my family's dreams, were just that. Perhaps I wasn't retarded or mentally ill, but I was far from college material.

All of our work—the village that pulled me through—those who cheered for me and mentored me and tutored me, for whom I was the hope of a college success story. I had failed them all. This man said I wasn't good enough, and I had to believe that he was right.

At this moment, I was alone and frightened. To this point in life, through every hardship and obstacle, I had had someone who cared about me close by to pick me up, dust me off, and lead me on my way. Always in the past, my mother was in the next room, or there would be an inspiring sermon from Reverend Carter at New Shiloh or an encouraging word from Coach Mack or Father Bart that would lighten my burden and I could push through. This time none of them was in sight. The shame inside me grew. All those demons of insecurity and uncertainty waiting just below the surface of my life were pushing their way to the top. I was ashamed that I had failed, ashamed even more that I was thinking about giving up, quitting.

SIX

# Letters from Home

To get where you want to go, you must keep on keeping on.

**—Norman Vincent Peale**

For eighteen years Clarice Pitts seamlessly raised me by combining a fierce demand for discipline and an equal measure of love. With the balance of a high-wire acrobat, she would dish out punishment with the same hand she used to hold her children when they needed comfort. Clarice was born with long limbs, but they could not stretch easily from East Baltimore to Delaware, Ohio. The miles between us now created distance and difficulties. My grades were suffering, and I was on the verge of flunking out. In her own way, she still needed to wage the fight for me, just the way she did when I was a kid. She had appealed to Dr. Lucas by phone and was left frustrated. She was not in the habit of being ignored. So perhaps in order to stay connected and still yield a high level of influence, she resorted to writing letters. She is not a casual woman; thus, these would not be casual letters.

School was tough. Clarice was tougher. It was her way of being supportive. To her, support meant brutal honesty. But now the opponent was my own lethargy and intellectual paralysis. If she had to punch through my soul to knock out the enemy, she'd do it.

While it may be hard for my children or many of their generation to believe, long before e-mails, text messages, or cell phones, people communicated regularly by handwritten letters. During my four years in college in the late 1970s, my family and I rarely talked by phone. It was too expensive. There was a pay phone at the end of the hallway in my freshman dormitory, but phone calls were sporadic. A roll of quarters would give me a few minutes on the phone with my mom, a call to my grandmother, and maybe a few minutes on the phone with my sister or girlfriend, Kim. But I could always count on at least one letter per week from my home. Between my freshman year and graduation, my mother must have written me at least 152 letters, one for every week I was in school. Included with each letter, in every envelope, would be a Bible verse typed on an index card. Occasionally, a second index card would hold some encouraging quotation she'd picked up somewhere. Things like: "It is not your aptitude, but your attitude that determines your altitude." She got a lot of these pithy self-help bromides from her new collection of books. Her dozens and dozens of letters became a minor sensation among many of my friends. Especially Pete. He jokingly began referring to my mother as Mother Clarice (as in Mother Teresa) and Colonel Clarice. He found it amusing that this black woman hundreds of miles away seemed to have so much influence over my life. A small circle of friends who were estranged from their own parents seemed to take real joy in her words. Her typed index cards often wound up tacked to the corkboard wall in someone else's room. I've kept many of them. I wish I'd kept them all.

Of all her letters to me and my siblings, the one that's taken on near-legendary status in our family was the one that came in the midst of my struggles with my freshman English professor, Dr. Lucas. My confidence had slipped as much as my grades, and in a few of my phone calls I started dropping hints that maybe OWU wasn't right for me. My mother was not a quitter. She wasn't having it.

Clarice had a unique system for identifying the purpose of her letters even before you read them. Black ink meant all was fine with the world, and there might even be some humor in her correspondence. Blue ink meant she wanted to discuss some difficulty in her own life, which she was more likely to share as her children got older. But if a letter from home came in red ink, that meant the recipient was in serious trouble. Red meant anger. So when the envelope arrived in my dormitory mailbox with my name and address written in red, I knew I was in for a verbal assault, a linguistic beat down. Her first line cleared up any doubt. Clarice Pitts has loved the Lord nearly all of her life, but she's always had great affection for profanity when it served her, especially when it came to making a point to her children.

*Dear Mr. Brain Dead,*

*Have you lost your fucking mind? You went to Ohio Wesleyan with the expressed goal of graduating, going on to live your dreams and God's purpose for your life. At the first sign of trouble you want to give up. Fine! Bring your ass back to Baltimore and get a job. Maybe if you think you're up for it, enroll in Bay College. There are plenty of places in the city for dummies. Yep, come home with your tail between your legs and get some half-ass job and spend the rest of your life crying about what you could have been. Maybe all you're cut out to be is a meat-cutting, cab-driving underachiever. Maybe I was wrong about you. Maybe you have worked as hard as you can, as you claim, and your best isn't good enough. Is that what you think? Here's what I know.*

*You are a gift from God. The Lord I serve does not make mistakes. You did not get to Ohio Wesleyan because you are so smart or worked so hard. You got there because of prayer and faith and God's grace. Yes, you worked hard in high school. But you only did part of the work. Every time you took one step, God took two. Is college harder than high school? It better be, as much as it cost. So what's that mean for you? Work harder than you think you are even capable of working. Pray longer than you've ever prayed. That's what I'm doing. That is what we always do. What has your grandmother told you? You can't climb that mountain without some rough spots. Maybe you're in a cave on the other side of your mountain. Don't get scared or lazy. Don't just cry. Figure out what God is teaching you, then get your ass back on that mountain and keep pulling hard and looking forward.*

*Son, you know your momma loves you. I believe in*

*you. I pray for you. I know you better than you know yourself. And I know a God who is able. You're not coming home. You're not going to give up. You're not going to fail. You are going to endure.*

*Love,*
*Mom*

*Whew!* That's my momma summed up in a single letter: angry, passionate, relentless, unbending, unedited, unforgiving, immovable in her faith, and unwilling to give an inch or give up on her son. Regardless of the times, whether or not the experts, the people around her, or even I doubted what was possible, she stood like stone. Thirty years later, it still makes me laugh a bit, even tear up every time I read this particular letter. She never simply pushed—she lifted. I know that now; I sensed it then. As I recall, back in 1978, I had three reactions. As I was reading the letter, I was crying, for obvious reasons, because it felt like she was piling on. It was symbolic of the tension between a kid growing into manhood and his mother. She didn't understand that I was trying.

Then it made me angry. Oftentimes my mother's tough love brought us together. This time it pushed us apart. I understood her point, but she was wrong about the particulars. Up until that point in my life, she had been right about everything.

I remember reading the letter again and finally it made me laugh. It reminded me how intense my mother is. As I read the letter over again and again, it was like looking in a mirror. I too was tough. It was okay to get angry, perhaps even curse a bit, then settle down, refocus, recommit, remember not simply who I was but whose I was. As always, included in the envelope was an index card with Scripture. Psalm 37: "Fret not thyself because of evildoers . . . For they shall soon be cut down like the grass, and wither as the green herb." I wasn't sure if that biblical threat was aimed at me or Dr. Lucas. Mom would later explain that negative thoughts and pessimism were like "evildoers." She was saying don't worry about things. Her bottom line was always, let God fight your battles.

Maybe it was the training that came with being a social worker or the innate skills of a good parent, but even when she was at her harshest, Clarice always seemed to know what was needed and when it was needed. She made a compelling argument. Did I want to return to Baltimore and cut grass on the interstate? Was I giving up? For weeks Clarice continued to write letters of encouragement while I wrestled with the decision to withdraw from school.

My mother was appealing to the dream of who she thought I could be. But Dr. Lucas spoke directly to who I believed I was. "You're not Ohio Wesleyan material," he had said.

My mother was being hopeful. But, in my mind, he was being realistic, more honest. Finally, I was exhausted and wanted to escape them both. If I left school, I would be done with him, and if I went back to Baltimore, I couldn't stay in my mother's house. On a chilly February morning I walked over to University Hall to pick up the forms to withdraw from Ohio Wesleyan.

Sitting on a bench outside, I had my book bag on one

shoulder and blank forms in my free hand. Somewhere between sadness and anger, my emotions provided insulation from the winter cold. I didn't seem to notice the temperature or that I was now crying. Not small tears, mind you, but nose-running, lose my breath, shoulders-shaking tears. How pathetic I must have looked. I guess that's why a plump woman with long brown hair and a heavy coat stopped in front of me.

"Young man, are you okay?" came a slightly accented voice.

"Yes, ma'am, I'm fi . . . fi . . . fine." It was almost guaranteed that whenever I was overcome by emotion, the stuttering would start.

"You don't look fine. Please tell me what's wrong," she insisted. By this time my spirit was broken, and I was too emotionally spent to make up a story, so I just started blabbing. I must have talked for several minutes because the woman in the big coat interrupted me and said, "May I sit down while you continue your story?"

I continued to ramble on for at least twenty minutes. This round-faced stranger just kept smiling and listening. Her body language assured me that what I had to say was somehow important. First I told her what Dr. Lucas had said, that I wasn't college material. I was failing his class, and it was his recommendation that I leave. "I guess I'm just stupid," I told her. "I was fooling myself to think I could make it here." I told her that I was tired of being embarrassed in class. But I knew that if I dropped out of school, it would embarrass my family. I told her I didn't feel as if I had any choice. All the while I was crying, sniffling, and stuttering.

Eventually she interrupted me and said, "I'm so sorry, but I must get back to work now. But can we continue our talk tomorrow. And promise me you won't drop out of school before we talk?"

"Bu . . . bu . . . bu . . . but I'm just stupid. I don't belong here," I mumbled.

Then she flashed a part of her personality I would come to see plenty of in the years to come: "That's just nonsense. Stop it. Stop that right now! Now give me your word you will speak to me tomorrow before you make any final decision on school! Give me your word! Look me in the eye and give me your word!"

Confused about why this stranger would be raising her voice at me, I simply said, "Yes, ma'am."

"Well, good," she answered with a reassuring smile. "My name is Ulle. My office is on the second floor of Slocum Hall. Can you come see me at around eleven?"

"Yes, ma'am."

"Then it is settled. Go on with the rest of your day, and we will speak tomorrow."

I welcomed the chance to delay what seemed like the inevitable. Clarice was always big on going to bed and allowing trouble to rest the night as well. Somehow I felt a bit relieved and finished the day. The next morning I made my way to Slocum Hall. Perhaps because of my own emotional state or her odd accent, I wasn't sure I caught her name correctly. Ohio Wesleyan is a small and friendly campus, and most people could put a name with a face. She did say second floor. Inside Slocum, I asked a student, "Do you know a lady who works in this building—she has long brown hair, friendly round face, a bit on the plump side . . ." (There are a number of plump women in my family, and "plump" was always the preferred description).

"Oh, you mean Dr. Lewes," the student responded.

I smiled. She must be mistaken. "No, this lady isn't a doctor." I thought to myself that maybe she was on the University staff in some capacity. Perhaps administrative or something clerical. Professors, I believed, looked and acted like Dr. Lucas.

"Well, you just described Dr. Lewes. Around the corner on the right. I gotta go."

With that, I was alone in the hallway with directions to a professor's office who couldn't possibly be the woman who listened to my sad and lengthy story the day before. Since I had nothing to lose, I walked to the office as directed, and there to my surprise on the door was the name DR. ÜLLE LEWES. Inside the office, behind the desk, was the plump woman with long wavy brown hair, her face buried in a book. With a knock at the door, I asked, "Dr. Lewes?"

"Good morning, young man," she answered with that familiar smile. "Please come in." It was a greeting that would change my life. The remarkable Dr. Ülle Lewes. If ever I doubted that angels really do exist, those doubts were now cast aside. In time, she didn't simply change my life—she saved it.

SEVEN

# An Angel from Estonia

. . . he shall send his angel . . .

—**Genesis 24:7**

ÜLLE LEWES RECOGNIZED MY struggle because she has survived a lifetime of her own struggles. I've never been to Estonia, but in my eyes Ülle Erika Lewes is the embodiment of her native land. Proud but not boastful, optimistic yet a realist, tough but easily wounded, loyal but at times distant, independent but willfully vulnerable, always prepared to fight for what she loves, and willing to love based on blind faith. She is like all the women I love. An inner beauty cast inside an outer toughness. A beating heart wrapped in warm steel. Open to all but truly welcoming only to a few.

Ülle was born in Tallinn, Estonia, during World War II, when the country was caught in the middle, with the Soviet Union pulling and bombing from one direction and Germany pulling and bombing from the other. Her earliest memories of childhood were running into the basement with her mother during aerial attacks by both sides. At the age of three, with her father off fighting the war, Ülle and her mother, grandmother, aunt, and a cousin escaped from Estonia on a barge. They eventually became refugees, first in Latvia, then Lithuania, Poland, Czechoslovakia, and finally in Germany. It was there that she took her first bitter taste of discrimination. She went to school with German kids who hated the foreigners. Surrounded by prejudice, Ülle would pass by police checkpoints and soldiers every day going to and from school. The innocence of childhood and each new day were often interrupted by slurs and intimidation. Her tales of life in a distant world drew me closer to her. The difficulties she had to overcome put my own in a new perspective.

Eventually, in November 1951, Ülle and her family would immigrate to the United States, with the promise of a better life. Sponsored by the Lutheran church for the first six months, they settled in Roxbury, Massachusetts. But amid the promise of the New World was an old and familiar problem: prejudice. On the postwar streets of a Germany scarred in battle, people had hated the Estonian girl because she was foreign. In the racially segregated city of Boston, on the awkward side of the civil rights era, black kids hated the nine-year-old white girl, who did not look like them or sound like them.

When she first came to the United States, it was the same as it was in Germany, the mean looks and crazy questions. But Ülle found peace and comfort in her schoolbooks and in words. Eventually, her family moved to Buffalo, where she graduated valedictorian of her high school class and earned a full scholarship to Cornell. She was fluent in Estonian, Spanish, French, Latin, and German. Ülle's first love was comparative literature. Soon the little girl from Estonia found her path. After graduate school at Harvard University and a brief time teaching at Temple University in Philadelphia, Dr. Ülle Lewes took a job in the English Department at Ohio Wesleyan University.

When I met her, Ülle was a full-figured woman, with thick, curly, reddish brown hair, round glasses, and a perpetual smile. Even on those days when her knees hurt or life did not treat her kindly, there was that smile tickling her eyes and stretching across her kind face, along her soft round shoulders down to the tips of her fingers. She was born to teach English. She taught it the way a good masseuse gives massages: with her entire body. During lectures she would actually extend her arms in the air, rub her fingers together like a sculptor rolling clay, as if the words were alive in her hands. That was Ülle, working to become one with the right word.

She started at OWU in the fall of 1978, the same as me. "I was a new-bee," she said, describing those early days. And soon the "new-bee" from Estonia and the freshman from Baltimore would cross paths on a cold morning outside University Hall. Perhaps it was Ülle's own encounters with disappointment or her feelings of being out of place that allowed her to notice me. Although Ülle has never considered herself a religious person, she acknowledges that some sort of spiritual guidance might have been at work.

At that first meeting in her office she made a commitment to help me. We planned to meet for two hours a week at first, and eventually it increased to three and then four hours. We would get together either in her office or in the Writing Resource Center set up across campus. In the early days, as I struggled with an English assignment, complaining and voicing doubt, she always reassured me. Ülle identified my two basic problems: not enough attention to (as she called them) stupid details; the other, a simple lack of structure. She began to work on my structure issues by organizing my life. Ülle never taught me a single class my freshman year, but she was the only professor I cared about pleasing. She set up something that resembled a shadow class to my scheduled English class. In one hour Professor Lucas would strip at my confidence like a craftsman stripping varnish off an old floor. I would go to Professor Lewes for a new coat of confidence. She rarely questioned the content of my work. She would patiently have me correct punctuation, grammar, and sentence structure. She insisted I pay attention to every detail. Secretly she would grade Dr. Lucas's papers with her own grading scale. While Dr. Lucas was still giving me Ds and Fs, Ülle would grade the same assignment and give it As or Bs. Dr. Lucas measured the outcome, and there was simply a right or wrong, black or white. Ülle graded in the gray area. She measured effort, creativity, and the slightest improvement from the previous assignment.

"He graded you on surface areas like punctuation and sentence structure. It's all important, of course. I graded you on rhetorical structure, development, and detail. Detail provides those vivid nuggets," she said.

With the improvements I was making, by the end of the semester, Dr. Lucas would mark my papers with Bs and Cs and an occasional A. Dr. Lewes, on the other hand, had changed her standards, and suddenly she was giving Cs and Ds. She had helped break Dr. Lucas's code, his standard. Now she was teaching me to set my own and continually move the bar higher.

"Never settle. Push! Push! Push harder."

Ülle showed the sort of kindness, optimism, and concern I had seen in only a handful of people till this stage of my life. She and my mother were from completely different worlds, but they shared this relentless faith in me and in hard work. Both would flash their tempers, not at results but at lackluster effort. Both would use profanity to lecture but never once to scold. It is a characteristic they shared with my favorite athletic coaches. And Ülle seemed inexhaustible. We would often meet at the end of a day after she had taught several classes and met with several other students.

When you are in Ülle's presence, you have her undivided attention. It was during one of those sessions that Ülle touched my hand and shouted, "Look at me! Someday you will write a book." I was eighteen, on academic probation, and a breath away from flunking out of college. A book seemed beyond impossible.

The closer we became as professor and student, the more she sounded like Clarice. I do recall at least one F from Dr. Lewes. On at least one occasion, she did not like my effort.

"Don't get lazy," she snapped. It was as if she had cut me with a knife. Laziness was rarely my problem, but impatience often got the best of me in college and in the years that followed. Why am I still struggling? Why do I still comprehend things so slowly? Why can't I read a chapter once and grasp its meaning? There were times I wanted to give up, not because I was lazy but rather because I was overwhelmed by impatience. The two-step forward one-step back dance often became tiresome. Ülle would always push me past those moments.

"Anyone who reads your work carefully can see you have a brilliant mind," Ülle said. "You have to make them see it and I will help you." Instructive and encouraging. That was her style. Over many years and a few meals, we have discussed Dr. Lucas. What could she see that he could not? "I don't know," she would answer modestly.

To his credit, Dr. Lucas had a wonderful reputation for working with and inspiring honor students. In fact, he was one of the leading advocates for raising the academic standards at Ohio Wesleyan. Standards quite frankly that would have kept me from ever being admitted to OWU. I am sure there are countless OWU grads who can attest to his brilliance and care. That is not my testimony or that of at least two other OWU graduates I've met over the years. Twice while giving speeches around the country, where I told the story of my experience at Ohio Wesleyan and without mentioning his name, a person in the audience would walk up to me afterward, shake my hand, and ask, "Were you talking about Dr. Lucas?" I guess I wasn't alone. We would exchange notes and quickly come to the conclusion that the experience only made us stronger. Perhaps it just serves to illustrate that even in a place as small as Ohio Wesleyan, there are the right people and the wrong people placed in a person's path. You must survive one and cling to the other. I was in Dr. Lucas's class, but I was never one of his students. That first year I was not in a single one of Ülle's classes, but I was most certainly one of her students.

As often as she would allow it, I would eat my lunch in Dr. Lewes's office. Sometimes she was there. Sometimes she wasn't. Her office had become my second home. There were even times I would sit outside her classroom and do my homework. Even her encouraging words aimed at other students would lift my spirits.

Ülle and my mother first met by phone and hit it off instantly, although there was some adjustment required in the beginning because college professors are not used to being treated like daycare providers. Clarice has always taken great pride in keeping tabs on her children. She has called teachers, professors, and a few news directors whenever she has seen fit. One of the few who never seemed to mind was Ülle. "Once your mother called me and asked, 'How is my boy doing? Is he getting an A?' I said no, but if he works hard he may get an A-," recalled Ülle. "She really wanted to understand. I liked Clarice right from the start. She wasn't pushing me—she wanted to understand. Her tone was, I want to understand what's going on. I could sense her heart," Ülle said of my mother.

Two women from different worlds who endured different hardships and whose paths intersected. There have been countless strong women in my life: my mother, sister, grandmother, aunts, and my wife. I revere Ülle Lewes as much as I do any of them. Others have been bonded to me by blood or marriage, but Ülle just showed up one day and never left. Because of her, I believe in angels.

While some students found Dr. Lewes's style odd, pushy,

and invasive, she did teach one course that was a particular favorite. Advanced English Composition. It was a class in which profanity was encouraged. Early in the semester Dr. Lewes would have us close our textbooks, and she would ask us to scream. Then scream and curse. Initially, students were reluctant and shy. Eventually, they would embrace the concept. Before long, she would have to temper their enthusiasm.

"I want to break you down," is how Dr. Lewes described it. "It takes half the semester to break students down. They're so stiff and proper, they're not writing authentically. Just writing school shit and not writing real shit. There is absolutely nothing worse than school talk. Almost all the talk we talk is fake talk. There is nothing wrong with curse words. They're only words. I want my students to write authentically. You can decide if it's [profanity] not proper for the audience and change, but first it must be raw."

I remember the experience. It was both frightening and fun. I had never, not once, cursed intentionally in front of an adult. Dr. Lewes always seemed to value effort and authenticity; perhaps that's why she questioned my occasional speech pattern. Thus far, I stuttered only when I was nervous, angry, or tired. I was never any of that around Dr. Lewes, but occasionally my enthusiasm would get the best of me, and I'd stutter, if only just a bit.

"I thought you were faking some odd British accent or something," Ülle would say many years later.

I believe God equips us all with different gifts and just a select number of them. Ülle Lewes's command of the written word would help shape and change my life. For stuttering, I had to go elsewhere. Fortunately for me, help with stuttering was actually in the next building. If Dr. Lewes was all things kind and encouraging, Dr. Ed Robinson was all things cranky and gruff. He was a professor in the understaffed, less-than-glamorous department of speech communications at Ohio Wesleyan. Simply put, it was a department few people on campus seemed to take seriously at the time. Dr. Robinson was a bear of a man. A few inches over six feet tall and with a thick Midwestern build, he was more old lion than cuddly teddy bear. His voice was just as loud and scratchy as the Harley-Davidson motorcycle he rode to campus. At a university where some professors rode bicycles, walked, or drove fuel-efficient cars, the sight of Dr. Robinson riding his Harley was often greeted with a turned-up nose or rolling of the eyes. Oddly enough, he always seemed to have a soft spot for the inner-city kid who, like him, didn't seem to fit in at this small liberal arts college in Ohio.

"I like you, Pitts," he'd say. "You're a tough kid."

Dr. Robinson noticed my problem with stuttering one day when he asked each student to declare what they wanted to do for a career after college. Many of my classmates were children of privilege or came from stable middle-class families. Their career plans seemed consistent with their upbringing. Some answered with ease and conviction. "I will be a teacher. . . . A lawyer. . . . I will work in my dad's company. . . ." When it was my turn, I said, "I want to be a jour . . . jour . . . jour . . . journalist." I could hear the whispered laughter around me. With a stone cold stare, Dr. Robinson looked at me and said, "See me after class."

Expecting harsh advice from yet another unyielding professor, I braced myself for Dr. Robinson's comments. "How long have you stuttered?" he asked.

"Sir?" I answered.

"You heard me—how long have you stuttered?" Dr. Robinson wasn't into pleasantries or repeating himself. "I think I can help you." That's all he ever said. It was a quick glimpse of kindness he would never betray again. I wish now that I had been looking directly in his eyes because perhaps they would have revealed more. Except for those six words "I think I can help you," I had all but missed a precious moment with a man who had joined the list of those who would change my life.

For the next year or so, Dr. Robinson, with the help of a colleague of his from Ohio State, worked with me patiently. He would force me to sit in a booth at the radio station for thirty minutes at a time and record my voice. The recording was easy. Speaking with pencils in my mouth was the challenge. There was no money in his budget to teach speech pathology, and I did not have the money or the means to drive to Ohio State University in Columbus, which had the resources I needed. So, with Dr. Robinson's help, we improvised. He would have me read Shakespeare or the sports page forward and backward. He insisted I take a theater course called The Actor's Voice. He also encouraged me to take on a hosting job at the radio station. Odd choice for a stutterer, but he believed in confronting the problem. And it worked. I never stuttered on the air. I used a technique of singing my sentences. It helped me transition between the words without taking a breath. I likened it to church, where the minister sometimes sings the words in a sermon. I did the same thing with my scripts. (It was a habit I had to break years later as a professional journalist.)

"You gotta keep working, keep practicing," he insisted. "You can lick this if you work at it," he'd say more as an order than as words of encouragement. I would often greet his directives with a smile. If I closed my eyes, ignored the smell of his cologne and the scratchy bass in his voice, he too sounded like my mother. Often my smile would turn into a brief and quiet laugh.

"Concentrate! Slow down! Breathe!" That was as detailed as his coaching ever was. I suspect he had little or no training as a speech pathologist. In the same way, he was not a trained motorcycle mechanic, but he tinkered and cursed over his Harley-Davidson and kept it on the road. Much the same way, he kept me on the path God was paving for me. Through the years I have talked with skilled speech pathologists who talk about the dark ages of working with people who stutter. Many of the things Dr. Robinson had me do were long ago cast aside as outdated. Today, there are a number of institutions across the country that work faithfully and skillfully with people of all ages who stutter. There are even associations for people who stutter. I have done a few news stories on stuttering but have never sought specialized training. I could certainly still use it. There are words with which I still struggle. Phrases I avoid. It has forced me, as best I can, to think before I speak. It has left me vulnerable in verbal confrontations. But the practice of pausing and gathering my thoughts before speaking has served me well as a journalist.

Life is always about choices. The choices we make for ourselves and the choices people make for us. Dr. Robinson and I lost contact. He left Ohio Wesleyan not long after I graduated. Some people saw him as bitter and outdated. His old school ways and unpolished manner suited me perfectly. I believe we are all instruments of God. There aren't many uses in life for an old rusty hacksaw, except when only an old rusty hacksaw will do.

Dr. Lewes and I continued our tutoring sessions for well over a year, but by the end of my sophomore year, most of my visits to Dr. Lewes's office were more social than academic. I'd go by her office for lunch, and we would shoot the breeze, sometimes talking about her life and not my academics at all. By now she was becoming my friend. She had helped me unlock Dr. Lucas's system, and she'd taught me to do two things that applied to every class: meet the instructor's expectations and do my best. Before college, my teachers and tutors and counselors had always come to my level to figure out my problems. What Ülle taught me was that now I had to meet the professors at their level. I had to learn to interpret what each professor needed and to deliver it, not always plead with them to help me understand or give it to me in smaller bits so I could digest it.

I began to select classes based not just on the credits I needed but on professors to whose style I could adapt. I even avoided the professors who had a reputation for easier courses because I recognized the need to challenge myself in as broad a way as possible. I had a philosophy professor my sophomore and junior years who loved his students to be engaged in class, challenging him in the discussion. So I would prepare for his class by having mock discussions in my dorm room, sometimes alone, sometimes with Pete. Spelling was a challenge, too. In the journalism department, one professor would give a red F for misspelling someone's name, lowering your grade by a full letter. Two red Fs and you could easily fail the class. Before Ülle, that kind of standard would have intimidated me, but after Ülle's counsel, I embraced it. Once I understood his standard, I worked harder to achieve it. Steadily my grades in all my classes began to improve.

With an unbreakable bond and affection, Dr. Ülle Lewes quickly became a permanent part of my family. She wept with my mother at my graduation and years later attended my wedding as a member of my family. The weekend my wife and I got married we threw two parties: a reception for family and friends and a luncheon for just family. Ülle showed up at both. My aunts and uncles loved her light Estonian accent. After the wedding, she danced and laughed with my mother and grandmother. Ülle Lewes taught me English in college, but she taught and still teaches me so much more. Perhaps more than an English professor, she is a life coach. I asked her once about her teaching philosophy, and after a long silence she said, "Challenge them [students] to be better than they think they can be."

Leaving the nurturing tutelage of Ülle at Ohio Wesleyan reminded me of what it felt like to break that childhood connection to my mother. Clarice had molded me and guided me, been there to fight my battles and level her expectations. I still carried a lot of baggage, emotional and otherwise, but we had gotten me this far by faith. But now I was heading into adulthood. Clearly not ready to stand all alone, I would need the counsel and support and mentorship of countless friends and colleagues. Many of them shared those characteristics of passion, toughness, and commitment that my mother and Ülle had. They all would have a pivotal role in shaping my future. But I was no longer simply a student of those around me; it was time to venture out. Apply the lessons learned. Fall and get up again on my own. Though fear and anger were still vital, a spiritual strength and optimism were growing inside me.

EIGHT

# Never Say I'll Try, Say I Will

Let not your heart be troubled, neither let it be afraid.

—**John 14:27**

Where the spirit of the Lord is, there is peace; where the Spirit of the Lord is, there is love.

—**Stephen R. Adams**

EVEN WHILE I WAS knee-deep in my struggles with college academics and working to overcome my stuttering, my mind and heart were growing in focus on a career in broadcast journalism. And why not? My love for words was a result of my struggles with literacy. I believed some good, a new strength, would also come from my difficulties with speech. Much more than belief in my own abilities, it was a belief in God's power. Thus, despite my shortcomings, I never doubted my chosen path. My faith teaches me that there are no obstacles, that all stumbling blocks are merely stepping stones and part of God's plan. It was my responsibility to remain faithful and see what God had in store on the other side of my difficulties.

When I left high school, having moved from functional

illiteracy to a solid transcript, I approached college with relative confidence and the assumption that I was prepared for whatever might come my way. The first year of college was like a blast of frigid air to my psyche. If there had been a basement class, at least one professor we know would have put me there. I was at the bottom looking up again.

Could read but couldn't read fast enough or smart enough.

Could write but my thoughts were a jumbled mess.

Could speak but couldn't speak clearly under pressure.

Knew words but didn't have a wide enough vocabulary.

Yet I was not the same kid I had been at age thirteen. That young Byron was frightened, ashamed, and angry. The older Byron was still angry but beginning to realize that there would always be hurdles. There might always be a period of starting over. I just needed to be patient and faithful and tough enough to work my way to the other side. Admit what I didn't know and ask for help when I needed it, but mostly roll up my sleeves and outwork those around me.

By my senior year at Ohio Wesleyan I was on pretty solid academic ground. I had decided to major in journalism and speech communications, with a minor in political science. Active in sports and school organizations, I had a column for the school newspaper, was news director for the school's cable television news show, co-hosted a nighttime radio show, and worked as a freelance reporter for the local area radio station. It was a big deal for me when I made the regional Associated Press with a story I wrote on a local city council meeting. I stayed up half the night to see my byline cross the wire. I was named one of the top three students in the journalism department based on academic achievement and contributions to the department. We all dreamed of big careers in newspapers or television, becoming the next Bob Woodward or Walter Cronkite. My hero was Ed Bradley. I knew his level of coolness would always elude me, but just maybe his caliber of work might someday be achievable. It was another Pitts family philosophy. Never say you'll try. Say you will. I was raised to believe that if you speak your dreams long enough and loud enough, eventually others will dream and speak with you.

My inspiration to pursue journalism had deep roots. First, there were my struggles with literacy and speech. I took those as signs from God that communication would play a major part in my life. I had convinced myself through Scriptures like Romans 12:21, "Be not overcome of evil, but overcome evil with good," that all the bad things in life had some good purpose if only I searched long enough. So I concluded that journalism was my purpose. In addition to commanding respect, journalists have a significant and valid place in our democracy. As a child, I attended any number of rallies related to social justice and civil rights or big events at my church. I always sat in amazement when the media would show up. The police would behave one way when cameras and reporters were present, often less aggressively. Journalists held the authorities accountable, and that appealed to me. In the days after Dr. Martin Luther King Jr. was assassinated in 1968, there were riots in cities across the country, including Baltimore. On our street, looters vandalized cars that failed to have a black cloth tied to the antenna. Police took that same black cloth as a sign the car belonged to some kind of troublemaker. My father and brother stayed up most of the night, running back and forth to the car to put up or pull down the black cloth, depending on whether there were police or looters on our block. The police were not as violent but they were certainly as aggressive as the looters. One evening, as the police made their way through our neighborhood (there was a police station just a few blocks away), pushing and shoving men and women on the street, a local television crew pulled up. Suddenly, the nightsticks were not being used as aggressively. That moment left an indelible impression on me. Journalists, simply by their presence, could keep the police honest. I wasn't so much bitten by the bug as saw that the bug had teeth.

Why would someone with a history of stuttering choose a career in television? Why not become a print journalist? There were a number of factors. I was a television junkie, having spent hours and hours watching television as a child, especially when the tension in my house was at its highest. Television also kept me company when I was home by myself. Much of what I knew about the world, I learned from television. When it came to gathering news, I was much more comfortable speaking to someone in person as part of a television crew rather than on the telephone, where my stuttering problems might be more apparent. Face-to-face, I could smile or even use my hands for emphasis. I was also a great listener. One of the things I learned in broadcast journalism was to allow the interview subject to fill the silence. That part was easy for me. But I knew I would need practice to overcome my lingering communication issues. I still spoke slowly and deliberately, using the sing-song style I had learned from Dr. Robinson. So I practiced being a television reporter in my dormitory bathroom with a glass and my toothbrush. The top of a glass is about the size of a television camera lens. A toothbrush doesn't resemble a microphone at all, but it's what I had. With a Magic Marker, I traced the edge of the glass on the bathroom mirror, and every morning before class and every night before bed I put on my own mini-newscast. Silly, I know, but since my early struggles with literacy and speech, repetition and routine are things I rely on. The bathroom routine was about practicing the mechanics of television news.

My decision to pursue a career in journalism was solidified after hearing the stories of the guest lecturers who appeared on campus during my time at OWU, such as investigative reporter Jack Anderson and network television correspondent Emery King. In the 1980s, King was one of a handful of African-American television network news correspondents. He served NBC News as its White House correspondent covering the Reagan administration, and later spent nineteen years as an anchor in Detroit. During my senior year King spoke at OWU as part of a university lecture series. He spoke of the highs and lows of broadcast journalism as well as his travels around the globe. I had the honor of picking him up at the airport with a few of my classmates. As was my pattern back then, I was still very shy about speaking in unfamiliar settings, without the opportunity to rehearse and with people who might sense my limitations and dismiss me. So I said very little in his presence. Too nervous, anxious about my stutter, and, frankly, convinced I had nothing worth saying, I certainly made no impression on the man.

But a notable thing happened after his lecture as we were walking him back to the car. One of my female classmates stopped him on the stairwell and said, "Mr. King, thank you for talking to us. We will always remember what you said."

Now here's the line that made Emery King stop in his tracks. "But I want you to remember one name," she said. "Byron Pitts. He will be at the network someday."

King seemed surprised by my classmate's bold prediction. I was stunned. Perhaps I had spoken my ambitious plan aloud so often people around me were beginning to believe it. My friend's words were powerful because it was the first time I had heard anyone, not even my mother to this point, affirm out loud what my career goals were. It was like a needle full of adrenaline in the heart. For years I had quietly claimed my future career as a network journalist, and now others were claiming it with me. Emery King politely smiled and got in his car. Years later I met him on assignment. He didn't recall the moment, nor did he have any real reason to. But I will always remember it. I have never stopped affirming (or claiming) what I want, and I have always found support from those who join me. It is amazing how you can transform a dream into a reality by saying it until you believe it and others believe it with you. It can become a call to arms. You say it. You believe it. You then devote your dreams and your sweat to it.

That May the dream of my mother, my grandmother, Dr. Lewes, and countless supporters back in East Baltimore came to pass. I put on a cap and gown and joined the 1982 graduating class of Ohio Wesleyan. I was grateful to be graduating on time. I remember the pride stitched across the faces of my family. My mother, brother, sister, and grandmother were in attendance. Remember we are not a big smiling family, but I did see a few teeth that day. It was a bittersweet day for me. I was not focused so much on what I had accomplished or where I was headed as on the people I was about to leave behind. I had grown close to people like Dr. Lewes, my friend Pete, and others. Those kinds of emotional separations had always been tough for me since the breakup of my parents' marriage.

As I left the stage with my degree in hand, I paused so my brother could take a picture. Since no one in my family could snap a good photograph before there was automatic focus, we had albums full of blurry memories. In the age of digital cameras, none of us have managed to frame very well. Today we have crisp family photos with little head room or odd angles.

After my brother snapped his picture, I handed my degree to my mother. "You worked as hard as I did," I whispered to her. "You deserve this more than me."

She hugged me to the point of discomfort, kissed my cheek, and handed my degree back to me. "God worked harder than either of us. This is His, but you hold on to it in the meantime," she said, with the corners of her mouth nearly touching her ears. We laughed. I walked back to my seat with my wrinkled robe blowing in the breeze. I was actually a bit sad when the day was done. I have always enjoyed the journey more than the destination.

That was a Saturday. The following Monday I started work at *The Carolinian* newspaper in Raleigh, North Carolina, where my mom had relocated a few years earlier. It was a weekly newspaper published by a local African-American businessman and aimed at an African-American audience. As a reporter, photographer, sportswriter, copy editor, and go-get-the-boss-cigarettes-when-he-called-for-them, I was paid handsomely: one hundred dollars every Friday, five twenty-dollar bills in a small brown envelope. I assumed the envelope was small so the rolled-up twenties would seem like a larger sum of money. It was modest pay for joyous work. Despite the minimal sum, I was now a working journalist. My mother was simply thrilled I had a job she could describe to her siblings in one sentence. "Byron is a reporter in Raleigh," she'd say. To hear her brag to her friends and family, it was as if I was a staff writer for *The New York Times*.

There were countless lessons to learn at *The Carolinian*. It was all hands on deck for every issue. I reported on everything from city government to sporting events to obituaries. And I covered a lot of crime. But included in those lessons was humility. It was tough showing up at those first few news conferences with a Polaroid camera, lined paper instead of a reporter's notebook, and a pen donated by a local funeral parlor. We weren't issued business cards, so my mother printed some for me on a copy machine at her job. Thus, my career in journalism started like most new phases of my life: modestly. There was only one way to look and that was up. I was not setting the world on fire, but I showed up on time, stayed late, and did whatever the boss asked of me, usually with a smile on my face. On its worst day, being at *The Carolinian* beat cutting grass on Interstate 95 in the summer.

Even though I lived at home with my mother, it was hard to stretch a hundred dollars a week very far. After four months at the newspaper, I reluctantly took a job at Shaw University in Raleigh as sports information director. It was a better-paying position but offered more shots of humility without a chaser. I was no closer to my dream of being a broadcast journalist and was concerned that I was, in fact, moving away from that career. I wanted to be a hard newsman, not some glad-handing public relations flak. My mother, who knew I was disappointed with my career moves thus far, and who had always found solutions in the past, had the idea that I should meet more people in the broadcast profession. When she once found out there was going to be a nationally televised college basketball tournament in town, with one of the legendary voices of sports radio attending, she encouraged me: "You should meet him. I bet he'd help you."

We got tickets to the tournament just to meet this famed sportscaster. I can't imagine the tickets were very expensive, but I am certain it was money for which we could have found some other use. Standing high in the stands (the cheap seats), my mother spotted the sportscaster down on the floor. "There he is, baby! Let's go meet him," she said with schoolgirl excitement. This was not a request. She had already pulled me out of my seat and we were heading downstairs. "Momma, can we at least wait until halftime? He looks busy right now," I said, with the embarrassment of a twenty-two-year-old being dragged by his mother, pained by every step.

"Well then, let's get close to him. He's a busy man, I'm sure." Clarice is nothing if not persistent. Keep in mind this is the woman who rarely smiles. On this occasion, you could count her teeth from the other side of the arena as she stood patiently for halftime and her moment to introduce her son to the sportscaster she was convinced would change her child's life.

The halftime buzzer rang, and Clarice made a beeline for the press desk. "Hello, sir. My name is Clarice Pitts. I'm a big fan of yours. This is my son, Byron. He just graduated from Ohio Wesleyan University with a degree in journalism. He wants a career in journalism. Could you offer him any advice?" she asked, with a degree of desperation I rarely ever heard in my mother's voice.

The sportscaster never took her outstretched hand. He barely looked away from his notes. He did size me up for a moment, cleared his throat, and said, "You should probably do something else. Broadcasting is a tough business." End of sentence. We were wasting his time. He stood up and brushed my mother's shoulder as he walked away. I wanted to kick his ass right there. Just jump on him and beat him until he learned common courtesy.

Finally, my mother lowered her hand, her smile painfully

melted away. "Let that be a lesson to you, son. When you make it, never act that way. I guess God didn't want us talking to him after all," she said as she pulled at my arm again, this time headed back up to the bleachers.

I still wanted to kick his ass. That thought may seem like an overreaction, and perhaps it was, but that moment took me back to my childhood. How many times had I watched some person in authority treat my mother disrespectfully? From store clerks, to bosses, to a construction worker on a street corner or one of the many therapists we met when I was in grade school. How many times had I been bullied in school or on the way to school?

I believe there are assumptions that some people in positions of power or influence make about those on the other side. As a boy, I was too small, too weak, and too frightened to stand up to their slights, but I was no less offended by them. All those moments from the past pressed on my shoulders, like a tight lid on a boiling pot, and often sent me into a rage whenever someone was less than respectful of my mother or any person they viewed as vulnerable. Without question, those feelings existed deep in the dark places of my heart. But I used them like fuel. I was keeping score. It always kept me pressing forward to prove myself or defend others.

Years later, after I had joined *CBS News* as a correspondent, I ran into this famed sports broadcaster again. We were both covering the Super Bowl in Miami. My credentials gave wider access to the field and to players. There's that old saying about revenge being best served cold. I have never sought revenge, never rubbed a slight in anyone's face, but I have always made a mental note.

"Byron, you do a great job. I watch you all the time," he said with a bright smile during our sideline encounter.

"Thank you, sir, awfully kind of you to say," I replied with a firm handshake. "My mother is a big fan of yours," I added, thinking the whole time I would kill him with kindness, though deep down I wanted to punch that smile off his face. To this day, his behavior toward my mother is one of the reasons I do my best to give as much time as possible to anyone who asks. Every college student and fledgling reporter gets my full attention and a few minutes of my time. I don't want to dampen anyone else's dream the way that sportscaster made me feel.

In many ways, working at Shaw was like a postgraduate year after college. Shaw is one of the nation's historically black colleges. It had a compact, friendly campus like Ohio Wesleyan. In addition to working at Shaw, I returned to WTVD, Raleigh's ABC affiliate, where I had interned during my junior year in college. I would work days at Shaw, writing press releases and logging sports scores, then I would spend my nights, unpaid, at WTVD pulling scripts for the eleven o'clock late news. During these days before computers, TV anchors read from typed scripts that entry-level staffers and interns manually loaded into the teleprompter. Although this was not hard-news reporting, it was a chance to keep a toe in the business. It also gave me the opportunity to reunite with my old friend Larry Stogner, my original mentor and a reporter's reporter.

When I first met Larry, he scared me to death. Looking more like a banker than a reporter, he always wore a white shirt and a suit and tie, and was almost always deadly serious. He was a chain-smoker with a demeanor as hard as the briefcase he seemed to carry everywhere. He had one of those TV voices that revealed decades of smoking unfiltered cigarettes and drinking coffee. He was probably in his thirties when we worked together, but Larry carried himself like a guy who had been on earth a very long time. He was the station's go-to guy, and as best I could tell, most of the other reporters and anchors on staff feared and respected him.

The night before my first day as an intern, I had gone to the local library and read back issues of the hometown newspaper, *The Raleigh News and Observer*. I wanted to at least sound like I knew something about the news. That morning my mother made me breakfast, we said a long prayer, and she dropped me off on her way to work.

"God bless you, son," she said as she drove away. We hardly ever wished each other luck, since there wasn't much in life we ever attributed to luck. With a full stomach, a head full of newspaper clippings and Bible verses read at home, and at least one verse typed on an index card and placed in my sports coat that morning by my mother, I walked into the Raleigh newsroom ready to conquer the world.

"You're late" is how Larry greeted me that first day.

"Good morning, sir. I was told to report here by nine o'clock. It's not nine yet," I said with a tone of confidence in my voice.

"Chickenshit reporters may get in at nine, but I get here at eight, and I expect my intern here when I get here," Larry said, with his feet on his desk, a cup of coffee in his hand, a cigarette in his mouth, and both eyes on the morning paper. "You don't want to be some chickenshit reporter, do you?" he said, as he glanced up from his paper.

"No, sir. Good morning, Mr. Stogner. I'm Byron Pitts," I said. My morning confidence left by the door, I was now in a puddle of sweat.

"Well, good. We all work hard in this bureau, and we are all serious about the news. You serious about the news, son, or do you want to be some chickenshit anchor someday?" he said.

"No, sir, I want to be a newsman," I answered, confidence creeping back up my spine.

"Then good, every good newsman knows how to make coffee. Coffee machine is in the back room. Get to it," he said in what would be our lengthiest conversation of the day. Perhaps I wasn't the fastest learner he had ever had in the office, but Larry seemed to take a liking to me. Within a few days I graduated from making the coffee in the morning to picking up Larry's cigarettes. Years of going to the store to pick up my mother's cigarettes were finally paying off.

"Wear a sports coat tomorrow. We're going to the state house," Larry yelled as I walked out of the office at the end of a shift.

That was Larry's style, similar to my mother: do what I say and we'll get along fine. And we did. It was one of the best summers of my life; the state house one day, a murder scene the next, and I had a front-row seat with one of the finest reporters in North Carolina. Actually, it was more like a back seat, crunched between camera equipment and old bags of fast food, but I felt like Edward R. Murrow or Ed

Bradley in the back of that news truck. Larry usually worked with a young cameraman named Eddie Barber. While I never saw Larry without a shirt and tie, I assumed Eddie didn't own one. A total free spirit, he was always smiling, always upbeat, and always willing to go anywhere to tell a story with his camera. He was a wonderful example of always having a good attitude. No matter how lousy the assignment or how foul Larry's mood, Eddie was always enthusiastically at his side. He was also a great encourager. He patiently listened to my dreams about a career in television and would end every conversation with the same words of encouragement: "Go for it."

While Larry was a father figure, Eddie was like an older brother. Larry and Eddie never seemed to care about the color of my skin. They worked hard and seemed to appreciate my desire to do the same. To the bosses and staff at the main building in Durham, they were the odd couple. They taught me some valuable lessons, including, Never judge a person by what you see on the outside. On the outside, the three of us had next to nothing in common, and they certainly had no reason to take any interest in me. But they did. When Eddie would get a call about a murder overnight, he'd give me a call and swing by my mother's house to pick me up, just so I could get some experience. And Larry protected me from the sometimes unpleasant realities of the language and biases in the newsroom. Like the time we went to a murder scene "in the ghetto," as someone in the newsroom described it on the car radio. "Those people are animals, so you boys better be careful." Turned out the crime scene was less than a block from my mother's home.

Larry could see the hurt in my eyes as he glanced back at me through the rearview mirror. "Don't be an idiot," he barked back into the radio. I met Larry's smile with a smile of my own. He winked at me and said, "Son, don't ever let idiots bother you." His advice has served me well my entire career.

Now, two years later, I was back in the WTVD newsroom, for a free stint after college. Larry was no longer interested in having me make his coffee. "You weren't very good at it," he later confessed. "We got to get you a job," he said. And he did. It was my first lesson in the age-old saying, "It's not always what you know, it sometimes helps who you know and who you stay in contact with."

How fortunate I was to stay in contact with Larry Stogner. Without any professional advice or support like Larry's, when I graduated from college I had sent out more than forty videocassettes with samples of my writing and on-camera work to small television stations across the country. Places like Toledo, Savannah, Jackson, Mississippi, and Cedar Rapids, Iowa. About a dozen news managers were kind enough to write back. Most were form letters. One was handwritten. They all said the same thing: Thanks but no thanks. One news director at a small station in eastern North Carolina was a friend of cameraman Eddie Barber. Eddie called to see if the news director had received my tape.

"Yep, got it," he told Eddie. "Tell your friend he's wasting his time. I see a lot of tapes. He doesn't have what it takes. He's wasting his time." I guess it was his idea of doing me or Eddie a favor.

Eddie's response to me was "Don't worry about him. Just

keep going for it." As fate would have it, sixteen months later this same news director at this same station in eastern North Carolina had a job opening. Eddie encouraged me to apply again.

"He hated my work before. Why would he like it now? I don't have a new tape," I insisted.

"Just go for it," Eddie said. "And have Larry call the guy."

With the same tape and a recommendation from Larry Stogner, I applied again. Oddly enough, the news director seemed thrilled to get a personal phone call from a big-name reporter in Raleigh.

"I love this kid's tape. If you vouch for him, that's good enough for me," he said to Larry. He never interviewed me, but he did give me the job. By the time I started, he'd been fired. Had I missed my chance to kill him with kindness? Not exactly. We met years later. It was a familiar reunion: "Byron, nice to meet you. I'm a big fan of your work." He clearly had no recollection of the actual role he had once played in my career.

"Good to meet you, sir," I said with a smile and another insincere but firm handshake.

I started at WNCT-TV in Greenville, North Carolina, as a general assignment reporter and weekend sports anchor for an annual salary of $8,600. I was thrilled. My mother was angry. I had been earning about $20,000 at Shaw with a small expense account and an assistant.

"It's okay to dream, son, but don't be dumb about it" was my mother's response to the news that I was moving out of her house to take my first paying job in broadcast news.

Oh, by the way, I could no longer afford my own car. It just meant I would have to live within walking distance of my first job in television.

"Your tuition was more than they're paying you. Are you sure you want to take a step back like that?" she asked.

Two steps forward, one step back. That's how it had always been. When I left for Greenville, my mother wasn't speaking to me. We did not talk for a few weeks. Now that I was out of college, there would be no more letters written in red ink. Mother would express her disapproval from then on with deafening silence.

My first news director was a guy named Roy Hardee. He was a forty-something news manager who had cut his teeth on Southern newspapers and Southern radio. He preferred penny loafers, button-down shirts, his weekly crewcut, and pork barbecue for lunch. He knew more cops by their first names and their favorite beverage than any other newsperson I have ever known. Roy was always suspicious of reporters more focused on polishing their résumés than on covering local news. Thus, he greeted most new (and most often from the North) reporters the same way. Using both hands to hitch up his pants, just before he sucked his teeth, he said, "So you think you can cover the news?" It always came across as less of a question and more of a threat.

Because it was a small station with a small budget, most people were hired to do more than one job. I was a weekday news reporter and weekend sports anchor. It looked good on the business card, but it was a tough way to make a living. I lived in a one-bedroom apartment with at least one roommate, and for a brief time two. We learned the finer points of macaroni and cheese, tuna fish, and on rare occasions grilled chicken. Since we were paid so little at work and were constantly hungry, searching out free meals was sometimes a motivation for covering stories. One way the staff would decide which press conference we would attend on any given day depended on which organization provided the best food. The East Carolina University football coach's weekly press conference was always a favorite: sandwiches and shrimp cocktail.

That was the best part of being a sports reporter. I was eating with the best sportscasters in the state. Unfortunately, when it came to actually being a sportscaster, I was, to put it gently, awful. I had assumed (there's that word again), since I had played high school and college football, had been around athletes and coaches all my life, that being a sportscaster would be easy. Wrong! You actually have to know something about all sports. I never liked or even understood soccer until my children played many years later, and I thought tennis was a sport you played to pick up girls.

Needless to say, my career as a sportscaster did not last very long. But it lasted long enough for me to discover that I loved news reporting. I was allowed to change beats. I became what was known at the time as a one-man band. I was the reporter, photographer, producer, and editor wrapped in one. The station gave me a big van with the station call letters on the side. Fortunately, since there were no side windows on my van, no one ever knew the only thing inside the manual-shift vehicle was a video camera, a few tapes, extra batteries, and a spare tire. It wasn't much to look at, but it was all the gear I was responsible for, and now my dream had a starting point: I was a television reporter.

My beat was the small town of Washington, North Carolina, affectionately known as Little Washington, with a population under ten thousand. I would spend my day between the courthouse and the jail. I pretended to be Larry Stogner: white shirt, tie, and a sports coat. Who could afford a suit on less than nine thousand a year? Only a breath ahead of the Carolinian newspaper in Raleigh, we occasionally had real notebooks. I no longer carried pens engraved with the name and address of the local mortician. I had upgraded to the local gas station pens or the ones I could swipe from the sales department. I also learned that napkins and fast-food lunch bags make for wonderful writing surfaces in a pinch. I was in heaven.

Reporting for television is not particularly an art form or a science as much as it is a craft. WNCT-TV in Greenville was my first apprenticeship, a place to learn the very basics. In athletics, there are people who have been described as naturals. The same is true in broadcast communication. I have had colleagues over the years who seemed as if they were born to be on television. For them, talking on television is as simple as inhaling. Nothing about broadcasting ever came easy to me. What I have learned to do, even the simplest things, I have learned through practice. One of the first things I worked on in Greenville was the proper way to hold a microphone. That may sound ridiculous, but consider this: John Wooden, one of the most successful college basketball coaches of all time, insisted on teaching his players the proper way to put on their socks. No detail is too small to practice. Because of my long thin fingers, there wasn't a natural way for me to look manly holding a microphone. Do I hold it in my fist? What about three fingers, as if it's a flute? Do I hold it directly under my chin or off to the side? That's how I spent many evenings at home in Greenville, North Carolina, working on the best way to hold a microphone. Is it more effective to stand directly in front of a speaker at a news conference or off to the side? After some practice, I decided it was better to stand off to one side. The person would have to physically turn his head in order to face you. It proved easier to sneak in a quick followup question once you had the person's attention, and it seemed easier to turn away from a questioner directly in front. As a one-man-band photographer/reporter in Greenville, I would practice setting up in different spots at news conferences. It was a game I'd play. I kept notes on where the speaker would look first to answer questions. Which side would they look to most often? Through trial and error, I discovered it was often better to start the question—if I was competing for attention—with the person's name. Make everything as personal as possible.

Once, for example, while covering a murder trial in Little Washington, I got to know the families of a victim and of the accused killer. Every morning before trial and at the end of the day cameramen and reporters would run outside the courthouse and yell questions at the accused. He would always just look straight ahead. During one recess, I was talking to his mother. She called the man by his nickname. Relatives called him Junior. I held on to that small bit of information until the man was convicted and sentenced to die. That day at the end of court I waited by the police car. Reporters yelled their familiar questions. No response. As he approached in leg irons, with my camera on my shoulder and my microphone in hand,

I had one chance, "Hey, Junior! You ready to die?" The man stopped and turned to the voice that had called his name; we made eye contact. "I don't want to die. What I did was wrong, but I don't want to die." He looked scared. After days of sitting in court acting like a tough guy, this convicted killer finally showed a glimpse of fear. That night I got a "way to go" from Roy Hardee. But, more important, I got a call at the station from the victim's family. They were glad to see the killer had finally shown some emotion. The lesson for me that day was to always look for some human connection, whether to saints or sinners.

For all that I learned in Greenville as a hungry young reporter, I probably lost about fifteen pounds. Call it the price of an education. The first time I went home to Baltimore to visit, I ran into my high school buddy, Joe Stumbroski.

"Hey, Byron, you've lost so much weight. I heard you were in television. Are you a model?" Joe asked innocently.

"Nah, man, I'm starting in the basement. Call it remedial reading for reporters," I answered without a hint of regret. We both smiled.

All I had ever prayed for was a chance. God was giving me that chance. By this time I had an army of family and friends praying for me and pulling for me. Greenville was a long way from East Baltimore or Ohio Wesleyan, for that matter. But I wasn't alone. I never had been. I was not just trying my hand in television. I was doing it. I am sure I didn't strike the most impressive pose as a young reporter: Razor-thin, big Afro, big glasses, high-pitched voice, the three shirts I owned all worn around the collar. I looked more like a backup singer for the Commodores hooked on crack than a credible reporter. But based on where I started? Faith had carried me this far, so I just kept my head up, pushed my shoulders back, and kept stepping out on nothing. What a glorious ride. Next stop, Norfolk.

NINE

# It Never Gets Easier—You Just Get Stronger

Consider it pure joy, my brothers, whenever you face trials of many kinds, because you know that the testing of your faith develops perseverance. Perseverance must finish its work so that you may be mature and complete, not lacking anything.

—James 1:2–4

"Where's the beer?" Phil Smith was holding the door to my refrigerator open, staring at its contents, which consisted of a single large plastic jug of sweet tea, a carton of eggs, and a well-used bottle of Tabasco sauce.

"I don't drink," I said.

Standing six feet six and north of 250 pounds, Phil looked around with a disgusted look on his face. "You are such a loser," he said. Everyone in the room laughed.

It was Norfolk, Virginia, 1984. I had invited several friends from my new job at television station WAVY-TV over to my apartment for pizza and a college football bowl game. We were all young and single and working jobs we loved in a great city. It was a collegial group. Since many of us had begun our television careers in smaller markets, like my experience in Greenville, Norfolk was a step into big-city news. After an intense week, the favorite wind-down activity was a night of conversation about work, listening to music, dancing, lots of laughter, and alcohol. I was not a drinker and never learned to dance, so I was often the odd man out on those occasions. This particular night, it became clear just how different I really was. After the football game was over, one of my friends suggested that we watch a movie. They started going through my pile of VHS tapes next to the television. Much to their surprise, every single tape in the stack was a recording of a network newscast.

My closest friend in the group shook his head and announced, "You really are a loser." Even I laughed this time.

Back in college, that's the way many friends would affectionately label me at parties—a loser. "He doesn't drink, and he can't dance" was how many male friends would introduce me to their female friends. To which I would respond, "But I will graduate on time." By my early twenties, being considered an outsider was a badge of honor. I was used to it, almost preferred it that way. For the longest time I had always felt that it was God, Clarice, and me against the world. Now that I lived in a different city, mostly it was just God and me, and God was doing all the heavy lifting. That is one big reason why I have often been alone but never lonely.

My faith was just one of the things that made me feel different from my colleagues. There were professional differences as well. The goal of many reporters is to be the station's next anchorman or anchorwoman. Not me. I wanted to be a reporter, eventually at the network level, and knew that it was going to take a singleminded focus to become the best in the business. I didn't really make time for distractions. Many of my colleagues had wide-ranging interests. One reporter loved riding his motorcycle. Another talked about his love for surfing. Another had a great wine collection. I arrived in Norfolk with a couch, a card table, two chairs, a television set, and a VCR that I used to record the *CBS Evening News*, *ABC's World News Tonight*, and the *NBC Nightly News*. Many thought my focus was too narrow, but childhood difficulties had taught me to keep things simple and linear. Through every obstacle, the keys to success for me have always been the same: prayer, grace, structure, hard work, and more prayer. Whenever I have succeeded, it was because I stuck to the plan. Whenever I have failed, it has usually occurred because I deviated from the plan. There was very little time in my life for distractions.

The move to a bigger market was going to mean greater scrutiny of my performance and greater expectations for the quality of work. In Greenville, my slow, deliberate process had not been a liability. Since I had been expected to deliver one complete report each day, I generally had time to write several drafts of my script until I was satisfied with the product. But in Norfolk I had to report at least two and sometimes three stories a day. This requirement exposed a process that I had managed to keep hidden. When I first learned to read, I read everything out loud. When I began to write my news scripts, I would "write out loud," reading to myself as I put the words on paper. In Greenville, because I worked alone, my process had never been seen or heard by anyone else. In Norfolk, I was now regularly teamed up with a cameraman, who was with me nearly all the time, and we had to work on much tighter deadlines. I felt self-conscious and uncomfortable. When I began to speak on my side of the van, at least one cameraman would turn up the radio in annoyance. But some seemed more amused by my process. "You know that's weird, don't you?" asked one photographer, Tom Costanza. Tom and I were often teamed together. He was on the short list of those who didn't mind my chatter in the news vehicle. "I get why you talk out loud while you write," Tom said, while we were out on another story, "but have you ever thought about whispering?" Maybe he was on to something.

While I continued to work on the mechanics of the broadcast craft, how best to hold a microphone or position myself at a press conference, the one natural talent I brought to my profession was the ability to understand the thread of humanity in every news story and find a way for the viewer to connect and relate. Most news stories are stories about struggle: a struggle for political or economic power, a struggle over land, a struggle over life and death. More than who wins or loses, I relate most to the struggle. Most of the reporters in Norfolk had more experience than me, better contacts, were better writers, and many had wonderful voices. But I decided that no one had an intrinsic understanding of struggle and could bring that experience to life as I could. Take what little you have and build on it. That was something Father Bart had taught me back in high school at Archbishop Curley. It doesn't matter where you start, only where you finish. I came to Norfolk with few material possessions and limited ability, but what I did possess I could build upon with God's grace. That was all I could do. And just as in the past, it would have to be enough. As a young general-assignment reporter, I had to learn in a hurry how to make those connections on a story.

One of my first such experiences in Norfolk was a fatal car crash that killed five young men in November of 1985, members of a basketball team driving home from a tournament. The accident had occurred over the weekend. I was assigned to the story with one of the best photographers at the station, Michael Ridge. There was no video of the accident scene, and the authorities would not allow us to take pictures of the damaged cars. None of the relatives wanted to talk on camera. It appeared that the opportunity to tell an important story in a compelling way might be lost. But we did not give up. We eventually convinced the grieving families to provide us with pictures of the five young men. At the home of one family, Michael persuaded those assembled to let us photograph the pictures on the kitchen table. Being in the house reminded me of the many times I had been in the home of relatives during the first few days of mourning. Some people wanted to be left alone. Some needed to talk.

These five families were no different from mine. I had found a human connection. We politely asked if anyone who wanted to say something in remembrance of the five young men would come into the kitchen, in front of the photo array, in front of our microphone, and just talk. We did not ask any questions. We just listened. A few of the mourners welcomed the opportunity. Ranging in age from late teens to early twenties, most of the five were lifelong friends. They went to the same church. Some were in college. One elderly man with a deep scratchy voice said something that has always stuck with me. He said, "Death is something you never get used to." The comment was simple yet profound. Like almost every other family in a similar situation, these families would survive what happened, but they would never get used to it.

That night we aired our story on the accident, using family photographs, the voices of relatives, and video from the highway. One of the anchors choked up on the air. Colleagues who had never spoken to me before complimented me on the piece. And some of the relatives called after the broadcast to thank us for honoring their loved ones respectfully. We had captured and communicated a human moment.

Despite some success early on, I still felt like a country bumpkin in the big city in Norfolk. Compared to Greenville it was a high-rise metropolis. I was not one of those twenty-something reporters who was full of myself, believing I could conquer the world or that I was ready for big-time television. I was a kid who simply believed I had the tools to work hard and make up for my shortcomings as a reporter. I was full of energy but not confidence.

Terrell Harris was a reporter at the ABC affiliate who covered the same beat. He was everything I wasn't—good-looking and confident, he wore expensive suits and drove a fancy car. All the girls in Norfolk seemed to be in love with him. I owned two blazers, three pair of slacks, two red ties, one yellow tie, two pairs of brown loafers, and one shirt collar extender. I walked to work. Every time I saw him on a story I felt intimidated.

In fact, the only time I have ever stuttered on the air was during a live shot, when I was standing next to Terrell Harris. We were both covering a case of government corruption in the county. We were lined up outside the government office doing our live shots for the noon news on our respective stations. My trick to avoid stuttering in general on the air—but particularly on live shots—was to carefully prepare and rehearse what I intended to say. I needed that repetition to ensure that I would say every word correctly. A few minutes before noon I was rehearsed and ready. But that morning it had been snowing, which was unusual for Norfolk, and rather than hearing the introduction I expected on the corruption story, the anchor asked me a question about the weather. I froze. I was unable to react quickly to the unexpected question. In trying to respond, I stuttered. I intended to say that it had started to snow when we first arrived this morning. But it came out as "s-s-s-s-s-s-snow." I looked at my feet to try to kick-start my brain. I saw the cameraman peek from behind his camera in amazement, and I could hear Terrell next to me delivering his live report flawlessly. I wanted to die. To my relief, the cameraman kindly moved the camera away from my face to take pictures of the snow. It gave me a moment to gather my thoughts. I produced a nervous smile, imagined I could see my grandmother's face (which calmed me down), and got back on the topic I was prepared to discuss.

That night I ate my dinner alone in an edit suite and watched that live shot over and over again. I made a copy on a VHS tape and took it home so I could watch it again. I wanted to study it to see if there was a way to prevent something like that from ever happening again. But the shame has never left me.

I went to every story thinking every other reporter was

smarter than me, knew more than me, and had more talent. I tended to fight my sense of insecurity by getting angry, and in my mind Terrell was the standard I needed to beat. I would purposely take offense at the smallest slight. If the police chief answered his question first, I would get angry. If he got more time for his story than I got for mine, I would get angry. But rather than raise my voice or force a confrontation, I used the anger as motivation to improve my performance. Because it often took me a bit more time to read through the press releases or the prep material, I had to apply a different set of skills to my work. Thus, if my competitor interviewed two people, I would interview four. I would always have to do my best to get to the story first. I would also have to make sure I left the story last to pick up any crumbs the other reporters had left behind. Like Terrell, I needed to develop some techniques for nurturing sources. Terrell was tight with all the secretaries in city hall and the police headquarters, so I worked the people in the maintenance department. Terrell knew the hot spots in town and could meet sources after hours, and I would just hang out at the police station at night with the people forced to work the night shift. Terrell had his ways, and I found mine.

At my station, there was a reporter named Ed Hazelwood. With a thick beard, glasses, and a deep baritone voice, Ed won numerous awards for his investigative work and for any number of reports on the U.S. military. But that's not what impressed me most about him. It was the notebook he kept with the names and numbers of every contact he ever made. He had them listed by title, profession, spouse's name, their girlfriend's phone number, and address if needed. His contacts were always at his fingertips. He'd call people just to check in. He called contacts on their birthdays, their children's birthday, a bar mitzvah, any special occasion, or just to say hello. In a business where we are often takers showing up at the doorstep in the midst of some personal tragedy, Ed was a giver. He respected the people with whom he came in contact. But that's not to say they were always thrilled to hear from Ed or were pleased with his reporting—just that he respected his contacts.

If Ed kept names and phone numbers and birth dates, so would I. Somewhere along the way, I picked up the idea of sending handwritten notes to people kind enough to give me their time or an interview. It's something I have done for most of my career. "Kindness will take you a long way in this life," my grandmother always used to say. Most people have never written back, but those who have always seemed to appreciate the simple gesture. Besides, a person interviewed today might become a source or an expert the next day, and on a few occasions they have even become a friend. It was one more vital tool for my tool bag, and I knew I needed a good tool bag. I had places to go and things God wanted me to do.

My goal was to make it to the network by age thirty-five. Based on my research, thirty-five was about the median age for a young network correspondent. But my journey required baby steps, or rather two steps forward and one step back. I wanted to become a network correspondent for two basic reasons. For one, it is the biggest stage for a broadcast journalist. That same stubborn child who wanted to read Hemingway now insisted that the most exclusive club in television would someday open its doors to him. The second reason was that it would be the only way my mother and grandmother would ever get to see me regularly on television. From 1982 to 1996, during my career in local news, I changed markets about every two years and worked in cities up and down the eastern seaboard, while my family was mostly based in North Carolina. Occasionally, I would send a videocassette to my mother and grandmother so they could see my work. Somehow, sending them a tape once in a while never seemed to satisfy them. When she did see my work, my grandmother had this sound she would make, like a single grunt, but she would hold it for several seconds, as if it were a song. She would make that sound with a high-pitched voice, and then say, "Baby, you sure look good on my television." No praise from a boss or a television critic ever meant as much as the sound she made and the smile that followed. She would have appreciated seeing me more often.

However, over the years my grandmother did express concern about how often I changed jobs on my way to the network. "What's wrong baby?" she'd say with her Southern drawl. "Why can't you keep a job for very long?" She was talking about my stops in Greenville, Norfolk, Orlando, Tampa, Boston, Atlanta, and Washington, D.C. As I said, I took the long way. I knew I needed a body of work and a wealth of experience to be ready for the network. I didn't want to end up in the revolving door I had seen for other journalists of color at the network level. I kept track of all the network correspondents, and with a few notable exceptions, I noticed what looked like a pattern for African-

Americans who would arrive and then disappear a few years later. When I asked why it happened, I received a variety of explanations, ranging from blatant discrimination to a shortage of opportunities to a lack of preparedness. It depended on whether I was asking a manager or another journalist of color. Since the odds might be against me, I wanted to make sure I was prepared in every possible way. That meant choosing my next jobs with a purpose.

In 1989 I had a chance to work in New York, Chicago, or Boston. I chose Boston, the sixth largest television market in the country. Though it was smaller than New York or Chicago, it was the perfect environment for things I needed to learn. The city had a reputation for producing some of the best writers in journalism, and I knew that one of the criticisms that followed many African-American correspondents at the network was that they couldn't write a good script. I wanted to polish my writing skills, and Boston was the place to do it. This newsroom was the first where my colleagues spent much of their time discussing sentence structure and phraseology.

I quickly learned one important distinction between the smaller markets and the top-ten newsrooms. There was no tolerance for using emotion as a substitute for good reporting. One of my first big stories in Boston was a house fire with fatalities, and I was the only one to secure an interview with a relative of the victims. The woman cried throughout the interview, and I thought I had done an admirable job in capturing the drama of the event. In my previous jobs I would have been praised for such an emotional delivery—but not in Boston. The next morning the news director called me to his office to chastise me for sensationalizing the story and wasting time with a crying interview when I could have been reporting more facts of the story.

In addition to writing, there was another important reason why I chose Boston. Of the three cities where I could have worked, the Boston station had the least diversity in the newsroom, and I wanted to test my skill and my temperament in such a setting. Within weeks of my arrival, I got what I asked for with a major breaking news story. A white man named Charles Stewart accused a black man of shooting and killing his pregnant wife. As the reporter on the night beat, I covered the initial report for our eleven o'clock newscast. By morning, it had morphed into one of the most sensational crime stories in Boston since the Boston Strangler. Stewart's depiction of the attack on his wife was chilling, and his claim that a black man was the perpetrator ignited the undercurrent of racial tension in the city. I was called in early the morning after the shooting to attend a special editorial meeting, where assignments were being handed out and where I happened to be the only African-American in the room. A manager turned to me and said, "We need reaction from the black community. Why don't you go call your contacts?" Since I had been living in the city only for a few weeks, my "contacts" were nonexistent. But his assumption remained: I was black, therefore I had black contacts, and I was to cover the black angle of the story.

I knew I didn't want to be pigeonholed into covering only race, but I wanted to appear to be a team player. My immediate response was "You want my contacts in Tampa?" (my previous station). There was nervous laughter and the realization that the request might have been ill conceived, given my brief tenure in Boston. But I agreed to take on the assignment and pursued it aggressively. Eventually, police uncovered the truth, that Charles Stewart had killed his wife and created a mythical assailant upon whom to place the blame. A year later, in the aftermath of that case, many journalists in Boston's newsrooms were forced to examine how a lack of staff diversity adversely affected the coverage of the Stewart case and how their own biased assumptions about class and race had become part of the coverage.

I will always remember the night a black family had their front door firebombed in one of the city's housing projects. The photographer and I walked up to three elderly white women. "Excuse me, ladies, my name is Byron Pitts. I'm a reporter from Channel 5. What do you think about what happened to one of your neighbors?" I asked. The women looked at me expressionless when one of them said, "We don't want any niggers living here. They should have known better." The photographer I was with turned to me, smiled, and said, "Welcome to Boston." It left an impression. I fought to make my own reporting more reflective of the population we served. For me, it was a challenging time but a growth experience, working in a racially charged environment, learning to keep my cool but not compromising what I believed to be my journalistic or moral integrity. I ended up spending five years in Boston, covering politics and crime, and doing some investigative reporting.

I have been asked plenty of times if racism exists in the news business. The simple answer is that racism and other -isms have always existed in America. Newsrooms are not immune. Like many people in many professions, I have bumped up against the low expectations of others. Whether you are black, white, brown, or yellow, low expectations can weigh you down like an anvil. For one thing, I was often hired as the "black" reporter. A black male reporter would leave, and then I would show up. I could see on the faces of many of my colleagues, white male colleagues especially, the suspicion that I was the "affirmative action" hire. Maybe in the minds of management, that is what I was. I have worked in many newsrooms where reporters were recruited and handpicked to be groomed for a big anchor job. That never happened for me.

In fact, about halfway through my tour of states and stations, I stuck my neck out and for the first time expressed interest in anchoring a broadcast. It had disastrous consequences. For reasons that will become apparent, I won't mention which city it was. I was actually up for a weekend anchor job since I had been filling in for weeks, but the station was delaying making a decision. The ratings were good and my work was fine, but the company would not pull the trigger. Finally, I pressed my news director, who was a friend. "What's the deal?" I insisted. His response shocked me. His boss, a station executive, had said, "A nigger would never anchor one of my broadcasts." My news director passed on the quotation reluctantly.

"You can sue if you'd like. Then you'll be blackballed and never work in TV. If subpoenaed by a judge, I'd testify to what was said. You can be angry and let it eat you up inside. Or you can press on," he said, with a mix of sadness and disgust in his voice.

It is the one and only time I have ever cried about a job. Not to his face, but when I left the newsroom. I had been polite and shook hands with my boss, and we agreed to revisit the subject in a few days. This was the first time I was hit squarely in the nose with racism at work. The first thing I did was call my mother. She yelled and fussed with me, and then we prayed. Next, I called my sister. She yelled and fussed with me, and then we prayed. Next, I called my brother. He yelled and fussed with me, then offered to fly into town and meet the offending TV executive in the parking lot, and then we prayed. (Funny yet reassuring thing about my family, regardless of the crisis, big or small, the response is always the same. Since I was eight years old, my older brother has always volunteered to fight my battles.)

The next morning my mother called me up early. "What have you decided to do?" she asked. Before I could offer an answer, she gave her opinion. "I think you should just get past it. You didn't go to that job to stay forever. It's just a stop on the journey. Hold your head up. Push your shoulders back. Learn what you're there to learn, and move on," she pleaded.

I knew she was not advocating that I back down. Lord knows Clarice Pitts never shied away from a fight. But, for her, the point wasn't about a man's judgment of me; it was about what God had planned. Later that day, I went to my news director, thanked him for his honesty, and asked for his support when the chance came to move along. He agreed. A few months later I moved on.

Perhaps I should rephrase that. I didn't move on. God moved me along. In fact, most of the jobs I have ever had in television I never applied for. They usually just came along. Trust me, it is not because anyone was beating the bushes looking for me. As best I can tell, I have never been the first choice for any job, rather the second or third choice, but I always tried to reward those who hired me with my best effort, and I thank God for the many second chances He has given me. Like most people, I have sometimes failed to live up to my own expectations. At other times, I have had to work beyond the low expectations of others.

Pretty far along in my career, I was having a pleasant get-to-know-you conversation with an executive at a new station where I had been hired. I had been in the news business for quite a while, had won a few awards, and covered a few major events. It was a discussion about the expectations of the job and where I wanted to take my career. By this time, I was focused on the goal of being a *60 Minutes* correspondent someday. For me, it was the promised land of journalism. I could do everything I wanted to do as a reporter, from investigative work to profiles of the famous and the infamous, and it would be a chance to showcase my writing and my interviewing skills. I expressed that wish quite forcefully. The executive's response surprised me. "Byron, the thing I like most about you is that you are so articulate," she said.

The bubble over my head asked, *"Articulate? Did she just say articulate? That's it? That's what you like most about me? Years of television reporting. And it's not my body of work, my investigative pieces, my writing, or my reporting? You like that I can speak clearly and string a few coherent sentences together?"*

For me, and for many people who look like me, the word

*articulate* is code for "We presume most black people can't speak, but you can." I have always considered that one of the greatest insults, because it assumes that we would not be able to speak to be understood. I have heard people describe a Colin Powell or a Clarence Thomas as articulate. As if it's a surprise that a secretary of state or a Supreme Court justice could express themselves. And they are the exception to the rule. I never heard anyone describe as articulate Ronald Reagan or Bill Clinton or a single one of my white colleagues. It's as if the greatest attribute for a person of color is that he can speak the English language.

Did this executive declare this because of some deep-rooted racism? Almost certainly not. Maybe she could not think of anything else to say. Or maybe her expectations for me were just that low. That the best I had to offer was that I could speak English. Granted, given my problems with stuttering, at one stage in my life if a person in a position of authority had labeled me articulate, that would have been a reason to shake their hand and shout Hallelujah. But she did not know about my history. That was not her point of reference. For a seasoned broadcast journalist, such a comment was ridiculous.

But in her office I smiled and nodded and thought to myself: She will set limits that I must overcome. Her expectations of me are so limited that she is just one more obstacle I need to remove from my path. From that day forward, I always outwardly respected her opinion but gave it no value.

At age thirty-eight, I finally knew that I was ready. I was hired to be a correspondent by *CBS News* to report the national news. I arrived at CBS with a mixture of gratitude and impatience. From day one on the job, I was already three years behind my own career schedule. But I quickly learned that just getting to the network was not enough to guarantee a successful career. Even though a correspondent has been hired, it is still at the discretion of each individual broadcast executive producer to decide if he or she wants to use that correspondent regularly on the broadcast. Executives have their favorites, who might appear five days a week, and then there are some correspondents who appear rarely. The criteria can be very subjective, ranging from writing skill to voice delivery. After being hired, one can experience a continual process of auditioning for work. It reminded me of Dr. Lewes's lesson in college about learning the style of each professor and then working to please them. I needed to learn what each executive producer wanted if I was going to become a regular part of their broadcast.

Part of that process included establishing personal relationships with the executives. After a correspondent is hired, protocol requires that he or she pay a visit to New York for a sit-down meeting with each executive producer to discuss expectations and any special needs of their broadcasts, from the *CBS Evening News* with Dan Rather to *Sunday Morning* to the (then) *CBS Morning News* (now called *The Early Show*). Essentially, you are shopping your skills.

When I was first hired in 1998, I was in the process of relocating to work in the network's Miami bureau. I was brought to New York for meetings with all the executives, and that visit led me to the office of a particular executive producer at *CBS News* whom I had never met. He had been running the morning program for a number of years. Apparently he was not impressed with what he had seen from me so far. On the day of the appointment, I had shown up at his office a few minutes early. His secretary told me to be seated. We could both hear him on the phone. He took at least three phone calls before finally calling me in to his office about thirty minutes after I had arrived.

"Please take a seat," he said, with his feet hanging over the corner of his desk. "Just give me another moment," he said as he made another phone call.

After a few minutes of cackling on the phone, he turned to me and said, "I don't have much time, so let's get right to it. I don't think you're very good. You don't write well enough to be on my show, and I want only the best correspondents on my show, and that is *not* you," he said, as he spent most of the time searching for something on his desk. He never made eye contact. He went on for a bit longer. When he finally looked up at me and said, "I hope this doesn't hurt your feelings. I'm just giving it to you straight. Nothing personal," he said with a smile. "If there's nothing else, I have some work to do," he said and stood up, gesturing me toward the door.

Like a kid educated in Catholic school, I jumped to my feet and said, "Thank you, sir. I appreciate your honesty and your time." On the inside I wanted to punch him in the nose. Then just before I turned for the door, I stopped, looked back at him, and said something I had never said to any human being before. "I respect what you've said and I respect your position, but please know this: When I'm on my knees praying in my room at night, not once have I ever called your name. My destiny is not in your hands, not now, not ever. Thank you for your time. I'll see you down the road."

He cocked his head to one side and gave me a curious look. I walked out of his office and never appeared on *his* broadcast again. Perhaps he had won the day, but I was not defeated. Funny thing about God, He apparently has a great sense of humor. Less than one year later, the executive was no longer at the helm of the morning program. There's an old Chinese proverb that I have always remembered. "If you stand by the river long enough, you will see the bodies of your enemies float by." It was my intention to stand at the shoreline of CBS for many years to come.

What I have lacked in talent, God has always made up for with His grace. He has fought my battles, protected me in good times and bad. He has given me an optimistic spirit. Optimism is a great gift. It can sustain you when everything around you is falling apart, and when you cannot read, when you are deemed a failure, or when you are considered second best. I have leaned on that optimism more than might have seemed reasonable, and it has always helped me. I needed every bit of my optimism on September 11, 2001.

"Get down to the World Trade Center. There's been an accident," yelled Marty Gill. I had just moved to New York from the South and had never been to the World Trade Center. I had no idea where it was. But since Marty was not normally a yeller, I knew right away something serious had happened. Martin Gill worked the assignment desk for *CBS News*. For years he had been responsible for handing out assignments in the Southern region. When I was based in Miami and later Atlanta for CBS, Marty's was often the voice on the other end of the phone sending me to hurricanes, tornadoes, or any other kind of spot news event. Probably just a few years older than me, he carried himself like a wise old man. Marty knew everything there was to know about satellite trucks and satellite truck drivers, feed points, which local stations had the best photographers, and where his people could get a steak in almost every city and small town in the South, Midwest, and along the eastern seaboard. Born and raised in Michigan, Marty brought Midwestern values and sensibilities to the New York office. He was not flashy or loud. He was just solid.

That morning I could hear the excitement in Marty's voice and see it in his eyes when he leaned into my office. "I need you down at the World Trade Center now, brother," he said with an increasing sense of urgency. I had not moved the first time he called me.

I had come to work early, before the crowds, intent on finishing up the script for another project. It was a profile of actor Harry Belafonte for the CBS broadcast *Sunday Morning*. I was not really up for chasing a spot news story.

"What happened?" I asked, with sarcasm hanging from every word.

"A plane hit the World Trade Center. You need to go," Marty said as he stormed out of my office and back to the national desk. With that, I grabbed my work bag and suit coat and walked outside.

"Can you get me to the World Trade Center?" I asked the yellow cab driver. Without turning around (New York cab drivers never do), he said, "Yeah! Did you hear what happened? A plane just hit one of the Twin Towers."

At this point, I was thinking that a novice pilot in a small plane must have gone off course and hit the building. But the closer we got, the more obvious it became that I was wrong. This was big. Fire trucks and ambulances rushed past the cab, and in the distance flames and billowing smoke were visible from both towers.

We were both stunned at what we were seeing. "I can't get you any closer. You gotta walk from here," the cabbie said when we got about twenty blocks from the epicenter of the disaster. He never asked for the fare. I never offered to pay. I just got out of the cab and started walking. People were in the street, running away from the buildings. Police officers had already set up barricades and were directing emergency vehicles in. It was loud and chaotic. There wasn't as much a sense of fear in the air as there was confusion. Word was spreading that it was two commercial planes that hit the buildings. Reality was sinking in. This was not an accident. This was terrorism. Any question of who did it and the why seemed irrelevant at the time. I finally was close enough to the buildings to talk with a group of police officers. One plainclothesman, the others in uniform. They were looking straight up.

"What is that?" one of them yelled as he pointed. We all looked. It resembled a large sheet of paper floating to the ground. I thought maybe it was someone from one of the upper floors sending a message, à la the Columbine High School massacre. Perhaps it was someone pleading for help. As this object dropped faster and closer to us, we realized it wasn't paper. It was a woman wearing a dress. She was falling. There were at least a handful of people falling. The officers and I watched in stunned silence.

"Look up there," another one of the officers yelled. High above, we saw what looked like two people standing on a window ledge. They took hands and jumped. They held on to each other for a short distance and then let go. We followed their fall. It was more horrifying than the first. One of the officers vomited. We all turned away.

As I was trying to keep it together, and beginning to think about what part of the story I would work on, I spotted my colleague *CBS News* correspondent Mika Brzezinski. By this time every reporter in New York was dispatched to lower Manhattan. Not long after Mika and I exchanged hellos, the story was about to change.

"It's coming down," someone yelled. Chunks of the World Trade Center's south tower were falling to the ground. In that moment, any sense of confusion turned to sheer panic. Every person was running, and that included Mika and me. Mika quickly kicked off her shoes and grabbed them; I grasped her hand and we ran as fast as we could. We made it to an elementary school that was being evacuated. The students were all but gone. We crowded inside with police, firefighters, and every other straggler who sprinted in. Chased up the street by thick black smoke, we all waited inside in dead silence. There was a rumbling that sounded like an earthquake. As suddenly as it started, it stopped. One of the firefighters walked out first, and then a few more were joined by police officers. Mika and I had found a phone in the school and managed to contact the national desk. All the networks were live on the air. Mika and I agreed that she would give the first account by phone while I walked outside to get more information. The air was so thick with dust and debris that it was difficult to breathe. I have long carried a handkerchief in my pocket for no good reason. I finally had a good reason. It felt like I was wandering around the surface of the moon. Everything was covered in white. A powdery soft dust covered the ground, cars, buildings, and most of the people.

I would later describe the day on the air this way: "Except for a few sirens, I have never heard New York City this quiet. Graveyard quiet." That is what it felt like those early moments after the first tower fell. It felt like I was standing in a graveyard or on the moon. Minutes later, the second tower collapsed, and once again everyone who could ran for cover. During the next hours I would see acts of bravery and kindness we do not spend enough time talking about in our country. Most people were so dusty it was hard to tell a person's race or even sometimes their sex. People of all description were helping the injured reach safety. I watched business people in suits and dresses tearing at their clothing to make a bandage or a brace. I watched one man kneel and pray in the middle of the street.

We interviewed a firefighter covered in dust from head to toe. He had brown eyes. I could see only a streak of his skin, revealed as tears rolled down from his eyes. "I lost my men," he told me. How many, I asked. "All of them," he said. With that, he turned away and walked back toward the pile. Within a few days, ordinary New Yorkers had formed a gauntlet down the West Side highway. At night they would applaud the emergency teams and construction workers as they changed shifts. People brought their children, and they carried food and water. This was rough, tough New York City, and for those first few days after the towers fell, I never heard a single word of profanity. There was a sense of peace and purpose and strength at Ground

Zero that is hard to fathom except for those of us who were there.

The world was upside down. I had witnessed the end of a life more than a few times in my career—a man put to death in Virginia's electric chair, a stabbing victim who bled to death in an Atlanta hospital. None of that prepared me for what I was seeing. But there wasn't much time to dwell on it or mourn. On September 11, 2001, and on many days like it, I found it best to hide behind my job. Reporters are supposed to keep some detachment from the people and the subjects in their reporting. It was that professional distance that kept me grounded in the notion that I was placed in this moment to cover history not get caught up in it. It was not about me or particularly what I was feeling, it was about the people around me and reporting on their experiences, their emotions, and not my own.

History will recall the horrors of that time, and there were many. As an optimist, I choose to also remember the good and decent people of that day.

TEN

# Valley of the Shadow of Death

Yea, though I walk through the valley of the shadow of death, I will fear no evil: for thou *art* with me. . . .

—Psalm 23:4

Do you know all the people you love most in the world?"

"Yes, sir, I do," I answered with a kind of awkward do-I-or-don't-I-smile expression one often wears in the boss's office. The boss in this case was *CBS News* anchorman Dan Rather. We were sitting in his office on the second floor above the newsroom, Dan in his leather chair and me in a straightbacked, stiff, wooden chair in front of his massive desk, discussing my upcoming trip to cover the post-9/11 war in Afghanistan. It was fairly standard practice that a difficult overseas assignment would merit a warmup pep talk from Dan.

"Okay, then write each of them a letter, tell them exactly how important they are to you. Address the letters, seal them up, and leave them in your desk drawer so someone will find them in case you don't come home," he said. Then he just let the words hang in the air for a while. If he was trying to get a reaction out of me, he didn't. I kept my expression calm. Inside, I was wondering how this conversation was supposed to help me. I was hoping to be encouraged, not frightened.

Since there was no natural light in the office, the cavelike darkness often made it difficult to make out all of Dan's features. In dramatic fashion, it was slightly reminiscent of a scene from *The Godfather*, dim light, dark wood, an imposing figure behind the desk, and a much-worn trench coat hanging on the door. Instead of a gun or cigar box, however, he kept a Bible on his desk, which left a comparable impression.

"When you go to a place like Afghanistan," he continued, "you might not come back. That may sound harsh, but it's true. If you can't handle that truth, then you shouldn't go. If you can, go with God's speed. And remember three more things about Afghanistan. Don't eat the meat, don't drink the water, and never look at the women," Rather said, with a smile growing on the edges of his lips.

"I'm glad you're going," Rather said. "Birds gotta fly, fish gotta swim, and reporters gotta go."

"Reporters gotta go." I certainly lived by that creed. By 2001 I had established myself as a network fireman, volunteering for every major story, both domestic and foreign. I had worked in both the Miami and Atlanta bureaus covering the 2000 election recount in Florida, the tug of war over Cuba's Elian Gonzalez, and numerous natural disasters. I had traveled abroad to Iraq, Central and South America, and Haiti. But less than two months after September 11, when the network was seeking volunteers for coverage in

Afghanistan, I had hesitated. For the first time in my professional life, I had to ask myself whether the job was simply too dangerous for me, whether I really needed to be in a place actively involved in bloodletting, like Afghanistan in 2001. Without trying to sound morbid, there are reasons to die, causes worth dying for, like family or one's faith. But did my career ambition require that I take this risk with my life?

I was afraid. Have you ever been afraid? So afraid you couldn't move? Have you ever been shaken by the kind of fear that makes your eyes water and your nose run? When I was a child, fear would usually take me by the hand and lead me away from danger and difficult situations. Fear, just like anger, was a friend of mine. Now in my early forties I had done a pretty good job of keeping my fears at a distance. Journalists at this stage don't talk much about being afraid. One of the things that drew me to this profession in the first place was the bravery associated with it. I remembered seeing and reading about reporters who endured threats during the civil rights protest era or those who went on countless patrols alongside soldiers in Vietnam. Those were the risky datelines of their generation, and America was better because of their courage. Now history was calling on my generation. Being a journalist in wartime does not compare to the hardships and risks facing America's sons and daughters in the U.S. military or the demands heaped upon their families. Theirs is a special calling, but reporting from dangerous places carries its own risks, and a number of journalists around the world have given their full measure in search of truth. So after some soul searching, prayer, and a few intense conversations with family, I put my name on the list of those who would go to Afghanistan.

And after Dan's "pep talk," I wrote the letters to my loved ones as he recommended. (They are still in my office desk, and I pray I get to turn those letters into paper planes with my grandchildren someday.) Normally I was excited to go away on big assignments, looked forward to packing my bags, and enjoyed the process of counting out batteries and socks and maps. This time I felt more like I was packing to go to a funeral. I wasn't excited. I was too nervous to be excited. In the past, my foreign assignments would have been dangerous only by accident. In covering the war in Afghanistan, death wasn't an accident; it was a consequence. But before my fears got the best of me, I did what I was raised to do: I prayed.

Days later, I left for Russia and traveled from there to the capital of Tajikistan for the long car ride to the Afghanistan border. I met up with a few journalists from other news organizations, and we took a short ride on a raft across the Amu Darya River. It felt a bit like traveling backward in a time machine: thirty-six hours earlier I had been in a fine Russian hotel near Red Square and then aboard a jetliner from Moscow. Suddenly I was floating across a fairly deep river, with strangers, on a motorized raft. No one said a word, which is unusual for a group of journalists. Usually there is at least one person in these groups who wants to share how much they know about the place we're going to. But except for the two Russian guides who spoke no English, no one on the raft had ever been to Afghanistan before. It's one thing to be scared. It's another to see it in the eyes of everyone around you. I had been to the developing world before, but as we floated to the shoreline, Afghanistan looked like a place struggling to reach developing-world status. I could see mud huts and decades-old vehicles. A stench of burning charcoal was in the air, and men huddled around small campfires were cooking what appeared to be goat.

My only instructions were that an Afghani would meet me on the shore to take me to the CBS compound. I walked up the riverbank carrying my own gear and dragging two cases of equipment for the crews. At this point I was more of a packmule than a journalist, bringing in fresh supplies. I guess I was expecting the kind of welcome greeting I would have gotten at an airport, a nice man holding a sign with my name on it. What I got was a thickly built bearded Afghan man with a Kalashnikov rifle on his shoulder, carrying a CBS mailbag. He looked like he was in a bad mood. I put my right hand to my heart and said, "Hello, sir, I'm Byron Pitts." His expression didn't change. He didn't move, just looked right through me. I stepped forward and extended my hand and repeated, "Hello, sir, I'm Byron Pitts from *CBS News*." That got his attention. He took two steps forward and pushed my chest with both hands. I hadn't come across that greeting in all the books I had read about Afghanistan. More than surprised, I was puzzled as to why this man was touching me. About that time, he took another step and pushed me again. I looked around and saw other Afghan men standing and looking at us. The other journalists had filtered away. Then I looked down and realized that I was standing on the edge of the riverbank. If he pushed me again, I would fall into the water. When he reached up to push me one more time, I grabbed his hands and pushed him back hard. I was half expecting him to raise his weapons. Instead, he smiled. I guess I passed the test. He turned and gestured toward his ancient Russian pickup truck. As I got into his truck, I thought about how unfamiliar this environment was, how aggressive this culture was, and how careful I would need to be.

*CBS News* had a base camp in northern Afghanistan, in an empty stretch of windswept land masquerading as a village called Khoja Bahauddin (we pronounced it *Hoja-Baha-Who-Dean*). The region looked like one of those planets from an early episode of *Lost in Space* or the way the Old West might have looked long before it was settled. Living was hard: the place was dry and dusty, with most of its people living at different rungs of desperation. On windy days some of us would joke about the time and money Westerners spent on exfoliates and such to clear up their skin. Spend a brief time in Khoja Bahauddin, and the mixture of desert sand and Mother Nature would buff your skin to a baby-soft shine. Spend too much time, and you could age dramatically. We would meet men in their thirties, windblown and sunburned, who looked to be in their seventies. We were indeed foreigners in a foreign land. Language seemed the least of our barriers.

Before 9/11, most Americans knew little and perhaps cared even less about Afghanistan. The United States had shown passing interest in the region during the 1980s when the country was at war with the Soviet Union. September 11 changed all that. Osama bin Laden had claimed responsibility for the terror attack on the United States, and his organization, Al Qaeda, had ties to Afghanistan and its ruling Taliban party. While the Taliban ruled, a tribal militia group called the Northern Alliance had been battling for control, region by region, for years. Their commander, Ahmad Shah Massoud, was assassinated two days before the terror attack in New York. Now the Northern Alliance had a friend in the United States.

We were assigned to the northern region of Afghanistan. Our job was to file news reports on the efforts by the Northern Alliance to push their way south to the capital city of Kabul, while they engaged in all-out combat or minor skirmishes with the Taliban fighters. We would get daily briefings from our colleagues at the Pentagon about the major movements of the battle, but we mostly relied on our local interpreters to tell us how close we could get to the front day to day. We filed regularly for the *CBS Evening News* and *The Early Show* the next morning. One day we reported on the fierce battle for a village. Another day it was the reopening of a village bazaar, where people could shop for goods and men could shave their beards. Other network teams were coming into Afghanistan from the east and the south. We were all hoping to meet in Kabul, where many of us naively thought the war might end.

To travel abroad for a major news organization is something akin to being a part of a traveling circus, a rock band, or a very large family. Engineers, technicians, photographers, producers, and editors—these are the people television viewers never see and rarely hear about—are all separated from their loved ones for long stretches of time, often longer stints than the on-air reporters. Their days can stretch from dawn until bedtime—preparing for daily assignments, coordinating the teams, and keeping in communication with headquarters. Back home, assignment-desk and logistics folks make it all work. Add to it the bad food, poor sleeping arrangements, bouts of dysentery, plus the occasional burst of gunfire and explosives. No one was under any illusion that this was a vacation in paradise.

On big overseas stories, technicians traveled from around the world, so we were sometimes meeting for the very first time. Francesca Neidbart, a sound technician from Austria, was partnered in Afghanistan with her cameraman husband, Alex Brucker. I had never met Francesca until I actually bumped into her one night inside the compound near the kitchen. She's a beautiful woman, with olive skin and thick black hair; I thought she was an Afghan woman roaming around after dark and remembered Dan's warning, "Never look at the women." Here was a woman with her hair uncovered. I panicked, bowed my head, and backed out of the room like an uncoordinated at the moon-walk. I knocked over a case of water, which knocked over a stack of pots and pans. The loud chain reaction woke up the entire compound. On top of all the built-in stresses, we were living on top of one another and couldn't escape for a moment's peace.

Leading the CBS operation was a legendary producer named Larry Doyle. If John Wayne had ever worked as a network producer, he would have trained under Larry Doyle. The kind of rugged toughness that Wayne symbolized in Hollywood, Larry, a captain in the U.S. Marine Corps during Vietnam, commanded in the field of journalism. He had nearly translucent, penetrating blue eyes, a voice like Humphrey Bogart, matched with thick, wavy black and silvery hair, and a solid frame. Larry was a mess of contradictions. If you saw Larry at work, he was almost always disheveled, like a guy who didn't care about his appearance. He had a perpetual three o'clock shadow closing in on four o'clock, usually a cigarette and a Heineken in hand, deck shoes, and an untucked open shirt. But if you met Larry at a social event outside work, at a colleague's party or at dinner, he would be dressed to the nines. In such settings he was a guy who seemed very fashion-conscious, with a wardrobe of delicate fabrics, like silks and linens. It was clear that besides the valuable experiences he had picked up in various war zones, he had also done quite a bit of shopping. He staffed the Afghanistan office, as he had other locations, with beer, cigarettes, candy bars, beef jerky, and the best local drivers and interpreters around.

During one innocent moment when I first met him, I asked Larry, "Do we have anything besides beer? I don't drink beer." He never answered, just stared a hole in my head with his bright blue eyes rimmed with heavy bags from a lifetime of little sleep. I finally got the message, opened a beer, and shut up. Less because of the age difference and more because of his demeanor, Larry was like everyone's favorite uncle on the road, a bit dangerous, worldly, protective, and wise. As a relatively young correspondent, I worked with Larry in Afghanistan, Iraq, Central America, and throughout the United States. He was at times a friend, a parent, a coach, a confidant, and on occasion a pain in the butt. Each and every time he was what I needed. He was a truth teller on those days when the truth was not particularly pleasant to hear. He taught me to never go into a story with preconceived notions; always have a plan of escape and a backup plan. He taught me the meaning of professional loyalty. If it is a bar, a knife fight, or a trip to Afghanistan, you want Larry Doyle on your side. For all the weeks we were in Afghanistan, he made my top-ten prayer list each and every night. "Lord, thank you for Larry."

The CBS compound was guarded twenty-four hours a day by a dozen armed Afghanis. In the middle of this desolate, poverty-stricken region was about an acre of expensive, high-tech equipment worth hundreds of thousands of dollars, plus a significant amount of cash. We were a potential target. But the guards never traveled with us on any of our assignments. After several days in the country, the storyline and the war forced us to head south toward central Afghanistan. That meant leaving the comfort and security of our compound behind. I left with Larry, cameraman Mark Laganga, and CBS radio reporter Phil Ittner, along with three drivers and an interpreter. For our team, getting to Kabul meant traveling over two hundred miles of open desert, through small villages and scattered towns, with more than a few pitched battles between the Northern Alliance and the Taliban along the way. The challenge was to stay close enough to track the ongoing battle but far enough away to keep safe. We often talked about the pros and cons of carrying a weapon for our own protection, but we were observers of this conflict, not participants. Having a gun might have emboldened us to take an unnecessary risk. We always felt safer with some proximity to the troops, because without weapons or the protection of military forces, as journalists we were fully exposed to the violence of the region. There was also the fact that we were known to carry supplies and money. Bandits were about as common as rocks. Every day we made a threat assessment before we ventured out to shoot our story. How close could we get to the violence without getting caught in the crossfire? How dangerous were the roads?

One day we woke up early, packed, and were headed down a road that we knew to be a shortcut to the next village. Suddenly a local farmer shouted to one of our interpreters, telling us to stop. The road had been filled with landmines by the Taliban. We couldn't see the mines, but we trusted his word and turned our vehicles around. It was difficult to comprehend that we were just a shout away from almost certain catastrophe. We were relieved to be alive but angry that our own interpreter had not known the terrain well enough to protect us. We were paying him not just to speak the language but to guide us where we needed to go.

About two days out from Khoja Bahauddin, we were standing on the wrong side of the Kokcha River and needed to cross. The only way seemed to be by horseback. We had too much gear and too few vehicles to handle the weight. We were at risk of sinking into the muddy bottom. To make matters worse, it was growing dark. We had to reach the nearest village, on the other side of the river, before nightfall. It never failed to happen that the darker it became outside, the shadier the characters would become around us. Our interpreter told Larry the mood along the riverbank was changing. Some of the new arrivals at the river were debating whether to rob us.

That's when we heard a voice in the distance. "Larry! Larry Doyle, is that you, mate?" The voice came from an Australian journalist named Paul McGeough, who was sitting alongside the riverbank. He recognized Larry from a previous encounter, on a trip to Iraq. McGeough quickly assessed our problem and called in some support vehicles to help us across a shallow stretch of water. We soon learned that Paul had just endured what we all feared as journalists, an attack that left three of his colleagues dead. The night before, Paul had been with a group of journalists traveling with a Northern Alliance commander. The group was ambushed by Taliban fighters. Of the six journalists, three were killed and three survived. Paul was one of the survivors. He was headed out, not for home, mind you, but just for some other part of Afghanistan.

"Never leave a story on a bad note," McGeough said. Paul and Larry greeted each other with great affection, like long-lost brothers. Clearly, Paul needed the emotional support after his ordeal. After introductions were made, we quickly decided that Paul's story should be part of our report for the next night's *CBS Evening News*. We interviewed him right where we found him, by the side of the river.

**(The *CBS Evening News*, November 12, 2001)**

*Today, United Front Soldiers counted their bounty after the bloodiest weekend in this war so far. In what seemed like 72 straight hours of rocket launches, attacks, and counterattacks, much was gained here and much was lost.*

*These were the rocket launchers and rifles, boots and sleeping bags, taken off the bodies of Taliban soldiers killed in battle.*

[Byron speaks with commander]
*"Your tanks killed 27 Taliban soldiers."*

*This tank commander boasted of running over 27 wounded Taliban soldiers. "It was easier," he said, "than taking prisoners."*

*There were prisoners and prized trophies. This letter was taken from a dead Taliban soldier written on the stationery of "The Islamic Front," one of bin Laden's terrorist cells in Pakistan.*

[Byron, with interpreter]
*"I know they are bombing on you. So be strong. I know God will protect you."*

*For the first time, civilians in Northern Afghanistan were allowed back into villages once controlled by the Taliban. Cross the Kokcha River, they were told. It's SAFE to go home.*

[Byron on camera]
*But safety is a slippery* word *in war. Sunday night six journalists accompanied a United Front commander to survey a town that had just been declared safe. Three of*

*the six journalists were gunned down. Shot to death as they scrambled for cover.*

[Byron interview with Paul McGeough of the *Sydney Morning Herald*]
*"Suddenly we were being fired upon from three sides."*

*Paul McGeough is one of three journalists who survived.*

[More interview with McGeough]
*"We were ambushed. And probably the nastiest thing of all, the bodies were looted by the time we got to them this morning."*

*McGeough admits he GAINED a story but LOST three friends.*

[More interview with McGeough]
*"But if you combine the losses on both sides on that ridge last night, apart from the media, there were 110 people killed."*

*What do you take from what you lived through?*

*"Thank God I'm alive. It was very scary and it doesn't make me want to pack up and go home. But it makes me, it makes me . . . I want to be close to someone."*

*Gains and losses. On one weekend in one nation at war. Byron Pitts,* CBS News.

That night over hot tea and two fried potatoes cooked with oil on our hot plate, the five of us ate. Larry had convinced Paul to join us. We were glad to have his company and his knowledge of the region. Now, five of us were slowly moving south toward Kabul. Every day was physically draining. We would work eighteen to twenty hours a day, with very little sleep. We used bottled water and wet wipes for hygiene. There was not much food. Some days we would climb for hours on the dusty hills to get a better view of the battle. Our vehicles were often breaking down. Three of us would have to hold up the truck while a tire was being changed. One night we'd sleep in an abandoned building, another night on the rocky ground under the stars. Then there was the constant stress of wondering if the Taliban would overtake us or if bandits might find us. On a night when we finally found shelter from the cold in an abandoned schoolhouse, we were in desperate need of a good night's sleep. It didn't take any time for all of us to fall into a sound sleep. But when we were startled awake by a scratching sound, our first panicked thought was that it was an intruder. Mark Laganga saw it first—a large rat. Mark sarcastically suggested we catch it and eat it. Phil and I were in the room with it and wanted no part of the hairy creature. Larry ended the discussion.

"That rat lives here! We're the intruders. Quit your griping and get some sleep!" Later that night, he whispered to me, "If you want to switch places with me, you can." We all got a big laugh out of it, which we needed as much as sleep. It made us feel normal and gave us something else to talk about for a few hours at least.

Eventually, Paul would leave us, after he filed his share of stories and could end his trip on a good note. We parted ways as Paul waited in an open field to catch a ride from a Russian-made helicopter, north toward the Tajikistan border. As we pulled away, Paul waved good-bye. A single black bag hung from his shoulder. All he needed he could carry on his back, like a seasoned war correspondent.

A few weeks into the Afghanistan trip, I came down with a wicked bout of dysentery. I could not keep anything down and spent most of the day on my back or in the makeshift bathroom Laganga had rigged up. We affectionately referred to him as McGyver. (For the uninitiated, that's the name of a nineties' TV show about a guy who could get himself out of the most dangerous situations with as little as a toothpick and a piece of string.) Laganga could fix anything. There were not many restrooms in northern Afghanistan at the time. Mark took four pieces of tin, a milk crate, a shovel, a coat hanger, and a roll of toilet paper, and built a toilet—with running water, sort of. Although there was not enough tin for an actual door, Mark came up with the idea of a red bandana. If the red bandana was hanging on a hook in front of the bathroom, that meant no one should walk in front of it lest they and the person inside be surprised. When I was sick, that bandana was always in use. After about four days on my back on a cot, Larry tracked down a local doctor who spoke English. Actually, he was a veterinarian, but desperate times called for creative measures.

"Mr. Byron, what seems to be the problem?" the doctor asked, with a gentle bedside manner that surpassed plenty of American doctors I had encountered. I explained my symptoms. "What medicine do you take, Mr. Byron?" he inquired. Each of us had been issued a supply of Ciprofloxacin in the event of a bacterial infection. The bottle said take two tablets per day. I remember the doctor back in the States insisting I take no more than the prescribed amount each day because of side effects.

The Afghan animal doctor asked how many pills I took per day, and when I said three, he asked with a puzzled look on his face, "Why just three, Mr. Byron?" When I explained the concerns raised by the American doctor, he burst out laughing.

"Oh no, Mr. Byron, this is Afghanistan! Don't worry about side effects. Please take eight pills tomorrow." With that, he shook my hand. "You will feel better in a few days, Mr. Byron, I promise. Inshallah [God willing]," he said, as he left my side. Sure enough, two days later I was up and running, as if I had never been sick. In good shape for the head-on collision that was about to occur.

Like many things in Afghanistan, driving seemed like another test of manhood and another needless escalation of tension. In a convoy of vehicles, drivers would take turns jockeying to be in the lead. On narrow dusty roads, drivers were often blinded by the dust created by the car in front of them. Larry had arranged for a convoy of Toyota-style pickup trucks to take us south. I ended up in a burgundy vehicle, in the hands of a teenage driver with a collection of bad local music. Funny thing about teenage drivers around the world; they are all about the same, hard of hearing and fearless.

Our vehicle was about fourth in line when my young

driver decided it was his turn to lead the pack. So he dashed out into oncoming traffic to make his way to the front. Most drivers coming toward us just moved aside and honked their horns. However, the driver of an approaching large truck with people piled on top did not appear willing to concede the road. In my calmest East Baltimore tone, I whispered to the driver, "Hey, brother, do you see that big truck?" I quickly assessed that the young man spoke no English, and I took a different approach with more attitude and bass in my voice. "Yo, man! Do you see that big-ass truck?" He looked at me and smiled. He didn't understand a word I said, but he seemed to enjoy the panic in my voice and on my face. He turned his attention away from me toward the road and waved his hand at the truck, like a guy waving a fly off the windshield of his car. The truck driver apparently did not take kindly to the gesture. Just as we were about to hit the truck head-on, both drivers gave just a little bit but a little too late. We collided. Not a full-on front-end collision, but the front-right corner of our truck hit the front of their vehicle, which was about twice our size. Our pickup did a 180-degree spin and was thrown into a ditch, facing the direction we had come from. The bigger truck came to a stop on the opposite side of the highway. A passenger hanging off the top of the truck was thrown into the desert.

Dazed and grateful, I was still conscious, with a fast-moving headache that started at the back of my neck. I waited for the dust and sand to clear. Thank God we were both wearing our seat belts. As I lay there, the driver began yelling and pulling at my seat belt. Did he think I was injured? Perhaps he was trying to help me? Then I realized he was not clawing at my seat belt. He was trying to climb over me. His door was jammed. To hell with the American, he was trying to get away. About that time I noticed the driver from the truck and a few other men running toward our vehicle with pipes in their hands. They were yelling. I couldn't make out the language, of course, but their volume suggested they urgently wanted a conversation with my driver. By the time the men got to our vehicle, the driver was out the door and running down the road. All I could see was the bottom of his shoes and a small cloud of dust. Larry and Mark ran to see if I was okay. I was shaken a bit but otherwise fine. We repacked my gear into one of the other vehicles. When we inquired about the driver and his car, one of our interpreters said, "Do not worry. Local justice." With that, we moved on.

The pace of our travel was determined by the progression of the Northern Alliance push to the south. Some days they would gain several square miles and any handful of villages. The next day they might lose a third of it, as the Taliban would push back. That give-and-take of war dictated our timetable and our travel schedule. We knew that a major battle would eventually take place in the large city of Konduz, currently a Taliban stronghold. The Northern Alliance had to take control of it to secure a major supply route to the south. We traveled through a series of nameless villages on our way to Konduz. Tribal clans ran each town, and we needed to get permission for safe travel or an overnight stay.

After a week of sleeping under the stars fewer than fifty miles from Konduz, we found comfortable indoor accommodations just in time for Thanksgiving. It was a compound that had been abandoned by a local doctor fleeing from the Taliban. Relatively speaking, it was a nice two-story mud structure. There were multiple bedrooms because the doctor had multiple wives. No beds, no furniture, but we each carried our own cots to our own private rooms. Generally, we did not allow ourselves much time to think about our families back home. But it was a holiday, and I think we were all a bit melancholy. Mark was the most recently married. He decided to make Thanksgiving a special meal. Mark spotted a bird, which we believed to be a duck. While we worked, the household cook killed it, plucked it, and grilled it. Add some rice and beans, and we were ready for the feast. We were thrilled, because it was different from the goat, rice, or noodles that we ate most days after we ran out of beef jerky and Vienna sausages. Yet it was like a bad picnic. The duck was dark, stringy, and kind of bloody, not really cooked all the way through. No one complained. It was as close to home as we could get.

It was a nice respite but a brief one. The Northern Alliance was moving, and we had to move with them. Konduz was a few hours away; the battle was now imminent. Leaving after sunrise gave us ample time to make the trip in daylight, if there were no delays, no transportation breakdowns, and nothing unexpected happened. But we had to decide if we were going to push into darkness. Larry, who had been on the most overseas assignments, had a few basic rules that he insisted upon for safety. Never travel alone, never flash money in public, and never travel at night. But if we did not get to the outskirts of Konduz in the next few hours, we ran the risk of missing the action entirely. We took a vote, and there was unanimous agreement to push the limit of daylight and get to the next location in time to make air. Our maps indicated that a fairly routine trip was ahead of us. If everything went right on the road to Konduz, we would make it before nightfall. Unfortunately, very little went right.

Our interpreters provided a handmade map, which indicated a well-traveled road leading to Konduz. What our map failed to show was that the primary route, a narrow gravel road through the region, had recently been destroyed by the Taliban. We had to turn our convoy around and return to the last village to ask for help finding the best way south. The villagers put us on a road that was traveled more by animals than vehicles. The craters and rocks were hell on our trucks' transmissions and tires. Of the five vehicles we started with, three broke down by midday. Two of the drivers refused to leave their broken-down trucks, and another driver abandoned us when he grew frightened by the unfamiliar route. In the next village, we downsized our gear, leaving behind water and some of our camping equipment. We bought another truck for cash and picked up a cocky sixteen-year-old driver who was willing to make the trip. Despite the language barrier, negotiations always came down to the number of one-hundred-dollar bills we were prepared to hand over.

We had lost a few hours, and it was now closing in on the afternoon. Mindful of the time pressure, with our new driver and a not-so-new vehicle, we set off on our way. We were still on a back road without any map to guide us. I was in the front car of the caravan, with the new driver and an English-speaking guide. Laganga was in the middle vehicle, with one of our original drivers and the fixer/cook/handyman. Larry was riding shotgun in the third vehicle, with a driver and our interpreter. The three vehicles stayed in contact by handheld radio. The road was more like a dirt path, carved by nomads, merchants, and drug dealers. Since it was too late to turn back and too dangerous to stop, we kept going amid growing darkness. No one in my vehicle spoke. The only sounds were loud Afghan music and the occasional groan from a pothole. Then without warning the driver slammed on the brakes. He spoke and gestured to the guide, who then turned to me with a pained expression.

"What's wrong?" I asked.

Through broken English, he explained that we had mistakenly driven into an area marked for landmines. During the war in the eighties the Russians had left an estimated seventy thousand landmines in northern Afghanistan. Someone would have to lead us out. I relayed the information by radio to Larry and Mark.

"Any volunteers?" I asked, hoping humor might disguise my fear. My request was met with dead silence. Then Larry spoke up.

"We're paying the guide to guide, so goddamn it, get out of the truck and guide!"

And so he did, on foot. He was a middle-aged man, with a thin frame buried beneath oversized clothes and a face worn by years of conflict. Guided by the headlights of our pickup and the words of the Koran, we crawled along this way with our guide, the human bomb-sniffing interpreter walking in front of three vehicles for about thirty minutes. The cars were barely moving, but we soon reached the end of the minefield. Before we could celebrate safe passage, our teenager driver had stopped again. This time he was pointing out of the car and shouting. It turned out we were completely lost and most likely in territory controlled by the Taliban. Not good news. The guide, who had just recovered from his hazardous duty outside the car, now explained that a house off in the distance to our right should be off to our left. In all likelihood we were driving on the wrong side of the nearby mountain. We had little time to figure out how it happened because he could see shadows moving about in the house and was convinced that they were Taliban fighters. I delivered this alarming news to my colleagues in the other two vehicles. As I was explaining our current dilemma, those shadowy figures off to our right (most likely a good half mile away, although it looked closer) jumped in the vehicles outside the house and appeared headed our way.

Larry screamed into the radio, "Go as fast as you can!"

In the desert, "fast as you can" sounded more impressive than it was. We moved at a crawl. The scene would have been comical if it wasn't so frightening. We were in a high-speed chase on an Afghan desert road, but we would have moved faster by foot. The terrain seemed to change with almost every heartbeat. One moment we were in a wide-open area, the next driving down a narrow path with only a few inches on either side of the doors. Not enough space to even open the doors but positioned perfectly to be ambushed. At other turns, we were forced to drive forward a few feet, make a hard turn in the direction we just came from, in order to eventually go forward. It felt as if we were rats in a maze. I have never been more frightened in my life. Then my fear turned to anger. I had promised my wife and children I would do nothing foolish that would risk my life and their future. Eventually, anger turned to sadness. I was about to die. It had happened before in this lawless, forsaken country. Why shouldn't it happen to us? Journalists had no protection here.

Then I began to think about Larry and Mark. What about Larry's wife and children? What had we done? As we bumped along, I actually began to cry. Quietly, with my head down and my fingers in a death grip on the driver's seat in front of me. The paralysis of fear was setting in. I was giving up. I had stopped looking out the window or communicating with Larry and Mark by radio. I should have been helping to navigate our path or offering words of encouragement. I couldn't speak. I couldn't move. Eventually, I closed my eyes and tried to pray. I was so afraid that I could not remember a single Bible verse, even my mother's favorite prayer. So I forced my eyes open to look out my window and see if the end was near.

It was then, for the first time, that I noticed the sky. It was clear. The stars were bright and we were in a valley. It was a breathtaking sight. And then it hit me like a blow to the chest. The Scripture began ringing in my ears. It was Psalm 23:4-6.

> Yea, though I walk through the valley of the shadow of death, I will fear no evil: for thou *art* with me; Thy rod and thy staff they comfort me. Thou preparest a table before me in the presence of mine enemies: Thou anointest my head with oil; my cup runneth over. Surely goodness and mercy

> shall follow me all the days of my life: And I will dwell in the house of the Lord for ever.

In the time it took to say those words, a peace I had never experienced before came over me. In an instant, I felt safer than I had ever felt. I began to realize that nothing Larry or I or Mark or the drivers might do right at that moment would necessarily make a difference. If it was God's will we die, then we would soon be dead. But if it was God's will we live, it would not even matter if the men chasing us caught us. My heart stopped racing. I stopped panting. I wasn't in danger. I was in God's hands, and I knew that was more than enough. What power comes from the sort of peace that no man can give and no man can take away.

The car chase went on for about forty minutes. As it happened, the men in the vehicles behind us never got close and eventually turned away. When we finally made it to the safety of our next desolate accommodation, I did not share my spiritual moment with Larry and Mark. Instead, Larry offered me more earthly solace, a shot of whiskey. Mark gave me one of his cigarettes. I gulped down the whiskey, lit and smoked the cigarette. Looking on in amazement at his colleague who does not drink or smoke, Mark jokingly said, "Byron, at this rate we'll have you snorting cocaine soon." We burst into laughter and then took care of the work that needed to get done. Within a few hours we were all asleep.

We would have other terrifying days and nights in Afghanistan. Not long after the battle of Konduz, a Swedish journalist was awakened by bandits storming a compound packed with journalists in the city of Taloqan. He was shot and killed. Our team was sleeping about one hundred yards away. The screaming of his friends woke us up. We spent the rest of that night comforting one another and talking about how soon we could go home. The next morning nearly everyone in the compound packed their gear and joined a caravan headed north, to leave the country. We had all agreed the story was no longer worth the risk. In all, eight journalists were killed in seventeen days in Afghanistan, including those who had traveled with our friend Paul McGeough. It was a staggering casualty rate for journalists working in a war zone.

When soldiers return home from war, they talk about their comrades, their brothers in arms. Theirs is a bond formed in mud and sweat and sometimes blood. For the rest of my life, I will have that bond with Larry Doyle and Mark Laganga. We don't talk much anymore, but we don't have to.

ELEVEN

# Love the Least of Us

For I was an hungred, and ye gave me meat: I was thirsty, and ye gave me drink: I was a stranger, and ye took me in.

—Matthew 25:35

WORKING FOR *CBS NEWS* has been a wonderful education. Veterans call it seeing the world on the company's dime. I guess that's true. As much as it's taught me about the places I've been, it's also taught me a few things about myself.

Fear was one of the biggest traits I carried from childhood into adulthood. Selfishness was another. All my life I have been blessed by people who had nothing to gain by helping me, but they did it anyway. I grew accustomed to receiving the help and support of my family, my network of mentors, and all those angels I've met along the way. In the current vernacular, it was all about me. I admit that I never spent much time putting myself in anyone else's shoes. I never thought about the sacrifices Coach Mack made for me, or the time it took out of Dr. Lewes's day to help me. I simply took their graciousness and kindness and used it to my advantage.

I was a needy child, a needy adolescent, and still needy well into adulthood. I was still learning what it means to give and what giving meant to those who gave so much to me.

I certainly can't fault my mother for failing to set an example. If ever there was a call for volunteers at our church, Clarice would volunteer not only her time but that of her children. If there was a family gathering at someone's house, she expected the Pitts children to help set up chairs and tables and break them down afterward. "Helping hands please God," she'd often say. Countless times she would make room for "one more" at our dinner table. Sometimes it was one of her clients from work; another time it would be a teenage mother or a homeless person. Like plenty of social workers and teachers, my mother saw her job as a calling that extended beyond the office or office hours. My mother always said that when we open our arms wide to give away the gifts we have, that only creates room for God to give us more. Serving others, she always taught us, is a valued virtue.

But in the midst of my own overwhelming needs, I lost the time and energy to extend compassion. I was too busy trying to fix my own flaws. It wasn't until I witnessed extraordinary acts of kindness by my colleagues and by those we met, many of them in remote corners of the world, that I began to actually look back and appreciate the sacrifices people had made in my life. Most of what I've seen has only reinforced the lessons I learned as a boy. Most people are good. Whether it's somewhere in the United States or some faraway place, there are always people willing to make a sacrifice for others. Countless acts of kindness go on every day somewhere on earth. Some of the most rewarding acts

I witnessed came from people who didn't really have the means or the time to help someone else, but they did it anyway. People who all had a willingness to step out beyond what might have been expected of them, and as a result they demonstrated amazing kindness. As I see it, they stepped out on a faith in something greater than themselves.

## IN AFGHANISTAN

Our team saw many horrible and violent things in Afghanistan that fall of 2001. But we also saw the goodness that lives inside. As I traveled from northern Afghanistan toward Kabul with producer Larry Doyle and cameraman Mark Laganga, we met bandits and beggars and one remarkable family. We met them in Khoja Bahauddin in northern Afghanistan, where they were forced to flee after the Taliban took over their home city. The Nazir family, a husband and wife with two children, were almost like a typical American family. Always well groomed, they had an air of confidence that especially stood out in Afghanistan, where so many people walked around covered in dust, with rounded shoulders and heads bowed seemingly with the burdens of the world. (I met an Afghan man early on in my visit, who, before I spoke, sized me up and said, "You're an American." I smiled and asked what made him so certain, considering that I could be African or European. He said, "You walk like an American, with long strides and your head in the air.") Every member of this family walked like Americans, especially the children. The parents were a hardworking, handsome couple whose primary goal was that universal desire to provide a better life for their kids.

Fahranaz, the mother, was a Soviet-trained electrical engineer, and so was her husband, Nazir. Their teenage son, Kambiz, had dark hair and teen-idol looks. He spoke English so well he became one of our interpreters. The daughter, Vida, who was probably about seven years old, was as precious as any child you could meet and always underfoot asking questions about the world beyond her own or toying with our television equipment. This one family in particular reminded all of us of our own families back in the States and the heavy toll war takes on loved ones caught in the midst of it.

After careful discussion with Nazir, Fahranaz, and our producer Larry Doyle, it was agreed that the family would be relatively safe with us. This was a presumption based simply on one rule of war, that there is usually safety in numbers. So Larry put them on the payroll. They were worth every penny. Nazir was a gifted engineer, who kept our equipment in tiptop shape despite limited access to replacement parts and a steady source of electricity. Not to mention the dust and sand that would constantly get inside the equipment. Mishaps that would send the average engineer back in the States on an angry tirade just made Nazir smile more broadly. Fahranaz was also a tremendous resource. She often pointed us in the right direction for a story or contacts. She provided access into an underground network of women who desperately wanted their voices heard but who were forced to balance their taste for freedom with the day-to-day struggle of staying alive. Back in Kabul, Fahranaz had been active in women's rights organizations before the Taliban took over. In Khoja Bahauddin, she was still doing activist work with women, running literacy programs and postnatal care seminars. Despite all the discourse about freedom from the Taliban in the north, the local warlords did not like Fahranaz teaching women about their rights. Soon there was the strong suggestion that some in the area wanted her dead.

To escape the threat, they traveled with our team for part of the trip south, but eventually the journey became too hectic and too dangerous for a family to keep up the pace. They stayed behind in a village where they would be safe. The Nazirs were always resourceful; they assured us they would be fine. When it reached the time to say good-bye, I thought that's what it meant. On this trip, like so many others, we had met people, depended on one another, lived together, and enjoyed an intense but brief relationship. Especially with the local population, good-bye usually meant forever.

Yet despite our twenty-hour days and our own adventures on the road, Larry stayed in touch with the Nazir family, as did another one of my colleagues, correspondent Elizabeth Palmer. Elizabeth did several tours in Afghanistan and worked with the Nazir family. When she returned home to London, she stayed in contact. It was a relationship Larry and Elizabeth nurtured long distance by phone, fax machines, handwritten notes delivered by strangers from one village to the next, messages passed along by word of mouth, and by what remains the most reliable source of communication around the world—cash put in the right hands. More than a relationship, the family's security had become a cause for Larry and Elizabeth. For more than a year they kept track of this one family with one goal in mind: to help them make a better life for their children.

In time, Larry and Elizabeth, with help from a network of friends and contacts around the world, managed to get Nazir and his wife and children out of Afghanistan. Today, they live in Canada. Their son is in medical school. Their daughter, as Elizabeth describes her, is a typical Canadian teenager. It says a great deal about Larry and Elizabeth. They helped a family they might have left behind. I asked them both why, and both agreed that it was because it needed to be done. They helped someone simply because it needed to be done.

Elizabeth added, "I liked them. I thought they were extraordinarily brave and honest. I think when such opportunities present themselves, it's important to grab them."

Few people inside *CBS News* ever knew what Larry and Elizabeth were up to. They spent their own time and their own money and sought nothing in return. It was not about winning an award, receiving special recognition, or even getting a story on the *CBS Evening News*. For them, it was more than that, it was about making a difference. They used their own gifts and gave them away. Who knows what a Canadian doctor born in Afghanistan will do someday? Look out, world, when Vida pursues her dreams.

Here's a footnote to the story. It almost never happened. When Larry first approached Fahranaz about her son working as an interpreter for CBS, she said no. She was afraid it was a trick to get her son to fight for the Taliban. That kind of watchful paranoia keeps people safe in wartime. Larry and Elizabeth were able to do their good work because they refused to take no for an answer.

## THE FALL OF BAGHDAD

Just days after the U.S. military invaded Iraq in 2003, the nation was given a sense of hope that the war would be brief. Most Americans woke on April 9 to images of Iraqis celebrating in the streets of Baghdad, as many of their countrymen pulled down and kicked a statue of Saddam Hussein in the middle of the city. That impression did not last long. I was a few blocks away from the celebration, along with Mark Laganga. We were embedded with the U.S. Marine Corps Lima Company out of Twentynine Palms, California. The embed program was put in place by the Pentagon after lengthy discussion about the best way to give major news organizations (and their audiences) the fullest and most unfiltered access to the war. The program would be widely criticized later on. But in the early days and weeks of the war, it gave America a front-row seat to war.

On this particular morning, *CBS News* gave viewers a split screen of the war. On one side, there were the hopeful images from downtown Baghdad of the capital city of Iraq apparently under the control of U.S. forces. On the other side of the screen and a few blocks away, U.S. Marines were engaged in an all-out firefight.

Earlier in the day, the Marines of Lima Company were assigned to clear the Iraqi Ministry of Oil building. They were cautioned to be on the lookout for snipers. Mark and I tagged along, actually hoping to see what was commonly referred to as "bang bang," American troops engaging the enemy. The early minutes of the mission were tense but uneventful. The Marines methodically went floor by floor looking for snipers or Iraqi fighters. Mark and I followed. We had been together for nearly six months by this time. We started our duty in Kuwait, where the buildup to the war began. By now Mark and I knew almost instinctively the other's movements and thought process. We could communicate without ever exchanging a word. So we split up that morning in order to cover more ground. Mark with his large network camera and me with a small digital video variety, the kind you would take to Disney World. It was one of the few days of my life I hated being over six feet tall. Besides being the oldest person with the group of Marines, I was just about the tallest. My fear was that I was an easy target, and at age forty-two I had the disadvantage of being a bit slow, alongside the twenty-something Marines. But it appeared that all of my anxiety was for naught. The building was safe.

An hour or so after storming the Oil Ministry, the Marines gathered on the front steps to catch their breath. Some rested. A few pulled out cigars. The day was almost over, and no one had fired a weapon. Our reverie ended with the crackle of gunfire and falling debris. In a war zone, the sound of gunfire begins to blend in with the background. We realized there was a problem only when plaster from the building overhead was starting to falling on our heads. "Holy shit," a Marine yelled. Someone was shooting at us. Everyone scrambled for cover. For weeks leading up to this moment, Mark and I had trained and studied with the Marines on how to respond to a chemical weapons attack, an air raid, trench warfare, and first aid. I do not recall a lesson on what to do in a firefight on the concrete in downtown Baghdad, so I got as low to the ground as I could and tried to keep up with the Marines in front of me.

While Mark videotaped the action, I placed a call to the New York office on our satellite phone to offer a live report. The first time I dialed in, a young person answered the phone. Sounded like one of the recent grads assigned to work the early shift back in New York. The person yelled into the phone, "I can't hear you; there's too much noise in the background." And they hung up. I looked at the satellite phone in disbelief. I wanted to curse, but there was no time. The Marines were about to change position. It was time to run. I was teamed up with a corporal and one of the company's staff sergeants. The corporal was young, thin, and athletic. The sergeant was just a bit younger than I, barrel-chested, with the classic Marine Corps tough-guy demeanor. I felt safe in his presence. The goal was to cross the outdoor mall beside the Ministry of Oil and make it to the wall surrounding the building. Run, stay low, then run again was the basic strategy. If cover was a necessity, there were cement tables scattered about. I imagined that workers in more peaceful times at the ministry might have sat outside at one of the tables enjoying their lunch. At the moment we would use the tables as temporary shelters. Somehow, the three of us—the corporal, the sergeant, and I—eyed the same cement table. The corporal got there first and the sergeant was a close second. I had the least amount of gear (flak jacket, helmet, small camera, satellite phone, and a notebook) but moved the slowest.

With no place safe to land, I dove on the sergeant's back—not intentionally—but I wasn't planning on moving right away either.

With gunfire above our heads, I buried my face in the back of the sergeant's neck, like a schoolgirl at her first horror movie. I wasn't particularly scared, mind you, but the sergeant was my security blanket and I was determined to stay wrapped up as long as I could. It was only a few seconds I'm certain, but it felt like much longer. As the gunfire temporarily subsided, the sergeant twisted his neck toward me. If not for our helmets, we would have been cheek to cheek.

In a calm voice inconsistent with the panic I was feeling, he asked me, "Are you okay? Are you bleeding? Any wet spots?"

I quickly did a hand check and fired back, "No, sir, sergeant! I'm fine."

In that same calm voice, he answered, "Are you sure?"

I answered, "Yes, sir, I'm fine."

Then, after a brief pause, perhaps for effect, the sergeant cleared his throat and in a very matter-of-fact tone said, "Okay, then fuck me or get off of me. But you can't just lay there."

If I had been eating, I would have spit out my food. He had detected tension in my voice and wanted to both reassure me and ease the mood. It worked. I sheepishly apologized, rolled to the side, and the three of us got up and ran to safety behind a wall. By now I had reconnected with the CBS office and was filing minute-by-minute reports to the control room for broadcast in New York. We did not have live pictures, only the sound of my voice describing the action, punctuated by bursts of gunfire and the shouting voices of the Marines around me. The gunfire aimed in our direction had not abated. The enemy was still an invisible target. In the midst of all the chaos came a moment I will remember the rest of my life. It was minor in the scheme of things, but it spoke volumes to me about the character of most of the men and women the American government sent into harm's way.

Lima Company was led by Captain George Schreffler from Harrisburg, Pennsylvania. He had the temperament of Tom Hanks in the movie *Saving Private Ryan*. His demeanor was often more professorial than warrior. Captain Schreffler was as calm as the quarterback in a church league flag football game, coolly calling out plays. Surrounded by a few of his Marines, including his radioman, he directed the movement of his unit and coordinated the call for support. A Marine corporal rushed over to tell the captain that his men had located the source of the gunfire. The corporal answered that he was certain of the location but could not confirm the identity of those firing. I for one was relieved by the news, but Captain Schreffler did not seem impressed. He instructed the Marine that no one was allowed to fire at the position in question until the threat was properly identified. I felt deflated by his strict instructions. We were getting pounded by gunfire, and I did not understand why he was reluctant to take out the target. But we soon realized that Captain Schreffler had made the correct call. He had been patient and protective of both his men and the potential enemy. It turned out that objects moving in the distance, once identified earlier as the source of the incoming fire, were actually members of an Iraqi family caught in the crossfire. If Captain Schreffler had given permission to shoot, that family would almost certainly have been killed.

Here's how I described those hours that night.

*The CBS Evening News*, April 9, 2003

*This morning the U.S. Marines rolled into downtown Baghdad . . . locked and loaded for a fight . . . when a party broke out.*

*Iraqi citizens chanting and screaming as they tore down this life-size statue of Saddam Hussein . . . on the steps of the Iraqi Oil Ministry . . . as the Marines were clearing this thirteen-story building. It was one of the last remaining symbols of Saddam's regime.*

Iraqi citizen: "*We hate Saddam! Thank you USA!*"

Staff Sergeant, USMC: "*I wish it was him they were tearing down, but the statue is nice.*"

Lieutenant, USMC: "*You know we've been fighting for days and to see this let's us know the Iraqi people are glad we're here, and maybe we're going home.*"

*But suddenly the celebration stopped with the crackle of gunfire. The party ended when these Marines were ambushed from three sides.*

*This wasn't warfare. This was a street fight. U.S. Marines . . . average age nineteen to twenty-two . . . each with an M-16 . . . versus Saddam's Fedayen paramilitary . . . also young men . . . with AK 47s.*

*Nearly two hours of small-arms fire . . . and rocket-propelled grenade launches. These Marines from Lima Company . . . based in Twentynine Palms, California, are flanked on three sides by sniper fire . . . when a corporal spots three heads bobbing behind a wall. He pleads with Lima Company's commanding officer to take the shot. But Captain George Schreffler from Harrisburg, Pennsylvania, orders his man to stand down. Wait until he can see a weapon. The captain made the right call. Those three heads were an Iraqi family—a husband, his wife, and daughter.*

*In the end, there were two Iraqi snipers dead . . . a third escaped. No American casualties. And a platoon of young Marines learned a valuable lesson: America is winning this war, but she cannot end it, at least not yet. Byron Pitts,* CBS News, *Baghdad.*

It was the most "bang, bang" I would see for quite a while. That night I unwound for a few hours with Mark and the captain. He walked us through the day's events. I was both curious and amazed by his calmness and clarity earlier in the day when so much was going on. "It's what I was trained to do," he said, without even a hint of arrogance or bravado. "I'm here to do a job. I'm not here to kill anyone I don't have to kill," he added.

Before we said our good nights, Captain Schreffler added, "I love my family, the Marine Corps, and my country. I would never do anything to dishonor them."

There were plenty of well-publicized low moments during the war in Iraq, moments that deserved the attention they received. I only wish moments like the one I witnessed the day Baghdad fell would have gotten more attention.

Acts of courage, decency, and humility often go unnoticed, and not just on the battlefield.

## HURRICANE MITCH

On October 29, 1998, category five Hurricane Mitch with 180-mile-an-hour winds hit the Central American countries of Honduras and Nicaragua. Over the next six days, the hurricane dumped a record seventy-five inches of rain, causing catastrophic flooding, killing nearly 11,000 people; another 11,000 were missing, and 2.7 million were left homeless. The damage was estimated at $5 billion. It was the second deadliest Atlantic hurricane in history. Those statistics provide the wide shot. For the closeup *CBS News* dispatched nearly the entire Miami bureau. That meant producer Larry Doyle, cameraman Manny Alvarez, soundman Craig Anderson, and me. We were a small office staff with eighty-two years of network experience combined. I provided the last two years. Manny is a Cuban-American who has the best sense of humor of anyone I have ever worked with. He can mix humor and sarcasm better than Larry can mix a drink. Larry had his rules for the road, and so did Manny. Never stand when you can sit. Never sit when you can lie down, and never just lie down when you can sleep. And a favorite of many a profession: eat when you can, as often as you can, because you never know when you will get your next meal. And then there is Craig Anderson. Built like a tank with the patience of Job, he has one of the best B.S. meters in television. Nothing got by Craig, and no one got one over on him.

Like many of these assignments, there was no road map. The assignment was to get on the ground as soon as we could and start sending in reports. We filed our first report along the Choluteca River in the city of Tegucigalpa, the capital of Honduras. The grim statistics that sent us to Honduras in the first place were mere echoes to the horror stories we heard on the ground. Survivors had poured into Tegucigalpa from villages miles away, with just the clothes on their backs. Many told of losing their entire families. Some set up makeshift tent cities along the river. Children were swimming and women washing clothes along one stretch of the river, while men, women, and children were relieving themselves along another portion. The place was rife with disease.

A few days into our trip, we traveled by small propeller plane and then by boat to remote parts of northern Honduras. We almost became part of the story. Never a big fan of flying, I was particularly uncomfortable in small planes. In a developing country after a major natural disaster, cash can get you only so much, so Larry rented the only plane available. It was a small twin-engine plane that could hold six people, including pilot and co-pilot. Larry, Manny, Craig, and I made four. After exaggerating about the weight of our gear and two additional Benjamin Franklins, the crew agreed to take us to a remote part of Honduras. We all assumed our usual positions: Manny in his own world, fussing over his gear; Craig and I talking about anything other than work; and Larry asleep in the back of the plane. As Manny was videotaping out the window of the plane and Craig and I were enjoying the view, we heard a loud noise. It sounded like flesh smashing together. We looked forward to see the co-pilot slapping the pilot for the second time. Neither Manny, Craig, or I had ever flown a plane, but we knew enough to figure out something was wrong. The pilot and co-pilot were screaming at each other in Spanish. Manny quickly filled in the gaps. The pilot was watching Manny videotaping, instead of watching his instruments. We were heading directly into the side of a mountain. The co-pilot slapped the pilot to gain his attention. The pilot pulled hard on the control, and the nose of the plane pointed skyward. Now we were all screaming, except for Larry who was still sound asleep. We barely cleared the mountain. When we landed, Manny, Craig, and I were still shaking and were soaked in sweat. Larry asked what was wrong. When we explained, he smiled and said, "Glad you didn't wake me."

There was plenty of death to be seen in the days that followed. Whole towns had vanished beneath the mud. We saw survivors living in trees and on slivers of land barely above water. In one place called Waller, we met Vicenta Lopez and her four children. She was twenty-eight but looked nearly fifty. Her oldest child was twelve, and the baby was barely old enough to walk. The family was practically homeless, except for a thin tin roof leaning against a stack of fallen trees, beneath which they slept and ate. She and her children were poor before the storm, but Hurricane Mitch had taken what little they had. Inside their makeshift home were three small stools, which the children used as chairs, a small table not much larger than a manhole cover, a few plastic bowls, cups, spoons, and one wooden spoon. A few days earlier an international charity working in the area provided Miss Lopez with rice and a large container of fresh water. She had a small fire burning just outside. Dinner that night for her and her children would consist of plain white rice.

Manny spoke to her in Spanish and asked her permission to videotape her preparation for dinner and the children sitting down to eat. She smiled and nodded yes. But then she did something that surprised us all. "Por favor [please]," she said in Spanish, "eat with us." She invited us to sit down with her family for dinner. Actually, she insisted. In a translated back and forth, we begged for them to eat without us. We were four healthy grown men who twenty-four hours earlier had slept in a hotel and had had three hot meals. Besides that, in about a week we would be back in our comfortable homes and comfortable lives.

Larry tried to seize control. "Let's go," he said, and the four of us backed up. "No! No! No!" she shot back as she moved to block our way. Wearing a worn apron around her waist, she used the edges to dust off the small table. She waved for her children to make room. With gap-toothed smiles and their almond-shaped eyes focused on us, they moved their small stools closer together to make room for their guests. Larry, Manny, Craig, and I all had tears in our eyes. I knew Larry was easy to tear up. Manny is passionate about most things, but Craig isn't. He was always the coolest member of our team. But the moment had even gotten to him. "Damn," Craig muttered under his breath. "I thought these things weren't supposed to get to us," as he wiped his eyes. This family had as close to nothing as almost any family you could imagine, and they desperately wanted to share. We were the American journalists who had come to this faraway place to tell the world of a horrific natural disaster and perhaps in some way help families like the Lopezes. And this poor woman with not even enough to properly feed herself and her children was offering to share with us. Finally, she relented and the family began to eat, a fistful of rice apiece. The gesture alone left our whole team emotionally spent for the rest of the day. We tried offering her some of our bottled water and some supplies, but she declined, though Manny did convince her to take our empty plastic water bottles so she could use them later to transport water back to her children. There must be a place reserved in heaven for people like Vicenta Lopez.

It's been my great joy to meet people with Vicenta's same spirit right here at home in the United States.

## THE NOTHING STORM

Some of the most remarkable things I have witnessed occurred in what some might describe as less than memorable or significant occasions. I guess it is all about perspective.

Meaux, Louisiana, is a spit of a town along the Louisiana coast. It is a speck on the map twenty miles southwest of Lafayette. In fact, you likely will not find it on most maps.

It's like my mother's hometown of Friendship, North Carolina. You normally go there for one of two reasons. Either you are visiting family or you're lost. I was traveling with *CBS News* producer Betty Chin on October 3, 2002, when Hurricane Lili hit the Gulf Coast. It was supposed to have been a major hurricane, but fortunately the winds died down, and Lili made landfall as a category one hurricane. To the bosses in New York, it was no big deal. When the morning began, Betty and I had the lead story in the broadcast. By lunchtime, our executive producer pulled the plug. Betty and I were given permission to head home, and most days that would have been the end of it. Hurricane duty usually means long days, little sleep, and bad food on top of the awful weather conditions and the sad stories you come across. Without the lead story, Betty and I were heading toward New Orleans for a decent meal, a nice hotel, and a good night's sleep before flying out the next day. We just happened to drive through Meaux. We were lost. Betty and I have probably logged more miles lost than almost any other correspondent and producer team at the network. My fault. Fortunately, Betty is incredibly good-natured, and we have always made the best of it. We weren't looking for a story in Meaux; the story found us. We had been in the car for hours and had not seen much storm damage when we saw a man standing in an open field littered with trash and a pile of debris on Abshire Road in Meaux. His arms were full of garbage, and he had a big smile on his face. He looked out of place. We wondered why this man looked so cheery when the weather was so lousy. Betty and I decided to stop and ask. We also thought he might direct us to the nearest gas station or at least get us back to the highway.

"Hi ya'll doin" is the way Jim Williams greeted us. He looked to be in his late twenties, an athletic young man with a cheery disposition. Come to find out he was a lieutenant in the National Guard. His unit had been assigned to help with storm rescue and cleanup. Since there was more cleanup than rescue needed, his commanding officer let him slip away for a bit to check on his own home. It was gone. That open field was Jim's yard. The trash and pile of debris scattered about was all that was left of his house. By history's high standard, hurricane Lili was a lightweight. But it was enough to destroy Jim Williams's home and leave him, his wife, and his three children homeless. Fortunately, Jim's family had gone to stay with relatives while he was assigned Guard duty. I asked him what he thought might have happened if they had all been at home when the storm hit.

"Boy, just looking at it, I'd be at the hospital or at the morgue right now, one or the other," he said, still smiling and with sweat gathering at the bottom of his chin.

Betty and I, along with our crew, helped him find a few valuables buried in what used to be the master bedroom. He found a few pictures and the family Bible. He seemed satisfied, like a man who had just eaten a good meal or finished building a bookcase by hand. Why appear so hopeful? I asked him.

"I have faith—that's just all it is. I can't attribute it to anything else but just saying, All right, God's not going to give you anything you can't handle, so, you know, I just wish He didn't trust me so much, you know," and his smile even broadened.

We spent about an hour with Jim Williams. The only time

his spirits appeared to falter was when he talked about his children. "It makes you want to cry when your four-year-old goes to your wife, her mom, and says, 'Mama, why are you crying,' " he said.

I have covered plenty of disasters, and you can always tell when someone has been crying. It did not appear that Jim Williams ever shed a tear. He thanked us for our help, and then said he had to leave soon. He was going back to his National Guard unit. "There are people who fared far worse than us, and they need our help," he said.

In reality, the Williams family had lost nearly as much as any family in Meaux. That did not seem to matter to Jim because he had a job to do. He cheerfully put the needs of others ahead of his own. As we pulled out of his driveway, Jim Williams was smiling and waving. He looked as if he didn't have a care in the world. We thought we had found a something story in this nothing storm. We pleaded with the executives in New York, and about an hour before the broadcast, they dropped another story and made room. Betty and I told the world about Jim Williams on the *CBS Evening News* that night. Funny, the wonderful golden nuggets God can lead you to when you are lost, with open eyes and outstretched arms.

## THE HUG DOCTOR WHO MAKES HOUSE CALLS

Dr. Regina Benjamin is one of the most beloved physicians in southern Alabama, partly because, for the longest time, she was one of the few. Dr. Benjamin runs a medical clinic in

Bayou La Batre, Alabama. She was just one of the many people I profiled for the *CBS Evening News* in stories about the recovery underway along the Gulf Coast after 2005's Hurricane Katrina. When I met her, she had 4,000 patients. You read right, 4,000 patients. And she made house calls. She drove an average of 300 miles per week across rural Alabama's shrimp country. She pulled fish hooks out of patients, delivered babies, and stabilized weak hearts. She had long days before Hurricane Katrina devastated the Gulf Coast. Her days got even longer in the months afterward. By some estimates, nearly 6,000 physicians were displaced from the region after Katrina. The hurricane flooded Dr. Benjamin's clinic. The following New Year's Day, the clinic caught fire and burned down. She stayed and rebuilt it. I asked her why not just close up shop and leave. She was a highly trained physician, a minority, and could practically name her price someplace else. She had a quick answer.

"This is my place. This is my price," she said without an ounce of regret, in fact, with a bit of an edge. Most people are fond of their primary-care physician. Dr. Benjamin's patients said they loved her. Everyone I spoke with used that word, *love*. Stan White, the mayor of Bayou La Batre, called her "the lifeblood of our community," adding, "I don't think we could survive without her." Certainly any number of people in the area would not have access to health care without her. Her clinic charged seven dollars per visit. Any treatments not covered by Medicare or Medicaid, Dr. Benjamin paid out of her own pocket or with federal grant money. She even dispensed hugs, as did her nurse. The patients affectionately refer to Nurse Nell Stoddard as Granny. She described the clinic this way: "We're a hugging office. We hug everybody. We'll hug you if you want to be hugged." And she did. I can count on one hand the number of times I've been hugged on a story in twenty-five years of reporting.

Dr. Benjamin talked a great deal about the character of her patients, especially the ones who could not afford to pay even the seven dollars. They lack money not pride, she said. They pay what they can when they can. More than just taking care of their health needs, it seemed that Dr. Benjamin was in the business of restoring her patients' dignity. She insisted she was well compensated.

"To know you made a difference, when a mother smiles after you tell her her baby is going to be okay. There's nothing like it," she said, smiling herself. "I've got the greatest job in the world," she said.

I agree with Dr. Benjamin. I feel the same about my job. It's allowed me to see my share of evil around the world, but it has also brought focus to the compassionate and caring spirit of so many. I can't look at my life now without recognizing that I too was once one of the "least of us" to whom so many reached out their hands. I won't live long enough to either repay those who've given so much to me or pay it forward. But it will keep me busy and always grateful. As for Regina Benjamin, in 2009, President Obama nominated the hug doctor to be surgeon general of the United States.

TWELVE

# The Power of Prayer and Optimism

God *is* my strength *and* power; And he maketh my way perfect.

—2 Samuel 22:33

As I BECAME ONE of the more senior correspondents at *CBS News*, people began seeking my opinion and my advice. Everyone from college students to up-and-coming young journalists, even established reporters and peers. They sought me out for encouragement and career counsel. For the longest time it seemed strange to me because I had always been the dependent one, in need of mentoring. I didn't consider my life or my career to be a model for anyone to follow. But I certainly saw this opportunity as one way to give back some of the time and attention I had been given. If I had the power to influence other people's lives, I needed to fully understand the source of my own strength. It took me more than forty years, but I was finally beginning to understand where my own power came from. One important factor was patience, the willingness to wait for my opportunities but remain productive in the meantime. As Coach John Wooden said, "Be quick, but don't hurry." As I've mentioned, long before I started at *CBS News*, the goal was to report for *60 Minutes*. It was my equivalent of the professional gold ring. Once at the network, I had to build a body of work and a reputation to get there, or at least get myself the chance. My prayer had never been "Lord, put me on *60 Minutes* someday." It was always just "Lord make me good enough to one day have the chance."

Not long after I moved to New York, I made it my business to find out where the *60 Minutes* offices were located. The staff works in a different building from the rest of *CBS News*. On lunch breaks, quiet days, and just for a change of scenery, I'd cross the street and make my way over to *60 Minutes*, where I'd see some of the most powerful figures in broadcast news: Mike Wallace, Morley Safer, Lesley Stahl, and Steve Kroft. Later, Bob Simon, Scott Pelley, and Katie Couric. I can still remember watching Ed Bradley gliding down the hallways. Ed made cool look good. I knew a few people who worked there, but I rarely stopped by their offices. I really just wanted to get a feel for the place, like a minor leaguer getting his first chance to walk around the field at Yankee Stadium. While some CBS staffers would walk down the street, smoke a cigarette, or go to the park to clear their head, I'd roam the hallways of *60 Minutes*. Long ago, when I overcame illiteracy, I discovered I needed to visualize things, have a snapshot in my mind of what I wanted to accomplish and where I wanted to be. I'd walk by the correspondents' offices just to peek in and see what they were doing and imagine myself there. That may sound childish, but remember I spent hours of my life staring into a bathroom mirror holding a toothbrush. Much to my relief, the *60 Minutes* guys were rarely around. I was often just staring at stacks of books and awards that lined their bookshelves. When they were in, I'd observe them buried in a book, crouched over a computer screen, scribbling notes, or conferring with a colleague. As a visual learner, I also spent a lot of time studying their video clips, watching how they conducted their interviews, how they interacted with their interview subjects. I carry a pretty good library of *60 Minutes* stories in my head. I knew I could only get to *60 Minutes* if I could see *60 Minutes* and put myself in the space. There is power in having the patience to visualize your path.

I've spent a good bit of my career covering power. The power of nature and the power of man to do good and cause harm. Still, the greatest forces I've ever experienced can't be captured by a television camera, just felt in the bones. As a Christian, I was raised to believe in other powerful forces, things that have become sources of both strength and comfort. These are all small things in size. You could fit them in a shirt pocket. I've come to believe they are fundamental to my strength: the power of prayer, the power of optimism, and, on more than a few occasions, the power of laughter.

I can't think of a single major decision I make without praying about it. I may seek the advice of my family, my friends, even respected colleagues, but I won't make a final decision until I've prayed. I have always believed that God could fill the gap between what I wanted to do and what was right for me to do—from my desperate prayers as a child for the ability to read to prayers for protection under dangerous circumstances. The war in Iraq tested the power of prayer in my life.

I've always prided myself on being physically and mentally prepared for every major assignment I've been sent on. I was part of the first wave of embedded journalists trained at the Quantico Marine Corps base in Virginia in December 2002 as the United States moved toward war in Iraq. We ran, hiked, exercised, and took crash courses in first aid, chemical weapons, and explosives. It gave all of us who participated a sense of what we might face overseas. It was the third war-training program I had attended. To prepare myself physically for the war, I also took five-mile walks around my hometown carrying forty pounds in a backpack to strengthen my back and toughen my feet. With flashlights, batteries, Band-Aids, a sleeping bag, and a big bottle of Tabasco sauce, I left for Kuwait in January 2003. I'd learned over the years that Tabasco sauce could make anything taste better, or at the very least mask the taste of whatever I was eating.

Most of us on assignment covering the buildup to war gathered at the Sheraton Hotel in Kuwait. From there, we could go back and forth into the desert where U.S. troops were massing at the Iraq border and still be back at the hotel in time for happy hour. Cameraman Mark Laganga and I teamed up and eventually joined a Marine Corps attack helicopter squadron in late February. The second Gulf War officially started on March 20, 2003. I was away from home for nearly six months. When my tour was over, I came back to the States hoping not to have to return to Iraq any time soon. Boy, was I wrong. I went back to Iraq twice more in less than two years. The first time, I was home for about two months when my bosses asked me to go back again. By that time, there wasn't a long line of journalists raising their hands for bureau duty in Baghdad at any of the networks, including *CBS News*. It was certainly understandable. It was dangerous and dirty work, but I took the assignment. I was still in pretty good shape and the dynamics of the war hadn't changed dramatically. After a month in Iraq, I was back in the States.

With the violence and the death toll in Iraq escalating in March 2005, and the United States deeply entrenched in battle, our executives were once again asking for volunteers to go into Baghdad. It had been nearly two years since I'd come home from Iraq the first time. I didn't volunteer, but when a colleague scheduled for Baghdad duty got sick, CBS needed a quick replacement. Reluctantly I stepped forward. "Reluctant" because I knew that I wasn't prepared physically or emotionally to go. With a week to get ready, there was no time for my exercise routine and no time to read all the briefing material on the war to that point. The weekend before I was to travel, I was more nervous than I had been that first trip. This time I knew the risks. Kidnappings, roadside bombs, and snipers abounded. Even the seven-and-a-half-mile trip from the Baghdad airport to the center of the city was treacherous, nicknamed Ambush Alley.

That Sunday I went to church with my wife and children. I did my best to put on a good face for the family. Besides, church was always a place of great comfort. After church, a group of deacons called me up front for prayer. A nice gesture, I thought, prayer is always a good thing. But this would be a new experience for me. The deacons, both male and female, placed me in the middle of a circle. They each put their hands on me, at least a half dozen people with their hands placed on my shoulders, chest, and arms. I admit to being a little uncomfortable at first. I'd certainly seen a number of prayer circles over the years, but this was the first time I had been in the middle of one.

One of the church ministers, Reverend Joseph Andrews, joined the circle. He did something that really made me uncomfortable: he put both his hands on my head. Since I'm an inch or two taller than Reverend Andrews, he really had to stretch to place both hands up there. Just before we all closed our eyes, I caught a glimpse of Reverend Andrews and he had a big smile on his face. Reverend Andrews has a booming voice, even in regular conversation. One by one, the deacons each gave a short prayer, asking God to keep me safe in Iraq and to keep my family safe and worry-free while I was away. The whole time Reverend Andrews kept his hands pressing against the top of my head. He prayed last. "Lord," he said with his Trinidadian accent, "be with our brother over in Iraq. Give him traveling mercy. And, Lord, let no harm come to him from the top of his head to the bottom of his feet."

When he finished, I felt a bit embarrassed for being so uncomfortable. But, more important, I felt a tremendous sense of peace. I could still feel Reverend Andrews's hands on my head and the hands of the deacons. I walked over to my family, standing in the back of the church, with a look of complete contentment. I may not have been quite up to Iraq physically, but I was, as military people are fond of saying, "high speed and good to go." I was ready spiritually.

Often, during the plane rides from New York to London,

London to Amman, Jordan, and Amman to Baghdad, I thought about that small prayer group. Security protocol called for a small private security team to meet me just outside the Baghdad airport. It was made up of three armed men traveling in two vehicles. There was one driver and two armed guards in one car, and then me with one armed guard and driver in the other. The drivers were all trained to maneuver in traffic and to take evasive action in case of attack. It was a high-speed sprint from the airport to the hotel CBS used as its headquarters. But this was an uneventful trip until we got there. Just as we were about to enter the secured gates around the hotel, we heard a loud bang. I could see people in the hotel courtyard running and diving for cover. The security guard in the front passenger seat ordered me to get down. I was already wearing a Kevlar vest, but I knew not to challenge him at that moment. Our car accelerated a short distance and then stopped abruptly. "Out of the car, mate, into the hotel straightaway," the British-born security guard yelled. Our hotel had just been hit by at least two mortars. One exploded and one did not. I wish I could say I started praying, but instead I asked God a question, "Lord, already? I just got here." I didn't wait for an answer—I ran for the hotel lobby. The unexploded ordnance was now resting on the ground outside the hotel. There's a good chance that if that mortar had gone off, shrapnel would have sprayed the courtyard and most likely hit the car I was in. "Boy, were you guys lucky," CBS producer Ben Plesser said, with his hand outstretched. "Welcome to Baghdad," he added with a smile. Perhaps we were lucky, but that's not how I saw it. For the next few minutes, my mind went back to my friends at St. Paul Baptist Church, who stood around me in a circle and prayed. I could feel their hands, especially Reverend Andrews's hands on my head and hear his words "from the top of his head to the bottom of his feet." When we settled upstairs in the hotel in the *CBS News* work space, Ben said with a hint of surprise, "You seemed awfully calm for a guy who almost got nailed by a mortar." My response was honest, "Not calm, just prayed up," I said. Later that night, when I finally went to bed, I again thought about that prayer circle. I slept like a baby.

It was, by the standards of war, a relatively uneventful month-long tour in Baghdad. We saw some "bang bang," as journalists are fond of saying, but no real close calls. Nonbelievers will contend those prayers had nothing to do with how things turned out. If safety and prayer were that easily tied together, why have so many people died in Iraq and elsewhere? My short answer is, I don't know. I do know the prayers of those friends comforted me the way prayers I had heard my mother and grandmother and others utter over the years. Prayers that remind us that whatever the eventual outcome, God will have a hand in it. When my mother prays, she often says, "Lord, not my will but Yours be done." That humble request has always worked for me.

I believe prayer works best when uttered from the bent knees of an optimist. A minister friend asked me once if my cup was half full or half empty. I stuck my chest out and proclaimed half full. His response was startling, Why are you optimistic only half of the time, he asked. Why not be optimistic all the time? Why not say your cup is constantly running over? That's always struck me as an awfully tall order.

Is it possible to be optimistic all the time? Over the years my life's been touched by a handful of people who have that kind of optimism, and they have helped me recognize and increase my own spirit of optimism. We all believe in putting the best face on a difficult circumstance and in anticipating the best possible outcome. We choose to be optimistic. At her core, my mother is one of these optimists. Despite what my grades showed or what a psychologist said, she believed my cup was running over, that I could do great things with my life. Optimists don't allow doubt to linger or to discourage them from their goals. There is something else this group shares, and that's toughness. Optimism isn't based on any pie in the sky naiveté. It is a hard-earned choice.

I believe that kind of optimism as much as anything got me to *60 Minutes* full time in January of 2009. Sure, I worked hard, and plenty of people had to sign off on it—from the show's executive producer, Jeff Fager, to the president of *CBS News,* Sean McManus, all the way up to the president and CEO of CBS, Leslie Moonves. They all had to be in agreement. Certainly my agent, Richard Liebner, played a role in negotiating the deal. But none of that would ever have happened without the spirit of optimism that's covered my life and the silent prayers of many people. Getting to *60 Minutes* was a thrill, but staying there, that now takes up most of my energies. It's never been about the destination for me. It's all about the journey. One of the best things about being at *60 Minutes* is the amount of time devoted to a single story. Research often takes months and on occasion years. Over time there's a chance to spend hours with the people you interview. Many of them are famous and have harnessed power in their own ways. A few I've met have reinforced or taught me things far beyond their professions.

Pete Carroll is my kind of optimist. He's the head football coach at the University of Southern California. His Trojans are one of the most successful college teams in the nation. Carroll certainly collects his share of high school all-Americans and has one of the top coaching staffs in the country, but he also has one of those contagious spirits. I met Coach Carroll while doing a profile on *60 Minutes*. The story was as much about what he does outside of football as about his success on the gridiron. He's part of an effort to reduce gang violence in Los Angeles through a program he started, called A Better L.A. One night he took us along when he went to South Central Los Angeles, into several neighborhoods known for gang violence. It was well past midnight, just a few days after a big win against Ohio State. Pete's been making such visits for several years, and this was the first time he ever allowed television cameras to accompany him. He chatted with gang members and gang wannabes, and with community activists who share his desire to make L.A. a safer place. Carroll's been criticized for his work, accused of being naive and in over his head. But he laughs it off. He has also been given credit by some in law enforcement in the city for helping to reduce the level of gang violence. He believes it's possible for a person to win at whatever they put their heart and effort into, from sports to business to living their life day to day. He doesn't just believe it—he lives it. Twice he was hired as an NFL head coach, and twice he was fired. A lesser person might have just curled up in a fetal position and turned the lights out. Not Pete Carroll. He said, "Okay, let me go. Let me move on to the next thing." He processed the criticism, learned from it, and moved on, just as Clarice would have prescribed. When *60 Minutes* first approached Carroll about a profile, he was hesitant. But in the end, he decided to cooperate. Wearing his perpetual big smile, he told me off-camera before the first interview, "I'm going to trust you guys and that means I'm in." That's another quality of an optimist, a commitment to give themselves fully to things they believe in.

An optimist takes stumbling blocks and turns them into stepping stones. Dr. Paul Farmer is a living example, and that's partly why I profiled him for *60 Minutes*. He's the cofounder of a group called Partners in Health, an organization that provides medical care to poor people around the world. He divides his time between his home in Haiti and Rwanda. Paul's childhood makes mine look like a day at the beach. He was raised near Weeki Wachee, Florida (near Tampa), by working-class parents. He was one of six siblings who spent part of their childhood living on a bus. I'll repeat that: they lived on a bus. Because he grew up poor, he recognized the lack of health care and the lack of dignity associated with poverty. He had spent a lot of time in Florida with migrant workers from Haiti, so his relationship with the country was part of his early development. He went to Duke on a scholarship and later earned a medical degree at Harvard, where he committed himself to providing both quality health care and dignity.

Like most optimists, he had great clarity about his purpose in life and therefore drew great satisfaction, no matter the difficulty of the moment, in just having the opportunity to live that purpose every day. The program Dr. Farmer started in Haiti has become a model around the world for providing health care to the poor. In fact, techniques Partners in Health mastered in Haiti are being used in parts of Boston to treat poor patients in one of America's great cities. Farmer, too, has a permanent smile etched on his face. Once, when I took a flight back with him from Haiti, as we were chatting, I realized he'd stopped talking. I glanced over and he was sound asleep. He had two books open on his lap, on top of notes he was preparing for an upcoming speech. His head was tilted back, eyes closed, and there was a slight smile on his face. He's optimistic even when he's dreaming.

There is a childlike quality to many of the people whose optimistic spirits shaped my life. In addition to their optimism, they all had the ability to laugh at life and just as easily to laugh at themselves. Laughter was often a miraculous ointment for the troubles in my life. It's one of the many and most valued things I learned from my mother. "Son, sometimes you have to laugh to keep from crying," she'd say, and that's exactly what we'd do. Often at night, just before bed, I'd sit on the side of my mother's bed with my brother and sister. Some nights we'd snuggle next to her. And somehow, no matter what had occurred that day, she would find a way to make us laugh. There was no topic too sensitive or serious that we couldn't laugh at it. From her failed marriages, to difficult bosses, to her own disappointments with relationships, nothing was out of bounds. She gave each of us a great gift, the ability to laugh at ourselves. It has served me well. At times, it's been therapeutic. Other days, being able to laugh at myself or at a situation was just enough to keep me from losing control.

One of those days occurred on July 22, 2003. I was sitting in the *CBS News* office in Baghdad. It was late, and I was filling time the way I often did on this particular assignment: I was losing badly to producer Mike Solmsen at cards. Mike was a great travel companion. He could find good fried chicken anywhere in the world, talk passionately about Syracuse basketball for hours, and recite the best lines from movies like *The Godfather* and *Pulp Fiction*. All valuable skills when you can spend hours waiting at airports, on stakeouts, or like this particular night, waiting out rumors that Saddam Hussein's two sons had been killed by U.S. forces in a firefight. The rumors had been circulating for hours. We couldn't confirm the story, and it was too dangerous to try to drive from Baghdad to Mosul, where the alleged shootout was supposed to have occurred. Mike and I did the next best thing; we sat in the office and played cards. For hours we played cards. The rest of our team of photographers and engineers had gone to bed. Mike and I were often the last ones up. Through the years we've probably played more than five hundred hands of cards. I've won twice. Once I cheated, and the other time Mike let me win. Mike and I were about to start another hand of cards, as we sat in the office, when we heard a loud round of gunfire. It was close, too close. We'd both heard enough gunfire over the years to recognize when the sound was too close for comfort. Someone was shooting just outside our building. Actually, it sounded like our hotel was under attack.

"What should we do?" I asked Mike. With a deadpan expression, he looked me in the eyes and said, "What should we do? It's pretty obvious. Get under the table, call New

York, and finish our hand." We both burst into laughter. We might be in serious trouble, but Mike was making jokes. It's just what we both needed. Laughing allowed us to at least temporarily block out the anxiety we were both feeling. We did call New York. Our cameraman heard the gunfire as well, and he had managed to ease outside to videotape whatever he saw. What he saw were Iraqis celebrating in the streets of Baghdad. It was official: Saddam's sons were dead. As is the custom in that part of the world, men celebrated by firing their weapons in the air. It wasn't a crisis we were hearing—it was a celebration. A brief moment of laughter had kept us from panicking. We later filed our story. As it had so many times before, laughter had gotten me past a difficult moment.

Prayer, optimism, and laughter are all wonderful gifts. They are part of the foundation my mother used to raise her children. "If you pray hard, work hard, and treat people right, good things will happen," she often said. She left out laughter, but it was certainly vital. Her foundation was now mine. I've found that status or wealth can last but so long and take one but so far. Patience, prayer, optimism, and laughter are their own renewable-energy sources. Mix in a relentless work ethic, and you might be surprised how far you can go.

THIRTEEN

# The Power of Forgiveness: When Father and Son Talk as Men

Forgive, and ye shall be forgiven.

—Luke 6:37

For if ye forgive men their trespasses, your heavenly Father will also forgive you.

—Matthew 6:14

CAN YOU TELL BY now that I'm an optimist? I choose to see the bright side of most any circumstance. My closest friends say I'm easygoing and almost never get visibly upset or angry. I carry my faith right out front and acknowledge that every good thing in my life has some connection to prayer, whether my own or someone else's. However, what is unseen is a heart that has been unwilling to forgive. I believe that God gives us power through our ability to forgive others and forgive ourselves. Nothing has drained me more of that power than my knot of unforgiveness. Like anger and fear, it kept me safe or, to my thinking, kept certain dangers at a distance. When TV's Tony Soprano said one of his enemies was "dead to me," I could totally relate. If someone crossed me personally or professionally, I would kill them off emotionally. I think that's one reason my anger never turned to violence.

I remember when a distant cousin offered me heroin when I was about eight years old. I got mad and never went to his house again. I never talked to him again and I never told my parents. When a girlfriend in college went out with another guy, from the moment I found out I never spoke to her again, ever. Back in my midtwenties in the mid-1980s, a colleague at a local station (a nighttime assignment editor) sent an e-mail to our news director criticizing my work and making a few false accusations. I got a copy of his e-mail. I never confronted him, but I also never spoke to him again. Mind you, this was the man who gave me my news assignments every day, but for more than a year I would not speak to him. I would not call his name. If he addressed me, I'd simply look at him and walk away. Not the best way to cover the news—and it still surprises me that I didn't get fired. I guess someone else in the newsroom was praying for me.

I could not forgive myself either. I can still remember every blown live report, every story where I've been beaten by the competition. For the longest time I kept a video diary of my worst work. Fortunately, I lost that videotape. An unwillingness to forgive was perhaps the coating on the masks I've worn most of my life. Like a hard acrylic, it kept most people and most things from getting too close or close enough to hurt me. In many ways, learning to forgive has been harder for me than learning to read or learning to speak clearly. It took only twelve years for me to learn to read. Speaking finally became easy at twenty. Forgiveness seemed beyond my reach for the first forty-five years of my life, and I was okay with that, or so I thought. For the longest time, my life was littered with people I had killed off emotionally for one reason or another. But, for me, there was at least one body that needed to be recovered: my father.

The conversation with my father was the most-thought-out, researched, prayed-over conversation I'd *never* actually had. Probably as early as middle school, certainly in college, and every few weeks of adulthood, I'd rehearse "that conversation I'll finally have with Daddy." I had discussed it with everyone in my family. They all encouraged me, but I just never could bring myself to call him and do it. The whole birds-and-the-bees conversation had long passed us by. All the big "man-to-man" conversations I had already had with my mother. For the longest time, I struggled just to remember the sound of his voice. I never remember him congratulating me, saying he was proud of me, or ever wishing me well in school, in sports, or, for that matter, in life. I wanted no part of him. My last significant conversation with my father was when I was about twenty-five years old.

Baltimore wasn't that far from Norfolk, where I was working at the time, so I had gone up there to reconnect with old friends. Out of respect for my mother, I often avoided my father, but my brother asked me to stop by and see him. I did, but I did not look forward to the visit with the joy and excitement one usually has for a long-distance parent. I dreaded it. I spent an afternoon with my dad and his wife. He questioned me about all aspects of my life and my job, even spoke proudly of me and my professional accomplishments. But what I waited to hear and wanted to hear was some acknowledgment of how he had behaved when I was young. I wanted him to tell me he was sorry. But he didn't. When the afternoon came to an end and he talked about staying in touch, I told him, "When I was a boy, you had no time for me. Now that I'm a man, I have no time for you." I was snarling when I said it, while my heart was breaking. I'd rehearsed those two sentences over and over again. Even down to my facial expression.

Another conversation I had contemplated having with him was one that involved the kind of violence I had witnessed between my parents. Instead of the two of them scratching at each other, this time it would be me, Byron Pitts, grown man, slapping my father around, forcing him with my fist to listen. Truth be told, those conversations in my head never lasted long or wound up any place productive. I've seen enough in my own life to know violence (although it might offer some temporary gratification) is never the long-term answer.

For twenty years there was nearly silence between us. We had perhaps five phone conversations, but I thought about him every single day. I often wondered if he was watching me on television. When I got to the network, I began wearing a white cotton handkerchief in my jacket pocket every day because I remembered that he always wore one. It's my daily reminder of the man I will always wish I had known better. Every time I glanced down at that handkerchief, I'd think of him. Outwardly, I was successful, but, inside, I felt incomplete. I was burdened by my unforgiving heart.

In the end, there was nothing courageous about my decision to talk with my dad again. I was simply paying off a bet with two of my workout buddies from my church. Dave Anderson and Darryl Carrington are two deacons at St. Paul Baptist Church in New Jersey. We would meet at the YMCA a few times a week to lift weights and for fellowship. On more than a few mornings, Darryl and I had to encourage Dave to lower his voice when he'd recite Scriptures while doing squats or bench presses. He was scaring some of the other people in the gym. Strong as an ox, Dave could also be as loud as one.

One week we got into a discussion about regrets—things in our past that pained us but which we hoped there was still time to address. I mentioned my father. The three of us talked about strained relationships with our fathers, though I seemed to be the most bitter. Darryl talked about his battle with his weight. Dave spoke of his temper. We agreed to pray for one another. Then Darryl challenged me. "If I start to lose weight," he said, "you have to start the conversation with your father." I refused. Refusing that challenge was as easy as lifting a twenty-pound dumbbell. But Darryl was relentless. Every morning for weeks he'd bring up the bet. Finally, I gave in. To his credit, Darryl didn't shame me into it; he nudged and supported me. "Jesus died for us, He laid it all on the line, what are you willing to give up?" he'd say as a smile crept across his face. It is hard for a Christian to think selfishly when one ponders that kind of question. It actually can be a strength builder and can be applied to most of life's struggles. Who can explain why after years of encouragement from family and close friends, I finally took a challenge from a friend in a weight room to push me toward a talk I had both dreaded and longed for most of my life? I guess God truly can use any of us in any situation. A sweaty weight room was the place for me. Days later, I called my dad on the phone. He was surprised I called. So was I.

We met at the Renaissance Harborplace Hotel in Baltimore for breakfast, just me and my dad, in 2005. He was seventy-seven; I was forty-five. It was the first time we had spent this much time alone, just the two of us, ever. Then it hit me. I didn't really know this guy, and he didn't really know me. Even those first eleven years, we were rarely alone. During my childhood we would almost always be with my mom or my siblings, people at church, members of my Boy Scout troop, or baseball or football teammates, but rarely was it just the two of us. Through most of high school and all of college, we never spoke or saw each other. During high school football games, I could always look from the sidelines into the stands and find my mother and smile. Secretly, I'd also look for my father, but he was never there, or if he was, I never saw him. Even when my father remarried, if I saw him I also saw his wife, a lovely woman who often tried but failed to get us to settle our differences. She always seemed more generous with her time than he was. So with enough baggage to fill an ocean liner, Byron A. Pitts sat down with William A. Pitts.

"Good morning, sir, how are you?" I greeted my dad as if it was a business meeting. That was the "Clarice" in me: be polite no matter what. We shook hands. As affectionate as my upbringing was, I don't ever recall my dad hugging or kissing me or ever saying he loved me. The last photograph we took together, when I was a child, was Christmas day, 1973. I was thirteen. He didn't put his arm around me, and I certainly didn't touch him. Now as an adult, I'll hug a tree, a dog, or a stranger if we're posing for a photograph. I simply love touching the people I love. But the notion of hugging my father had always seemed as foreign a notion as speaking Chinese.

"Good morning, son. You look good. How's the family?" As long as I can remember, my dad's always been a pleasant man in public, with an air of elegance (not Park Avenue elegance, more Rampart Street in New Orleans after-dark elegance). This day was no different, except looking into his oval-shaped eyes, I saw a flicker of innocence and sadness I'd never noticed before. There we were, father and son, the same last name, the same blood—we even look somewhat alike. Both six feet one, both balding, he a few shades darker, the stride of a once-confident young man long gone. Yet we share the same awkward gait. And our hands; identical, even down to the few strands of hair above each knuckle and to the length and shape of our fingernails. But it was still as if we were from different planets.

I motioned him toward the elevator and the ride up to the restaurant. For the first time in my life, I was suddenly looking down on him. Age had bent his spine, rounded his shoulders a bit, and left him with a slight limp. Had he been in an accident? Was it some degenerative condition? Does he have any major medical issues? Is this how I'll walk in thirty years? These and about a hundred other questions filled my head as we walked the forty yards from the lobby to the elevators. In the ride up one floor, not a word passed between us. We both looked straight ahead, studying the details of an elevator door without any significance other than as a focus for our discomfort. The doors opened and I ushered him out first, touching the middle of his back. I wanted to put my arm around his shoulder. As a boy and later as an adolescent, I was repelled by the idea of touching my father. Now, as a man, the boy inside me longed for the moment. I'd seen fathers and sons do such things in the movies, at ball games, and at church. Each time, I had longed for the same moment, but when my chance came, I let it pass.

My father walked into the restaurant like a man out of place. His clothes and shoes hadn't appeared so worn when we stood in front of the hotel. Why was he still wearing his hat? When I was a boy, he always seemed so stylish. Now he looked like the man he'd been most of his life, someone who worked with his hands, unaccustomed to fine linens. He remarked in a surprisingly loud voice, "This is a fancy restaurant." This was the kind of restaurant I'd eaten in a hundred times over the course of my career. It was no big deal. I felt both a tinge of shame and unexplainable joy. I was finally standing with my poppa in public. We were in my world and one beyond his reach. We took our seats.

"Everything here is so expensive," he said, visibly uncomfortable.

"Please order whatever you'd like," I said, in as encouraging a voice as I could muster. Suddenly I couldn't breathe. "Please excuse me," I said and pushed away from the table and made my way to the restroom. Once behind closed doors, I splashed my face with cold water only to realize that my hands were shaking. I'm not one to succumb to nerves very often, but here I was on shaky legs with trembling hands. I could feel my heart pounding through my tailored sports jacket. I was a mess. After several deep breaths and a quick prayer—"Lord, be with me. Hold me in Your hands."—I returned to the table. My father appeared so engrossed in his menu he hardly noticed I'd been gone.

"What are you having, son? I don't know what I want," he said, expressionless.

"I'm going for the buffet. When the waiter comes, please order whatever you'd like." I'd never fully appreciated the value of comfort food until that moment. I crowded my plate with smoked salmon, strawberries, blueberries, and grapes, oatmeal and brown sugar—all my favorites but in unusually large portions. Much to my disappointment, I was uneasy being alone with him. I'd felt more comfortable with convicted killers and Afghan warlords than I did with my own father. Perhaps they could hurt me physically, but this man could wound me emotionally like no other. In desperate need to gain control, I decided to sit across from my father, as if he was just another interview on a run-of-the-mill story. He could have been a politician, a corporate executive, or a criminal. I'd decided to fill the time with as many questions void of any emotion for as long as possible.

"So how's your health? Are you a fan of the Baltimore Ravens [they were the Baltimore Colts the last time he and I were alone together]? Doesn't the Inner Harbor look nice?" Meaningless questions fired off with machine-gun frequency. I barely paused long enough to give the man a chance to answer. I'd leave no room for silence. Silence was awkward, and the occasion was already awkward enough. The silence left space for feelings and emotions, and I wanted no part of that.

"Your order, sir." Thankfully, the waiter interrupted with my father's breakfast. My goodness, it was a heart attack special: scrambled eggs, white toast with a small mountain of butter, hash browns, slices of bacon, ham, *and* three sausage links, with a cup of coffee. He looked pleased. I felt sorry for his arteries. Now my father was ready to push back, take control of the conversation.

"How's the family? How's work? Where have you been lately?" His questions were as pointless as mine. Then the conversation shifted. "So can you lend an old man some money?" I shifted uncomfortably in my chair. I was no longer nervous. "You know your old man is getting up in age. Now that you're doing so well, I'm sure you can help me," he said, with a big toothy grin. It was an odd sight, no one else in our immediate family could ever gin up that kind of smile. Maybe we weren't related after all. I wanted to shut him down, refuse him point-blank, and leave. Not this time.

"How much, Daddy?" I said, more resigned than angry or even annoyed. "A few thousand bucks would be nice." As the words left his lips, I flashed back to a painful moment from my childhood. This is the same man my mother had to take to court in order to make him pay seventy dollars per month to provide for his two sons after their divorce. I remembered the shame of being in court, my mother making sure my brother and I were dressed in our Sunday best. My father showed up with his girlfriend and his youngest son, Myron, insisting he couldn't afford the money because he had "other responsibilities." Thirty years later, he was asking me for a few grand with the same tone a co-worker might ask a colleague to borrow their stapler.

I felt something odd. The edges of my mouth were slowly turning up. I was smiling. It was the same menacing smile I'd seen on the face of bullies just before they pounced. Or the knowing smile of Wile E. Coyote as he was about to devour the Road Runner. This was my opportunity to savage this old man, belittle him with three decades of anger and shame. Instead, for reasons I can't easily explain, and in a modest tone reserved for reading Scripture during a church service, I said, "Daddy, I'm not here to give you money." His face fell a bit, but I just kept going. "I'm here to talk to you, man to man. I want you to know something. I want you to know a few things. I love you. I've always loved you and wanted you to love me. I've never felt your love, and for most of my life I've felt cheated. I've been angry. Everything I've done I did in part to prove to you I was worthy of your love." A lifetime of hurt and anguish and anger were pouring out of me like well water from my grandmother's old bucket.

I felt lighter with each word. "Daddy, I want you to know I'm not that angry little boy anymore. People who love me have forgiven me time and time again. God has forgiven me more times than I can count. I can't seek forgiveness unless I can give forgiveness. So, Daddy, I forgive you. I forgive you with all my heart." I never took my eyes off his face. At one point, I put one hand on top of his and used my other hand to grip the edge of the table for balance. Near the end, my voice cracked a bit. But I held on. I stopped talking, took a heavy breath, and smiled.

My father sat back in his chair, wiped his mouth with his napkin, then leaned in toward me. I leaned in to him. Might this be the moment we embrace? Would he whisper some pearl that would change the trajectory of my life? For the first time during all of breakfast his eyes met mine. Was the moment I'd longed for about to occur? He put down his fork, cleared his throat of scrambled eggs, and said, "So you're not going to give me the money?" As my mouth slowly dropped, he continued, "Then can I taste that," as he pointed toward the smoked salmon on my plate. By now my jaw and heart were falling in the same direction. Without thinking, I motioned down at the salmon and said, "Sure, it's yours." He smiled in appreciation.

That was it? The moment I'd convinced myself would change my life had come and gone. As I often do in an awkward moment, I dropped my head a bit and put my hand to my mouth like a student in class who'd just made a startling discovery. Then suddenly I was back in my father's car. I was a little boy again. Stone-faced. Expressionless. Then something odd happened. The passenger side door of my father's old Buick opened, and I got out. What happened next surprised me. I burst out laughing. Then I smiled. It was an earlobe to earlobe smile. I clapped my hands and continued to laugh. The couple at the next table looked a bit startled. It was in that moment that the last few pounds of what had felt like an unbearable weight lifted from my shoulders and across the width and length of my back. All my life I had been waiting for some miraculous healing moment, and that was it? It actually made me laugh when I realized that I didn't need my father to release me from the pain. With God's grace, I could release myself. For the first time, I no longer felt inadequate. I no longer felt inferior. I no longer had anything to prove.

In that moment, it felt as if I'd been born again. I had finally let go and it felt good. It felt better than good. It reminded me of my own baptism at the age of twelve, when I was submerged in water. I remember the weight of the water as it covered my body and the fear I felt as water filled my nostrils. My pastor used one hand to brace my back and the other to hold my hands against my chest when he dipped me in the pool behind the pulpit of our church. When he raised me out of the water, I squealed with relief. The weight was gone. Those seconds after my father's words reminded me of my baptism.

Sitting in the restaurant of the Renaissance Harborplace Hotel in my beloved hometown, I was suddenly enjoying a moment and was unwilling to let it go. I've never laughed longer. I reached across the table and touched my father's cheeks. He looked puzzled and said nothing. "Thank you! Thank you, Lord," I said again to the distraction of the couple next to us. "Thank you, Lord, for lifting this burden," I said, with my head tilted slightly back and my hands raised above my shoulders. All these years, and the answer to my anger had been right there, right where the answer to every question in my life had always been.

In that moment, sitting across from my father, I stepped out on faith, not in the words I had long rehearsed but in the words God had placed in my heart. I could finally stop beating this man up and, more important, stop beating myself up. My dad wasn't a great father, but he did what he did and that was okay. I'd always had a Father who loved me and valued my life, a heavenly Father, who'd been there for every ball game, every disappointment, and every achievement. This man sitting across from me was just that, a man. As I watched him finish his meal, all of what he had meant began to flood my memory. Like everyone else in my path, God had His reasons for our relationship to be what it was. God doesn't make mistakes. How many times had my mother told me that? So there was no reason for this man to apologize. No reason for him to even acknowledge my selfish offer of forgiveness.

Instead of being angry with my father, I wanted to thank him. Thank him for the things he did do and even the things he'd never done. He never abused me physically or emotionally. He never said a particularly unkind word to me. This man born in the segregated South with little more than a high school education had taught me things in both words and actions no college or university could ever teach. Like my mother, he was a hard and reliable worker. That was his gift. He had a curiosity about life, and perhaps that too was a part of my DNA. For the years my parents were married, my father was the one avid reader in the house, newspapers and magazines mostly. Perhaps he had more to do with my career choice than I'd ever given him credit for. For all the tears he caused, he had the ability to make people laugh. He was good at pleasing people, if only in short spurts. He wasn't a monster, just a man. He was the one who first introduced me to football, which had long been one of the great loves of my life. How many times had football kept me sane, kept me out of trouble? The game of football had given me a stiff measure of discipline, confidence, and social significance that helped fill the void of my father's emotional and physical absence. For all the years and all the things I blamed him for, there were reasons to show him gratitude. For the first eleven and a half years of my life, I lived in his house, ate his food, lived a modest working-class lifestyle.

We finished breakfast, and I walked him outside and waited as the valet brought up his car. I tipped the valet and gave my father the rest of the cash in my pocket, about forty dollars. We shook hands, I touched his face again and walked away. He drove off, the sound of his muffler eventually disappearing in the distance.

I wish I could say that was the beginning of a wonderful relationship. It wasn't. We talk from time to time. He still asks for money, and my answer remains about the same. But things are dramatically different. I am no longer angry at the man. I see him in a different light. I can see God's goodness even in him. I finally accepted that his relationship with my mother was their relationship. They were right that day in the car, when I was a boy, outside his girlfriend's house. I had nothing to do with their troubles. He is no longer the fuel that gets me going in the morning or drives my personal or professional ambitions.

Admittedly, it was tough letting go of the anger. It was like the first few weeks of wearing contacts after years of wearing glasses. I felt naked without my glasses. That thin piece of glass provided a nice wall between me and the outside world.

Anger had provided the same kind of protection. It kept the world at a distance and a frightened boy safe. I even worried for a time whether I could function without it. I had never considered my own anger as destructive but rather as instructive. I knew God was the real source of my strength, but anger was like a set of jumper cables. It provided a boost in the moments when I felt estranged from God. When I finally said the words "I forgive you" to my father, it freed me.

The Bible speaks of the power and the necessity for forgiveness. Jesus said we should cast the wrongs of others "into the sea of forgetfulness." I'm not there yet, but I'm gaining ground. I still keep score but no longer feel compelled to punish my opponent or relish their struggle. I'm not angry today; I'm grateful, fully grateful for the many blessings God has given me. There's a banquet of blessings for all of us. I still have my struggles. As a minister I know is fond of saying, "We all have skeletons in our closet, and some still have meat on the bone." Some of mine are still fully dressed. That's okay too. What are the things you struggle with? Where in life do you feel inadequate? Whom would you like to forgive? If you step out on nothing, you may be amazed at what you may find.

My wife remarked once with a smile in her voice, "Don't tell me God ain't good. He took a boy who couldn't read and put him on *60 Minutes*." We laughed. We laughed in part because hearing such terrible diction coming out of the mouth of a Stanford-educated woman with a brilliant mind was comical. But my life and the people who've blessed it, do speak to the power of God's grace. There are grand stories of men and women who pulled themselves up by their own bootstraps to achieve great things. That is not my testimony. I've been fortunate to grab on to the boot laces of others, and they were kind enough to pull me along. There are world-class athletes with phenomenal physical gifts who through shared effort and opportunity have set records and achieved greatness. That is not my testimony.

As an individual, there is nothing remarkable about my abilities or my intellect. I was simply blessed to be born in the greatest country on earth and blessed to have been surrounded by wonderful people who stood in the gap at every vital moment in my life. They, too, are ordinary people, and most readily admit they serve an extraordinary God. I'm not smart enough or wise enough to advocate a religion to anyone, but I know what's worked for me. I know that in all the darkest, loneliest moments of my life, when I felt the world was against me and the winds of conventional wisdom were in my face, in those moments, God held me in the palm of His hand. His Son, Jesus Christ, died so I might live. His sacrifice set the stage for every success I've been blessed to achieve thus far. When to the outside world it appeared I was stepping out on nothing, I was standing in the center of God's hands. He's got big hands. There's plenty of room.

Next to Scripture, my mother's sage advice, and my grandmother's wisdom, there are few words that move me more than Maya Angelou's poem "Still I Rise," especially the line "I am the hope and the dream of the slave." As an African-American man that line speaks to the trajectory of my life. The connectedness of unnamed generations marked with grand achievements, setbacks, and days of little consequence. But it is a journey forever moving forward. Regardless of one's race or ethnic identity, we are all on a journey. Who knows what the Lord has in store for me or for any of us. I'm more excited about the journey than I've ever been. I recently discovered my purpose. When I was a boy, my grandmother prophesized I'd become a preacher. She had high hopes for me. My mother always believed I could and would do great things. Thus far, being a parent, a husband, a brother, and a child have been the greatest accomplishments of my life. But I now know my purpose. I know it with the same clarity I knew as a child that I would one day learn to read. God put me here for two reasons: be a storyteller and be an encourager. I have friends who are avid runners, and few things bring them more joy than running outdoors with the air stroking their faces and the rhythm of their heartbeats as they take each step. It's that same joy I feel whenever I have the opportunity to tell a story or encourage someone else. All the struggles with literacy and speech, and even the difficulties in my relationship with my father, were placed in my path to teach me, to prepare me for my purpose: to encourage someone else to overcome their obstacles.

There is a purpose for all of us and a path for each of us to follow. Every path has a few potholes, and some of those potholes look like craters. There is a burden each of us must carry. My grandmother would also say, "God doesn't put heavy burdens on weak shoulders." My mother's response would always be, "Then God must think I'm a twin." She was trying to be funny. Her point was that she often felt she was carrying a burden meant for someone else. My mom might tell a few jokes or even rest a bit, but eventually she'd just take a deep breath and push on. Today, when I visit my mother down in North Carolina, we often sit on her porch, just me, her, and her dog. No matter where the conversation starts, it almost always goes back to those days when she struggled to raise her three children practically on her own. She'll remember something that will make her angry. Fast-approaching eighty years old, she's still fiery. But the anger passes. Then she'll remember something that will make her laugh. Almost always, she'll remember a day long gone that will make her eyes water: whether it's the memories of a day of financial hardship or a day she felt emotionally spent. They've never been tears of sadness but rather tears of gratitude and tears of amazement at what God can do. My mother taught me many things. Perhaps, most important, she taught me less with words and more by the way she's lived her life. She taught me that in times of uncertainty, step out to a place where only God is. Step out on nothing, and it will take you far. Safe journey.

# Epilogue

She was an immigrant from Haiti who had lived with the shame for thirty-six years. He was a prominent banker who wiped tears from his eyes as he admitted the truth about his adult son. They were telling me their stories because they knew that I would understand. I shared their secret and their pain. A history of illiteracy. But we shared something much greater. We were survivors. We had triumphed over a debilitating and shameful struggle despite tremendous odds against us.

For two years now, I've been traveling the country lecturing on illiteracy and the difficulties I've had to overcome. The stories I've heard have saddened and heartened me. We are the most educated nation in the world. But we have a staggering rate of illiteracy. If you think you don't know someone who is illiterate, think again. Perhaps you have an older relative who calls you to write things down because he or she "can't find my glasses." Or perhaps you know someone who is grateful for the car GPS because, truthfully, they can't read a map or written directions.

As an adult, imagine hiding for a lifetime something so fundamental to your everyday life. Never able to fill out a job application or take a driving test. Imagine raising children who have read more books than you. If you're a child, what about taking homework home from school and never understanding it. Or experiencing the humiliation of being caught by your friends. How do you start your education over? In whom do you confide? These are questions I faced as a young teenager. But today I'm an avid reader. Books are a lifeline, and words are the foundation of my professional life.

People laughed at me when I told them I wanted to work in television. It might have seemed impossible, since I could barely speak. But in my silence and beneath my shame, I had a burning belief that all things are possible. A faith that God would make a way. I think there are lessons to be learned from my journey and the steps I took, even as a child, to put myself on a path to success: self-discipline, hard work, the power of prayer. The importance of finding and nurturing mentoring relationships. My story may be no different from yours or someone you know. I want to encourage you to have faith, to believe in the impossible.

I also want to encourage the "angels," like my Dr. Lewes. I've met them all across the country at luncheons and dinners. They speak to me through tears about their challenges and often thankless responsibilities in trying to bring light to a world without words. They tutor, they read, they fundraise, and they encourage. They need to believe in the difference they are making in people's lives and in this world. And they must know how much we love and appreciate them. I would not have made it through college without my buddy Peter Holthe. Recently, our friendship was tested in ways neither one of us would have expected back in 1978.

"Dear wise and almighty God, we come to you as humbly as we know how, just to say thank you, Lord. Thank you for blessings seen and not seen. Thank you, Lord, for our family our friends and even our enemies. Lord, please put your arms of comfort around my dear friend Pete. Let him know that he is loved. Be with him, Lord, when he goes into surgery. Be with the doctors. While they will hold the instruments, let them know you will be holding them in the palm of Your hand. Lord, so many people love and need Pete. Let Pete feel our love and our strength. Give him peace. Give him comfort. Give him strength where he's weak. Give him comfort where there may be fear. Lord, we who love Pete and love You are claiming a miracle right now. We proclaim it in Your name. These and all other blessings we ask in Your name and for Your sake. Amen."

When I finished praying on the phone, my friend Pete said, "Thank you, brother. I love you. I'm not sure I believe in prayer, but I know you do. I've watched it work in your life. Maybe it'll work in mine."

"I love you, too, Pete." We hung up the phone. We were both crying.

Now in our late forties we have been facing a difficult

time together. This time it's Pete who's facing one of life's greatest challenges: a rare and deadly form of cancer. As always, Pete's taking the analytical approach to the problem. The faith part is up to me, his wife, Kara, and a host of relatives and friends.

There are countless people who have shared their personal stories or told me about their children. I wrote this book to celebrate our victories and the successes of so many like us. I wrote this book for the adults who are faking it, for the children who are being left behind, and for every child who sits in the basement class in his or her school, labeled "slow" or "unteachable" when, in fact, they may be hiding an inability to read.

In 1978 I was on the verge of dropping out of college. In 2006 I was invited to Ohio Wesleyan as their commencement speaker. Cap and gown, doctor of humane letters, the whole deal. What an improbable journey. It happened to be Dr. Lucas's final commencement. He was retiring. I had always wondered what I might say or do if he and I ever crossed paths. When the moment came, I braced my back, took a deep breath, looked him in the eye, and said, "Thank you, Dr. Lucas. I would not be here without you. Bless you." Then I took his hand, gripped his shoulder, and said, "I wish you well." He smiled. I couldn't be sure if he even remembered me. He'd served a valuable purpose in my life. Nothing more. Nothing less. That day as part of my speech, I told the story of my experiences with Dr. Lucas. I never mentioned his name. The goal wasn't to embarrass him, but rather to share that part of my journey with the graduating class; success is often preceded by struggle.

Just as it was on my first day of college, little was going as planned. It was mid-May, but it felt like mid-November in Ohio. It was cold and rainy. The graduates and their guests were soaked. But adversity and I were old friends by now, and it was time for the commencement speech. So I took the "opportunity" God had given me and made the best of it. Here's some of what I had to say that chilly day:

*I know many of us prayed for sunshine and clear skies today, but thank the Lord He made umbrellas. To the graduates, President, Faculty, staff, the Board of Trustees, honored guests: It's a privilege to be with you today as we mark this historic moment in the life of our beloved university, and the lives of these young people. As uncomfortable as conditions may be, we're still blessed. It's Mother's Day. There are few gifts greater one could give a mother than to fill her cup, fill her heart with pride. Graduates, many of you may not have a dollar in your pocket, but the gift you've given your families today is priceless. . . .*

*I know we've come to honor the ones receiving the degrees today. But I believe graduations are also moments to honor those who paid for those degrees. Graduates, despite what some of you may think, you did not get here by yourselves. I would ask the parents, grandparents, aunts, and uncles—anyone who made a tuition payment and prayed a prayer for one of these children—to please stand. Parents and relatives of the class of 2006, please stand so we can applaud you. This is also your day. I'd especially like to acknowledge the single parents here this afternoon. As a father, I know it's not easy for two parents to raise a child. But as the proud baby boy of a single mother, I too know the unique sacrifices that single moms and dads make. On behalf of your sons or daughters, thank you for your many sacrifices.*

*I'd like to thank my own mom, who, just as she did twenty-four years ago, sits in the audience today, beaming with pride. My mother, Clarice Pitts.*

*A newspaper reporter interviewed my mom once for a story about me and asked, "Mrs. Pitts, how did you manage as a single parent, a divorcée, to send three kids to college?" Her answer: "It was simple. I said, 'Go to college, or I will beat you to death.'"*

*Simple parenting is good parenting. Thanks, Momma. I'd also like to thank my brother and his family for joining us today. . . .*

*Let the record show I believe in Ohio Wesleyan University. The liberal arts education provided here is second to none.*

*Graduates, please know you are well qualified to compete in any field, against any competitor, from any college, at any place in the world.*

*As a correspondent for CBS News, I've interviewed the last five presidents of the United States, reported from thirty-three countries, covered three wars and natural disasters of biblical proportions, from the tsunami in Indonesia to Hurricane Katrina in New Orleans. None of that would have been possible had it not been for the four years I spent here in Delaware. Not possible without professors like Verne Edwards, the head of the journalism department until his retirement. Mr. Edwards is here today with his lovely bride, Dolores. Thank you, Verne. Can I call you Verne now? For four years I was always nervous just to be in your presence. Today I'm grateful to call you my friend.*

*None of the dreams I had for my life would have been possible if not for many of the friends I made at OWU. Friends like Peter Holthe from Minnetonka, Minnesota. Pete was the whitest white guy I'd ever met. We were hallmates in Thomson Hall freshman year and suitemates sophomore year in Welch Hall. Pete told me that before we met, the only black people he'd ever seen were in Ebony magazine. Pete and I remain close to this day. That's the beauty of OWU. Children of the working class and children of the wealthy can meet in this corner of the world to learn of history's great philosophers while studying the forces that went into making an igneous rock. I had a geology class (I hated geology and, for the most part, geology hated me). But my first time in the mountains of Afghanistan, the country was foreign yet the rocks beneath my feet were familiar.*

*Class of 2006, you are 401 strong. You represent 21 different countries of the world. You are 401 of the estimated 1.3 million college seniors graduating in America this spring. According to BusinessWeek, you are about to enter the best job market for college graduates in at least five years. You have much to feel good about. Feel confident but never arrogant. Arrogance, I believe, is the cloak of cowards. Stay humble. My mother always told us, If you work hard and pray hard and treat people right, good things will happen. But, above all else, stay humble. Humility has its place.*

*It is with that sense of humility I'd like to share a few*

*final thoughts with the class of 2006. I know all of you are smart and computer-savvy. In this computer information age, you laugh at people like me and your parents as we still struggle with the VCR back home, and you stay connected with your friends by Skype, Facebook, MySpace, and Xanga. What the heck does Xanga mean? I bet most of you own an iPod, laptop, and a cell phone. And all those gadgets are wonderful.*

*But when you leave this place, there are a few old-fashioned tools you're also going to need in order to survive in this ever-changing world. Here are two:*

*Please and thank you. Knowing how to give a PowerPoint presentation may take you far. But human decency and politeness will make the landing easier when you get to wherever you're going. Please and thank you. Powerful words. Empowering words. Make them part of your permanent vocabulary. It worked for your grandparents. It will work for you.*

*If I had a speech title today, it would be "Follow Your Dreams and Find Your Passion." I believe in dreams. Progressing from academic probation during my freshman year at OWU in 1978 to Commencement speaker in 2006—I have to believe in dreams!*

*Whether you graduate today Phi Beta Kappa, Summa Cum Laude, Magna Cum Laude, or just plain "Thank you, Lord," you must believe in your dreams. You see, America is at a crossroads. We need new dreamers—not daydreamers but dreamers. Daydreamers play and procrastinate, but dreamers plan their work and work their plan.*

*So, my future fellow alumni, dream and dream boldly.*

*When good men and good women dream, a runner breaks the four-minute mile. An astronaut steps foot on the moon. A doctor finds a cure for a terrible disease. A colored girl from the segregated South becomes Secretary of State. . . .*

*Class of 2006, what is your role? What do you dream? And you can't dream without faith. Young people, degrees are good. But when trouble comes—and for you just entering the world beyond college, trouble will surely come—please know this. If you take one step, God will take two.*

*Have faith in something greater than yourself.*

*Now, I'm a Christian and proud of it. But whether you turn to a preacher or a priest, an imam or a rabbi, have a name you can call other than your own. You can't dream without faith. And faith without love is empty love.*

*Now, I'm not talking about that kind of love you think you may have found on Fraternity Row during freshman year or at your first party in the Cave. I'm talking the kind of love I've seen on the battlefields of Iraq and Afghanistan. It's the kind of love angels bring. It's the kind of love I experienced here at OWU, second term, freshman year. This is my testimony. I'm sure each of you has yours.*

*That term I was on academic probation. I had an English professor—for the record, he no longer teaches here.*

*To tell you how slow I was, I got a D in his class, first term, and took his class again the second term. This English professor knew me. I knew him. One day in class he handed out test scores in small blue notebooks, and when he handed me mine, he announced in a loud and clear voice to all my classmates, "Mr. Pitts, congratulations! Your best work thus far." With a bit of surprise and a sense of relief, I opened that blue book, and there at the top of the page, in bold letters, was a D+. Seeing my anguish, the professor leaned forward and said, "Mr. Pitts, come see me after class."*

*I did, and that English professor who no longer teaches here, said, "Mr. Pitts, may I speak frankly?" Before I could answer, he went on and said, and I quote (I carried this quote in my heart ever since). He said, "Mr. Pitts, your presence at Ohio Wesleyan University is a waste of my time and the government's money. I think you should leave."*

*"A waste of my time and the government's money." I was eighteen years old, and this man, this teacher, crushed my dreams. So taking his advice, I walked over to the admissions office and picked up papers to withdraw from school.*

*It was clear to me I was not worthy, so I sat outside Slocum Hall with tears running down my cheeks, filling out the forms to drop out of college. At that moment, a stranger walked by—a woman with a round face and a warm smile. She said, "Excuse me, young man, are you okay? May I help?" With nothing to lose, I explained my situation. She listened and said, "Come by and see me tomorrow. Do not leave school before talking with me." I would soon find out that this stranger, another English professor, was not just a professor. She was my angel.*

*Dr. Ülle Lewes, please stand. Dr. Lewes. That day you didn't simply soothe my tears. You saved my life. Thank you for believing in me when I didn't believe in myself. Thank you for being my angel.*

*Class of 2006, each of you have angels to thank for bringing you this far. I encourage you to thank each one. And don't just thank them. By being a high achiever you can thank them. And you can thank them someday by being an angel for somebody else. Graduates, real success is not measured by how much you take from this life but by how much you give to it.*

*For those of you going on to graduate school, I say, give yourself to your studies and study the way Michelangelo painted. For those beginning careers or just taking summer jobs, learn to work like Martin Luther King. Live each day as if it's your last. Don't simply be good—be better. Better isn't good enough, so be the best. Don't settle for your best. Be an angel.*

*If you haven't figured it out by now, I'm an optimist. I believe in each of you. I believe in the promise of America, despite her many warts. America is still the greatest country on earth. Be good to her and she'll be good to you. Love her and she'll love you back. Be dreamers and be passionate about your dreams.*

*I leave you with the words of Horace Mann, the founder of nearby Antioch College in Yellow Springs, Ohio. He told Antioch's first graduating class: "Be ashamed to die until you have won some victory for humanity."*

*To the graduating class of 2006 from Ohio Wesleyan University: Congratulations and God bless you. Today you make your family proud. Now go and make your world better—because you live.*

# Acknowledgments

THIS BOOK WOULD NOT have been possible without the kindness, patience, and hard work of many people and the whispered prayers of many more. I first would like to thank my wife, Lyne. Thanks to her, I married well. She's been an encourager and a confidant. When I needed a push, she gave it. When I needed a hug, she gave one. Thanks to my family of course. My beloved grandmother, Roberta Mae Walden, who left us in 2000. My mother, sister, and brother; my aunts Gladys, Diane, Rebecca and Pat, along with uncles Albert, Alton, Fred, and Luther; and my late cousin Marian Sanders. Thanks to Dr. Ülle Lewes, who is an honorary family member, and to Dorthey Daniels and Andre Jones, who are the best friends a person could ever ask for.

I want to express my gratitude to all of my friends and colleagues at *CBS News*, who have made the last twelve years of my professional life the most rewarding. A special thanks to producers Betty Chin and Rodney Comrie, who have traveled the country with me in search of important truths worth telling. I'm also grateful for the support of Jeff Fager, Sean McManus, Les Moonves, Bill Felling, Terri Stewart, Larry Doyle, and (the late) Martin Gill. Thanks as well to Richard Liebner at N. S. Bienstock, my agent and my friend.

This book would have remained just a dream without Jan Miller and the team at Dupree/Miller and Associates. My thanks especially to agent Nena Madonia. They were all an answer to my prayers. I'm so grateful to St. Martin's Press and my executive editor, Kathryn Huck. She has made the rough places smooth. I'd also like to acknowledge Howard Kurtz at the *The Washington Post,* because it was an article he wrote that set this project in motion, and Lisa Dallos, who believed in my story.

A special mention for college professor Verne Edwards and a dear friend in Boston, Maceo Vaughn.

To Daniel, Tiffani, Benjamin, Angela, Brittni, and Christiani, I hope I make you as proud as you make me.

And thanks to all of you who have allowed me into your homes and into your lives to tell your stories. You have taught me more than you will ever know.

# Index

BP stands for Byron Pitts.

INDEX

# Light on Saint Matthew

# Light on Saint Matthew



A Commentary on the Gospel

Maharaj Charan Singh

RADHA SOAMI SATSANG BEAS

*Published by:*
Sewa Singh, Secretary
Radha Soami Satsang Beas
Dera Baba Jaimal Singh
Punjab 143204, India



Sixth Edition 2003

ISBN 81-8256-015-2

Printed at: Baba Barkha Nath Printers, New Delhi.

# Contents

# Preface

*Happy is he whom Truth by itself doth teach, not by figures and words that pass away; but as it is in itself.*

These words of Thomas à Kempis, speaking of his spiritual ideal, Jesus Christ, in *The Imitation of Christ,* express a unique characteristic of a Son of God. Self-realized and God-realized beings, true spiritual Masters teach from what they know and have experienced within themselves, not from scriptures, hearsay, or from "figures and words that pass away".

All such teachers have one message to give to the world, though the language and terminology they use may be different. They teach that God's kingdom is an inner reality to be found within each and every human being. God, the supreme reality, is love. God is spirit, the living Word. To find God and to worship him "in Truth" we must find a way to be in touch with that Word or spirit within us. Like them, we need to turn within ourselves, reach beyond the limitations of the physical plane and raise our consciousness to spiritual realms.

If we go deeply into any of the great world religions, we will find this one message in all. No Son of God, no true Master, claims his teachings to be new, unique or exclusive. Jesus himself said, "Think not I am come to destroy the law or the prophets; I am come not to destroy but to fulfil" *(Matthew 5:17).*

Through his ministry he was reminding his disciples of that same law and teachings already there within their scriptures.

History shows us, however, that when the great seers and mystics leave the physical plane, the subsequent generations of their followers rarely attain the same heights of spiritual wisdom and understanding as their Master. Lacking understanding of the truth within, not having any personal experience of union with God at the level of spirit, they have to depend upon doctrine and external "words and figures that pass away".

Thomas à Kempis, in the same passage, goes on to say: "Our own opinions and our own senses do often deceive us, and they discern but little." In the natural course of things, as the followers of the Master rely on intellectual understanding rather than mystic experience, outer practice and worship gradually replace inner practice and worship, rituals arising from cultural considerations are confused with spiritual reality, and the original message of one spiritual truth and a common inner path is obscured. This is how religions are born.

The saving grace for humankind is that saints, Sons of the one Father, keep coming to the world to remind us of what is real. They answer the longing of those who crave for a truth that is eternal, who want answers that make sense to people from every faith, time, country and clime. To reveal this timeless truth, the mystics refer to the scriptures that are familiar to their audiences, drawing their attention to the spiritual reality they no longer understand.

*Light on Saint Matthew* was the fourth book prepared under the guidance of the Master, Maharaj Charan Singh, to explain to people of a Judeo-Christian background the mystic teachings of Jesus Christ. The preceding three books were *The Master Answers* and *Thus Saith the Master,* both addressing topics of general and biblical interest, and *Light on Saint John,* which explains Christ's mystical teachings from the point of view of the *Gospel According to Saint John.*

The present volume, including the Introduction and Conclusion, was prepared from discourses given by the Master on passages from St Matthew's gospel. The manuscript was compiled from tapes recorded in India between 1967 and 1972, and in America during the Master's tour overseas in 1970. On such occasions it was the Master's practice to first elaborate on a specific text and then respond to questions from the audience to further clarify the passage in question.

Since those days, much research has been made public in the field of the Christian scriptures. Maharaj Charan Singh never claimed to be a Bible scholar. He took the gospels as they are given in the King James version and explained them from the ordinary person's point of view. But being a mystic, not only did he understand the inner truth buried within them, he also saw how people come to misunderstand the teachings. He understood how the human mind behaves. He would smile when he related how his own words or actions were sometimes misrepresented by his own disciples—incidents taking on a miraculous colour before coming back to him.

Without any background in the Christian scriptures, his assessment of the gospels was remarkably accurate. Observing for example that *Mark, Luke* and *Matthew* had large sections in common, he chose *Matthew* as being the most authentic. Generally speaking, and reaching their conclusions through research and analysis, most scholars would agree. They have noted that while *Luke* tends to paraphrase its sources, often diluting the original message, and *Mark* is more interested in miracle stories than in the teachings, *Matthew*—although it has its own particular point of view—reproduces its sources most accurately. The Master simply chose the gospel that presented Jesus' mystic teachings in the clearest manner.

He also selected particular passages for explanation. He would point out that the gospels were not written by the direct disciples of Jesus and had also passed through the hands of many copyists, translators and others who had their own opinions of what Jesus taught, before coming to us as they are now, two thousand years after Jesus lived. It is interesting to note how often the passages he chose to ignore are those which scholars have also come to regard as least authentic.

As a mystic, the Master was able to see many things in the gospels that escaped or baffled a common understanding. There are times when he brings out meaning on what might appear as the flimsiest of evidence. Yet a study of other literature of early Christian times shows that this is the way that some early Christians also understood the texts.

His reference to reincarnation with regard to "Agree with thine adversary quickly" *(Matthew 5:25* on), for example, is not without precedent in early Christian literature. Similarly, his explanation of the parable of the sower may differ from a traditional interpretation of its meaning, yet early Christian texts clearly explain the seed as the creative Word of God just as Maharaj Charan Singh does in his commentary.

Many examples of the Master's insight could be given. They all point to his unerring perception as a mystic, to the spiritual accomplishment that distinguishes the living Master from the ordinary person. In touch with "Truth" directly, in contact with the living Word of God within themselves, these Sons of God are able to draw from that "spring of water welling up into everlasting life" *(John 4:14)*. They come to earth for this purpose, so they can guide others to the same.

Since most of the discourses were given in different places or addressed to different audiences, there was naturally repetition within the tapes. Where this repetition serves to enhance the meaning of the explanations of the gospel, it was retained in the manuscript. Where the questions put by members of the audience related to a passage in the gospel, they were included and placed in the appropriate sections of the book. To organize informal spoken language into a written commentary for publication, the editors, working under the Master's guidance, had also to consider the arrangement of passages for ease of reading and continuity, and the appropriateness of idiomatic phrases associated with the Master's spoken rather than written style. For this revised fifth edition, some minor, non-substantial changes have been made in these areas. The presentation of the text has also been reconceived to make the movement from discourse, to question, to answer, and back to discourse, more transparent and smooth-flowing.

To the many people who have put their time and effort into the book since it was first conceived by the Master, the members of the Society would like to express their thanks on behalf of the sangat. And to the Masters who provide us with the precious opportunity to learn how to serve, we cannot begin to express our gratitude, nor can we presume to comment on the real significance and value of their presence among us.

Sewa Singh
*Secretary*

Radha Soami Satsang Beas
January 2000

# Introduction

Saints may come at any time, in any country. Every mystic or saint has the same teachings to give, the same message or spiritual truth to share with us. Saints do not come with any new teachings, nor to lay the foundation of any religion or to condemn past mystics. But we forget their teachings after they leave this world, so saints again come in some other place to revive the same teachings, the same spiritual truth. No saint comes to create a religion. They just come to share their spiritual experience with us, to put us on the path and take us back to God. Therefore, if with an unbiased mind we try to go deep into the scriptures written by any mystic, or into their sermons, we will find the same spiritual truth.

First they try to explain to us that whatever we see in this world has not sprung up by itself. There is some power at its back, someone who has created this creation—call that power God, call it Lord, call it anything else. He, and nobody else, has created this whole creation. All that we see is nothing but his own projection. After creating us, he has shared the same life with every part of his creation. He is everywhere in it. And yet, being part and parcel of it, we do not see or realize the Creator who is living within every one of us.

Why do we not see the Creator? Because we have forgotten him. We have become blind as far as he is concerned. We are attached to this world, and our attachment brings us back to it again and again. So due to that attachment, we are all blind and see nothing but darkness within ourselves. Unless we are able to eliminate that darkness, we will not be able to see him. And unless we meet the Creator within ourselves, we will not be able to escape from birth and death, from the transmigration of the soul.

How can we eliminate the darkness and see the light or life which the Lord has kept within every one of us? When the Lord wishes, by his grace only can we eliminate that veil of darkness. When the Father wants to pull any soul from the creation to his own level, he sends somebody from himself to our level. After having sent him—call him a saint or a mystic, or the son of God, give him any name—he is like us in the flesh and is also at the level of the Father. He has access to him and also experiences the same light within himself. There is no veil of darkness between him and the Father.

Why has the Lord given the saints this privilege of seeing that light of life while being at our level? Because the Lord wants that, through them, we should also experience the same light which they experience within themselves. It is through their living guidance and help that we also can eliminate the veil of darkness from within ourselves and see the light.

So unless we see that life or light within ourself, we do not escape from this creation and we cannot become part and parcel of the Creator, who can be realized nowhere outside until we have realized him within. Having created us, he is within every one of us. That is why this body is referred to as a temple of the living God, or as a house of prayer, or the house of the Lord.

Mystics come to explain to us the necessity of going back to the Father and put us on the path leading back to him. They not only baptize or initiate us; they help us travel on the path to go back, to merge into and to become one with the Father.

That is the main purpose of the coming of a mystic. They do not come to create peace in this world. Their work is not that of a social reformer. If that had been their purpose, this world would have been reformed long ago and there would have been peace by now—because when we read history, every country and nation has had the privilege of producing great mystics, great souls. But in spite of them, the world is the same as it was probably thousands of years ago. We have not improved in any way at all. So their purpose is not to improve the lot of the world or to create peace in it. It will go on as it is. Their main purpose is to take us away from this miserable world, this creation, and to make us one with him.

Christ also had the same teachings and spiritual truth to give us, and I will discuss the teachings of Christ from *Saint Matthew*, in that light. I am holding here the New Testament, the King James Version printed in your country. I am very well aware that I am no authority on the Bible because that is not my background. I have hardly read the Bible except during the last few years. But as I am very fond of reading the writings or the scriptures of past mystics or saints, the Bible has also become one of my favourites. When I read the Bible, I find the same teachings which have been given to us by other mystics of past ages and which Christ has also tried to give us.

You are probably quite aware of the history of the Bible. It was not written by Christ. What you read in the Bible are not the exact words which he spoke, nor were any notes taken by anybody during his lifetime, nor was the Bible printed during his lifetime. I am told that it was written quite some time after his demise. And then, it does not contain the teachings given by the direct disciples of Christ, but what was known to people through those first disciples. That is why you read that it is *according* to Saint Matthew, *according* to Saint John. So you cannot interpret the Bible literally as you would interpret a book of law.

For example, you heard the lecture yesterday. You know that the sermons given by Christ were to very simple people. They were poor farmers, fishermen and carpenters, not men of letters or intellectuals as we find people are now in this world. So if today you try to bring the speech onto paper, try to write down notes of what was said yesterday, with your best intellect and intelligence you will only be able to reproduce exactly on paper perhaps a small portion of what was said. And that too will not be the exact words which you have heard, but only the gist of the lecture. And that is after hearing it with your own ears. You personally listened with all your attention because you came to the lecture for that purpose.

So if today you go home and tell a friend what was said to you yesterday, only twenty-four hours ago, and if he, after twenty-four hours, tries to reproduce that lecture on paper, he will not be able to reproduce word by word what you told him. At best, he will be able to reproduce only a portion of what he heard from you. His words, especially, will be his own, according to the ideas he may have been able to grasp. And then, if that same writing were to be translated from one language to another, and then again to another, you can imagine how much would remain of what was said. When you translate anything, a lot of the beauty and much of the meaning of the words is lost. Where the translator does not understand, he 'straightens' the language or eliminates a word or gives his own meaning to it. Hence, many things are lost in translation.

Even with our own Sant Mat books,* some are translated from Hindi or Punjabi, or from my discourses, and many things

* The Radha Soami Satsang Beas publications.

are lost, misquoted or misinterpreted. As you know, the Bible has passed through so many interested hands, and many things have been eliminated, suppressed or added. People have twisted some of the teachings of Christ for their own selfish ends. So what you read in the Bible today are not the exact words of Christ, nor of Saint John, nor of Saint Matthew.

And of those people who heard Christ lecture and were attracted to him, some were diseased, some were lame, some were lepers. They were only attracted to him because he performed certain miracles; it was that which brought them. They did not even come to him with the intention of knowing his teachings, but all the same they did get the teachings from him because that was his main mission in coming to this world.

It was through those people that we now know the teachings of Christ! And then their version was translated into so many languages. Therefore you cannot take every word of the Bible as if it were the spoken word of Christ. You have to understand the teachings by reading the whole of it because his teachings are scattered throughout the Bible. They are like scattered jewels, and you have to collect them together to know the gist of Christ's teachings. So one should always try to read the Bible in that light, not as if it were the direct words of Christ.

## ⥽ ONE ⥼

# Discourse on Matthew 3–5

You know the New Testament quite well. Perhaps your knowledge is much better because you have a background of Christianity, but I will discuss with you whatever little I know about it.

> *And now also the axe is laid unto the root of the trees: therefore every tree which bringeth not forth good fruit is hewn down, and cast into the fire.* (3:10)*

First of all, John the Baptist tells us the importance of this human form. He says that if a tree does not yield good fruit, then it is not kept in the garden. With an axe we cut the roots of the tree and throw it into the fire. What is the 'axe'? It represents the sins or karmas with which we are born. And the 'tree' is our life. Similarly, he says that this opportunity of human birth is given to us by the Lord. This human form is bestowed on us to yield good fruit. And what is the good fruit? To realize the Lord within ourself, to become one with the Father. So if we do not yield good fruit after getting this human form, we will be thrown into the fire or cut down, just as a tree is cut down by an axe.

* All Biblical quotations are taken from the Authorized King James Version (1611), with the spelling, capitalization and punctuation of that version.

By coming to this world and forgetting the Lord, whatever sins we do, whatever karmas we are born with and collect, they become the axe. Then our sins become our master and we become their slave. As you know, a slave has no free will. He has to follow the command of his master. So at the command of our sins or karmas we have to shift from 'house to house', from flesh to flesh, from body to body; and we cannot be at peace nor find any comfort.

So do not think that just by chance we get this opportunity. In the Indian scriptures it says that even the gods and goddesses pine for the human form. It is not so very easily that we get it. The human body is given to us for only one purpose, and that is to realize the Lord, to go back to him, and thus escape from this cycle of birth and death. If we are not attending to our real purpose, not following the spiritual path, not trying to reach our destination, to achieve our goal, then the axe will cut down the tree. Then the sins that we have committed during the span of our life will deprive us of this human form and we may have to go back into the lower species and miss our opportunity. This human form is the top rung of the ladder. If we try, we can go back to the Father. If we slip, we go down to the lower species. So John the Baptist tells us to make the best use of this opportunity by removing the axe from the root of the tree.

*I indeed baptize you with water unto repentance.* (3:11)

Then he explains to us how to make the very best use of this human opportunity and achieve good results in this lifetime. He says: *"I indeed baptize you with water unto repentance."* In order to yield good fruit, in order to reach the Lord, to make the best use of this opportunity, we have to be baptized or initiated by a mystic or a saint. Mystics or saints do not come by their own will to this creation or to our level. They are sent by the Father with a particular purpose in view, that through them we may also experience that light which the Lord has kept within every one of us. So he says that in order to experience that light, to become one with the Father, we have to go to a mystic, to a saint. And what will he do? He will baptize or initiate us. He will put us on the path and will tell us the technique or method of how to withdraw from the world and go back to the Father.

What is 'baptizing with water unto repentance'? 'Water' means the living water, the nectar within. The Master initiates us so that we may have that living water. By tasting that nectar which the Lord has kept within every one of us, we will be able to repent for our sins. Unless we do this, the soul can never shed all its dross and shine in all its glory.

Repentance means to regret and be sorry for our previous sins and not to repeat them again. But we do not know what we have been doing in our past lives, so how can we repent? And how can we cease repeating those things when we don't know for what we are suffering now? This repentance can only be done by meditation, by bringing the mind back to its own source with the help of the Holy Ghost and thus releasing the soul from the clutches of the mind. That is why John the Baptist also says:

*Repent ye: for the kingdom of heaven is at hand.* (3:2)

He says that the Lord cannot be realized outside anywhere; he is within every one of us. If there is any laboratory in which you have to research to go back to the Father, it is only this body. You do not need any church or synagogue, any temple or mosque to seek the Father. He has created this temple for himself and he is residing within it. So you should only search for him there and nowhere outside.

When we are baptized by a mystic and he puts us on the path and attaches us to the Holy Spirit within, by hearing and worshipping that voice of God within ourself we repent for whatever we have done now in this life and in the past. And when we are able by meditation to repent for all that, then this veil of darkness will disappear from within ourself and we will be able to see the light. Unless we see that light we can never find comfort, nor be at rest, nor ever go back to the Father. So he says that mystics come to baptize us so that we may be able to repent for all our sins.

John the Baptist knew that he would be beheaded, and it was according to divine law that he had to leave a successor behind. Since he wanted his successor to be successful, so that through his successor the teachings should reach people, he began preparing the disciples for his exit and for bringing another Master or successor in his place:

> *But he that cometh after me is mightier than I,*
> *whose shoes I am not worthy to bear: he shall baptize*
> *you with the Holy Ghost, and with fire.* (3:11)

He is saying all this in humility only, because he baptized Christ. He put him on the path and initiated him, so actually he was Christ's Master. But he said it because he knew that he was going to leave this world and that Christ was going to be his successor; and unless a Master prepares the masses, they will not accept or pay any heed to the successor. Some people might think, 'He is my relative', 'He is my friend', 'He was my companion', 'He was my classmate', 'He was my schoolmate'. They always take him in the same light as they have known him previously.

So every Master praises his own successor. Similarly, John the Baptist is also trying to impress upon the disciples not to take Christ lightly, saying: *"He…is mightier than I."* John the Baptist wanted them to have faith in a living Master. Not that Christ was greater than John the Baptist, because no disciple can be greater than his Master.

Somewhere it is mentioned that Christ said: Right from Adam until John the Baptist, woman has not given birth to a greater soul than he *(11:11).* So for Christ, John the Baptist was the King of kings because he put him on the path. He brought Christ into touch with that Spirit and witnessed the Spirit descending on him.

And Christ also refers to John the Baptist where he says: "He was a burning and a shining light: and ye were willing for a season to rejoice in his light" *(John 5:35).* 'For a season' means for a particular time or period only. Every mystic or saint comes to our level for a particular time, not forever. So John the Baptist and Christ and Moses came for a particular period. After finishing their allotted task of putting their disciples on the path and showing them that light, they merged back into the Lord and became part and parcel of him.

But now they cannot help us. As long as saints are in the flesh and, being at our level, are experiencing that light within themselves and are also at the level of the Father, only then, through them, can we experience that light and become one with the Father. That is why John the Baptist is trying to prepare the seekers, saying: The one who is coming after me is greater than I because he will show you that light. I know that

I will be beheaded and will leave this world and merge back into the Father. After that I will not be able to help you and you will have to turn to Christ to show you the light.

And how will he initiate you? *"With the Holy Ghost, and with fire."* 'Fire' means the light, because light comes to us from fire. And what is this light? It is the light which gives us life, that *jyoti* or flame which shines within every one of us. And 'Holy Ghost' means that Spirit which is within every one of us. It is the same thing as before. 'Baptism with water unto repentance' is the same thing as 'baptizing with the Holy Ghost and with fire'. And that is what every Master does. It means initiating us with the light and the sound, putting us on the path of light and sound.

Why does he call it Holy Ghost? Because you never know how a ghost appears before you. Even though all your doors are closed and you are under lock and key, the ghost can still appear before you. You do not know whether he has come from the roof, or through the floor, or the wall, or from which side he has appeared. Similarly, when you withdraw to the eye centre, you hear that sound, the divine melody, but you do not know from which direction it is coming. But you hear that sound, which to begin with is like the rushing of the wind, as Christ described it.* And since it has the characteristics of a ghost and is holy—because it takes you back to the Holy Father—so the translators have referred to that Shabd or Nam, that Word or Logos, as the Holy Ghost.†

So he says that when you go to a mystic, he will put you on the path and will help you to withdraw your soul current to the eye centre where that light is shining, that Shabd is

* *John* 3:8; *Acts* 2:2.

† *See* Glossary for explanations of Indian-language terms.

ringing. And when you are able to withdraw your soul to the eye centre, you will hear that sound within yourself and see that light.

Our soul has two faculties—those of hearing and of seeing. The faculty to hear will hear the sound, and the faculty to see will see the light of that sound. With the help of the sound we are able to know the direction of our home. With the help of the light we have to follow the path and see our way and reach our destination.

For example, if in the evening you go out for a long walk, it becomes pitch-dark and you forget in which direction it was that you left your house—what do you do? You quietly stand in the darkness and try to hear some sort of sound or voice coming from your house. It may be your tape recorder, or somebody's radio, or somebody singing. By hearing that voice you will at once know whether your house is to the right or the left, or in front or behind. When you catch the sound and know the direction of your house, then because there is darkness and there may be a fence or pond in the way, if you have a flash-light you can see your way through and reach your destination. So what brings you back to your house is sound and light.

Similarly, we have forgotten our home, we have forgotten the Lord, the Creator who is within every one of us. In order to call us back, he has kept that sound and light within each of us. That is why Christ says: "If therefore thine eye be single, thy whole body shall be full of light" *(6:22).* When you are able to hold your attention here behind the eyes, then you open that single or third eye and see nothing but light within yourself. As long as your attention is downwards, towards the senses, you see nothing but darkness. So in order to eliminate the darkness and see that light, we have to seek the company of some saint or mystic. He tells us the method and technique of how to withdraw to the eye centre, how to hear the sound and see the light.

Therefore John the Baptist tells us that when you go to a mystic, he baptizes or initiates you with the Holy Ghost, with fire. He puts you on the path, and you will be able to hear the sound and see the light. With the help of that sound, you will know the direction of your house within your body. And with the help of that light, you will be able to follow the path and reach your destination.

> *And Jesus, when he was baptized, went up straightway out of the water: and, lo, the heavens were opened unto him, and he saw the Spirit of God descending like a dove, and lighting upon him.* (3:16)

When Christ was initiated he was absolutely ready. If a candle is ready, you only have to put a little spark or another candle to it and it at once starts giving light and becomes just like the first candle. So Christ was absolutely ready because he was sent by the Father for that very purpose or mission. But still he needed a spark to become a lighted candle. And unless the spark was there through John the Baptist, that candle would have been useless to people. So from one candle there became two. And the necessity for the second was because the first was going out of the spiritual drama, back to the Father, and the second candle was required to give light to the seekers. That is why it is said here that the moment Christ went into the company of John the Baptist and was initiated by him, he could at once ascend to the Father—because his vessel was clean. But we are not even candles as yet. First, there has to be wax, wick and a mould. Only then can we become candles and get the light from a candle that is already lit.

So it says: *"The heavens were opened unto him."* The moment he was initiated, he had access to heaven and to the Father. *"And he saw the Spirit of God descending like a dove."* As a dove from a high place very smoothly and gracefully alights, similarly the moment Christ was initiated and brought into touch with that voice or spirit of God, with its help he could go back to the Father. At any time he could be at the level of the Father or at the human level—the level of the flesh. But this was only after he had come in contact with John the Baptist, had received a spark from him, and had been initiated with the Holy Ghost and with fire.

> *And lo a voice from heaven, saying, This is my beloved Son, in whom I am well pleased.* (3:17)

As soon as we are able to hear the Spirit within ourself and see the light, we become the beloved sons of the Father. Then it is only a question of time before we realize the Father within ourself. So whosoever hears that sound and sees that light, whosoever is on the path and is travelling in the right direction, will ultimately become the son of the Father, and his beloved.

When Christ was baptized or initiated, the gates of heaven were opened to him. He was able to withdraw his consciousness to the eye centre, and with the help of the sound and light could travel on that spiritual path within. Then he at once became the most 'beloved son' of the Father, and naturally the Father was pleased that his son had access to him.

Then he says:

> *It is written, Man shall not live by bread alone, but by every word that proceedeth out of the mouth of God.* (4:4)

This human form is given to us for a much higher purpose than just to eat, drink, be merry and spend our life in sensual pleasures. And what is that higher purpose? How can we make the best use of this human form? *"By every word that proceedeth out of the mouth of God"*, which is that Spirit, that Shabd, that Holy Ghost.

The thing peculiar to this human form is that having come into the flesh, we can become God. So he says, do not take your having a human form lightly and waste your time unnecessarily in worldly pursuits and pleasures. Make the best use of it by hearing that Word which is coming from the mouth of God. If you catch hold of one end of a rope, you can be pulled up with it to the other end of the rope. Likewise, he says, that Spirit, that Shabd and Nam, is coming from the Father, at the eye centre. When, with the help of a mystic or a saint, you are able to withdraw to the eye centre and are brought into touch with that Holy Spirit within yourself, then with its help you can ascend to the place from where it is coming, merge into it, and by so doing, become God.

*From that time Jesus began to preach.* (4:17)

And this was the first thing he said when he started preaching:

*Repent: for the kingdom of heaven is at hand.* (4:17)

This word 'repent' covers a lot. It means not to repeat the same old mistakes which are bringing us back and attaching us to this earth, this world, again and again. For whatever seeds we sow here, we have to come back here again just to get their result, their fruit. So he says, first you must repent and not go on adding to whatever load of karmas you have already collected. You should abstain from evil deeds, evil acts, evil karmas, and only then can you do the practice which will take you back to the Father. If you are always here clearing your old debris, your old load of karmas, then when will you get the opportunity of travelling on the path which leads back to your Father? The main and first thing is *repent.* And all the four conditions on which we should be steadfast in order to live in meditation or in Sant Mat are covered by the word repent.

The first condition is that we should abstain from meat, fish and eggs. These should not be a part of our food any more because when we kill, we expose ourself to be killed. If we cut others' throats, naturally the time will come when they will cut ours. In addition, these items incite lower tendencies of the mind and senses. Then we have to abstain from all intoxicants because they always lead to vice and lower types of action. Also, we must have a good moral character. Unless we repent for what we have done in the past and remain steadfast on these three principles, we do not make much spiritual progress. The fourth condition is to devote two and a half hours daily to meditation.

And after we have repented and taken a vow not to repeat those mistakes again, he says: "*For the kingdom of heaven is at hand.*" Then you should try to seek your Father. And the Father whom you want to meet is nowhere outside. He is just near you, nearer even than your right hand. There is no sense in running to the synagogues or to the church, or in leaving your children and retiring to the mountains or a forest to find God. The Lord, who has created us and who is our Father, is within every one of us. This is another very important principle of Sant Mat, that we have to seek the Lord within, and nowhere outside.

So Christ says that if you want to escape from this prison of birth and death, you must understand these two things.

First you have to repent for whatever you have done. Do not go on sowing seeds that will bring you back to this world again and again. Whatever has been done is done. That can be cleared only by meditation. Then seek the Father within yourself, in your body: This body is the temple of the living God.*

Then, as you know, Jesus performed many miracles. And his purpose in doing so, in healing those people who were lunatic, or diseased, or were otherwise not well, was not for his own glory or fame. Actually he did it to attract the crowds, the masses, because these things easily lure them to the saints. They gather for their own material needs, but saints make use of that gathering and give them spiritual truth. This is very clear when you read:

> *And Jesus went about all Galilee, teaching in their synagogues, and preaching the gospel of the kingdom, and healing all manner of sickness and all manner of disease among the people.*
> *And his fame went throughout all Syria: and they brought unto him all sick people that were taken with divers diseases and torments, and those which were possessed with devils, and those which were lunatick, and those that had the palsy: and he healed them.*
> *And there followed him great multitudes of people from Galilee, and from Decapolis, and from Jerusalem, and from Judea, and from beyond Jordan.*
>
> (4:23–25)

---

* Guru Nanak, Adi Granth. See also *John* 2:21; *1 Corinthians* 3:16–17, 6:19; *2 Corinthians* 6:16.

Those are all places around Israel. When people heard of the fame of Christ, that he could heal them and make them healthy so that they were no longer sick or diseased, they all went to him just to get cured, or to have their worldly desires and ambitions fulfilled—not for any spiritual truth or because of any spiritual hunger.

> *And seeing the multitudes, he went up into a mountain: and when he was set, his disciples came unto him.* (5:1)

When he saw that a lot of people were coming to him, he was not keen to cure them physically any more, he wanted to give them spiritual truths. So it says that seeing the multitudes, he went up a mountain:

> *And he opened his mouth, and taught them, saying…* (5:2)

What did they get in return from Christ? Seeing the multitudes, he began giving them spiritual teachings. And the first thing he impressed upon them was:

> *Blessed are the poor in spirit: for theirs is the kingdom of heaven.* (5:3)

'Poor in spirit' means those who are humble and meek, who have been able to eliminate ego from within themselves. They are the fortunate people and the blessed ones because they are entitled to go back to the Father. That is the blessing of the Lord, that they have become humble. It is only our ego and attachment to this world which stands in our way and is bringing us back every time. So unless we become poor in spirit, unless we are filled with love and devotion for the Father, we will not be able to go back to him.

When are we humble? In the presence of a superior person, we always become humble. So when you see nothing but the Creator in this creation and are filled with his love and devotion, you naturally feel humble.

> *Blessed are they that mourn: for they shall be comforted.* (5:4)

We mourn when we are separated from somebody and want to meet him; when we are anxious to be one with him and cannot reach him, then we start crying and mourning. So he says that those people who are filled with love and devotion for the Father, who are longing and yearning to go back to him, they are the blessed ones. *"For they shall be comforted."* What comfort do they get? They will be able to go back to the Father. As long as the soul is shifting from one body to another, from one species to another, the soul can never get any comfort. Wherever we go, we are miserable. We feel most miserable in separation. We only get rest and escape from this misery when the soul merges back into the Father.

> *Blessed are the meek: for they shall inherit the earth.* (5:5)

The meek will feel happy and contented on this earth.

> *Blessed are they which do hunger and thirst after righteousness: for they shall be filled.* (5:6)

If you are hungry and thirsty for worldly things, if you have worldly desires, you will have to come back to the world to fulfil them. Those attachments will always pull you back to the level of this creation. So he says that if you are hungry and thirsty for the Father, you are fortunate people. Then in order to satisfy your hunger and thirst, you will seek the Father and be able to go back to him. And he says: *"They shall be filled."* When we are hungry and thirsty, we are filled when we eat bread and drink water. So Christ says that if you feel the separation from the Father, you will be filled with his grace. His grace will be there to satisfy your longing and desire to become one with him. Unless we feel the separation from him, we will not try to realize him within. So he says that to have this longing and to feel his separation is not an ordinary thing. You are blessed and fortunate people.

*Blessed are the merciful: for they shall obtain mercy. (5:7)*

The merciful are the kind-hearted ones and those who are always anxious to forgive and take pity on others. And in spite of the great provocation and hurt which they receive, they do not want to take any revenge, howsoever much anybody has injured them. If one wants revenge, he will have to come back to this world. Whether you come as a debtor or as a creditor, both have to go to the court for judgement. So he says that they are the blessed and fortunate ones who are willing to suffer at people's hands but do not want any revenge. *"For they shall obtain mercy"*—they will obtain mercy from the Father. If we forgive people for their trespasses, our Father also forgives us whatever offences we commit against him.

If I do not want to take anything from anybody, whatsoever another person may be owing to me, then what is left is whatever I owe to other people. So the Lord will forgive me that, if I forgive others whatever they owe to me. If I do not, how can he forgive me what I owe to others? So that is what he is trying to explain.

*Blessed are the pure in heart: for they shall see God.* (5:8)

So far he has not talked about seeing God, he has only said that you are the fortunate and blessed ones—you will be filled, you will find comfort and will be forgiven. Now he talks about seeing the Father. He says that by doing these things, by eliminating your ego, by having a pang and longing and desire and real love for the Father, and by forgiving people and asking the Father to forgive your sins—by these methods your heart becomes absolutely pure. Nothing will be left in it except love for the Father, who is love. You can only go back to the Father if your heart is filled with his love and contains nothing of this world. Only when there is no dross in a cup can it be filled with milk, or with anything else. If a cup is dirty you never even put water in it. It has first to be clean. So your heart has to be clean before it can be filled with love and devotion for the Father.

This is the right way of repenting. And with this repentance we see, or realize, the Lord within ourself. He says: *"Blessed are the pure in heart: for they shall see God."* When do we become pure? Only when the soul gets release from the mind and there are no coverings over it. As long as the soul has association with the mind, and the mind is the slave of the senses—and by running to the senses we are committing sin and collecting karma day and night—the soul cannot become pure.

In our body, in the waking state, the seat of the soul and mind, knotted together, is at the eye centre. The soul, a drop of that divine ocean, has taken the association of the mind and become part and parcel of it. And the mind has become the slave of the senses, because it is fond of pleasures. Thus, whatever the mind does, the soul has to suffer for it. So first the mind has to withdraw from the senses and become pure. Then the soul can leave the mind and be ready to go to its source. Then only are we pure in heart and can see the Lord within ourself.

A diamond has its own innate lustre and value. If that same diamond is thrown into the dirt and is covered with mud, it has lost neither its value nor its lustre, but we do not see them. When you wash it and remove the dirt, you will find its original lustre and value. Similarly, the soul is a drop of that divine ocean. It is immortal and eternal. But having taken the association of the mind, and the mind being a slave of the senses, it has taken on many coverings and has lost sight of its lustre and value. But when, with the help of a saint or mystic, by meditation we are able to withdraw our consciousness to the eye centre and attach ourself to that Spirit and see that light within ourself, then all the coverings are removed from the soul, and its lustre and value are visible.

Attachment to the Holy Ghost detaches the mind from the senses and makes it pure, and it returns to its own source, the second stage, which we call Trikuti. And as soon as this happens, the soul gets release from the mind. Then all the karmas which you have committed in past births become ineffective; or you may say that they have been washed off or burned. Then they cannot pull your soul back because it is no longer in the clutches of or in association with the mind.

So Christ says that fortunate people are those who become pure in heart, who become whole and clean and free, because only they will be able to see God within themselves.

*Blessed are the peacemakers: for they shall be called the children of God.* (5:9)

We are peacemakers when we are able to obtain peace within ourself. We obtain peace within when the soul gets release from the mind and we are able to realize ourself. As long as the mind is dominating, we are always miserable and at war with ourself. And as long as this is so, the whole world looks miserable and is at war with us. When we are at peace within ourself, the whole world looks peaceful to us. So we cannot create peace in the world, but we can definitely find our own corner of peace within ourself. When you have no malice against anybody at all, then only can you live at peace within yourself. So he says that those people are fortunate who are living at peace within themselves.

If I am happy, whosoever comes into my company, naturally I will make him happy. If I am miserable, whosoever is near me, naturally I will make him miserable. Therefore, those people who have obtained peace within themselves by love and devotion for the Father and by forgiving and having mercy on other people, are the blessed ones, because they also spread peace in the world. They radiate peace around them and share that peace with others.

Saints are at peace within themselves, so they are peacemakers, because they also create the same peace within us. Whosoever is able to obtain that peace within himself from a mystic or saint, and is able to hear and worship the Spirit and see the light within himself, becomes a son of God, one of the children of God.

*Blessed are they which are persecuted for righteousness' sake: for theirs is the kingdom of heaven.* (5:10)

It is the same thing as before. Those who are willing to face persecution and hardship, and to make all sorts of sacrifices for the sake of the Father, are blessed and fortunate people. Then he also explains to them:

> *Rejoice, and be exceeding glad: for great is your reward in heaven: for so persecuted they the prophets which were before you.* (5:12)

He says, do not mind if the world criticizes you, pours scorn on you, hates you, or lets you down. You have to rise above these and face all such things, because the reward is very great, which is that the Father will love you and will take you back to himself.

*"For so persecuted they the prophets which were before you."* He says that these people have even persecuted the prophets. You know what hardships they have had to face at their hands. Even Christ was crucified. And of other saints—some were burned alive, some were flayed alive, some were slain, some were made to sit on hot iron plates. So he says, when worldly people can deal with prophets and saints in this manner, what can you expect from them? They will not be good to you, because your way is different from theirs. Their way is outwards, your way is inwards; so you are the blessed people. Do not worry how the world deals with you.

> *Ye are the salt of the earth: but if the salt have lost his savour, wherewith shall it be salted?* (5:13)

If the ground is not fertile and gives no yield, it is of absolutely no use. Only if it is fertile can you sow anything and get crops from it; and that ground is very high-priced. He says that you are the salt of this earth, you are the few selected ones in this world who are following a mystic and are filled with love and devotion for the Father. But for you, this world is like barren ground, because there is no use in coming into this human flesh if you are not filled with love and devotion for the Father. So *"ye are the salt of the earth."* Only through you does this world exist, so to say, as far as the Father is concerned. For others the world only exists as far as the creation is concerned; they are only giving themselves to merrymaking and all those things. But you are the blessed ones, because you are selected by the Father.

> *Ye are the light of the world. A city that is set on an hill cannot be hid.*
> *Neither do men light a candle, and put it under a bushel, but on a candlestick; and it giveth light unto all that are in the house.* (5:14–15)

He says, if you have that light within yourself, if you are full with love and devotion for the Father, you will also be able to radiate love and devotion to others. You will become just like a torch, like a candlelight, which can be seen from a distance. That happiness, contentment and peace will radiate from your face, and wherever you go in this world you will spread that light and that peace and contentment among people. You not only follow the path, but by your own living example, you can influence others also to follow it. You can become a source of strength to others to remain firm on the path and to enjoy that bliss and light within themselves.

> *Let your light so shine before men, that they may see your good works, and glorify your Father which is in heaven.* (5:16)

There is no need of arguing or fighting or quarrelling with anybody in the name of the Lord, or of converting anybody to the path. Be a living example and people will automatically be influenced when on meeting you they realize how much you have changed.

And if you become a living example in this world, then not only do you glorify yourself, but you glorify your Father, your Master. People are impressed and happy that you are disciples of a very good Master, that you are filled with love and devotion for the Father.

> *Think not that I am come to destroy the law, or the prophets.* (5:17)

It is something very beautiful. 'Law' means the law which governs the soul in its going from the creation back to the Creator. And that is what the teachings are about. He says, do not have the least idea in your mind that I have come to condemn or make you forget the teachings given to you by previous saints or prophets, nor have I come to tell you that I am superior to the mystics who have come before me. That is not my object at all in coming to your level. No mystic comes into this world with a new teaching.

> *I am not come to destroy, but to fulfil.* (5:17)

You have forgotten their teachings and have given yourself to rituals and ceremonies. I have only come to remind you about those same teachings. I have only come to fulfil them—to give, to share with you their spiritual truth in the right way. And the right way to worship the Father is to worship the Spirit. And that Spirit, the Lord has kept within every one of us.

So do not think that I have brought new teachings or a short cut for you. Every mystic has the same thing to say, and I want you to follow those same teachings. And I also want reverence in your heart for those prophets.

> *For verily I say unto you, Till heaven and earth pass, one jot or one tittle shall in no wise pass from the law, till all be fulfilled.* (5:18)

He says that right from the beginning to the end of the creation, the teachings remain the same. It means that nothing can be added or taken away from them. The law which governs this universe, the law according to which the soul goes back to the Father, will always remain the same. Some mystics may emphasize certain points, other mystics may emphasize other aspects of the teachings. Their approach can be different according to our background, but the main teachings will always be the same. Their examples and parables can differ, but fundamental principles themselves cannot differ.

> *Whosoever therefore shall break one of these least commandments, and shall teach men so, he shall be called the least in the kingdom of heaven: but whosoever shall do and teach them, the same shall be called great in the kingdom of heaven.* (5:19)

He says that anyone who distorts, misinterprets or changes the teachings of any mystic will never get admission to the kingdom of heaven and be able to go back to the Father, because the teachings belong to the Father. If anybody is giving his own teachings, then he has not brought them from the Father; he is only doing his own will. Only he is great who gives you the same teachings as previous mystics, who tells you the plain spiritual truth. Then he refers to the old teachings:

> *Ye have heard that it was said by them of old time,*
> *Thou shalt not kill.* (5:21)

This is one of the commandments of Moses.*

> *And whosoever shall kill shall be in danger of the*
> *judgment.* (5:21)

*"Danger of the judgment"* means that whosoever kills will also be killed. He says that Moses made it very clear to you, and I also want to remind you of the same teaching. His commandment was: *"Thou shalt not kill."* He does not say, thou shalt not kill men or women. 'Kill' means to destroy whatsoever has life, whether it is an animal, or a fish, or an insect. We have no right to destroy that life. They are all part of the creation, all have been created by the Lord.

> *But I say unto you, That whosoever is angry with*
> *his brother without a cause shall be in danger of the*
> *judgment: and whosoever shall say to his brother,*
> *Raca…* (5:22)

That is, whosoever will abuse him—

> *…shall be in danger of the council: but whosoever*
> *shall say, Thou fool, shall be in danger of hell fire.*
> (5:22)

* *Exodus* 12:13; *Deuteronomy* 5:17.

Christ tells us, what to say of killing—killing is something very serious—but you should not even become angry with your brother, nor even abuse, hurt or annoy him. Because if you do, you create a karmic bond with the person and you may have to come back to this world to face that judgement. If today you have annoyed him, then he may have to annoy you, and for that both you and he may have to take birth. So you should not even use abusive language to anybody. Under no circumstances should you hurt anybody. Whatsoever the other person may do, you should not lose your self-control. You must always be loving and good.

> *Therefore if thou bring thy gift to the altar, and there rememberest that thy brother hath ought against thee;*
> *Leave there thy gift before the altar, and go thy way; first be reconciled to thy brother, and then come and offer thy gift.* (5:23–24)

He says, when you are going to the altar, to the church or synagogue to offer some gift, and on the way you remember that you have made somebody angry or have unnecessarily gone out of the way to rebuke somebody or injure someone's feelings, do not worry about giving your present to the Father. First go and reconcile yourself with that person. That is much more important than giving a gift. Forgive him or ask for his forgiveness. Then only can the purpose of your going to the synagogue be served. Otherwise you are just deceiving yourself.

Your gift will not be accepted unless your heart is without any malice. If you go with a closed heart to the Father, with malice and blackmailing thoughts against anybody in your heart, or you are thinking that somebody has hurt your feelings and you must take revenge, how can your heart be pure? How can your Father accept your gift? Only a clean heart can receive what the Father wants to give. If a cup is upside down, however much it may rain, not a drop of water can get in. If the cup is in an upright position, one or two falls of rain will fill it.

So he says that your cup is closed by injuring and unnecessarily offending people, and day and night killing for your palate, for your stomach. And your Father is not going to hear your prayer at all. You cannot receive his mercy. First you must be good enough to make amends with the other person. Then only will you be heard and can receive his blessings.

> *Agree with thine adversary quickly, whiles thou art in the way with him…* (5:25)

*"In the way with him"* means while both you and he are in the body, still living in this world. Then there is the opportunity to ask for his forgiveness. And if he asks for your forgiveness, you should always be happy to forgive him. But if you or he die, then you have no opportunity to ask for his forgiveness.

> *…lest at any time the adversary deliver thee to the judge…* (5:25)

'Adversary' means the other person. 'You will be delivered to the court to face judgement' means that after death you will have to go to the judge, to Dharam Rai where the karmic account is examined, and face the consequences of the karmas you have done.

> *…and the judge deliver thee to the officer, and thou be cast into prison.* (5:25)

Into which prison are we cast? That of transmigration of the soul. This whole world has been called a prison of eighty-four or *chaurasi*. Indian mystics have also used the words prison or jail for it, and Christ has used the same word. Whether you come as a debtor or a creditor, you will have to face judgement and return to this prison.

> *Verily I say unto thee, Thou shalt by no means come out thence, till thou hast paid the uttermost farthing.* (5:26)

He says that you cannot escape from this prison of birth and death until you have cleared all your karmas, all the seeds that you have sown, because even a little thing can pull you back to this world: "Render therefore unto Caesar the things which are Caesar's" *(22:21).* So unless we are able to uproot that seed, we have to come back to reap the result of whatever we have sown. If the seed is no longer in the ground, then there will be no result or harvest. If you have planted a chilli seed and, before it grows, you uproot it, then you will not have to go to the field to harvest it. So Christ says that if, unfortunately, you have injured anybody's feelings, go and apologize to him. Clear that seed so that you do not have to come back to this world. Then he talks about another thing:

> *Ye have heard that it was said by them of old time, Thou shalt not commit adultery.* (5:27)

He says that every mystic or saint impresses upon us that we must lead a good moral life, for unless we do this, our heart cannot be clean. Unless our heart is clean, we cannot receive the grace of the Father. So you must be clean even in mind and thoughts. You should not commit adultery at all. But it is very sad that people take moral laws so liberally these days. They live as man and wife without even getting married. They do not try to enquire about or read the teachings of the mystics or saints. Christ says that if you are living an adulterous life, you should know that you will not be able to go back to the Father.

> *But I say unto you, That whosoever looketh on a woman to lust after her hath committed adultery with her already in his heart.* (5:28)

He says, there is no question of committing adultery; if you look at anybody with a lustful eye, with adulterous intention, you have already committed adultery. How so? Because if you have a lustful tendency towards anybody, you create a desire to satisfy that lust. And that may be able to pull you back to this level for its satisfaction. So you have already committed it. Even the desire, the lustful tendency, is bad. You must rise above it, otherwise you will not get the Father's grace. Then further on he will tell us how to get rid of such desires.

> *And if thy right eye offend thee, pluck it out, and cast it from thee: for it is profitable for thee that one of thy members should perish, and not that thy whole body should be cast into hell.* (5:29)

What he means to say is that if you have committed adultery or any karma, it is better to clear it now. If, out of your whole body, one portion of your finger gets septic and diseased, it is better to cut that off rather than allow the septic area to spread throughout the entire body. It means that one little desire may bring you back into this world, and the whole of yourself may have to suffer and burn here. It is better that you make amends now for that one sin, either by meditation or by asking forgiveness from the Father. And if we are able to wash off or burn that sin now, then we are only 'cutting off a limb'—it means that we are clearing that particular karma.

So Christ says, do not commit adultery. For whatever you have already done, try to meditate. Try to wash off your sins by means of the Holy Spirit, the Holy Ghost within. And that spirit or voice of God will help you to rise above this karma, to make your soul and your heart pure, and to realize the Father within.

> *Ye have heard that it hath been said, An eye for an eye, and a tooth for a tooth.* (5:38)

It means that whatever actions you do, you expose yourself to the same type of actions from other people.

> *But I say unto you, That ye resist not evil: but whosoever shall smite thee on thy right cheek, turn to him the other also.* (5:39)

Nobody could give a better philosophy of non-violence than has been given by Christ. He says, if anybody slaps you on the right cheek, there is no question of returning the slap. You should even turn your left cheek to him, let him slap that one too. It means that under no provocation should you offend or strike another person. Let him do whatever he wants, but do not think of taking any revenge. Always be non-violent and approach him lovingly and kindly. You must be absolutely clear in your heart. Be good and noble to others and put them to shame by your nobility and goodness. Just be patient and calm and let him suffer for his own folly and mistake, for his karma. If you retaliate, then you are also behaving the same way. So he says that at least you should be good. You should try to rise above these things and behave like a noble person, rather than becoming like him.

> *And if any man will sue thee at the law, and take away thy coat, let him have thy cloke also.* (5:40)

If anybody sues you or tries to injure you or wants to defame you in this world, do not try to take revenge. Even give him those other things of which you have surplus. Do not create any karmic relationship with him under any circumstances, because a small karma may bring you back into this world. Then he says:

> *But I say unto you, Love your enemies, bless them that curse you, do good to them that hate you, and pray for them which despitefully use you, and persecute you.* (5:44)

What better philosophy of non-violence could Christ give than this? He says that there is no question of hating an enemy. You should love your enemies. If he is hating you and you are also hating him in return, then you are both at the same level. The beauty is that he is hating you and you are giving him love in return. So he says: *"Love your enemies."* Fill them with love and devotion and with affection. It is very difficult to live like that. But if we are able to live the life that is explained to us by the mystics, we will at once become pure and merge back into the Father.

*"Bless them that curse you."* If somebody hates you and curses you, you should rather take pity on him. You should bless him, win him over with your love and kindness and greatness. *"Do good to them that hate you."* Just show them love and understanding instead. *"And pray for them."* Just pray to the Lord to give you strength to bear all that and to forgive them, because they do not know what they are doing. Think: 'O Father, they are blind. Give them understanding, give them your love and your devotion. Give them your grace.' Then they may also behave in the same way in which you are trying to behave with them.

> *That ye may be the children of your Father which is in heaven.* (5:45)

Christ says, why am I giving you such a high philosophy? Because you want to become the children and the beloved of the Father. The Father has all these qualities, so you must also possess them if you want to become his children.

> *For he maketh his sun to rise on the evil and on the good, and sendeth rain on the just and on the unjust.* (5:45)

When the sun rises it shines on everybody, whether he is a thief or a saint. When the rain comes, everybody benefits from that rain. You should also try to possess the qualities of the Father, and just be good to your enemies as well as to your friends. Do not say: 'This person is my friend and that one my enemy. This person did this bad thing to me and I am going to hate him, and that one did that good thing to me and I am going to love him.' You should be one and the same to everybody. Just be loving and good to all. Then he gives a very beautiful explanation:

> *For if ye love them which love you, what reward have ye? do not even the publicans the same?* (5:46)

It is easy to love a person who loves you, but very difficult to love one who hates you. He says that the beautiful thing about becoming my disciple is that you also love those who hate you. If anybody is good, kind and loving to you, naturally you also give him your love. There is nothing special about you if you are good to a person who is good to you. The beauty is that with those persons who are not kind and good to you, you are still loving and good. If you are living with a person who is very difficult to live with, who has no understanding, who does not want to listen to you, your goodness is that you are still living with him in love and peace. He says that that type of attitude you should develop in your life.

> *And if ye salute your brethren only, what do ye more than others? do not even the publicans so?* (5:47)

If anybody respects or greets us, we also respect or greet him. But we should also greet those people who even turn their face away from us when we come across them, who do not want to talk to us. Greet everyone lovingly, with a smile. Everybody is eager to get the favour of an important person and to do good to him, or to a friend or relative. We always like to greet them first. But try to be good to those people about whom nobody bothers. If you are their superior, do not let them feel that you are their superior, their boss, and much higher than they. You should also respect them in the same way that you respect and show regard to your elders and seniors.

> *Be ye therefore perfect, even as your Father which is in heaven is perfect.* (5:48)

He says, why am I advising you in this way? Because you want to become perfect. Unless you become pure and perfect, you can never merge back into the pure and perfect One. If a child is dirty, will the mother take him in her lap? First she gives the child a bath, dresses him, then she takes him in her lap and kisses him and loves him. She does not embrace the child until she has cleaned him. When we are so particular not to even lift up a dirty child, how can we expect the Father to lift us up when we are so dirty and so engrossed in maya?

We have to become perfect like our Father in heaven is perfect. Unless we become like him, we cannot merge back into him. That is why Christ said to that man whom he had cured: You have become whole, go and sin no more *(John 5:14)*. I have attached you to the Word, the audible life stream, and now you are in the process of becoming whole, provided that you do not add any more sins to your load of karmas. Unless we become whole, we cannot merge back into the Whole, the Father.

That is why Socrates said: "Know thyself." Unless we realize ourself, we cannot realize the Lord. And realizing our self means getting release from the mind and going beyond the realm of maya. Then the soul becomes perfect.

And that is why Christ is emphasizing that you have to become as perfect as your Father in heaven. Unless you gain such qualities and attributes in life, and achieve the same type of perfection on the earth here, you can never become perfect and merge into the Father. He has sent us here to become like him, so that we may become him. We have to become like him while we are here in the flesh, and then we become him who is in heaven.

When a drop merges into the dirt, it becomes part and parcel of the dirt and cannot merge back into the cloud. It must first leave the dirt by evaporation, then only can it merge back into the cloud, which is pure water. Similarly, we are also a drop of the divine ocean, that divine bliss. Potentially every soul is God, but in this realm of maya, we have become very, very dirty, and become part and parcel of maya. Unless we detach ourselves from maya, become pure again and separate ourselves from the attachments of this creation, we cannot merge back into the Creator. Thus, separating ourselves from the creation is becoming perfect. Merging back into the Creator is to become the Creator. So he says that that is why I am trying to give you the teachings from all aspects, because you have to become perfect in order to go back to the Perfect One.

Some people say that Christ used to take fish, and he did not stop us from eating meat. But a person who was so loving, so compassionate, so noble and kind, who could not even tolerate hurting or annoying or being angry with anybody—how can you imagine that he would kill his creation, or eat fish or meat? It is completely contradictory to the other things which he has tried to tell us. So, "Thou shalt not kill" *(5:21)* covers everything: whatsoever has life should not be destroyed. The question of our justifying the taking of meat does not arise at all.

Then he explains that unless you clear all your karmas, you will never be able to escape from this prison. But by killing we are just adding more to our load. So the stories which we tell about a saint, that "he took meat here" and "he went there", must be proved from the teachings which he has given to us. They must be compatible with the events in his life. If they are contradictory, then either the teachings or the life story which we have constructed about the saint is wrong. There is some mistake somewhere.

## Questions and Answers

### *The birth of Christ (1:18–25)*

Q. Master, when you were in London, sir, you made a very significant statement about the manner in which the Lord Jesus was born. You said that he was born not by the will of his father and mother, but of the will of God. Now I know that many existing brothers and sisters of mine, who I have thought might have been in search of truth, have disbelieved this, and have tried in vain to prove it in the laboratory, with the use of test-tubes and bunsen burners and flasks. But I know that what the Master said is perfect in its truth. But may I know, sir, from you, whether all Masters of the order and status of Lord Jesus who preached Shabd and Nam, have they all been born in a similar manner?

A. How do we take birth? Our father and mother are just instruments. Whatever karmas and sins we have committed in past lives have become our master, and wherever they force us, we have to go and take birth there. Then those karmas bring about the union of our father and mother, and we are there. So 'by the will of the Father' means that saints do not have their own karmas at all—they come by the will of the Father. It is not that their karmas are their master and that they are a slave of them.

> Q. Maharaj Ji, please would you explain about the birth of Christ. The gospel says that Mary was a virgin.

A. Actually this is a misinterpretation. What is meant in the Bible is that he was not born of a man and a woman, as others are born. His peculiarity was that he was the Word made flesh; the Word had taken abode in him. So he was a son of the Word. But now they interpret it that probably he was born without a father. It is absolutely a wrong interpretation. I do not think that that is right. Why should he come in an unnatural way? Where was the necessity to even select a mother then, if he could avoid the father? These are just our ways of looking at things. Actually, he was the Word made flesh—the manifestation of the Word. It is absolutely wrong to think that probably he will not be respected or we are not giving him proper respect if we accept that he had a father. Why should we think that way? Every mystic or saint had a father. You read in the Bible, everywhere he says 'son of man'—so it means that the man was there. The question of not having a father does not arise.

### *"He that cometh after me is mightier than I"* (3:11)

Q. I was thinking of when a saint goes beyond and leaves the body. For some of them who are contemporaries of the one who follows, don't they have a hard time recognizing that he is also a saint?

A. That is what I tried to hint, when Christ said that John the Baptist came to prepare a way for me. Unless the predecessor prepares the way for his successor, the successor cannot be successful; nobody will pay any attention to him.

Q. In other words, they could not recognize him unless…

A. They will not. Even after the predecessor's nominating him during his lifetime, telling the people publicly about him, even then they will refuse to recognize him—because they are so much attached to their own Master. No doubt that is a good thing; but for a successor to be accepted, it is not so easy. People will care more for the Master's shoes, the Master's bed, the Master's table, the Master's well and the Master's house, than they will for the Master's successor—people are so used to giving importance to this type of thing. But since Masters do not want them to forget the real teachings and give themselves to these unnecessary rituals and ceremonies, they always prepare the people for their successor. That is why John the Baptist said that the one who is coming after me is greater than I. He was preparing the people to accept Christ.

### *"Blessed are they that mourn: for they shall be comforted"* (5:4)

Q. [on shedding tears for the Lord]

A. Even Christ has tried to express the same thing when he said "*Blessed are they that mourn.*" When do we mourn? When somebody dies. When somebody is parted from us, we cry and weep in separation. So he says, blessed are those people who are mourning for the Father, and who are shedding tears in love, are missing him, dying for him day and night, who have intense longing, *birah*, love and devotion—they are the blessed ones. Whenever we mourn, tears generally flow from your eyes, we cannot help it. Christ says that those who miss the Lord, who are mourning for him, they only are the fortunate ones.

Those who cannot bear the separation and are shedding tears in his love and devotion *"shall be comforted"*. 'Comforted' means that they will be able to go back to the Lord. Their longing will take them back to the Father and they will get real comfort when they are with him. Without him, whatever he may give them, they are never in comfort. So he says, blessed are those people who mourn. The same thing is expressed by all the mystics, in one form or another.

### *"Blessed are the meek"* (5:3, 5)

Q. Could you talk about humility?

A. Humility means absence of ego. If you are able to eliminate ego from within yourself, naturally you are filled with humility, and humility will also bring love within you. If you really have love, then automatically you will become humble. And if you are full with love, then ego has no place in you. So elimination of the ego will fill you with love and humility. And unless we become humble we cannot travel on the path, because the obstacle in our way is nothing but the ego.

And the term 'ego' is generally meant in a very wide sense. It is an instinct of possession, and that comes into almost everyone. We want to possess. We always declare: It is *mine*, *I* want it. We are obsessed by the possession of those things. So that is all '*haumaiŋ*' or ego.

But when the mind is attached to the light and sound within, then naturally attachment to that creates detachment within us from worldly things, and automatically humility and love fill us. That is why Christ has laid so much stress on humility and meekness, and says that you must become like a babe, just as meek as a child. Anything can please a child. He has no pride. Similarly, we have to become simple and innocent like a child.

### *"Blessed are the peacemakers" (5:9)*

> Q. Master, it says in the Sermon on the Mount: "Blessed are the peacemakers" and that you should be like a light shining on a hilltop. I find this a bit difficult to reconcile with the principles of self-defence where, for instance, we guard our country against H-bombs.

A. What he means by 'peacemakers' is not worldly peacemakers—the politicians and humanitarians and people who are trying to bring nations together and bring a truce in this world. Christ does not mean these people. He refers to the devotees and lovers of the Lord as peacemakers. Those who have developed peace within themselves, who are in union with the Lord—only then do we get peace—*they* are peacemakers, because they create peace among us. They radiate peace around themselves.

He makes this point clear elsewhere in the Bible when he says: "Think not that I am come to send peace on earth: I came not to send peace, but a sword" *(10:34)*. Otherwise, these two things would be contradictory. At one place he says that the peacemakers are the blessed ones; at another he says, do not think that I have come to create peace in the world. But he is exactly right in both places. Saints do not come to create peace in the world, they come to take us away from the world. They do not interfere with the administration of this creation, they do not worry about this world. They are only concerned with their allotted sheep, to take them out of this world, back to the Father. And as for the rest, they do not touch the world; it will go on as it is. It is as imperfect today as it was in the past. They come to give and create peace within us.

### *"Thou shalt not kill"* (5:21)

> Q. We know we must not kill, and nobody likes to be killed, and the young men of today do not like to serve in the armed forces because there is a danger of their being killed. And many of them violate the laws of their land by either tearing up their draft cards or going to other countries. Would you care to comment on that?

A. Well, sister, the first thing Moses told us in one of the commandments was: *"Thou shalt not kill."* It is written there. If you kill, you expose yourself to be killed. But those people who do not want to join so that they may not have to kill, do they not kill otherwise? They take meat; they do not hesitate to murder people and hurt their feelings. Is it with this intention that they do not go, or is it an escape? If one really thinks that he should not kill, then it is all right. But if it is just an escape, it is wrong, when otherwise they are killing all around. If one really, honestly, does not want to kill, the Lord's grace and protection is always there, which you can depend on. We have so many of our people in the army, and you know that they do not want to kill. And somehow with the Lord's grace they do not even get the opportunity, however much on the front or in whatever position they may be.

I know about one of our satsangis—he has retired now from the air force. He said: 'I was so scared about having to bomb anything and was always escaping from such situations.' But he was caught up in the war and ordered to go and bomb certain places. He said: 'I could not refuse, so I went up in the air and just prayed to Maharaj Ji: I can't and will not do it. While I was taking off, I got the order: You come back to the control room and take over the duty of the officer here because he has been taken ill. Somebody else will go in your place.' And he said: 'I have never bombed anyone.'

> Q. Master, my husband is a professional soldier and has been for thirty years, and he said that just within the past two years the army is changing. More and more of the soldiers are saying: 'I don't want to kill.' And I have seen the change in him. He has been through wars, he has killed people, feeling that he was just being led by the Lord wherever he was, and now he is changing and he says like everyone else, that we do not want to kill any more.

A. It is a good thing, sister. If we can all learn one thing, *"Thou shalt not kill"*, the whole world can be at peace today.

We say it only in the synagogues or churches, but when we come out of them, then we find excuses to kill people. Nation is against nation, country against country, people against people. As long as the mind dominates, they will just be trying to kill one another. If we could just literally follow the commandments given by Moses, what to say of spirituality, this world could be at peace today. But we do not; they are only meant within the four walls of the synagogue or church, or of any other holy place. Outside of them we do not bother about what we have heard, or what we say or read.

You have lived through so many wars. In the First and Second World Wars they were all Christian countries that were at war with one another and probably both sides were praying to Christ to help them. What should Christ have done? Whom should he have helped? The Germans were praying to him; the Americans were praying to him; the English and the French were praying to him: 'Help us to kill people of another country; to conquer, crush, and bombard another country.' And what should he have done? Imagine his position—because all were Christians.

It is just self-deception. When there is a mass prayer for victory and success, what is that mass prayer? To destroy another people or another nation? What should God do? Everybody belongs to God. Everybody is praying to the Lord. So the Lord has to be accused by one party or another for not hearing them. It is just self-deception, trying to make fools of people to set them against one another, that is all—to justify their fights and quarrels.

If we really mean *"Thou shalt not kill"*, the question of wars does not arise. And why are there so many armaments, and tanks and bombs? For what are we making all these things, day and night? Only in our private life, we are all devout Christians and devout Jews, and so on. These narrow loyalties are all the play of the mind. We do not take the world, or humanity as a whole, or the spiritual values of life as a whole. "Love thy neighbour as thyself", as Christ said. He gave only two commandments: "Love the Lord thy God with all thy heart, and with all thy soul, and with all thy mind" *(22:37).* Then he said: "Love thy neighbour as thyself" *(22:39).* If you just follow these two commandments, where is the question of fights and quarrels and hatred? We say it, but actually we do not follow it. We say that the Father exists in every one of us, that the Lord exists in every part of the creation, that he is omnipresent, omnipotent; and yet what do we not do in this world?

If there is a five-year-old child standing before us, we do not dare to even steal a candle. We say we are being watched and that he will call us a thief. Does the Lord not watch what we do—and what we think? Do we not give more importance to a child than to the Lord? Is he nowhere around us when we do all these things? They are just things that we say, that we want to feel satisfied that we believe in. Actually we do not believe in them at all. They are just sayings meant to be said, that is all; nothing else.

If we really believe even a little of the teachings given to us by the mystics—and we claim we are their followers—then the whole world can be set at peace, what to say of spiritual progress. Spiritual progress is something very high. But if we can understand these teachings, even then we can be at peace in this world.

Perhaps the Creator does not want that peace, and neither do the mystics come to this world to create that type of peace. That is why Christ said, do not think that I have come to create peace; I have come with a sword *(10:34).* I have not come to make this world a paradise for you to live in; that is not my purpose. I have come to take you away, to cut your chains to this world. You are so much attached to one another, and with my sword of light and sound, or Word, I will cut all your attachments to this world, loosen your chains, and take you back to the Father. That is my mission in coming to this world.

Peace is within. Nations will not be at peace; in the world there can never be lasting peace. When we read history it does not encourage us. When there has not been peace in this world during the last so many thousand years, how can we expect that we can create peace in this world today? We cannot.

### *"Whosoever shall smite thee on thy right cheek, turn to him the other also" (5:39)*

Q. Master, in the portion of the Bible about turning the other cheek, which is a very difficult philosophy, what about if you are, let us say, attacked by somebody without provocation, and it is a question of protecting your home or your family. Should you even then not try to defend them?

A. Well, brother, do whatever you feel like, but whatever Christ has to say about it I have told you. I do not think he is ambiguous; he is very clear about it. We may act any way we feel like, but mystics or saints have to say what they want to. His philosophy is very clear—that there is no question of taking any revenge.

Q. In the Bible when it says that we should turn the other cheek, does that mean that no matter what people say or do to us, we should accept it?

A. What he means to say is, if anybody harms or insults or talks ill of you or shows hatred against you, you should not retaliate in the same way. If he slaps you on the right cheek, you should turn the other to him also. But generally if anybody slaps us, we try to retaliate. You should just keep your thoughts absolutely clear. Kabir also says that if somebody sows thorns in your way, you should sow flowers in his path; for you the flowers are flowers, but for him the thorns will become spears. That is, it is he who will suffer for what he has done. For you the flowers will always remain flowers.

## TWO

# DISCOURSE ON MATTHEW 6

In the Sermon on the Mount, Christ has covered practically all aspects of the spiritual life, and here he talks about charity. We generally think that perhaps we will be able to reach the Lord by giving things in charity. But Christ tells us in what way we should give charity:

> *Take heed that ye do not your alms before men, to be seen of them: otherwise ye have no reward of your Father which is in heaven.* (6:1)

You know that some people are of a very charitable nature. They always want to help and give to others and be useful to them in their time of need. Christ indicates that we often give things in alms, in charity, just to please the Father. But if we give just to show off to the public that we are doing so much for the needy and the poor, it will do nothing but inflate our own ego.

The purpose of giving something in charity is not for the satisfaction of our ego, but to create humility in us. The Lord has given that wealth to us and we are only sharing it with his creation because we have a surplus—their requirements being more than ours—and so that we may detach ourselves from it and not feel so possessed by those material things or by that money.

So try to please the Father, try to be grateful to him. Nothing is yours in this world. Everything belongs to the Father. You have given that money in order to win the grace of the Lord, not for fame or to win the pleasure of people.

> *Therefore when thou doest thine alms, do not sound a trumpet before thee, as the hypocrites do in the synagogues and in the streets, that they may have glory of men. Verily I say unto you, they have their reward.* (6:2)

What reward do they have? They only want to give money to people to please their ego, so that their name should be in the newspapers and people should shower praise on them. If that is their only object, people will give them that reward—and they will get nothing more than that. However, Christ teaches us:

> *But when thou doest alms, let not thy left hand know what thy right hand doeth.* (6:3)

He says, do not blow your own trumpet if you help anybody or give in charity or in alms. Do not even let your left hand know. It means that nobody should know about it. Do not dwell upon it, do not feel the least bit egotistical about it. Otherwise, though the Lord may even give you ten- or a hundredfold, all the same you will have to come back to the world to get it.

> *That thine alms may be in secret: and thy Father which seeth in secret himself shall reward thee openly.* (6:4)

He says that the Father will not withhold any reward for whatever you do in his name. Whatever help you give to anybody in secret, its result or reward will be that the Father will openly give you his grace, or will take you back and make you one with himself. Because he sees every action of yours, he knows what you are doing. By blowing your own trumpet you will not be able to get more of the Father's attention.

Then he tells us about praying:

> *And when thou prayest, thou shalt not be as the hypocrites are: for they love to pray standing in the synagogues and in the corners of the streets, that they may be seen of men. Verily I say unto you, They have their reward.* (6:5)

He says, when you go to a synagogue, or a church or a temple or mosque, the priest prays openly in a public place, so that people who go there should know that he is praying. We also try to pray in public before people. We try to impress them that we are very noble, very religious, very spiritual people. We want to go to the church or synagogue to pray, so that people may see us there on Sunday or any other day and should also respect us, thinking: 'He is a great lover of God. He attends church every day or every Sunday. He is a very nice person.' We are not trying to impress the Father, but only the world. We are doing it for our ego. So Christ says: *"They have their reward."* We only want worldly honour and praise from people, and they give it to us. That is the be-all and end-all of our praying, and it takes us nowhere else.

But you have a direct relationship with the Father. You should pray to the Father to be in communion and contact with him. Just *be* with him! Just talk to him. When you pray to the Father, you should be unconscious of the world. Nothing should stand between you and him. You should forget the whole world. There should be only you and the Father, and none other. That is the right kind of prayer.

Prayer does not mean that you sit with a thousand people and start praying to the Father. If your attention is spread all around and people are coming and going, what is the sense of that prayer? And sometimes you try to pray or meditate sitting together, twenty or thirty people. But then we are always conscious of the people and of our surroundings, so how can we concentrate, how can we be one with the Father? And if anybody is between you and the Father, how can the prayer be accepted? You are wasting your time and not achieving any results because you are just doing it for your own glory and fame. You are not doing anything that pleases the Father.

So that is what Christ is warning us about, that prayer should be a communion between you and the Father. Nobody else should be in between and nobody else needs to know what you are doing.

> *But thou, when thou prayest, enter into thy closet, and when thou hast shut thy door, pray to thy Father which is in secret; and thy Father which seeth in secret shall reward thee openly.* (6:6)

He says that if you pray in seclusion, in a lonely, solitary place where you are not noticed, there will be no distractions. You will not be conscious of anybody else around you. Then you will only be conscious of the Father, so you will be receptive in your praying to him and will get its reward openly from the Father. It means that he will openly take you back into his lap.

*But when ye pray, use not vain repetitions, as the heathen do: for they think that they shall be heard for their much speaking.* (6:7)

He says, in praying there is no need for any set prayer. My prayer may be different from yours or another person's. You think that perhaps the Father is deaf and unless you speak very loudly or very much, he will not hear you. The Father is nowhere outside. He is sitting right within you. Nobody is nearer to you than the Father. Even when an ant walks, he hears its footsteps! So why are you speaking so loudly?

Why are you wasting your time in reading set prayers, as there are in almost every religion? Your heart should speak, your heart should pray, for which no language is required. It should only be a language of love, an expression of your love for the Father—that is real prayer. There is no use in repeating the same sentence again and again. That is just like a tape recorder, just mechanical repetition without any love and devotion.

*Be not ye therefore like unto them: for your Father knoweth what things ye have need of, before ye ask him.* (6:8)

Now he tells us, do not pray to him for worldly objects, achievements and desires, because he knows what you need. The One who has given us this birth, he knows what we are wanting and what we need. He knows much more than we. We do not even know what we need. Our mind deceives us; we think 'I need this thing or that thing', and if we get those things, we then have to pray again to the Father to get rid of them. So when we are so blind that we do not know what is best for us, then why not leave it to the Father? If he thinks that this thing is to my advantage, let him give it to me. If he thinks that ultimately it is not going to help me, let him deny it me. I should have full faith in him.

So just be in love with him. Do not show your lack of faith by knocking at his door again and again with the same request. Only pray to the Father for the Father, so that you may go and merge back into him. That should be your prayer: 'O Father, make me one with you, and take me back to where I was before the creation began.' And you can ask the Father to give you strength to face the results of the actions which you have already done in past births, to go through your destiny cheerfully and happily. And if you meditate, you will get the strength to face all those karmas cheerfully without losing much of your balance.

You do not have to ask for anything from a loving father. He always knows the needs and necessities of the child. Without even asking him, he is always happy to give. But if the child is always asking and asking and does not show any respect and love for the father, the father becomes tired of that child.

> *For your Father knoweth what things ye have need of, before ye ask him.*
> *After this manner therefore pray ye: Our Father which art in heaven, Hallowed be thy name.* (6:8–9)

He says: O Father, you are in heaven. I just want to merge in you, to live in your Name, in your will. In whatever way you want to keep me in this world, I am happy. What I want is just your love and devotion in my heart, that is all that I need. Give me what you want to give me. Take from me what you do not want me to have. I have absolutely and unconditionally surrendered to you because you have eyes and I am blind. I do not know what is best for my soul.

Why put a demand list before him every day in the morning? 'I want this and I want that.' He says, that is no prayer at all. These are your desires that you want the Father to fulfil. You are not trying to live in the will of the Father, you are asking the Father to live in your will. You are not a devotee of the Father, but only of your mind. And if you pray to the Father for these things, he will send you back to the world, to that place where you can best fulfil those desires. So he says, pray to the Father only for his grace, for his love, for his forgiveness and mercy.

Whatever time we devote to meditation, we are devoting to prayer. Meditation is prayer. Repetition of set words is no prayer at all. Withdrawing our mind to the eye centre and being one with the Holy Ghost, with the Spirit within ourself, is the highest prayer. Submitting our mind to the Father, trying to live in the will of the Father by attaching ourself to the Spirit, is prayer.

*Thy kingdom come. Thy will be done in earth, as it is in heaven. (6:10)*

He means: 'Your will prevails in heaven where you are, and I also want to live in your will while I am on this earth, in the flesh.' And that can only be if we eliminate our mind and our ego. Otherwise, as long as the mind is dominating, we are just living in the will of the mind.

*Give us this day our daily bread. (6:11)*

'Daily bread' means the daily necessities. Kabir Sahib also says: I ask from the Lord only for so much that I may not be hungry, and if any beggar comes to my door he may not go away hungry. He says just what Christ said—daily bread. We only want our daily necessities because they are essential before we can sit in meditation. We can increase them to any unlimited extent, or we can decrease them to the barest minimum. We can curtail our needs or we can expand them, it just depends upon us.

We cannot live without food or clothes or shelter. These three things everybody needs. And we can go on expanding these necessities, go on demanding more and more. Instead of one bed, we can have ten or twenty beds. We can have a wardrobe full of clothes, our whole house can be full with provisions, with all varieties of things. And we can also have many houses to live in. We are not satisfied with one room. We can go on enlarging our desires and wishes; there is no end to them. So he says, just ask the Father for the daily bare necessities and no more.

*And forgive us our debts, as we forgive our debtors.*
*(6:12)*

For this also we have to pray. This is the grace that we want from the Father, that he should *"forgive us our debts"*. It means whatever karmas we have done in this world, please forgive us, because they are what is forcing us to come to this world again and again. So ask forgiveness for your *sinchit* or store karmas, and your fate karmas. They are the debts which you are carrying from birth to birth.

*"As we forgive our debtors."* If anybody owes anything to us, we should forgive him. And if we owe anything to anybody, please, Father, forgive us, so that we may not have to come

into this world either as a debtor or even as a creditor. Whether somebody has done something against you or you against somebody, unless all that is cleared and that relationship is finished, you cannot escape from this prison.

So he says that if you have to pray to the Father, pray to him to help you to get rid of this load of karmas, to help you in rising above them, that they should be finished, should be burned.

For what else should you pray to him?

> *And lead us not into temptation, but deliver us from evil.* (6:13)

Pray to the Father: This world is very dangerous, and my mind is very weak. I am always attracted by worldly temptations. At every step there is the temptation to fall. So, Father, give me the strength to remain steadfast and away from those temptations, to withdraw from the senses. *"But deliver us from evil."* As long as the attention is running downwards, it is under the influence of the mind, the negative power. He says, pray to the Father always to save you from evil, to help you remain firm in this world, so that you may not have to come back to account for all those acts which you do when you become a slave of the senses.

> *For thine is the kingdom, and the power, and the glory, for ever.* (6:13)

He says, unless the Father helps us to come away from evil, from temptations and sensual pleasures, we can never go back to him. He is the only one who can help us out of these things. So let us pray to him to help us, to guide us. The Father can forgive anything. He can help in every way. He is the mightiest of the mighty, the most powerful of the powerful. He has the power to protect, and can give the strength to save us from evil temptations.

> *For if ye forgive men their trespasses, your heavenly Father will also forgive you.* (6:14)

This has a very deep meaning. It is always our karmas which pull us back to this world, and if we forgive people and clear our karmas by meditation, then the mind becomes pure. As Christ said at the beginning, only the pure ones will see God. When my mind becomes pure, then the Father forgives me from going through birth and death and I merge back into him. That is his forgiveness, that is his grace.

What anyone has done against me, I can forgive; but what I have done against anyone, I cannot forgive myself for that. When we have asked a person's forgiveness for any wrong we may have done to him and we have forgiven him for whatever he has done to us, then only can we expect the Father to forgive us for what we have done against one another. Some of those whom we may have wronged may no longer be in this world and some of them we may not have the opportunity of seeing again to ask them for forgiveness, so we pray to the Father to forgive us. And this we can only do by meditation. We should harbour no ill will or have any desire to take revenge.

> *But if ye forgive not men their trespasses, neither will your Father forgive your trespasses.* (6:15)

The Father has sent us here, and it is for him to take us away from this world. But he will only take us back to himself when we forgive people what they owe to us. Not only should we say we forgive others, but we should also not harbour any feeling of animosity or vengeance. Otherwise, God will not forgive us. What other people have done is no concern of mine, but if I keep my conscience clear and really forgive others, then I have done my duty and the Father will also forgive me for any wrong I may have done.

Then Christ talks about fasting:

> *Moreover when ye fast, be not, as the hypocrites, of a sad countenance: for they disfigure their faces, that they may appear unto men to fast. Verily I say unto you, They have their reward.* (6:16)

He is just telling us what the real purpose is of fasting, or of giving anything in alms, and of meditation or praying to the Father. He says, many people go on very long fasts and just try to make a show of their fasting through certain signs. So he says, where is the necessity of disfiguring your face? You are fasting so that your mind should become pure and think about the Father. Those people who used to fast did so, so that they might feel light and might spend the whole day in meditation, in love of the Father. So he says that now we do not think about the Father or pray to him or meditate on him; we only fast and disfigure our faces just to show people that we are fasting. It is nothing but ego and there is no sense in it at all.

> *Lay not up for yourselves treasures upon earth, where moth and rust doth corrupt, and where thieves break through and steal.* (6:19)

In whatever way we are trying to deceive people—by fasting, by praying, or by giving alms—we are only laying up a treasure in this world. People have left millions, and they spent their whole life in collecting that money. Day and night they sacrificed high principles of their life to become wealthy. But then were they able to take it with them? The same wealth remains here and has come down to us today, and they have gone empty-handed from this world. He says, what is the use of collecting a treasure which is always a source of worry and misery to you here and which you are also not able to take with you? If our ancestors could not take it with them, we also will not be able to take it with us.

So he says, what is the use of building a treasure on earth, because it will rust, it will become corrupted, and thieves will *"break through and steal"* and take it away. This is another point that he is making, that all the people around us are thieves—our relations, our friends and so on. They are always trying to rob us. Rob us in the sense that they are always trying to draw our attention towards them and away from our real aim or object in life, God-realization; trying to pull our attention to themselves and not letting us go towards the Father. He says, what is the use of toiling for these thieves?

> *But lay up for yourselves treasures in heaven, where neither moth nor rust doth corrupt, and where thieves do not break through nor steal.* (6:20)

He says, build that treasure in heaven of which nobody can deprive you. Whatever time we devote to meditation, whatever time we spend in his love and devotion, we are building a treasure in heaven. And that treasure will give peace of mind to us while being in this flesh and will be able to take us back to the Father. So try to get that treasure!

*For where your treasure is, there will your heart be also.* (6:21)

Our attachment is always from the heart. He says, wherever you build your treasure, you are attached. Your heart is with that, and after death you go straight to that place. If you are attached to the sound current or voice of God within, if you are building your treasure in heaven within, then your heart is in that light and sound. That audible life stream will pull you back to the Father, and you will be able to escape from birth and death. If you are attached to this creation, howsoever you may behave in this creation, all those attachments will again pull you back to their own level.

Then Christ explains to us how to get rid of this attachment, how to detach ourselves from worldly faces, possessions and objects.

*The light of the body is the eye: if therefore thine eye be single, thy whole body shall be full of light.* (6:22)

In our body, the seat of the soul and mind knotted together is at the eye centre, which is also known as the single or third eye, and has been referred to by mystics by so many names. From here our mind is being pulled downwards towards the senses, through the nine apertures.* And the mind is fond of pleasure and runs to the senses to find it. So the mind has become a slave of the senses; and the soul, being a slave of the mind, has also become their slave. So by running towards the senses, we are building a treasure in the world. And if we

* The eyes, ears, nostrils, mouth and two lower apertures.

become a slave of the senses, we always take birth in this world in one form or another.

So he says, if you want to detach yourself from the senses and want your soul to dominate the mind, and the mind to control the senses, then there is only one thing to do—withdraw your consciousness to the eye centre. And when you are able to still your mind at the eye centre with the help and grace of the Master, you will see light and hear the spirit of God, the voice of God within yourself. When your mind is attached to that Spirit, when you have become one with that light, then you are building a treasure in heaven, not in the world at all, because your mind is getting something much better, much finer than the sensual pleasures.

Only attachment can create detachment in you. Detachment will not be able to create attachment in anyone. If you were to tell a girl before she meets her lover to forget her parents, her relations and her friends and then get married, it would be difficult for her. But when she falls in love with a young man, she forgets everybody else in the world. Attachment to one man detaches her from all others in the world. This is the nature of the mind.

So Christ says, unless we attach ourself to the light which the Lord has kept within every one of us irrespective of caste, creed, religion or country, it is impossible for us to detach ourself from the sensual pleasures.

He says: *"The light of the body is the eye."* If you want to see that light, you have to see that light in the body and nowhere outside. We often go to the church or synagogue or temple and light candles there. Why? There is enough light otherwise. Where is the necessity of lighting a candle in a church? This body is the real temple of the living God, and that candle is always at the eye centre. We do not try to reach *that* light. We make our own temple or synagogue or gurdwara or mosque, where we light an outer light and just waste our time in ritual and ceremony.

So Christ says that if you want to be one with the light, the light is in the body. And if you want to see that light in this body, the temple of the living God, open your single eye. Be here at the eye centre. Close these two eyes, detach yourself from the whole world and open the inner eye, the third eye. Draw the attention back to the eye centre. Focus it there. Open this door. Then you will see the light. There is nothing but light in your body.

Our soul has two faculties—those of seeing and of hearing. The faculty to see is known as *nirat*, in our Indian language, and that of hearing as *surat*. Our soul hears the sound within ourself and sees the light. The light comes from the sound, and we hear and see that spirit of God, that voice of God, within ourself. So with the help of the sound and light we will be able to follow the spiritual path, and slowly and slowly, stage by stage, be able to reach our destination.

Christ says, if you run to the forest or the mountains, or to the church or synagogue, or if you read scriptures day and night, you are trying to discipline your mind by austerities. These are temporary things. It is just like putting a snake in a basket. As long as the snake is in the basket, we are safe from its poison. The moment it comes out from the basket again, we are faced with its poisonous bite. But if you take the poison sac out of the snake, then you can even put the snake around your neck. It becomes absolutely harmless. So running away from our worldly responsibilities and doing all these things is just like trying to put a snake in a basket. We think that our mind has become pure and that we have been able to control it, but the moment we have to face this world again, those desires spring up and our mind again makes us dance to its own tune.

Christ says that if you want to make your mind absolutely harmless, then there is only one thing that can do it, and that is to see that light which the Lord has kept within every one of us. Now when we close our eyes, we see nothing but darkness within ourself. We do not see the light because "The light shineth in darkness; and the darkness comprehended it not" *(John 1:5).* There is a veil of darkness created by our attachment to the world, by the ego. So in *The Gospel According to Saint John,* Christ says: "There was a man sent from God, whose name was John" *(John 1:6).* When the Lord wants the state of ego to be eliminated from within us so that we should be able to pierce through this state of darkness, he sends someone from himself. And he tells us the method, the technique, of how to withdraw to the eye centre, how to be one with that light and sound. Then the mind gets so much absorbed in the light and the voice of God within ourself that it no longer turns to sensual pleasures at all.

> *But if thine eye be evil, thy whole body shall be full of darkness.* (6:23)

But if the tendency of your mind is downwards, if your consciousness is below the eye centre, then you will see nothing but darkness in this world. If you are a slave of the senses, you always live in darkness. The darkness of ignorance, of illusion, will always be there.

> *If therefore the light that is in thee be darkness, how great is that darkness!* (6:23)

When we live in darkness outside and inside, we come back to this world again and again because nobody can find the way to his home as long as he is in darkness. Only in light can we find our way and our destination. So he says, if you want to go back to the Father, you must see that light.

> *No man can serve two masters: for either he will hate the one, and love the other; or else he will hold to the one, and despise the other. Ye cannot serve God and mammon.* (6:24)

It is very beautiful. He says that your mind cannot love two masters. The first master is God, the second is the senses. Either the mind is a slave of the senses and goes down, or it is attached to the light and sound and goes up. You cannot please both masters. You have to leave one and be faithful to the other. So he says, either be a slave of Kal, the negative power, or a devotee of the Father. When your attention is downwards, you are serving Kal. When your attention is upwards, you are serving God. When you are with God, you will go back to God. When you are with Kal, you will come back within the realm of Kal. So he says, you cannot serve both God and mammon.

> *Therefore I say unto you, Take no thought for your life, what ye shall eat, or what ye shall drink; nor yet for your body, what ye shall put on. Is not the life more than meat, and the body than raiment?* (6:25)

He says, do not always go on planning about your worldly possessions, about how to live in this world. We are always obsessed with 'How am I going to spend the fifty or seventy years of my life?' or 'How many houses, how much property, how many dollars do I have?' He says, do not worry. The Father knows what is best to give you. Go on doing your duty in this world. Keep your object and destination in view. The Father knows your needs in this world and he will give you those things.

> *Behold the fowls of the air: for they sow not, neither do they reap, nor gather into barns; yet your heavenly Father feedeth them. Are ye not much better than they?* (6:26)

Christ gives a very beautiful example. He says, look at the birds—you have never seen them ploughing the fields, sowing seed or harvesting the crops, yet the heavenly Father provides them with food and they are living in this world. He says: *"Are ye not much better than they?"* They are only animals, fowls and birds; you are the top of creation. Will he not provide for you? You are a temple of God, and the Lord is living in that temple day and night. Does he not know what his temple needs? The One who has created you is more anxious about you and takes much more care of you, is more concerned about you, than you are about yourself. He says, have faith in the Father.

> *Which of you by taking thought can add one cubit unto his stature?* (6:27)

He says that even if you desire all the things of the world, and day and night you are hankering for worldly possessions and achievements, with all your efforts you cannot add even a cubit, even a comma, to your destiny. Whatever is destined, whatever is in store for you in your fate karmas, you are going to get, whether or not you ask the Father. Neither can you add to it, nor can you decrease it. You may worry and plan and pray to the Father all day and night, but only that will happen which the Father wants to happen. He has given you a certain destiny, a certain role to play in this life, and you cannot escape from playing that role.

So he says, why waste your time in always praying to the Father for the fulfilment of worldly desires and achievements, and in day and night running about in this world to gain possession of things? It is a waste of labour. Leave it to the Father. Just keep yourself, your mind, always detached from worldly possessions.

Then he gives the same example about the lilies of the field:

> *...how they grow; they toil not, neither do they spin:*
> *And yet I say unto you, That even Solomon in all*
> *his glory was not arrayed like one of these.*
> *Wherefore, if God so clothe the grass of the field,*
> *which to day is, and to morrow is cast into the oven,*
> *shall he not much more clothe you...?* (6:28–30)

He says, we have no faith in the Father. We think that only by our efforts, only by our worrying and working day and night and wasting our time, will he be able to look after us, otherwise he will not bother about us. He says, look at the grass; it just grows for a very short time, just for a month or two. The Father also feeds that little part of his creation. He gives it food and it flourishes. It becomes green, and the next day people cut it and burn it. So even the thing which lives for such a short time is being looked after by the Father. He reminds us, we are at the top of the creation; will he not look after us?

> *O ye of little faith.* (6:30)

You say you are a devotee of the Father. You say you are worshipping the Father, but you have absolutely no faith in him. He says, why do you show such lack of faith in the omniscient Father? He has given you so much in this world and he is looking after you. Why can you not live in his will? Why do you not eliminate the desires of the mind and just face what is in store for you and be happy in that, rather than creating desires and always remaining unhappy?

> *Therefore take no thought, saying, What shall we eat? or, What shall we drink? or, Wherewithal shall we be clothed?* (6:31)

He says, do not always remain worried with future problems. Do not always go on brooding and thinking: 'What will happen to me tomorrow? What will I wear? What will I eat?' and so forth. You are always worrying about the future, about the past and about the present, always thinking of spending your life in this world, always obsessed and possessed by these thoughts. He says, do not waste your time in this foolish way.

> *For your heavenly Father knoweth that ye have need of all these things.* (6:32)

God knows what you need and he will give it to you. He will give you the opportunities and facilities to get all he wishes to give you.

> *But seek ye first the kingdom of God, and his righteousness; and all these things shall be added unto you.* (6:33)

He says, the Father has not given you this opportunity of being in the human form to worry about all these things. He has given it to you for a far better purpose, and that is God-realization, to go back to the Father, to become free from birth and death. In previous births, when you were in lower species, even then you ate and drank and had some hole to live in. Everything that you have now you have had here before. The peculiarity of getting this human birth is that now you can go back to the Father. It is the top rung of the ladder. Either you can slip down or you can go up to the roof. So do not neglect that purpose. Always keep that in view and then the Father will always take care of whatever you need in this world.

He says: *"And all these things shall be added unto you."* Hazur Maharaj Ji* used to tell us that if you bring a carpenter home, there will be no dearth of chairs, tables and so forth—he will always be there to make them. Instead of asking or worrying about getting a chair, bring the carpenter home; he will make all you desire. When we realize the Creator within us, then his whole creation is ours. We are hankering for his creation and ignoring the Creator. We want his blessings for material advantages, but we do not want the One who is blessing us with these things. If we bring him home, all that he can give we will automatically get because he is the giver of everything and we have brought the Giver within ourself. So similarly, Christ says: *"All these things shall be added unto you."* If you bring the Creator home, the whole creation will come along with him, and then you can take anything that you need.

> *Take therefore no thought for the morrow: for the morrow shall take thought for the things of itself. Sufficient unto the day is the evil thereof.* (6:34)

* Maharaj Sawan Singh (1858–1948), the Master of Maharaj Charan Singh.

He says, do not worry unnecessarily about your future or dwell on what you have done in the past. Make best use of the present time. Keep your mind always in love and devotion, and do not waste your time in these foolish ways or in building your treasure in this world.

## QUESTIONS AND ANSWERS

### *"When thou prayest, enter into thy closet"* (6:6)

Q. Excuse me, I have a question about when in *Saint Matthew* Christ says: Pray not in public places to be seen of men, but go to your closet and pray alone. Now is he speaking of meditation there?

A. Naturally. You see, he explains before that, what he means by prayer. By prayer, mystics always mean meditation. The time we devote to meditation, actually we are praying to the Father for his grace, to be one with him. That is real prayer.

Q. Master, that also means that one should not speak about one's meditation, then?

A. In what way?

Q. In this sense that 'Oh, I meditated so long last night, and I have meditated so long' and so on. A person should really not speak about it.

A. What is the use of speaking about that? Why do you want to speak about it?

Q. Well, then it is also a case of wanting to impress somebody.

A. Then? It is of no use. You are doing it for your own good and not for impressing other people. It means that you want other people to know that you are a great devotee of the Father. You want them to praise you and you want to inflate your ego unnecessarily.

### *"Give us this day our daily bread" (6:11)*

Q. Does the 'daily bread' that is promised to us by the Lord at the time of our birth apply only to satsangis or to everyone?

A. What do you mean by 'daily bread'? If we need only bread it is all right, but we also want jam and butter on it! Our 'daily bread' means our simple needs of the day. Now how much we have complicated this 'bread' is due to us. We have created so many desires. What Christ meant is that you should just worship the Father for the sake of the Father, not for your daily bread or to fulfil your worldly desires. He has already given you in your karmas what you are to get and you should be happy with that.

Life itself, if you analyse it, is a very simple affair to live and to lead. But we have complicated it so much today and are now trying to solve our problem of complication. And we feel frustrated when we cannot solve it and cannot fulfil our desires. Then we try to commit suicide and run away from these people and the world because we are not able to live with the desires which we have built within ourself. Otherwise, if we take life as it is, it is a very simple thing to go through. But we are not used to accepting simple things in a simple way. Unless the mind complicates simple things, it is not satisfied. Simple truths, for example, we can never accept in a simple way. They must be put in a very intellectual way, in a very complicated way, before we think about them.

So if you read that prayer, it is very simple. And it is to be read along with the whole chapter, the whole text, not just those four or five lines only. Christ is giving parables to explain to us that the Lord who has created us knows best what we need and we should try to live in his will.

### *"For where your treasure is, there will your heart be also" (6:21)*

> Q. In *Science of the Soul*, there is a passage that says that the Master saves not only the disciple, but also saves the family of the faithful disciple. I guess there are lots of us who hope that our families will be saved, so we wonder how?

A. Sister, we go where our attachments are. Christ says that if you build your treasure in heaven, you go to heaven. If you build your treasure in the world, you come back to the world. So if a satsangi is attached to the Shabd, the voice of God, and is building a treasure in heaven, naturally with the help of that Shabd he has to go back to his destination. If the relatives are attached to the satsangi, and the satsangi is attached to the Shabd, the relatives are also helped. They also find their way onto the path which leads to that destination. On the other hand, if the satsangi is not attached to the Shabd but to the relatives, then they will pull him to their own level.

If you are attached to a bulldozer and are holding the chain of a dog, the dog can never pull you back. The bulldozer will pull you and will also pull the dog along with it. But if you are not attached to the bulldozer and the dog is strong, then the dog will pull *you*.

So in order to help our relatives, we must first help ourselves, and whatever we are doing to help ourselves by attaching ourselves to the Shabd and Nam, we are also helping our family members and friends who are attached to us. Some are influenced by our meditation, our atmosphere, our company, and automatically come onto the path. Others who die, who leave us, but were attached to us, also find their way towards us. Wherever I go, those people who are attached to me will automatically come to me. And if I go to my Master or to the Lord, naturally they will also find their way through me towards him. In that way you can help them; but by being attached to them you cannot help them.

Q. Does that mean that in the next life they will meet a Master?

A. They will definitely be on the path some day, and will slowly and slowly find their way to the same destination, howsoever slow it may be.

That is why Christ says: You have merged into me and I have merged into my Father, so you have merged into the Father.* It means that you are attached to me and I am attached to my Father, so you are also attached to the Father.

---

* *John* 14:10–11, 20; 10:30, 38.

Then he further says: You have seen me and I have seen the Father, so you have also seen the Father *(John 14:9)*. It means that you have come to me and are attached to me. You are in love with me because you have seen me, and I am in love with my Father. So I have to merge back into my Father when I leave this body, and you have to come back to me. Therefore, through me you will also find your way to where I will be.

This is how relatives are helped.

Q. Would the same position not arise with the physical form and the Radiant Form: that one is inclined to hang on to the physical form and not try and reach the Radiant Form?

A. Ultimately, the affection or love and devotion for the physical form will lead us to the inner Radiant Form. Ultimately it will come to that because both the Master and the disciple will leave their physical forms. Physical forms do not go beyond this world. The association which the soul creates with the Shabd, the light and sound, which is our real Master, is permanent. But the soul cannot come into contact with that Shabd unless both the Master and the disciple are in the physical form at the time when the disciple is initiated.

That is why it is said that the real saint, our real Master, is Shabd. But since we can only be attached to the Shabd through the physical form, so we have respect and love for the physical form. Except for that, we would never have been brought into touch with the Shabd, the Radiant Form of the Master within us. But ultimately love and devotion for the physical form will lead us to the real form of the Master—and that is Shabd.

Christ also told them that for a little while I am with you and then I will leave you, and then again I will be with you *(John 16:16).* It means: Now I am in the flesh, I am with you, but I will leave you. But again, in the form of Shabd I will be manifested in you. I am not going to leave you. Then he also said that it is in your interest that I leave you now *(John 16:7)* because the love which you have developed for me, being in the physical form, will now turn your attention towards my Radiant Form, my Shabd-personified form, within yourself.

He says: Now you have so many doubts and questions, but when you see my inner form you will have no doubts and no questions at all to ask *(John 16:22–23).* He makes it very clear in *Saint John* that he is referring to his Radiant Form. It means that the disciple, being in the physical body, becomes filled with love and devotion for the Master. And then, when the Master has left this physical, mortal body, the disciple cannot find him outside in the world. But he says: You know the way, you know the truth and you know where I am going *(John 14:4, 6).* The disciple knows where to seek the real Master, and his love for the physical form of the Master now drives him to turn his attention inside to find the real Master. It means that then we concentrate and see the Radiant Form of the Master inside.

So this outside love has helped us to go inside. That is why he said: "It is expedient for you that I go away" *(John 16:7).*

### *"O ye of little faith" (6:30)*

Q. Maharaj Ji, you have said that a disciple must not use his initiation for acquiring worldly wealth or satisfying desires, but surely the Lord would not allow him to misuse this precious gift?

A. You will be just misusing your spiritual powers if you use them for that. I have discussed this very point from the Bible.* Christ has made it very clear: he says that the fowls do not sow anything, yet the Lord takes care even of them. Why do you use vain repetition to the Lord and pray to him for worldly things? Does he not know your need?

You know that when we have a maidservant or helper in the house, if she is doing her work devotedly, faithfully, honestly and diligently and we are happy with her work, then we are always anxious to please her and to give her something, or to increase her wages or say a few kind words to her. And we are always appreciative of what she does. If on the other hand she does not work and is always asking for an increase in wages and wanting gifts, we prefer to get rid of her.

Accordingly, if we are meditating, living in his love and devotion, he is anxious to give us as much as we need. But we are never his obedient seekers or lovers. We do not try to resign ourselves to his will. He knows all about us. Christ says: *"O ye of little faith."* You have no faith in the Father. That is why you are asking him daily. If you have faith in him, you will not need to ask him—he will give you what you need.

So it is the love and loyalty which will invoke the Father's grace, not knocking so much at his door for worldly things. We sit for barely fifteen minutes in meditation, but we spend at least one hour in asking the Father for the reward of that meditation, and our demand list is always very, very long.

---

* *See* discourse on *Matthew* 6:25–34.

## ⇶ THREE ⇷

# Discourse on Matthew 7–9

Christ continues with his Sermon on the Mount:

> *Judge not, that ye be not judged.* (7:1)

We are always anxious to judge others, but we forget that if we want justice, we also expose ourself to justice. If a complainant goes to court, no doubt the accused will come, but the complainant will also have to be there. The judge will be able to say who is right, but both have to knock at the door of the court.

So if anybody owes you anything or has injured your feelings and you want judgement, then for that judgement you also have to take birth to get from the other person whatever is due to you. And do not forget that when you come to this world, you also owe so many things to so many people. You will suffer for that too. So if you want to escape from justice, do not judge anybody else.

> *For with what judgment ye judge, ye shall be judged: and with what measure ye mete, it shall be measured to you again.* (7:2)

Whatever treatment we give, we have to face the same treatment in return.

*And why beholdest thou the mote that is in thy brother's eye, but considerest not the beam that is in thine own eye?* (7:3)

We should not desire justice. We should want remission and mercy so as to clear all our accounts. A condemned or guilty person cannot sit in judgement on another condemned or guilty person. We are all guilty or we would not be part of this creation, so how can we sit in judgement on one another? The condemned are the sinful. That being so, we are a part of the creation and we have no right to sit in judgement on anybody. We must look to our own weaknesses and try to get rid of them.

Christ says that we do not see the big beam in our own eye, but try to magnify the minor faults of others. We do not realize what serious sins we commit under the cover of darkness, not wanting to expose ourself to the world. But we are always anxious to pronounce judgement on others, not on our own self, howsoever wicked or evil-minded we may be. So he says, you are full of weaknesses yourself. And with all your deception you are trying to hoodwink others. You are just a hypocrite, deceiving yourself and others.

*Or how wilt thou say to thy brother, Let me pull out the mote out of thine eye; and, behold, a beam is in thine own eye?*
*Thou hypocrite, first cast out the beam out of thine own eye; and then shalt thou see clearly to cast out the mote out of thy brother's eye.* (7:4–5)

He means that when you have removed your weaknesses, have become pure yourself, then only will you be able to judge whether or not the other person has any weaknesses in him or has really done anything against you. Otherwise when you yourself are so impure, how can you judge another person? Your own judgement is blinded by your sins and karmas, and you cannot see clearly.

He advises, first improve yourself, help yourself. Then you will be in a position to help others. Now you just judge people in order to criticize them, to humiliate them, to tell them that you are superior to them—that you are rid of these weaknesses and that they are slaves to them. You are trying to find out their weaknesses from that point of view. But, he says, first try to help yourself. You yourself should rise above all these weaknesses, then try to help others also to rise above them.

Therefore, we must come to the eye centre and be one with that light. When we are able to become one with that light, one with that Spirit, then we can lovingly explain to others that they can also follow the same way and escape from sensual pleasures and the resulting sins.

> *Give not that which is holy unto the dogs, neither cast ye your pearls before swine, lest they trample them under their feet, and turn again and rend you.* (7:6)

What he is saying is that everybody is not meant to understand such holy and beautiful teachings. They are meant only for the chosen few, the allotted souls. So he says: *"Give not that which is holy unto the dogs."* If the Lord is showering his grace on you and you are able to make yourself pure, do not be anxious and enthusiastic to share the teachings with everybody. Do not argue or try to force them on another person, on an undeserving person who does not want them. The Lord knows best whom to give and what to give and how to give to them. Do not try to convert others.

Then, when you meditate, the grace of the Father is there. You will definitely get spiritual wealth within. But try to digest that wealth within. Whenever we share our spiritual experiences with anybody, we always do it at our own cost. Our whole progress is blocked.

He says, why give such a precious treasure, the grace of the Lord in you, to others? We should never discuss our spiritual experiences with anybody and should never encourage anybody to discuss their spiritual experiences. They are our personal treasure, between us and the Master and the Father, and nobody else should share these.

He says, 'do not give unto the dogs that which is holy'. All spiritual experiences are holy. So we are not to waste them nor publicize them. Do not be tempted to use supernatural powers and start performing miracles or try to impress people by showing them your petty tricks or by trying to show them that you are very holy. Do not waste your energy like that. The world will, at the most, praise you and take you to be a very holy man, and that is all. But you lose all that you have. So he says *"neither cast ye your pearls before swine"*, because swine will not be able to appreciate pearls. They do not value what you are giving them. So why unnecessarily waste such beautiful spiritual wealth and spiritual experiences?

Then he says, you must invert yourself within:

> *Ask, and it shall be given you.* (7:7)

'Ask' means to pray to the Lord; *"and it shall be given you"*—then the Lord will definitely give you whatever you ask from him. If you ask for his grace, for the strength to go through your karmas, the Lord will definitely give it to you.

*Seek, and ye shall find.* (7:7)

If you have a real desire to go back to the Father, you are honest in your devotion, in your love for him, then you will definitely find him. Then there is no question of not finding him. Our desire and devotion must be intense. We must have deep devotion, deep love for the Father, to go back to him. Then it is for the Father to pull us towards himself.

You know, we give our children to babysitters and if the child cries and weeps, the babysitter tries to please him in every way. Sometimes she will give him some toffees, sometimes she will try to get his attention by telling him fairy tales, and sometimes she just plays with him and gives him toys and so on. As long as the child is happy with the babysitter, the parents are free to attend to their work in the home. When the child is not happy in being with the babysitter, does not want to play with any other child and starts to cry for his parents, they at once run to the child and just embrace him. Then they do not continue their work in the home because they cannot bear the cries of the child.

Similarly, as long as we are engrossed with the toys of this creation, the Lord pays no attention to us. When we withdraw our attention from the creation and are really sincere in our desire to go back to the Father, are full with love and devotion only for him and feel the separation from him, then he also pulls us up to his own level.

*Knock, and it shall be opened unto you.* (7:7)

He says, if you knock at the door, it will definitely be opened to you. This is the door, at the eye centre. We have to knock by withdrawing our consciousness to the eye centre. Then this door will be opened to us and we will find the way which leads us back to the Father. As Christ explained in the last chapter: "The light of the body is the eye: if therefore thine eye be single, thy whole body shall be full of light" *(6:22).* It is the same point that he is referring to here also, that you must knock at the proper door. Then only will it be opened to you and you can get admission. Whenever you enter any house, you have to open the door. In order to open it, you always knock from the outside, and the door is always opened from the inside.

Why does he call it knocking? Because simran and dhyan are nothing but knocking. Knocking is always repeating the same action again and again. Again and again we try to collect and still the mind here at the eye centre, and the mind again runs out. Again we bring the mind here, again it runs out. Similarly, Christ says that your mind is running wild in this world. Try to still your mind again and again at this point. Ultimately you will succeed. Then you are able to knock at this door properly and it will be opened to you.

With the help of simran and dhyan, you are knocking at the door of your house day and night, you are trying to control the mind. Ultimately you will definitely succeed in stilling your mind and then you will be able to see that light and hear that sound. And that light and sound will pull you back to the Father.

> *For every one that asketh receiveth; and he that seeketh findeth; and to him that knocketh it shall be opened.* (7:8)

Whosoever is honest in asking for the Father definitely receives showers of his blessings. Whosoever is trying to seek the

Father, the Father definitely puts him on the path. Whosoever is trying to knock at the door, the Father definitely opens the door for that person. There may be something lacking in us, in our desire, in our longing, in our devotion, if the door does not open. But the Father is always anxious to put us on the path and to open the door for us because he himself is very anxious to meet us. Then Christ gives a very beautiful example:

> *Or what man is there of you, whom if his son ask bread, will he give him a stone?* (7:9)

He says, we are worldly people, but still we are so kind and generous and good to our own children. And if our son, out of love, asks us for anything, even for bread, we never give him a stone in return. We are always anxious to give him whatever he wants because we love him. So he says, the Father also loves you. You are also his children. If you really want the Father from the Father, he will definitely shower his blessings on you.

> *Or if he ask a fish, will he give him a serpent?* (7:10)

For no father will give you a serpent if you ask him to give you a fish.

> *If ye then, being evil, know how to give good gifts unto your children, how much more shall your Father which is in heaven give good things to them that ask him?* (7:11)

Being 'evil' means being a slave of the senses and of Kal. If we, being at this level, are so good and loving to our friends and children as to give them what they want, imagine how much the Lord, who is all love and all compassion, will be loving and good to you, how eager he will be to give you what you want from him.

> *Therefore all things whatsoever ye would that men should do to you, do ye even so to them: for this is the law and the prophets.* (7:12 )

It is very beautiful. He says, whatever behaviour you want from a person, you must behave in the same way with him. If you want to be honoured and respected, first you should learn to honour and respect others. If you want your debts to be forgiven, you must first learn to forgive others whatever they owe to you. Then others will also forgive you whatever you owe to them. We have to clear all our accounts, all the karmic debts that we have collected while being in this world.

*"For this is the law and the prophets."* Every prophet who has come to this world has given us the same law, the same teaching, that this whole universe is governed by the law of karma: Whatever you sow, so shall you also reap *(Galatians 6:7).* And do not think that you have not done anything in this world for which you have to account.

> *Enter ye in at the strait gate: for wide is the gate, and broad is the way, that leadeth to destruction, and many there be which go in thereat.* (7:13)

What he means to say is that the way back to the Father is very narrow and difficult, but the gate to destruction is wide and is always open. It is very easy to fall prey to temptation, to sensual pleasures, but very difficult to withdraw your consciousness back to the eye centre and to knock and open that door and get admission into your house.

> *Because strait is the gate, and narrow is the way, which leadeth unto life, and few there be that find it.* (7:14)

He says that the path is very narrow. It is extremely difficult to enter that path because the wind of karma and temptation is always blowing. Sometimes you go this way, sometimes that way. It is just like walking on a razor's edge, as Kabir said. So Christ says, the way leading to destruction is very, very wide and easy. But the way back to the Father, which gives us everlasting life, is most difficult for us to follow. However, the reward is great.

He says: *"Few there be that find it."* Do not think that everybody will be able to walk on this razor's edge, that everybody will be able to seek the Lord, will be able to knock and open the door that leads back to their home. He says: *"Few there be that find it"*—not everybody.

Guru Nanak says that one or two in a million will be able to find the Lord. Otherwise people are just moving towards the way of destruction: rituals, ceremonies and dogmas, or becoming the victim of passions, always being evil, always going in the other direction. Very few are really honest and sincere in invoking the grace of the Father on them. Very few are walking on the narrow road back to the Father.

> *Beware of the false prophets, which come to you in sheep's clothing, but inwardly they are ravening wolves.* (7:15)

'False prophets' means the priests of the organized religions. They are always trying to mislead you, always tempting you to perform rituals and ceremonies. They say: Take a bath here and all your sins will be washed away. Read these holy books and you will be able to clear all your karmas, wash away all your sins and go back to Father.

Many pseudo-saints appear in the world, gather an army of followers and collect wealth for their own personal glory. It is a case of the blind leading the blind. Christ warns us against such masters. Then he continues:

> *Ye shall know them by their fruits. Do men gather grapes of thorns, or figs of thistles?* (7:16)

He gives an example. He says, we always know a person by his deeds, his actions, his karmas.

> *Even so every good tree bringeth forth good fruit; but a corrupt tree bringeth forth evil fruit.* (7:17)

He says, if you remain in the company of good people, you will also be influenced to become like them and be filled with love and devotion for the Lord. If you remain in the company of evil or bad people, you will be affected by their company because one is influenced by the company one keeps. We can be easily led astray by wicked and bad company, but it takes a very long time for us to be influenced by noble and good company.

> *A good tree cannot bring forth evil fruit, neither can a corrupt tree bring forth good fruit.* (7:18)

If you have the company of godly people, you will not be tempted to evil or bad things and you will always keep improving. If you keep the company of bad people, whatsoever you may do you will never think about the Lord.

> *Every tree that bringeth not forth good fruit is hewn down, and cast into the fire.* (7:19)

He says, look at what we do in this world. Those trees which give us good fruit, we always water, fertilize and take care of them. But if a tree is absolutely barren or is yielding bitter or sour fruit, we never keep it in the garden, but cut it down and throw it in the fire. Similarly, after having taken this human form, if we are not able to bring forth good fruit—to see that light, to hear and to worship that Spirit within ourselves and to go back to the Father—then we will be *"cast into the fire"*. It means that we may have to face hell-fire, or come back to this world again and again in birth and death, and may even have to go down into the lower species.

> *Wherefore by their fruits ye shall know them.* (7:20)

So if you devote your time to meditation, to love and devotion for the Father, then you are yielding good fruit. Then you make the best use of this human opportunity.

> *Not every one that saith unto me, Lord, Lord, shall enter into the kingdom of heaven; but he that doeth the will of my Father which is in heaven.* (7:21)

He says, if you just profess lip service, saying 'I am a disciple of Christ and he is my Master', but do not follow his teachings, do not live in his will, he says I will not be able to save you. Just proclaiming that you are my disciple and that you accept me as a Master will not help you.

So he says, if you come to me and you understand but do not follow my teachings, nor try to see that light and become one with that Spirit, and think that by calling yourself my disciple you will be able to escape from this hell-fire, it will not be so. We have not only to hear these teachings; our whole life is to be based on them. We have to rise above the level of mind and maya. Then only will we know the will of the Father. We have to unconditionally surrender to him. Whatever karma or destiny is in store for us, we have to face that cheerfully and always keep our attention in the Shabd and Nam, in devotion and love of the Father—that is the will of the Father. So only those will get admission into his court who live in his will, not everyone who just pledges allegiance without properly worshipping him.

> *Many will say to me in that day, Lord, Lord, have we not prophesied in thy name? and in thy name have cast out devils? and in thy name done many wonderful works?*
> *And then will I profess unto them, I never knew you: depart from me, ye that work iniquity.* (7:22–23)

He says that only those people are entitled to go back to the Father who follow the teachings of the mystics implicitly, have faith in them and always keep themselves attached to the Shabd and Nam. As for the other people who do not understand or try to live in my teachings, Christ says, I will refuse to own them in my Father's house. I will say that I never knew them.

> *Therefore whosoever heareth these sayings of mine, and doeth them, I will liken him unto a wise man, which built his house upon a rock.* (7:24)

Christ says, who will be the blessed people? Only those are the fortunate ones, the wise men, who are building their house upon a rock so that it has a strong foundation and not even an earthquake can shake it.

> *And the rain descended, and the floods came, and the winds blew, and beat upon that house; and it fell not: for it was founded upon a rock.* (7:25)

What is meant by *"the rain descended"*? He is just giving an example. It means that sometimes a spate of bad karma comes. Sometimes devotees have to face very hard karmas. But even then their faith is never shaken. They are always steady, always loyal and faithful to the Master; such people will be able to stand all the miseries and worries and hardships of life.

> *And every one that heareth these sayings of mine, and doeth them not, shall be likened unto a foolish man, which built his house upon the sand.* (7:26)

Those people who just hear my teachings but do not try to live that way of life, do not keep their attention at the eye centre and attach it to the voice of God, are foolish people. They are building their house upon sand and it cannot stand. Unless a house has a deep foundation laid on very solid ground, it can never continue standing.

> *And the rain descended, and the floods came, and the winds blew, and beat upon that house; and it fell: and great was the fall of it.* (7:27)

If you just hear the teachings and do not attend to meditation, then you can fall very easily. Then you are just building on sand and any time that the wind or rain comes, the house will fall. It means that any time that a little temptation comes, we are at once swayed by it off the path. And you will not be able to stay on the path unless you devote your time to meditation, live the teachings and follow these principles. So always try to keep yourself attached to that Holy Spirit within yourself. Then nobody in this world can shake you. No temptation can take you away from the path. He means that before we try to follow and live the teachings of Sant Mat, we must understand them very thoroughly. We must build our foundation and our meditation on an absolutely deep rock. So every initiate is building a house. But some are building on a rock, some on sand.

> *And it came to pass, when Jesus had ended these sayings, the people were astonished at his doctrine.* (7:28)

Because the purpose of those people in coming to Christ was not to get the teachings from him, but only to get their diseased ones cured, they were astonished at the type of teaching he was giving them.

> *For he taught them as one having authority, and not as the scribes.* (7:29)

Christ was speaking all these true teachings from his heart, as one who had authority to teach, because he had experienced what he was trying to teach them.

Then, as you know, when he performed any miracle, he always told those people not to tell anybody. He did not want people to blow a trumpet about whatever he had done for them or cause his miracles to be known to the world. But as I have told you, miracles do happen in the lifetime of a saint.

> *And, behold, there came a leper and worshipped him, saying, Lord, if thou wilt, thou canst make me clean.* (8:2)

The leper said, I know you have the power; if you will, I can become clean.

> *And Jesus put forth his hand, and touched him, saying, I will; be thou clean. And immediately his leprosy was cleansed.*
> *And Jesus saith unto him, See thou tell no man.* (8:3–4)

He did not want people to run to him just to get their diseases cured, but wanted them to come to him for his spiritual message or teaching. So he told that man: Do not tell anyone that I have healed you.

> *But go thy way, shew thyself to the priest, and offer the gift that Moses commanded, for a testimony unto them.* (8:4)

On the contrary, he advises him to go to a synagogue and give a gift to the priest or to the synagogue, as is commanded by Moses, so that the priest may feel flattered or happy that the leper had probably been cured by him and that is why he is giving a gift. Christ did not want it to be known that he had cured someone and did not want to accept anything in return for cleansing that leper. Then we read:

> *Now when Jesus saw great multitudes about him, he gave commandment to depart unto the other side.*
> *(8:18)*

Many people were following him just out of curiosity, so he said to them: 'You had better leave me alone and go your own way.' Then Christ prepares us for how much sacrifice we may have to make in order to follow this path of love and devotion:

> *And a certain scribe came, and said unto him, Master, I will follow thee whithersoever thou goest.*
> *(8:19)*

Naturally, when he was giving the teachings, people were impressed with them and were filled with love and devotion for the Father, and somebody said: 'Master, I am going to follow you wherever you go.' It means: 'I will follow your teachings. Whatever you command me to do, I will obey.' So Christ warns him, saying:

> *The foxes have holes, and the birds of the air have nests; but the Son of man hath not where to lay his head. (8:20)*

He says, I know you are very sincere and anxious to follow me. But remember one thing—it is not so easy to love the Lord. Do not think that it is a bed of roses. It is very difficult to follow where I am going. He says: *"The foxes have holes."* Even the foxes have a resting place, a hole to sleep in at night. *"And the birds of the air have nests."* Even the birds who are flying all day get time to rest at night, because they have made their own homes where they can go for rest. *"But the Son of man hath not where to lay his head."* But the lovers of the Lord will get no rest anywhere in this life unless they are able to achieve their destination. They are not a part of this world and live in the agony of separation until they meet the Father.

So you must think twice before you say that you want to follow me. It is a path of hardship and sacrifice. You will have to walk on the razor's edge. You will have to face many difficulties if you want to become a lover of the Lord.

> *And another of his disciples said unto him, Lord, suffer me first to go and bury my father.* (8:21)

One disciple said: Just wait, let me bury my father—he has just died. Then I will follow you.

> *But Jesus said unto him, Follow me; and let the dead bury their dead.* (8:22)

He says, if you want to follow me, *"let the dead bury their dead."* Why are you worrying about your father who has died? He has finished his life. You have no relationship with him now. How can the dead bury the dead? Those people who never think about the Lord, who are always day and night worrying about and attached to the things of this world—they do not even know whether the Creator really exists. While living in this world, they are already dead. He says, let them deal with the dead people. You are not dead. If you have love and devotion for me, then why think about your dead father? Just forget about the world. If you want to follow me, leave everything immediately and come and live in my teachings. Detach yourself and do not think about anybody at all. Do not worry about who has died and what your duties are under such a situation. Let the worldly people do their own duties. You have to live in my teachings. Then only will you be able to go back to the Father.

What he means to say is that these people are attached to the world and are therefore not fit to follow me. For them the Lord is dead and the world is living. If you want to follow me, you have to be living. For you the world should be dead, and the Lord living.

> *And it came to pass, as Jesus sat at meat in the house, behold, many publicans and sinners came and sat down with him and his disciples.*
> *And when the Pharisees saw it, they said unto his disciples, Why eateth your Master with publicans and sinners?*
> *But when Jesus heard that, he said unto them, They that be whole need not a physician, but they that are sick.* (9:10–12)

One who thinks he is healthy, naturally does not need a doctor. Only one who sees that he is sick will go to a doctor. So he says, one who does not see the necessity of the Father will never seek the company of a mystic or saint. One who thinks that he is already upright and good, already at the level of the Father, why should he come to me? Those people who know that they are sick, are not whole yet, only they will search for me.

So he says, many people in the world do not seek the Father at all. They say: 'We are upright and noble and highly moral. Why should we seek the Father? Our goodness is enough to take us back to the Father.' They do not bother to go to mystics, but just live and die in their ego.

*But go ye and learn what that meaneth, I will have mercy, and not sacrifice: for I am not come to call the righteous, but sinners to repentance.* (9:13)

Christ says, I have only come for those people who realize that they are sinners and are part and parcel of the creation because they have sinned in past births and are always taking birth along with those sins. They realize that they have a load of karma on their heads and unless they are able to shake off that load, they will never be able to go back to the Father. I have not come for those who are egotistical, who think they are very noble and upright, and think 'Why should we need a mystic?'

But those who realize their weaknesses—that they are slaves of the senses and are being dominated by the mind and are too helpless to travel by themselves, and that they must get rid of their weakness—only they need help. And I have only come for those people, so that they may repent for whatever stands between them and the Father. And the real repentance is meditation. Whatever time we are devoting to meditation, actually we are repenting for the karmas which we have done in past births.

*Then came to him the disciples of John, saying, Why do we and the Pharisees fast oft, but thy disciples fast not?* (9:14)

It seems to have been quite customary among the religious practices of those days that people used to fast. So somebody asked him, even the disciples of John the Baptist and Moses fast, but your disciples do not. Christ gave a beautiful answer:

*Can the children of the bridechamber mourn, as long as the bridegroom is with them?* (9:15)

He says, as long as the father and mother are living, as long as the protecting and guiding hand of their parents is there, why should the children worry at all? When the parents are dead, then the child will weep and cry and mourn. Christ says, as long as I am living and I am a living example for them, their living guidance, why should they foolishly waste their time in fasting and such things? They have much better things to do.

> *Can the children of the bridechamber mourn, as long as the bridegroom is with them? but the days will come, when the bridegroom shall be taken from them, and then shall they fast.* (9:15)

He says, they will also be misguided and tempted to do all these things that you are doing—rituals, ceremonies and austerities, running to the synagogues and churches, reading holy books, and all that sort of thing—when I will not be with them. Then they will claim to be my disciples just as you are claiming to be the disciples of John the Baptist, even though you have never met him. You do not try to understand and live his teachings, and you think that just by fasting in the name of John the Baptist you will be able to go back to the Father.

So he says, why should my disciples fast and waste their time when I am there with them all the time to tell them what to do and what not to do? I can guide them at every step. I have much better things to give them. I have a path for them to tread. I have shown them the real thing. When I am with them to give them something definite and positive, why should they waste their time and worry about superfluous things? But when I leave the scene and go back to the Father and they do not have the real teachings and living guidance with them, then they also may give themselves to rituals and ceremonies and hold on to organizations, to these shells. The essence will be lost.

Then he gives a beautiful parable to explain this:

> *No man putteth a piece of new cloth unto an old garment, for that which is put in to fill it up taketh from the garment, and the rent is made worse.* (9:16)

He says that nobody tries to mend a rotten old tattered cloth by taking a piece from a beautiful new cloth. Whatever you may do with the old cloth, it will still be tattered and torn and remain an old cloth, and you make a big hole in the new cloth. You will only make a bigger hole in the old garment and spoil the piece of new cloth as well. Similarly, he says:

> *Neither do men put new wine into old bottles: else the bottles break, and the wine runneth out, and the bottles perish: but they put new wine into new bottles, and both are preserved.* (9:17)

He says, nobody wastes such precious new wine by putting it into old bottles. They always like to keep such a valuable thing in good containers which will not break, lest the precious wine be lost.

What he means to say is, I am just like new cloth. My disciples do not want to leave me in order to mend old cloth—in order to do these unnecessary rituals. The real devotees and lovers of the Father, when their mystic or Master is with them, do not waste their precious time in useless pursuits. They are always busy in attaching themselves to the Shabd and Nam within themselves.

> *And, behold, a woman, which was diseased with an issue of blood twelve years, came behind him, and touched the hem of his garment:*
> *For she said within herself, If I may but touch his garment, I shall be whole.* (9:20–21)

A lady wanted to touch Christ's garment because she had faith in him, thinking that 'The moment I touch his garment I will become whole.' It means: I will be on the way to becoming whole, to becoming clean.

> *But Jesus turned him about, and when he saw her, he said, Daughter, be of good comfort; thy faith hath made thee whole.* (9:22)

He says, there is nothing in my garment. But your faith that you will become whole at the moment you touch my garment has made you whole. Because you have faith that I have come from the Father, that there is no difference between him and me, and that the moment you touch me you are touching him, and that the moment you touch him, you will become whole—this faith in me which you have developed will make you whole, not just touching my garment.

Unless we have faith in the Master—that he can cure us or save us from worldly temptations and can lead us back to the Father—we do not receive much result in our meditation. Whatever you do, do it with faith that 'If I live in these teachings, if I follow the instructions of my Master and attach myself to the Spirit within myself, then I will become whole.' So we must do our meditation with faith in the Master and in the path. Then only can we be cured.

> *The harvest truly is plenteous, but the labourers are few.* (9:37)

It means that the Lord is always there at the eye centre, giving us his grace with both hands, but the labourers are very few. Very few people are really full with love and devotion for the Father. Very few people really work hard to come back to the eye centre.

If somebody is giving alms at the fourth storey of a building and we are sitting down below, unless we go up, how can we have those alms? So we have to labour in order to go up to get from the Lord what he is anxious to give us. Day and night he is waiting for us to give to us, but we never knock at that door where the grace is being bestowed.

If it is raining day and night but the cup is upside down, not a drop of rain can come into it. The moment you turn the cup upwards, it will be filled with rainwater. So he says that the labourers are very few, but there is no dearth of grace, no dearth of the blessings of the Father.

> *Pray ye therefore the Lord of the harvest, that he will send forth labourers into his harvest.* (9:38)

We must become labourers so that we may be able to collect that harvest. The harvest is always there, but we do not put in the labour that is necessary in order to collect it.

# Questions and Answers

### *"First cast out the beam out of thine own eye"* (7:5)

Q. If during meditation we picture somebody—mainly if we know of some problem or trouble that they are going through—and ask the Lord to put them on the right path, does that help them at all?

A. You mean, if we pray for them?

Q. Yes.

A. It is all right to pray to the Lord to help somebody, but first we must pray to the Lord to help us. When we have helped ourself, then we may ask for help for others. But we ourself need so much help, so much grace and blessings of the Lord to be fit for him that, to be honest with ourself, it is hardly sufficient for our own self. Why worry so much for others? We have sufficient problems of our own—I do not think we are short of them. So we should try to help ourself first. When we have helped ourself, then of course we should try to help others too.

Q. But if we do this, are we taking on karmas, so to speak, if we are—I mean, Master, if we are praying for another person, do we take on karmas?

A. Sometimes we do, because we involve ourself so much in another person's problems that we also start suffering along with him. We get so much obsessed with his problems that we cannot feel free of them. Then of course we are involved. We create a great groove in our mind and we may have to account for all that.

That is why Christ said in the Bible that you do not see the beam in your own eye, but you see the mote in another person's eye. It means that you must remove your own beam first. We think our weaknesses are not known to anybody and we therefore pray for others. That is a sort of self-deception.

Q. In Maharaj Jagat Singh's book, *Science of the Soul,* we read that if a disciple criticizes another, it is a very bad sin. What is the consequence upon a person who criticizes others?

A. Every mystic has been telling us the same thing. Christ also says that you do not see the beam in your own eye, but you see a mote in another person's eye. What Sardar Bahadur Maharaj Ji meant was that instead of criticizing others, we should criticize ourself—what is our weakness that we cannot live with another person? Rather than criticizing him for not cooperating with us, cooperation has to come from us. We have to adjust to a situation; the situation cannot adjust to us. We have to be good to another person and not expect him to be good to us. We always expect others to be good and nice and loving to us, but we never realize that it has to start with us. That is what he means, that it is sinful to criticize anybody unnecessarily and not to look within our own self and find our own faults and try to remove them.

Q. Maharaj Ji, speaking about discrimination, it seems to me that there is a fine line between being too critical of a situation or a person and having to use understanding of that person or situation, and I would like to know just where that fine line is. How should we discriminate in these cases—between becoming critical of a person and trying to understand?

A. There are two types of criticism—constructive and destructive. Constructive criticism is all right. It is to help another person to improve. Destructive criticism is to run down another person. You can understand the difference. And the same thing can be said in different words. If you have the intention to make constructive criticism, then you can put it in a much better way, in a pleasant and loving way, because you want to improve the situation. You do not want to give vent to your ego, thinking that you are superior and another person is inferior, and wanting to run him down in the eyes of others. That is destructive criticism, which is wrong. So it depends upon our approach. Sometimes, we are so near to some people that we do not like to see them going wrong. Our intention is not to humiliate them before others but to improve them because we love them so much. So then we give them practical suggestions for improvement. When we want them to improve, it means that we have love for them, whereas in destructive criticism there is hatred.

Q. Should we always try and hold the truth in our minds when we make any criticism?

A. Well, brother, I do not say that we should compromise with the truth, but there is a way of putting it to another person. If we want to hold the truth in mind, and our object is that the other person should also see that truth as we are seeing it, then our approach should be of love, of helping him to come to that level. But if we are trying to use the truth just in order to humiliate him, then we are not really trying to hold the truth in mind. Then the ego is coming in, we think we are superior, and we are only using the truth to humiliate him. That approach is not right.

Q. Better say nothing at all?

A. It depends upon the situation. Sometimes silence is golden. Most of our problems in this creation are due to our tongue! If we were to know how to hold it or use it, I think we would have solved most of our problems. Control is something very good, and to use it rightly is better still. If we cannot use it rightly, at least we should try to control it.

Q. Master, there is a saying, 'The truth hurts.' You can often hurt another man's feelings by telling him something that is contrary to his way of life or against what he believes.

A. It depends upon your approach—how and with what intention you are trying to reach him, with what motive you are trying to give the truth to him. You can say the same thing either with the intention of hurting him or of making him understand, and he may appreciate and love you more for that.

Q. Maharaj Ji, there was a play acted on the stage, I suppose it must have been fifteen years ago, called *The Truth, the Whole Truth and Nothing but the Truth.* And the object of the play was to point out that human beings are incapable of living together and telling the truth the whole time. In any case, in this play the whole cast started to tell the whole truth twenty-four hours, and in the end there were divorce cases, cases for defamation of character and so on.

A. You are perfectly right. There was a one-eyed king, Maharaja Ranjit Singh, who used to hold open court or durbar, and somebody said: 'If, in durbar, anybody were to tell him that he is a one-eyed man, we would think him very brave.'

Then a man who, as you said, was very truthful, and brave too, went straight to the court and said, 'You are a one-eyed man', and naturally the king was very cross. The man had not said anything that was a lie, but naturally how could the king bear to be told before all the courtiers that he was a one-eyed man?

Then another man went with the same object and said, 'Look at the grace of God: however mighty these people may be, even they, with two eyes, are bowing at your feet!' He said the same thing and was given a reward; the other person was put in prison! And both spoke the truth. So it depends on your approach, how you say a thing. It does not always pay to speak out the blunt truth.

### *"Beware of false prophets" (7:15)*

Q. Maharaj Ji, would you explain the verse in *Saint Matthew* here which is often quoted by people as being against living Masters. It is the verse which says: "Beware of false prophets, which come to you in sheep's clothing, but inwardly they are ravening wolves."

A. Actually Christ said at that time to his disciples that many people may profess that they are prophets and may try to misguide you and deflect you from the path, but do not listen to them at all. I have given you the right path. I am the right Master for you, to take you back to the Father. Many people may even try to imitate me, to give the same type of teaching which I am giving. That is what he means by imitating Christ. But he says, do not pay any heed to these pseudo-masters, because you are my allotted sheep, you are marked for me. Whatever you are to get, you will get from me, so you should always be careful and not be misled by these people. That is what he is trying to brief his disciples about.

But people generally give the interpretation that after Christ many saints will come but they should not listen to them because they will all be false prophets. It does not mean that. He is warning them against pseudo-masters who are always present in the world.

### *"See thou tell no man" (8:4)*

Q. I was under the impression that Masters do not perform miracles. Didn't Jesus perform miracles?

A. Well, sister, Masters do not come to perform miracles, neither do they intend to perform any miracles; but, as you know, they are very kind and gentle, and miracles do happen in their lifetime. If you read the Bible, you will find that Christ also said 'Go and tell no man'—do not tell anybody at all about these miracles. And so much so that he even said to go to the synagogue and give an offering to the rabbis and tell them that it is through them that you were healed *(8:4)*, because saints do not want to publicize those miracles at all. They do happen here and there, but that is not their main purpose for coming to this world. Neither do they encourage people to perform miracles. They want us to digest our spiritual progress and spiritual development within ourselves. The more we digest, the more grace of the Lord we receive. If we waste it in performing miracles, then our whole labour is lost unnecessarily.

That is why Christ said to the sincere seekers that you have been attracted to me and are following me not because you have seen these miracles, but because you are real seekers. You have been filled with the 'bread' which I have given you *(John 6:26).*

Christ did perform some miracles, I do not deny that, but not as many as are generally attributed to him. It is said that he raised the dead; but to him 'dead' means something different. He does not mean physically dead, but spiritually dead—just living for the world and dead to the Father. So he put life in them. When he filled them with love and devotion for the Lord, they became alive as far as the Father is concerned. So generally we misinterpret these things and just link them with the miracles that he performed.

Also, when you read *Saint Matthew*, it says that Christ's fame spread to other countries—Syria and Jordan and many other places. On hearing about him, people were attracted by his miracles and they all came to him. But making use of their gathering there, he gave them the Sermon on the Mount. It says: Seeing the multitudes, he climbed a hill and gave them a sermon *(5:1–2).* That was his main purpose—to give them the teachings, not just to perform a few miracles. But probably that was the only way to collect the crowds then, because people generally come to saints only to see miracles.

The majority of people run after a saint just for the miracles' sake; very few are real seekers who just go to him for the sake of love and devotion for the Father. Otherwise we always have some desires or something in us which we crave and want, and we run after the saints for that purpose. But saints sometimes grant such things just to keep us on the path; and ultimately they detach us from all those things and fill us with love and devotion for the Father. That is their main purpose for coming.

> Q. Maharaj Ji, if one of the boons that the Lord gave to Kal is that saints will not perform miracles, does it mean that Masters have to pay for the miracles they perform?

A. Yes, they have to pay for the miracles they perform. The Master stands as a ransom for the souls which he takes out of the realm of Kal. The ransom is that whatever is due to Caesar must be paid to Caesar *(22:21)*, whether the Master pays through his own body or he makes the disciple pay. So if saints want to perform miracles, they have to pay for them through their body, they have to share the karma. When they share the burden and karma of their disciples, if the disciple is weak and cannot pay, they have to pay for it, definitely.

But generally, there are hardly one or two instances in a saint's life where so-called miracles are performed. Generally they do not perform them because they like to live in the will of the Lord. Miracles come when the lower mind comes in, and at every step Christ says that I have merged my mind into the will of the Lord, I have no will of my own; I do not do anything for my own fame or glory *(John 8:50)*. One who performs miracles does it for his own fame. But Christ says that I do what my Father wants me to do; I am happy to live in his will *(John 4:34)*. So when living in the will of the Father, the question of miracles does not arise. The Lord can do whatever he feels like, and saints are happy to live in his will.

What greater miracle can come in a disciple's life than that his whole attitude towards life is changed? What greater miracle can there be than that? He becomes blind to the world and opens his eyes towards his home. He gets life! When at first he was dead, now he is living; what better miracle can there be than that? People who were running after worldly pursuits and worldly things and desires, now they do not want to look at them or see them, they have no time to even talk about them. Day and night they are filled with love and devotion for the Father, and now they are running after the Father in the same manner and with the same zeal. Where other people weep and cry and lament, they become contented. Not the slightest sign of sorrow comes to their face when a loved one departs or dies, where other people may even commit suicide if any relation or friend of theirs dies.

So that is the miracle which comes into every man's life when he comes to the path. And there are some other times also, just to convince the disciple that he should remain on the path and be on the path, that they do a miracle. But when such a thing happens in a disciple's life, he should not broadcast it; he has to digest all those things within himself, because that is a personal experience he is getting. That is a personal miracle for him, a personal grace from the Master, or from the Lord, for himself.

Q. It is not quite clear to me how it is that spiritual healing is not appreciated in Sant Mat.

A. If you are praying to the Lord to set another person right or to cure another person, you are creating a karmic link—a desire or a wish in your mind that he should be cured. He is to be cured according to his karmas, and if the person is not cured, you become so much attached to him by praying for him day and night that you cannot bear to see him sick; you want him to be cured. So you create a mental association with the person and you want to use your own spiritual power to cure him. And whenever you use your own spiritual power, it is always at your own cost.

Spiritual power is acquired after very hard effort and much sacrifice, and it is meant only to take us out of this creation, back to God. When we use this power for material advantages—even for the good of others, like healing them—we lose this power and our main purpose of life suffers. The more we keep this wealth to ourselves by using it for our inner spiritual progress, the more the Lord gives us to make further progress.

Even if we have no spiritual power, whenever there is a desire, there is always attachment because we want that desire to be fulfilled, and that can bring us back to this world. That is not living in the will of the Father; it is living in the will of the mind, which is not good for our spiritual progress.

Q. But then, the healing which was performed by Jesus Christ, was that not spiritual healing?

A. That was spiritual healing, but he had much spiritual wealth. He could give it to anybody—there would be no deficiency in that. If a millionaire gives two thousand rupees to somebody, there is no deficiency in his treasure. But a person who has only two thousand rupees in his pocket and gives all of it becomes a pauper.

The healing by Christ was something very different. Those were miracles that he performed and there was a purpose behind them: perhaps to attract some seekers so that they would give their attention to what he wanted to say. People are so selfish in this world that they do not like to listen to you unless they are convinced that you can give them some material benefit. They are never attracted just by the simple teachings. But the purpose of Christ was not to show miracles or juggling tricks. When he gave the Sermon on the Mount, he never performed any miracles or tried to impress people with them. He just gave them the simple teachings. That was the purpose of those miracles, not to heal people. Otherwise he could have healed everybody. But still there were lame, blind, and diseased ones; he healed very few, actually.

And those few miracles always happen in every saint's lifetime. What happened in Christ's lifetime was nothing new. That came into the limelight without his consent. Miracles of other saints may not have come into the limelight, because no saint wants to advertise them. Their purpose is to give faith to people, to give them the teachings, to reach their heart and fill them with love and devotion for the Father. Their purpose is nothing different from that.

> Q. But that in itself is spiritual healing—to bring real knowledge in people's hearts.

A. That is different, that is not physical healing. We are all sick in this world, and in that sense saints always spiritually heal us. It is a spiritual healing of the soul, not of the body. They come to heal our soul which is diseased, which is sick, which is lame. But outside also, sometimes they do perform miracles; or because they are so gentle and kind, these happen in their lifetime. But their main purpose for coming to this world is not to spiritually heal people of physical diseases.

But regarding these mediums and spiritual healers, their main purpose is to heal people's mental and physical ailments.

You can only help another person if you have helped yourself. If you are not able to help yourself, you cannot help another person. So those healers have not helped themselves spiritually yet and whatever little power they have, they use it to try to heal people—and it is always at their own cost.

### *"Let the dead bury their dead"* (8:22)

> Q. Maharaj Ji, in the passage from the Bible where Christ said to the disciple whose father had died, "Let the dead bury their dead", you mentioned that he should have nothing to do with worrying about his—

A. He said, 'Master, I want to follow you', and at the same time his heart was with the dead, thinking 'Let me bury him.' So Christ said, 'If you are thinking so much about dead people, how can you follow me? Let them do the burying. Do not waste a moment if you wish to follow me.' Saints only try to find excuses to give us certain teachings. We should not try to analyse such things and think, 'He stopped him from doing his worldly duty.'

To another person he gave this advice: If you want to follow me, you should be prepared to follow me, because there may be many hardships in the way. Even the foxes have holes and the birds have nests to rest in at night, but you will have no such place, because love and devotion for the Father may consume you day and night and you may not even get sleep. So it is not so easy to follow me *(8:20)*. He is explaining it to him so that the next day he should not think of another worldly problem. He tells him that the path is not as easy as he thinks. He is just explaining the teachings to him with one excuse or another.

And to this disciple he said that if you are so much attached even to the dead, how much more will you be attached to the living? So how can you follow me? Not that he had not to do his duty; he had to do it.

## FOUR

# Discourse on Matthew 10

After the Sermon on the Mount, when Christ had gathered a few disciples, he beautifully briefed them to go to the masses, to the villages, to share and explain the teachings to people in the same way that we hold discourses or satsangs here:

> *These twelve Jesus sent forth, and commanded them, saying, Go not into the way of Gentiles, and into any city of the Samaritans enter ye not:*
> *But go rather to the lost sheep of the house of Israel.*
> *(10:5–6)*

By 'lost sheep' he means marked souls, but ones who are lost in rituals and ceremonies and do not know the real path. But they are marked, so they are sincere seekers. They want to go back to the Father and are very honest and sincere in what they do to reach him, but they do not know which path to follow. He says, go and approach only those people and do not run after other people.

> *And as ye go, preach, saying, The kingdom of heaven is at hand. (10:7)*

He says, the first thing which you have to impress upon a real seeker is that he cannot find the Father in synagogues, in churches or anywhere outside. He has to seek the Lord within, in his own body. That is the first thing which any saint will teach.

> *Heal the sick, cleanse the lepers, raise the dead, cast out devils: freely ye have received, freely give.* (10:8)

The healing of the sick and raising of the dead and such things referred to here are not outside miracles. They are all spiritual miracles. *"Heal the sick"* means that we are all sick—because, while God has given us this opportunity as a human of being with him, we have given ourselves to the senses. The Lord has given us such a healthy body, but day and night, being slaves of the senses, we are crying and weeping and have invited all sorts of sickness, worries and miseries upon ourselves. So he says, you must *"heal the sick"*—you must help them to give up all their sensual pleasures.

And by *"cleanse the lepers"*, he means that we have all become lepers because we have made this body absolutely diseased; it is smelly, emitting a bad odour. We make such beautiful houses of prayer for the Father—such beautiful synagogues and churches and mosques, because we think that the Father is going to live in them. But the Lord has made a much more beautiful house for himself to live in, and we have made it absolutely dirty by putting wine and meat in it and by becoming a slave of the senses. As a result, this whole body has become like that of a leper. So he says, help those people to clean their body, help them to make this body a place that the Lord will find worth living in.

And then he says: *"Raise the dead."* We are all dead because we see only the world and not the Lord. So we are dead as far as the Father is concerned and living as far as the world is concerned. That is why he says: *"Raise the dead."* Put life into inert souls. Make them live again. Fill the worldly people with love and devotion for the Lord; then only will they be living. And *"cast out devils."* The devil, the negative power, the mind, has taken control of them. They are day and night being tempted by this devil. Help them to get rid of and save themselves from those temptations.

He says: *"Freely ye have received, freely give."* I have not charged you anything for these beautiful teachings, for putting you on the path. So if you also want them to go back to the Father, do not sell my teachings because you are preaching to them and helping them. Do not commercialize my teachings.

> *Provide neither gold, nor silver, nor brass in your purses.* (10:9)

Never take a single penny from anybody in return for the teachings. You should accept nothing in exchange for these teachings which you give to people.

> *Nor scrip for your journey, neither two coats, neither shoes, nor yet staves: for the workman is worthy of his meat.* (10:10)

You have to give only the teachings to them. You must not charge them anything in any way. You must not justify your accepting anything from them in any way.

> *And into whatsoever city or town ye shall enter, enquire who in it is worthy; and there abide till ye go thence.* (10:11)

It means that whenever you go to any village or city, always find out if there is any real seeker, which he calls the 'worthy' one. He means those who are sincere within themselves, but lost in rituals and ceremonies.

Do not try to convert and feel how many people you have converted. There is no question of numbers at all. Try to contact only the worthy souls. Do not unnecessarily argue with those people who are very orthodox and stick to their own position and are always willing to argue, quarrel and fight in the name of religion. He says, avoid those people. There is no need to waste your time on them.

*And when ye come into an house, salute it. (10:12)*

He says, when you approach the people who are living in a house, you should always show them respect and be humble. Do not try to give them the impression that you are superior to them and are full with love and devotion for the Father and possess all the spiritual knowledge, and that they are ignorant; that they are blind and you have opened their eyes. So always meet every seeker with humility, with love, with devotion. Think that the Lord's grace is with you and you are only trying to help him. You have to become a living example to those people—that you have so much within you, but even so you are humble.

*And if the house be worthy, let your peace come upon it. (10:13)*

If you think that they are real seekers, then share your peace with them. You have obtained peace within yourself by following this path, by meditation. You are contented because you are attached to the Shabd and Nam. So radiate peace to them. Fill them also with love and devotion for meditation. Make them realize the necessity for meditation, so that they also may share in that peace which you have. You must make them just like yourself.

> *But if it be not worthy, let your peace return to you.* (10:13)

If you find that the man is not prepared to listen to you, is not interested in sharing your peace or bliss, he says, do not offend him. Do not lose patience or your peace of mind. Very calmly, lovingly and affectionately try to explain to him, and if he is not interested in listening to you, do not feel offended. Do not feel angry or cross with him and think 'He never even thanked me for coming all the way to his house only to help him.' He says, do not have any such feeling. Return with the same peaceful feeling that you went to him with.

> *And whosoever shall not receive you, nor hear your words, when ye depart out of that house or city, shake off the dust of your feet.* (10:14)

Christ says that if the man has not responded to your teaching, was not attentive to what you wanted to say to him, do not mind if he is not willing to share that happiness you are carrying and do not have any grudge or grievance against him. The Lord knows best. You have done your duty. Just forget about it.

> *Behold, I send you forth as sheep in the midst of wolves: be ye therefore wise as serpents, and harmless as doves.* (10:16)

He says, I am sending you to the 'wolves'—those people who have taken up an orthodox position, who have closed minds, who do not want to hear about anything else at all. Whatever rituals or ceremonies they are doing, they do not want to leave them. They are like wolves—adamant, stubborn and hard-boiled. You are just like sheep—humble and gentle. They have authority and intellect and can be violent with you. If you try to share these beautiful teachings with the people, they will just come upon you like wolves because what they do is their business and commerce. They are exploiting people. So they will not tolerate your putting them on the path.

*"Be ye therefore wise as serpents."* I advise you to be intelligent, be wise like a serpent. A snake will not attack unless it feels that it is going to be attacked. It means that the moment you find that a man is not interested or wants to argue with you or harm you, just avoid the situation. But be *"harmless as doves"*. Do not be harmful like a serpent, be harmless like a dove. A dove can do no harm to anybody, it is such a gentle bird.

So what Christ means to say is that you are evolved souls, you are going to give the teachings to the seekers. But if they do not listen to you, do not feel annoyed and start cursing and abusing them. 'Be wise like a serpent, but harmless like a dove.' You should just be innocent, but wise enough to get out of the situation. Do not unnecessarily create trouble for yourself.

> *But beware of men: for they will deliver you up to the councils, and they will scourge you in their synagogues; And ye shall be brought before governors and kings for my sake, for a testimony against them and the Gentiles.* (10:17–18)

He says, naturally people who are at the helm of the organized religions cannot tolerate their clientele slipping away from them and that people should not listen to them any more. They are concerned only with their prestige and with their money. So for filling people with love and devotion for the Father, for telling them the right path, you may be persecuted or taken to the governors and kings for punishment and you may be sent to jail. Do not think that a red carpet will be spread before you. You may have to face all sorts of hardships in order to reach people's hearts and share these teachings with them. So you should all be prepared for that.

> *But when they deliver you up, take no thought how or what ye shall speak: for it shall be given you in that same hour what ye shall speak.* (10:19)

He says, even if you have to appear before a king or a court and are charged with corrupting or misleading people, do not feel frightened. Do not try to prepare your defence, to put your mind into it and think, 'I will give this answer to this question and that answer to that question.' Do not let your mind interfere at all. Have faith in the Lord, because he is sending you to that person and he will himself make you say what he wants you to say. Give yourself to the Father.

*"It shall be given to you in that same hour what ye shall speak."* He says, the Lord will help you because you have only tried to create love and devotion for the Lord in their hearts. So the Master will always be there to help you at that time, and whatever he wants you to say, those words will automatically come out of you. Just think about your Master. Just keep your attention in that audible life stream, the sound current within

yourself, and then whatever explanation comes to you at that hour, just give that explanation.

> *For it is not ye that speak, but the Spirit of your Father which speaketh in you.* (10:20)

He says, at that time *you* will not be speaking. It is the spirit of the Father that will speak in you. Let the Shabd, that divine guidance which is with you and always part and parcel of you, let him guide you. Let the voice of God say whatever it wants to say through you. You should not let your mind prepare any defence for yourself. Just depend upon the grace of the Master.

> *And the brother shall deliver up the brother to death, and the father the child: and the children shall rise up against their parents, and cause them to be put to death.*
> *And ye shall be hated of all men for my name's sake: but he that endureth to the end shall be saved.*
> (10:21–22)

He says, people will despise you and hate you. They will not like you, because you do not belong to them—you belong to God. God loves you, the Master loves you, so why worry about the love and respect of the people? You are not meant for them, you are meant for the Father, for the Master.

If you are able to face all these hardships at their hands in the name of the Father, what will be your reward? *"He that endureth to the end shall be saved."* You will be saved from all the worries and miseries of the world, from birth and death, and from coming back to this world again.

*But when they persecute you in this city, flee ye into another: for verily I say unto you, Ye shall not have gone over the cities of Israel, till the Son of man be come.* (10:23)

He says, if anybody is not prepared to give you a hearing, do not try to force the teachings on him. Leave that city and go to another. Do not quarrel and fight with them. Do not make it a personal cause and feel disheartened. Do not have that attitude at all. Hurry away from that city to another and do not worry about anything.

*The disciple is not above his master, nor the servant above his lord.* (10:24)

He says, when these people can persecute and hurt me, you should not expect any better treatment from them. You will also have to face the same thing at their hands. You are not greater than I. When they do not spare me, how can they spare you?

*Fear them not therefore: for there is nothing covered, that shall not be revealed; and hid, that shall not be known.* (10:26)

He says, do not worry about or be afraid of anything at all, because there is nothing which is hidden. You are only playing the part that is in your destiny. Everything is already laid out for you; you are only doing what you are meant to do. If you have to face persecution, it is already written there, so face it boldly and cheerfully.

> *What I tell you in darkness, that speak ye in light: and what ye hear in the ear, that preach ye upon the housetops.* (10:27)

He says, I am explaining all these things to you in darkness, meaning in such a small group. But you should be bold enough to explain everything openly. Do not feel humiliated before the world, thinking 'What will my father or my brother or my friends and relatives say if I follow this path or the Master? They will think: he is not a Christian any more, he is not a Sikh any more, he is running away from the traditional family religion.' Do not feel frightened by anybody at all. If you feel convinced about these teachings, do not try to conceal them, or feel ashamed or shy to admit that you follow them. You should be bold enough to say: 'This is my conviction. I am following and believe in this path. He is my Master and this is the way in which I worship God.'

> *And fear not them which kill the body, but are not able to kill the soul: but rather fear him which is able to destroy both soul and body in hell.* (10:28)

He says, at the most what can they do? They can kill your body but not your soul, and my teaching is meant for your soul. You should be more concerned with the soul than with the body. Ultimately, everybody has to leave the body. If you are not dead today, you will be dead some day. So why worry? Try to save your soul, not so much the body.

He continues: Fear Satan, because he can destroy the body, no doubt, but he can also put your soul in hell. If you do not follow and live this path, you may have to be sentenced to hell. In any case, some day you will have to leave the body. But now if you leave the body or they deprive you of it, your soul will go to heaven. Otherwise, even if you live another ten years in this world, you may have to be cast into hell. So he says, fear the devil, your own mind, not the worldly people.

How can the Father 'destroy the soul'? The soul is eternal and can never be destroyed. It means that the soul may have to go back to the lower species and take birth in the form of an animal or an insect or a plant. So try to be bold and do not worry about public criticism and public opinion. You yourself should be free and be convinced and happy with your teachings.

> *Are not two sparrows sold for a farthing? and one of them shall not fall on the ground without your Father.* (10:29)

It means that everything is destined. He gives a very beautiful example:

> *But the very hairs of your head are all numbered.* (10:30)

He says, what to say of all these things, every little thing is destined in this world. Even the seemingly worthless sparrows are looked after by the Father, and the hairs that we have on our body are numbered. If such little details are destined, then no harm can come to you without his will. Do you think you can be easily killed or deprived of this body? Nobody can touch you if the Father does not want it. You cannot leave this world even a moment before the time which the Father has fixed for you. So why worry about these people and be afraid of giving them these true teachings? Whatever has to happen has already been planned. Nothing happens without the will of the Father. So become fearless and steadfast in your faith.

> *Whosoever therefore shall confess me before men, him will I confess also before my Father which is in heaven.* (10:32)

If you publicly admit and proclaim before people that I am your Master and you are my disciple, if you are proud of me and proud to be my disciple, I will openly own you before my Father: This sheep belongs to me, and I have brought this soul into your lap.

> *But whosoever shall deny me before men, him will I also deny before my Father which is in heaven.* (10:33)

If they are shy to accept me as their Master here in this world, Christ says, I will also deny that I ever knew them in this world. And unless I accept them in this world, my Father is not going to accept them. So it depends upon me. If they do not accept me here, I am not going to accept them in heaven. If they accept me here, I will accept them in heaven. Then he says:

> *Think not that I am come to send peace on earth.* (10:34)

In the beginning, when he started giving the sermon, he said "Blessed are the peacemakers" *(5:9)*, and now it seems absolutely contradictory when he says 'I am not come to send peace on the earth.' But it is not so. What is meant is, do not think that mystics come to reform this world or to make it a paradise. There has never been peace in this world, nor can there ever be. The Lord's creation is such that there will always be conflict—nation against nation, country against country, men against men, brother against brother—we are always at war with one another. The world has to remain imperfect if it is to exist. The moment we become perfect, we merge back into the perfect Being.

*I came not to send peace, but a sword.* (10:34)

I have come with a sword, not to create peace. You are so much attached here and have such deep roots in this earth that I have come with a sharp-edged weapon, with a sword, to cut all those roots, to set you free, and then to take you to the Father. And the sword is that of the Shabd, the voice of God. I have come to take you out of this world forever so that you may not have to be born in it again. Then he explains it in a little more detail:

*For I am come to set a man at variance against his father, and the daughter against her mother, and the daughter in law against her mother in law.*
(10:35)

What he means is, we are all attached to one another. A father is attached to the son, a mother to the daughter, a daughter-in-law to the mother-in-law, and he says: *"I am come to set a man at variance against his father"*, and so on. I want you to detach yourself from these worldly relationships. I have come to detach you from one another, from all your relations and friends and all your loves of the world. That is my main purpose in coming to this world.

*And a man's foes shall be they of his own household.*
*(10:36)*

He says, who is our enemy? Our own relations, the members of our household, are our foes because they keep us so much absorbed in their own love and affection that they have even made us forget the Lord. They have become an obstruction in our main purpose for coming to this world. They always keep our whole attention towards themselves and never even give us time to think about the Lord. Therefore our own family people to whom we are attached, however much they may love us, are not our friends; they are our enemies.

Our friend is one who always thinks about our betterment. Christ means that the Master is your friend because he wants you to detach yourself from everybody, wants to take you back to the Father. And he who is holding us back from the Father is our worst enemy. Soami Ji* calls these relations 'beloved thugs' because they deprive you of everything and are so sweet in their ways that they do not even let you know of what they have deprived you. They deprive you of the main opportunity of seeking God which you have when you come into this world as a human. Similarly, Christ says, you have no real relationships in this world—they are all karmic. So do not get attached to them and forget the real purpose of your coming.

In this life we need relatives and friends but we do not really belong to anyone, nor does anyone belong to us. It is self-deception to think that someone belongs to me or I belong to someone. In everybody's life a time comes when one realizes that one is really alone and no one belongs to him. Actually

* Seth Shiv Dayal Singh of Agra, a nineteenth-century Master who taught the path of Shabd or Word.

that is his grace. But for that, no one would turn to the Father—the one to whom we actually belong.

> *He that loveth father or mother more than me is not worthy of me: and he that loveth son or daughter more than me is not worthy of me.* (10:37)

He says, if you are strongly attached to your parents, your sisters, brothers, other relatives and friends, then you cannot come to me because you go where your heart is. If your heart is in those relations, you will always remain part and parcel of them, you will go to them, where they are. Wherever they take birth, you will also take birth along with them. If your heart is in me, that attachment to me will be able to pull you away from everything, just as you can easily remove a knife from soft butter.

The Master fills us with his love and devotion. And that attachment to the Master can be created only when both the Master and the disciple are in the physical body. And this can pull the disciple away from all the attachments of the world and take the soul back to the Father. That is what Christ is trying to impress upon us.

> *And he that taketh not his cross, and followeth after me, is not worthy of me.* (10:38)

Those who attach themselves to the Shabd and Nam, who withdraw their consciousness from the nine apertures of the body back to the eye centre, 'taking the cross of Christ', only they are worthy of me. Those whose consciousness is below the eye centre and are attached to the world are not taking the cross. They are not worthy of me, not fit to become one with me, to merge into me. Unless we become one with the Master, we cannot become one with the Father.

Our forehead is like this. [Here the Master showed how a horizontal line across the eyebrows and a vertical line from the forehead down the bridge of the nose form a cross, with the intersection at the eye centre.] So you see, we have to withdraw back to this point.

> *He that findeth his life shall lose it: and he that loseth his life for my sake shall find it.* (10:39)

*"He that findeth his life shall lose it"* means that he who has given himself to sensual pleasures, to worldly loves and attachments, is losing the golden opportunity of being in this human flesh, of going back to the Father. *"And he that loseth his life for my sake shall find it"* means that he who is sacrificing all these things and abstaining from them and lives only for me, is gaining everlasting life. He is not losing anything.

> *He that receiveth you receiveth me, and he that receiveth me receiveth him that sent me.* (10:40)

He says, because *I* am sending you to give this teaching to the masses, to the public, if anybody hears you and accepts what you teach, he is not hearing you, but me. Because after hearing you he will come to me, and when he comes to me he will come back to the Father. So through you they come to me, and through me they go back to the Father.

> *He that receiveth a prophet in the name of a prophet shall receive a prophet's reward; and he that receiveth a righteous man in the name of a righteous man shall receive a righteous man's reward.* (10:41)

Those who go to a saint and take him as the incarnation of the Father, as a real saint or prophet, will get a prophet's reward, and that is—to go back to the Father. Those who only think that he is a very good person, a righteous and noble person, will only get a righteous man's reward. At the most they will benefit from having been able to appreciate a gentleman, a noble soul, a good person. But we have to get *"a prophet's reward"*. And that we can only get when we have full faith in the saint that he is an incarnation of the Father, that he has come from the Father to guide us on the path and will be able to take us back to him. Therefore, it depends upon how we look in that glass. A saint is just a mirror, and it depends upon us how we look at him. We benefit according to the attitude or intention with which we go to him.

> *And whosoever shall give to drink unto one of these little ones a cup of cold water only in the name of a disciple, verily I say unto you, he shall in no wise lose his reward.* (10:42)

He says, those people who show even a little respect to you, give a little of their time to you and serve you with an ordinary thing such as a cup of fresh water—even for doing that small amount for you, they will also get their reward. The Father will help them also and shower his grace on such people because they were considerate to you—they at least showed their respect for you. Because in my Father's house not a single thing goes unrewarded; everything is rewarded.

And then, this also means that if you put a lost sheep on the right track, if anybody is a slave to sensual pleasures and you with love and affection are able to help him to shed those weaknesses and put him on the right path, you will definitely get its reward. So he says that whosoever receives you, ultimately will be receiving me.

## QUESTIONS AND ANSWERS

### *"Be ye therefore wise as serpents, and harmless as doves" (10:16)*

Q. Lao Tsu, the Chinese sage, said that the ideal man is strong like a lion, gentle like a woman, and simple like a child. Is this not quite perfectly in line with Sant Mat?

A. It is the same thing. Christ also said when he briefed his apostles to go out and spread his teachings that you should be harmless like a dove and shrewd like a snake. He also used the same words. You have to be intelligent and shrewd so that nobody may deceive you. When a snake hears any sound or fears an attack from any side, it always crawls away. So he says that you have to be shrewd like a snake and tactfully avoid any ugly situation. Every wise man has said the same thing.

### *"But the very hairs of your head are all numbered" (10:30)*

Q. I am still not too clear about free will. I wonder if you would mind going through that again?

A. I have often said that from a higher point of view, there is no free will. As Christ said, even the hairs on your head are numbered. When so much detail is prearranged already, when even your hair is numbered or destined, then practically there is no free will. But we have conditioned free will—within our own circumstances. If we also include the environment in which we have been brought up, the way in which we have been moulded to think, then we have absolutely no free will. But if we eliminate our background, our environment, our education and circumstances, then we can say that we have free will—a conditioned, limited free will.

It is not in our hands to select our parents, and most of our characteristics—our way of thinking—we inherit from our parentage. Then our education and our environment also influence and mould our way of thinking, and we act accordingly—according to our heritage, according to the influences in which we have been brought up. If you eliminate all that, you can say that you have free will. If you also include that, then you have no free will in the way that you are acting and thinking now.

You have often seen people playing chess. The first move is free will, then every other move is conditioned by the first and subsequent moves. The player has no option. So, firstly, we are not part of this creation by our own free will. We were part and parcel of the Father, the Lord. We were in the Creator and he projected himself—and we are here and he is still there where he was. It is not our will that we are away from him. To begin with we had no free will, otherwise we would not have come here at all. And having come here, we have gathered so much dirt in this world of illusion that we all act accordingly now. In whatever way we may act or think today, we cannot eliminate our past.

That is why Guru Nanak says: "Even a leaf does not move without his order"—even that leaf has no free will. It moves according to his orders, not by its own self. Christ has similarly said that even every hair on the head is numbered; our destiny is fixed in such detail. So when we have no option even in having more or less hair on the body, what free will can we have?

It is very hard to digest this thing, that having got so much education and having developed so much intellect, yet we are not free, yet we are slaves of our background. But it is a hard fact we must swallow, that we have no free will and still we are responsible for our actions.

Guru Nanak said: "Whoever you want to remain misguided and in this illusion will always remain misguided in this world. Whoever you want to meet you, he will search for you." Where is the free will? Then Guru Nanak says: "Whatever he does, he does of himself"—he does not consult us at all. We have no free will, we are all puppets in his hand. All we can do is to realize that we are puppets in his hand, but the ego is so much there within us that we do not realize this. We think, '*I* am dancing. *I* do this thing. Who can make me dance? Who can make me do this? *I* did it.' But we forget the string behind the curtain—there is somebody who is pulling our strings and we are dancing according to those tunes.

Our karmas are the strings and the Lord does the pulling. According to our karmas we act, we behave, we meet, and we weep. Where is the free will? We can only have free will if we absolutely eliminate the karma theory. As long as the force of karma is at the back to make us do certain things, where is the free will? Practically speaking, we have no free will, while at the same time we cannot use that as an excuse to justify our weaknesses. We should use our intelligence and act as if we had free will, but leave the results in the hands of the Lord.

### *"I came not to send peace, but a sword" (10:34–36)*

Q. Master, it seems to me that we sometimes really suffer from our attachments.

A. That is right. We know that we suffer, but still we do not want to get rid of that suffering. For example, if we have to face much hardship from our husband or wife, or we are unhappy with our children—they do not obey us or they are ill—would we like to get rid of them? We would not like to be separated from them even then. We may be day and night crying because they are upsetting us—perhaps our son does not obey us—but our love and attachment to the child is so much that we cannot get rid of it and are still worrying about him. We are suffering, we are crying, but we do not want to give up these attachments.

Even a pig, in the lower species, who is always feeding on filth and that kind of thing and is suffering in that life—but if anybody were to ask him, 'Would you like to be killed in order to get a better birth? Let me shoot you', he would not like it. We may be ill and not even able to get up, but if anybody tells us, 'You will get a birth as a better human, with better facilities, so let me put you to sleep', we would not allow him to deprive us of our life.

We are suffering in this world. We cry, no doubt, but we are so much attached to our sufferings that we do not want to get rid of them. We get hurt so much in our attachment to one another. Yet we cannot leave them and want to be with them, to possess them, to own them, and to be possessed by them. We get so hurt; we cry for them and are day and night unhappy. But we do not want to get rid of those sufferings because we are so much involved and possessed by them.

Saints realize that we are very much attached to our suffering, so they help us and make us realize that we are suffering, that we should try to get rid of it, detach ourselves from it and get peace and bliss within ourself. As Christ said: 'I have come with a sword. I have not come to create peace in this world'. The purpose of a sword is to cut. I have come to cut your bondages to this world forever, not to make it a paradise for you. He says: I have come to set a father against a son, a man against his wife, a daughter against her mother—just to detach you from each other.

Q. But what about our duty in this world?

A. We have to discharge our responsibilities. We do not say that we have to run away from them, but that does not mean that we are not suffering within our surroundings. We are suffering.

Q. We suffer in love, too.

A. Yes, this love only makes us suffer. We would never suffer at all without love. These attachments make us suffer. If we did not have them, we would not suffer. If my child is sick, I do not sleep all night. If my neighbour's child is sick, I do not bother about it—I just switch off my light and sleep. I am attached to my child, not to my neighbour's child. Where I am not attached, I just take a detached view of it; but where I am involved, I suffer.

That is why saints say that you cannot make this place a paradise. Suffering is prevalent here. So they always advise us to detach ourselves from this world. They know, and we also realize it, but they know it more clearly—that we suffer but do not want to leave that suffering. However, they want us to leave this suffering and the suffering world.

Q. Like Buddha said?

A. Every mystic will say the same thing. Suffering is there because the inclination of the soul is towards its own origin. And unless we allow our soul to go back to its own source, it can never be happy. Howsoever rich you may be, whatever material things you may possess, whatever worldly love you may have—in spite of everything you have in this world, you are lonely. You cannot get rid of that feeling of loneliness. When you sit alone and try to realize that you have every conceivable thing, you are still not happy within yourself and feel that you are missing something. That feeling of loneliness does not leave you. This is the inclination of the soul towards its own origin. Unless we let it fly to its own source, it can never be happy.

Saints say that you are all playing with these toys and trying to get happiness out of them, but you can never get happiness here. You are suffering in this creation however much you may think that you are not. Saints want us to get real bliss and peace. That is why Soami Ji says that when we realize we are suffering and want to get rid of it, the saints put us on the path of bliss and peace, of detachment. This is why Christ said that I have come with a sword, to detach you from this world. That is the purpose of the saints—not to give us those things which keep us tied to this world.

Take for example a mother nursing her child. There can be no stronger love, no stronger relationship, than that of the mother and child—a blood relationship. But if the child is ill and wants some sweets, the mother will not give any to him. Not that the mother does not love the child; she loves him so much that she cannot bear to see him suffering by eating them. The child does not know what is best for him. Nobody but the mother knows what is best for the child. She may give him a bitter medicine, but she will never give him a chocolate or a sweet under those circumstances.

The purpose of the saints is similar. They love us so much that they do not want us to suffer more by getting these worldly things. They say that we have already made a mess of our life in this world by getting more and more. So now they want us to become detached from it all. Not that they do not love us or think about what we need. As Christ said, the Lord takes care even of the fowls, the birds who have never sown. Even the grass which just grows for a few days and then is cut down and thrown into the oven, even that is fed by the Lord . So the Lord knows what we need. Christ said that he knows about it even before we need anything. He knows so much about us. We desire today, and he knew yesterday what we were going to desire, what we would need *(6:25–34).*

He gives us what we need, but we do not know what is best for us. We are wanting those things from the Lord which are keeping us tied to this world. Saints come, and their main purpose is to detach us, so they will never give us that which keeps us here. They will rather take those things away from us which are binding us to this world.

So, the grace of the Master, the grace of the Lord, is not in his giving us all that we want—for that may not be his grace at all. His real grace is to divert our whole mind and attention towards himself, to detach us from the world and fill us with his love and devotion, to put us on the path and make us travel and complete our spiritual journey. His grace is not his giving us something which even makes us forget the Lord; that is no grace.

> Q. But Master, we create another attachment even when we find the Master, don't we? Because if the Master is taken and merges back into the Father, and the disciples have not yet been able to see the Radiant Form, there is still this feeling of loss.

A. Christ explains this point very beautifully. He said that it is expedient for you that I leave you now *(John 16:7)*, because you know the way and the destination, and you will have no alternative but to find me within. As long as I am with you, you are all running after me. But then, since I will not be with you, you will have no option but to find me within. So you will divert all your energy within. Then he says: After a little while, I will again be with you *(John 16:16)*. Just as a mother giving birth to a child weeps and cries, but then her happiness is so great after she has delivered a son; so he says, no doubt you will weep and cry when I leave you physically, but when you see me within in my Radiant Form you will be so happy, just like a mother after she has delivered a child *(John 16:20–22)*.

Then he says, I am not leaving you orphaned at all—I will again be with you and I will take you unto me. There are many mansions in my Father's house, and according to your spiritual development I will place you there *(John 14:2)*. Ultimately it will be all one big fold, one big family, you and I and the Father *(John 10:16)*. So the question of leaving does not arise. It is the attachment which we have with the mystic or a Master which ultimately is going to take us back to the Father. Christ says: You have merged into me and I have merged into my Father, so you have merged into the Father *(John 14:20)*. You have seen me and I have seen the Father, so you have seen the Father *(John 14:9)*.

FIVE

# Discourse on Matthew 11–12

You know that John the Baptist was imprisoned and later beheaded, and he appointed Christ to carry on his teachings. And when John heard what good works Christ was doing, he sent some of his disciples to check up and get first-hand knowledge to confirm that all the stories he was hearing about Christ were right.

> *Now when John had heard in the prison the works*
> *of Christ, he sent two of his disciples,*
> *And said unto him, Art thou he that should come,*
> *or do we look for another?* *(11:2–3)*

Are you the Christ to whom we have been sent? Or should we go somewhere else to find that man?

> *Jesus answered and said unto them, Go and shew*
> *John again those things which ye do hear and see.*
> *(11:4)*

He said, I have nothing to say. Go to my disciples. Ask them whether I have been able to give them the right teachings as given to me by John the Baptist. Listen to them and see how much I have done of what John the Baptist told me to do. Then you can go and report to him.

*The blind receive their sight, and the lame walk, the lepers are cleansed, and the deaf hear, the dead are raised up, and the poor have the gospel preached to them.* (11:5)

He says, what do I do? *"The blind receive their sight."* Having eyes, we do not see the Lord. He is everywhere in this world. He is within every one of us. But neither do we see him within, nor outside, so we are all blind. So those people who had become blind in this mesh of maya, now have their inner vision opened, and they are seeing the light within and the light of the Lord outside.

*"And the lame walk."* Those who were only giving themselves to sensual pleasures and did not walk straight in this life—were crooked in their dealings with the world—have now become noble, simple and honest people and have learned to walk straight in this world.

*"The lepers are cleansed."* We are all lepers because this body is given to us as a temple of the Lord. How clean we keep those temples for the Lord which we are always building! We polish and beautify and decorate them because we think that they are a place of prayer, that the Lord resides there. Similarly, the Lord has built this body as a temple for his residence, but we have made it diseased like that of a leper. Sometimes we put wine in it, sometimes meat, sometimes we give ourself to sensual pleasures. We fill it with greed, lust, jealousy, ill will and so forth. So he says, the lepers are being cleansed. Those people who day and night were slaves of the senses are rising above their weaknesses, are realizing the beauty of this body and are trying to seek the Father within.

*"The deaf hear."* The voice of God, the spirit of God, is ringing within every one of us, but we do not hear it. We have

ears, but they only hear the voices of the outside world. He says, since people have started coming to me, they can hear that voice, the spirit of God, within themselves. So the deaf have started hearing.

And *"the dead are raised up."* He says that those people who, though getting this human birth, never even thought about the Father, and day and night gave their whole time and thought to the world—they were dead as far as the Father was concerned—they are now being raised up. Slowly and slowly, love and devotion for the Father is coming in them and they are rising from their graves. They are raising their consciousness from the body towards the Father. So Christ says, tell John the Baptist that the dead are being raised up.

*"And the poor have the gospel preached to them."* As you know, only the rich people who could give good gifts to the priest or the rabbi and who could give big donations to the temple or the synagogue had the privilege of getting the teachings. Poor people could not even get admission into those places where the Lord was talked about. So he says, go and tell John the Baptist that now the teaching is given to everybody, irrespective of poverty or wealth. Freely I have received the teaching from the Father and freely I am giving it to people. My teaching is meant for everybody, and everybody is most welcome to follow it.

> *And blessed is he, whosoever shall not be offended in me.* (11:6)

He says, those are the fortunate people who come to my company and live in my teachings, have faith in me and always feel happy about me.

Then Christ pays a compliment to his Master:

> *For this is he, of whom it is written, Behold, I send my messenger before thy face, which shall prepare thy way before thee.*
> *Verily I say unto you, Among them that are born of women there hath not risen a greater than John the Baptist.* (11:10–11)

He says, John the Baptist is not an ordinary man. In my experience of life, I have yet to see a greater person ever born of a woman. It means that, to Christ, in the whole creation there can be no greater man than John the Baptist. He is the noblest of the noble, the King of kings—that is the compliment that Christ pays to him. Because for a disciple, no one is greater than his own Master. There may be other Masters, but he is not concerned with them. Whatever he is to get, he is to get from his own Master. Those past Masters may have been of a very high order, but they are of no use to us today. They will not come to our level now to put us on the path.

So Christ says that John the Baptist is a very great teacher, a great mystic; and all that I have, all that I share with my disciples, I have received through him, by his grace. Then he pays still more homage:

> *From the days of John the Baptist until now the kingdom of heaven suffereth violence, and the violent take it by force.* (11:12)

If there are many people who want to see a movie or attend some other entertainment, you know what a great rush there is at the gate. Everybody wants to get to that place first. Similarly, Christ says that since John the Baptist came to this world with his abundant spiritual power and started putting people on the path and attaching them to the Shabd, the light and sound within, they are going in great force back to their Father's house. It means that many souls are readily going back to their Father; they no longer desire to stay in this world.

> *For all the prophets and the law prophesied until John.* (11:13)

Every prophet, every saint, has been saying that the Messiah will come, that there will always be Masters coming to this world. So he says that every prophet has been prophesying about John the Baptist.

> *He that hath ears to hear, let him hear.* (11:15)

He says, if you have eyes you can see, if you have ears you can hear from people, how much advantage and how many blessings people have got through John.

> *At that time Jesus answered and said, I thank thee, O Father, Lord of heaven and earth, because thou hast hid these things from the wise and prudent, and hast revealed them unto babes.* (11:25)

He says, this spiritual enlightenment, these spiritual heights, are not meant for intellectual people, because they are always bothered by their intellect and wisdom and are proud of it. They have so many doubts and questions, their intellect does not let them understand the simple reality. They are always lost in arguments and reasoning. Spiritual truths are not for those who split hairs or want to overcome people by arguments or by reference to authorities. It is for the 'babes'.

*The babes* are simple-minded and innocent and have no ego or intellect to bother them. They accept whatever is given to them without question. Intellect and scholarly attainments are a great barrier in the path of spiritual progress. Similarly, Christ says that unless we become innocent and simple like a babe, a small child, and eliminate all our intellect and ego, we cannot reach that spiritual height.

So he says, I am grateful to the Lord that he has hidden these things from the wise and prudent—from intellectual people who are proud of their learning and intellect. Intellect does not let faith develop, and without faith there can be no love. And without love and faith, there can be no practice at all. So he says, intellectual people are deprived of those spiritual heights and spiritual truths. But the babes, the simple people, have immense faith. They accept whatever the Master says and put it into practice. And only they progress on the path and are able to enjoy spiritual experiences within.

> *Even so, Father: for so it seemed good in thy sight.*
> *All things are delivered unto me of my Father: and no man knoweth the Son, but the Father; neither knoweth any man the Father, save the Son, and he to whomsoever the Son will reveal him.* (11:26–27)

Now he tells us how to shed our intellect and become innocent like a babe. "*All things are delivered unto me of my Father.*" He says, whatever experience or knowledge I have of heaven or of the Father has been given to me by the Father, by his grace, not by my own wisdom and intellect. I could not have reached the Father by my own effort.

He says: "*And no man knoweth the Son.*" Nobody in this world knows that the Son knows so much about the Father.

Because having been sent by the Father to the level of the world, I still have access to him. So both my Father and I know that I have access to him. *"Neither knoweth any man the Father, save the Son"*—that is, nobody knows the Father except me. People think that they are worshipping the Father, but actually it is only an emotional state built up inside. They have their own mental concept of God and of worship of the Father. They do not know the Father. Unless we know somebody, we cannot worship him, give our respect or show him our devotion or love.

So he says, nobody in this world knows me or the Father, *"save the Son, and he to whomsoever the Son will reveal him"*. Nobody knows the Father, because they do not know me. And me they do not recognize because I am just like them in the flesh, and their intellect is the barrier. So he says, my Father has given me the privilege of leading souls back to him because I know the Father and my Father knows me. And only that disciple to whom the mystic reveals himself knows that my Father is an ocean of spirituality and wisdom, and that the Son is one with the Father. And I will reveal it to them who have been drawn to me by my Father, who have been sent to me and marked for me by him.

> *Come unto me, all ye that labour and are heavy laden, and I will give you rest.* (11:28)

We are all crushed under the load of our karmas. So Christ is telling us: *"Come unto me"*—follow my teachings, have faith in me, live the way of life that I am trying to teach you. Your load is too heavy for you to carry by yourself. *"And I will give you rest."* He will give us rest from going from one house to another, from one body to another, from constant birth and death. From that our soul will get rest, when we follow a mystic and worship the Father according to our Master's instructions. As long as we are loaded with karma, we do not get rest anywhere. So our karmas are the axe at the root of our life. Unless they are cleared, there is no permanent life for us.

> *Take my yoke upon you, and learn of me; for I am meek and lowly in heart.* (11:29)

The 'yoke' is the teachings. Whatever I am teaching you, try to live in that, try to keep yourself attached to the spirit of God, to the Shabd and Nam within yourself. *"And learn of me."* Whatever my teachings are, learn from me. *"For I am meek and lowly in heart"*—because I have no load of my own. I have made my heart pure. My heart is filled with humility and with love and devotion for the Father.

> *And ye shall find rest unto your souls.* (11:29)

If you just surrender yourself to me, I will take your load and you will become light. Then your soul will find rest. Christ says, I am full with spirituality because my Father has sent me to your level, so do not worry about me. Give your load of karmas to me and I will share it, provided that you surrender yourself to me, you do not let your intellect interfere, and you learn what I have to teach you.

> *For my yoke is easy, and my burden is light.* (11:30)

Only that person can help another who has no burden of his own. If I am crushed by my own load, I cannot help another person to lift his load—I have sufficient of my own.

So he says, I have no burden, no karmas of my own. I was not born by the will of my parents. I have come to the flesh by the will of the Father. And having come to the flesh, I still have access to the Father. So if you come to me, I can lead you out of this darkness back to him. I will be able to take your load from your shoulders and to help you. Just as I am free, so will you also become free.

Then he explains his teachings by beautiful stories:

> *At that time Jesus went on the sabbath day through the corn; and his disciples were an hungred, and began to pluck the ears of corn, and to eat.* (12:1)

All these incidents are given from only one point of view. Saints do not believe in unnecessary rituals and ceremonies—that 'On this day you have to fast', and 'This is the time for eating, and after sunset you must not eat', and 'Today is a sabbath or a church day', and so forth. They always want us to give up such things. That is why these incidents have been given by Christ.

> *But when the Pharisees saw it, they said unto him, Behold, thy disciples do that which is not lawful to do upon the sabbath day.* (12:2)

Probably among the Jews nobody is permitted even to pluck or prepare food on the sabbath day.

> *But he said unto them, Have ye not read what David did, when he was an hungred, and they that were with him.* (12:3)

Masters always try to explain by giving examples from history, from the life of the mystic in which people believe. And Jews generally believe in David, so he explained to them: Look what David did on that day—

> *How he entered into the house of God, and did eat the shewbread, which was not lawful for him to eat, neither for them which were with him, but only for the priests?*
> *Or have ye not read in the law, how that on the sabbath days the priests in the temple profane the sabbath, and are blameless?*
> *But I say unto you, That in this place is one greater than the temple.* (12:4–6)

David also proved that these traditions, rites and rituals have no spiritual value, by transgressing them himself. Even the priests transgressed them. As for the sabbath, it is also stated in the Bible that the sabbath was made for man and not man for the sabbath.* He says, why are you worrying about rituals which forbid you to do certain things in the temples? There is one here who is greater than those temples. There can be no better temple at all than the human body. You are carrying the temple of the Lord always and everywhere with you. So you are greater than all these man-made temples. Temples are made for your convenience, not you for them.

> *But if ye had known what this meaneth, I will have mercy, and not sacrifice, ye would not have condemned the guiltless.*

---

* *Mark* 2:27; *Exodus* 23:12, *Deuteronomy* 5:14.

> *For the Son of man is Lord even of the sabbath day.*
> (12:7-8)

One who has realized the Lord within his body, within himself, is the highest and greatest in the temple. So he says that I have become Lord of this temple and I am not bound by these rituals and ceremonies. These things are only meant for worldly people, not for the lovers of the Lord. Then he gives a beautiful example:

> *What man shall there be among you, that shall have one sheep, and if it fall into a pit on the sabbath day, will he not lay hold on it, and lift it out?* (12:11)

He says, if on the sabbath day your only sheep falls into a ditch, do you not lift it up from out of the ditch? So if you are prepared to do such a thing on a sabbath day, then what difference does it make if you are hungry and gather or prepare some essential food?

> *How much then is a man better than a sheep? Wherefore it is lawful to do well on the sabbath days.* (12:12)

So these are just small incidents by which he tries to give us examples and tries to help us leave these unnecessary rituals and ceremonies.

> *But if I cast out devils by the Spirit of God, then the kingdom of God is come unto you.* (12:28)

How can I help you? How can you realize the Lord within yourself? He says, by 'casting out devils' that stand between you and the Father. 'Devils' means the mind and its tendencies. Mind is the agent of Kal, the negative power, which is possessing us. The Lord has created this creation and he has given it to the negative power, or Kal, to govern. So unless I help you to purify and control your mind, you will never be able to go back to the Father.

By 'the Spirit of God' he means the Holy Ghost, or the light and sound within. If I attach you to the Holy Spirit and you are able to eliminate your mind, "*then the kingdom of God is come unto you*"—then automatically you will reach the kingdom of God because now there is only one obstacle in your way, and that is the negative power. And you can only conquer the negative power when you attach yourself to the Holy Ghost.

> *Or else how can one enter into a strong man's house, and spoil his goods, except he first bind the strong man? and then he will spoil his house.* (12:29)

If you go to a strong man who has your wealth and you want to retrieve your treasure, he says, how can you be successful unless you are able to capture and bind that person? That strong man is our mind, the negative power. Our mind is extremely active and very powerful. It is always running to the senses, always taking us outside. It never lets us sit at rest. It never concentrates at the eye centre. It is always wandering and running about.

Christ says that unless you capture and bind your mind, unless you conquer the devil or Kal, you can never get whatever the Lord has kept for you within your body. And the Lord has kept his love and devotion and that treasure of light and sound within every human body. And without realizing that treasure you will never be able to go back to the Father. So that is your primary duty—to conquer your mind, to eliminate the negative power.

> *He that is not with me is against me; and he that gathereth not with me scattereth abroad.* (12:30)

He says, he who is not with me outside in this world will never be able to be with me inside. So if you want to go with me to the Father's court, you must live my teachings and have faith in me.

> *Wherefore I say unto you, All manner of sin and blasphemy shall be forgiven unto men: but the blasphemy against the Holy Ghost shall not be forgiven unto men.* (12:31)

He says, even if you have slipped and committed some bad action or any serious crime in this world, that can be forgiven because attaching yourself to the Shabd and Nam will help you to clear all your karmas, to get pardon for all the sins you have committed in this life and even in your previous lives. But if you turn your back to the Shabd and Nam, to the Holy Ghost within yourself, then you can never be forgiven. Even God will not be able to forgive you.

'Never be forgiven' means you can never go back to the Father. Howsoever intellectual or clever you may be, however much a man of wisdom or a moralist you may be, whatsoever you may give in charity, you can never escape from birth and death if you turn your back to the Holy Ghost. That is why Christ says that to worship the Father is to worship the Spirit. There is no other way of worshipping the Father and of going back to him, but to attach yourself to the Spirit within.

He refers to the Shabd and Nam as the Holy Ghost because the Shabd has the characteristics of a ghost. As Christ explained in *Saint John*, a ghost just appears. So with the Shabd also, you just hear that sound but you do not know from which direction it is coming or when you may hear it within yourself.* And this sound is something which purifies us and makes us worthy to go back to the Father.

> *And whosoever speaketh a word against the Son of man, it shall be forgiven him: but whosoever speaketh against the Holy Ghost, it shall not be forgiven him, neither in this world, neither in the world to come.* (12:32)

He says, even if you turn against the Master, you can be forgiven because you are in the flesh and I am also in the flesh like you, in this world. So if you have no faith in me, if you do not realize or even think that I have come from the Father, then your sin against the Master can be pardoned, provided you are giving your time to the light and sound to which your Master has attached you, you are attending to your meditation. Because then you will yourself realize who I am.

So he says, do not turn your back on the Holy Ghost, even if you have no faith in me or are sometimes doubtful about me. Do not bother about it, because when you attach yourself to the Holy Ghost within, that Holy Ghost will itself fill you with faith in me. At another place he says that since I am at your level, all sorts of doubts come to you, but when you "have lifted up the Son of man" *(John 8:28)*—when you have lifted up your consciousness to the level of the son of man—then

* *John* 3:8, *Acts* 2:2–3.

you will have no doubts about me. Then you will know that 'I am in the Father and the Father is in me' *(John 14:11)*, and that "I and the Father are one" *(John 10:30)*.

> *Either make the tree good, and his fruit good; or else make the tree corrupt, and his fruit corrupt: for the tree is known by his fruit.* (12:33)

By 'tree' he means our life. "Whatever a man soweth, that shall he also reap" *(Galatians 6:7)*. If you do good deeds in this world, you will get good results. If you do bad deeds, you will get bad results. 'The tree will be known by the fruit': your life will be judged by the type of actions you do in this world.

> *A good man out of the good treasure of the heart bringeth forth good things: and an evil man out of the evil treasure bringeth forth evil things.* (12:35)

If you go to the company of good people, they will influence you. If you go to the people who are meditating, who are holy, who are noble, who are one with the Spirit within, you will also be influenced by them and will also tread the same path. Slowly and slowly, you will also be filled with love and devotion for the Father. And if you go to evil and worldly people who are always giving themselves to sensual pleasures, always blind to the Father, always living for the world, you will also be influenced by them and become a victim of vices. We say 'A man is known by the company he keeps.'

So he says, in order to meditate, in order to go back to the Father, we should always try to seek good company. We should always try to live in a good environment which is healthier for our meditation and for growing in love and devotion to the Father, and should always try to shun the company of worldly people.

> *But I say unto you, That every idle word that men shall speak, they shall give account thereof in the day of judgment.* (12:36)

You will have to account for every act and every minute that you waste in worldly, foolish pursuits, because only the time which you have devoted to meditation, in love and devotion to the Father, in his worship, will be to your credit. Therefore whatever time we are foolishly wasting in idle gossip and idle pursuits, we will have to give account for on the day of judgement, at the time of our death.

> *For by thy words thou shalt be justified, and by thy words thou shalt be condemned.* (12:37)

You will be judged by your acts. If you do good deeds you will justify your having been given this human body. And good deeds means attaching yourself to the Holy Spirit within. If you do bad deeds you will be 'condemned'—you will have to come back to this world again and again. That is the greatest condemnation a soul can have.

Then, another very beautiful teaching he gives us:

> *While he yet talked to the people, behold, his mother and his brethren stood without, desiring to speak with him.*
> *Then one said unto him, Behold, thy mother and thy brethren stand without, desiring to speak with thee.*

*But he answered and said unto him that told him,*
*Who is my mother? and who are my brethren?*
*And he stretched forth his hand toward his disciples,*
*and said, Behold my mother and my brethren!*

(12:46–49)

When Christ was talking to his disciples, somebody pointed out to him that his brothers and mother were standing outside to speak with him. Christ said: "*Who is my mother? and who are my brethren?*" My only mother and brothers are those who live in the will of the Father, who follow the path and are attached to the Shabd and Nam. They belong to my family and I belong to theirs—because that is an eternal relationship in which we do not part from each other. We all become one. Then we are all tied together with the bonds of the Holy Spirit, of love and devotion for the Father. We always remain together.

This earthly life is only a karmic relationship. Sometimes one is my mother, at another I may be her brother. Sometimes a person comes as a wife, a husband, a friend or a child. We have no real relationship with these people. It is only for a certain time—fifty, sixty or seventy years. Nobody knows when the other person will leave or where he will go. It is not a permanent relationship; it is only for adjustment of the karmic account.

If we look back, God knows how many mothers, brothers, wives, children, friends and relations we have had in previous births. If we have forgotten them, if we do not remember them today, we are not going to remember our present mother, brother, father, child and so on, to please whom we are in this life sacrificing such high principles and wasting our time day and night. We have to act according to our responsibilities, according to our duties as a mother or brother or sister. But we should not get so much involved with them that we forget the real purpose of our coming to this world, for which the Lord has bestowed upon us the boon of being in this human form.

> *For whosoever shall do the will of my Father which is in heaven, the same is my brother, and sister, and mother.* (12:50)

The real relationship, Christ says, is between those people who live in the will of the Father. Those who are in touch with the Shabd and Nam within themselves ultimately become real brothers and sisters, real relations. Ultimately, there will be one big fold and they will all live together with their Master.

Just as actors appear on a stage and whatever part is assigned to them by the director, they play that part, but when they leave the stage they have no relationship with each other; similarly, this whole world is nothing but a stage, and we are all playing our parts according to our karmic relationships with each other. But the moment we leave this world, we have no relationship with anybody.

When a soul takes birth at one place, all the family members and neighbours rejoice that the soul has come, that the child has been born in that house. But the same soul left its former home and there was weeping and crying and wailing because their dear one departed. And you can imagine whether that soul in the new arrival should be happy or miserable, should look ahead or look back.

Christ is trying to explain that I have no relationships in this world. It is just an adjustment of karmic accounts. My real relationship is with my disciples because that relationship is permanent. We are not only together here, we will also be together hereafter. We will always be together because they will merge into me. And because I am merged into the Father, so through me, they will become one with the Father.

## Questions and Answers

### *"Whosoever speaketh against the Holy Ghost, it shall not be forgiven him" (12:32)*

Q. Master, what is the most practical method that we have of securing that love that is so essential?

A. You mean, how to strengthen your love? Real, deep love will only come by meditation—from inside. But outside love you get from the company of satsangis and the Master, by satsang, reading the books, or understanding the necessity of going back to the Father. All these things combine together to create love in us, and faith also, for the Master. Outside love is always wavering. Sometimes you feel you love the Master, and at other times you feel you are blank and have no feeling. Sometimes you have a lot of faith, sometimes it is lost. The mind is always wavering. But the real love will only come by meditation, when you see the Master within.

Christ also says in the Bible that now you have all sorts of questions to ask me, but when I come again and meet you, then you will have no questions to ask and will have no doubt at all.*

* *John* 16:23–26, 14:26.

And 'coming again' means meeting the Radiant Form of the Master within. This is what Christ meant when he said that if you sin against me you can be forgiven, but if you sin against the Holy Ghost you can never be forgiven. To 'sin against me' means that if your mind is wavering and you have not much faith in me, you can be forgiven because you are under the sway of the mind, and sometimes the mind does deceive and cheat you. Sometimes your thinking is blank, sometimes it is full with love and devotion. But if you refuse to attend to meditation and slowly you just forget about meditation, that sin can never be forgiven you because then you will never be able to detach yourself from the world and go back to the Father. However, if you have no love for me, but you are attending to meditation, meditation will create that love and devotion in your heart for me. That is what he is trying to explain.

So real love we can only get by meditation. And that is all the Lord's grace. We think that we love. Actually the Lord is the one who is creating love in us, and we just respond to that love and feel we love him. But actually, he is the one who is pulling us always from within and diverting our attention towards himself. He is the one. He is the sower of the seed. He is the one who creates love and devotion in our heart.

## ⇻ SIX ⇺

# Discourse on Matthew 13

Here is another beautiful incident:

> *The same day went Jesus out of the house, and sat by the sea side.*
> *And great multitudes were gathered together unto him, so that he went into a ship, and sat; and the whole multitude stood on the shore.*
> *And he spake many things unto them in parables.*
> (13:1–3)

Why does he use parables? He has explained that everybody is not meant for my teachings. These are meant for the allotted souls, the allotted sheep—for a few—and only they will understand my parables. Those who are not meant to understand or follow my teachings will not understand them.

> *Behold, a sower went forth to sow;*
> *And when he sowed, some seeds fell by the way side, and the fowls came and devoured them up:*
> *Some fell upon stony places, where they had not much earth: and forthwith they sprung up, because they had no deepness of earth:*
> *And when the sun was up, they were scorched; and because they had no root, they withered away.* (13:3–6)

He says, when a farmer went to a field, he bundled up the seed in a piece of cloth, put it on his shoulders and walked to the fields. So, from that piece of cloth some seeds just fell on the roadside, and the birds came, took those seeds and flew away, hardly giving them a chance to grow in the ground. Other seeds fell on stony places where there was not much earth and they could hardly take root. So when they came up and the sun shone and there was no rain, the seeds soon withered away.

> *And some fell among thorns; and the thorns sprung up, and choked them.* (13:7)

And while he was passing through marshy places, some seeds fell where there were already thorns and weeds; so the seeds did grow, but the thorns did not let them grow fully and they could not produce any result or fruit.

> *But other fell into good ground, and brought forth fruit, some an hundredfold, some sixtyfold, some thirtyfold.* (13:8)

Naturally, the main intention of the sower is to take the seed to the fertile ground which he has prepared for sowing. But of those seeds, he says that the result is not always the same: *"some an hundredfold, some sixtyfold, some thirtyfold"*. What he means to say is that when the Master comes to this world, he attracts many seekers, he initiates many people, but everybody is not able to go back to the Father in that very birth. Everybody is not ready to receive his teachings. Some people have closed minds. They come seemingly by accident or chance to the company of a mystic. They hear the teachings, and while they are in his company they understand them and feel convinced. But the moment they go away, they forget about the teachings and the mystic.

And there are other people who do not have much depth of understanding about the teachings, but somehow, due to the influence of their relatives and friends, they are initiated. They try to follow the teachings and are very happy as long as they are around the mystic. But the moment they go away from him to the company of evil or worldly people, they find it very difficult to deny themselves the sensual pleasures, to remain on the diet and to give time to meditation, and they slip from the path.

And the third type of people, he says, are those who have certain weaknesses in themselves. They are not prepared to leave them and make any sacrifices, but yet they are also interested in following the real path to God-realization since they have, to some extent, love and devotion for the Father. They try to meditate on the one hand, but on the other, they cannot leave their weaknesses and the sensual pleasures. They are the seeds which fall among thorny bushes.

And the fourth class of seed—there is another kind of people whose ground is absolutely prepared and fertile, their mind is receptive and the moment the seed falls there, it starts yielding fruit. They are the right type of people, prepared for the right type of life, but the result, he says, is *"some an hundredfold, some sixtyfold, some thirtyfold"*. It does not mean that every person whose ground is fertile for initiation must go to the Father in that very birth, at that very time. Some get a hundredfold result. They are the people who will in that very birth, when given the opportunity, go back to the Father at once. Others get a sixtyfold result. These people will not come back to this creation but are placed in a spiritual region according to their individual development. From there they make further spiritual progress within and eventually go back to the Father.

Some get a thirtyfold result. They are able to make some progress, but still they are left with a certain type of attachment to the world and they may come back. Though their ground is fertile—the seed is good and is well sown—still they are not destined to go back in that very life. Enough opportunity is not given to them to make sufficient spiritual progress as to be able to achieve their goal in that very birth. So they may come back again to the world to clear those attachments and then make much better progress and go back to the Father. The seed is the same, the ground may be the same—fertile ground—yet the result cannot be the same.

That is why he says: "But many that are first shall be last; and the last shall be first" *(19:30)*. There is no seniority on the path. Progress is not related to the number of years one has been initiated. Everybody has an individual type of load to shed, an individual type of karma to clear. After being initiated, some are able to clear it in one birth, some in two, some in three; some clear all that burden in the inner regions.

So that is why Christ is trying to explain to us in a very beautiful parable that when saints come, they give the teachings to many, but everybody is not prepared to accept the teachings fully. Some have full faith, some have shaky faith, some have no faith, but somehow their karmas brought them into the company of the mystic and they were initiated. Some that are not marked but are just influenced by others and come for initiation are rejected by the mystic. Everybody will definitely get some advantage, but only those people will get the full advantage in that life whose ground is fertile.

Ultimately, those people who were not even prepared but the seed was sown will also go back to the Father, but they may have to come back a second, a third or a fourth time. Wherever the seed has fallen, it must sprout eventually. The result must be there. Every soul, whosoever has been initiated, must finally go back to the Father.

Now he explains:

> *Who hath ears to hear, let him hear.*
> *And the disciples came, and said unto him, Why speakest thou unto them in parables?* (13:9–10)

They said, why are you explaining things to us in very deep parables? Why can you not be very plain and clear to us?

> *He answered and said unto them, Because it is given unto you to know the mysteries of the kingdom of heaven, but to them it is not given.* (13:11)

He says, there is a great multitude around me and everybody is not meant to follow the path. It is given to you to understand the mysteries of going back to the Father, so you will be able to understand my parables and try to follow my teachings. Others will just take them as stories and parables and go away from me.

> *For whosoever hath, to him shall be given, and he shall have more abundance: but whosoever hath not, from him shall be taken away even that he hath.* (13:12)

He says, those to whom the Father wants to give, to them he will give in great abundance, without reservation. Unlimited wealth of Nam or Shabd will be given to them. Those who have love and devotion for the Father and are attending to meditation will be given more and more of it. As Christ said in *Saint John,* it will be just like a spring flowing from his belly *(John 7:38).* The grace and love will never dry up.

But those who are not meant to follow the path, to whom it is not meant to be given, even whatever little they have will be taken away from them. The 'little' we have is the human birth with its opportunity of going back to the Father. This privilege of a human birth will be taken away from them and they may have to go to the lower species because they are not meant to go back to the Father.

> *Therefore speak I to them in parables: because they seeing see not; and hearing they hear not, neither do they understand.* (13:13)

He says, I have to tell all these things to them in parables, because they see me but they only see my body. They do not really see me, they do not understand my reality, they do not recognize me, they do not know who I am and from where I have come. They do not know what relation I have with my Father and what I have come to give them. They just take me as a good man, a noble man, a man of wisdom. They see me with their physical eyes, but they do not really see me at all.

They hear my words, my speech, but they do not understand. It is too deep or is meaningless for them. They also do not understand that what I am saying is the truth. They hear my sermons, they are attentive to me, but they do not find any necessity or need for going back to the Father. So unless the Lord gives you that understanding, you cannot understand the mystic or saint fully.

> *And in them is fulfilled the prophecy of Esaias, which saith, By hearing ye shall hear, and shall not understand; and seeing ye shall see, and shall not perceive:*
> *For this people's heart is waxed gross, and their ears are dull of hearing, and their eyes they have closed; lest at any time they should see with their eyes, and hear with their ears, and should understand with their heart...* (13:14–15)

He says: *"This people's heart is waxed gross."* Their hearts have become coarse and impure. *"And their ears are dull of hearing."* They have not opened their inner ears, so their ears are just given to the outside noise and gossip of the world. They have become dull and are not in tune to hear the spirit of God. *"And their eyes they have closed"*—they have eyes, but they have closed them as far as the Father is concerned. They do not try to see the Father or seek him within themselves. *"Lest at any time they should see with their eyes, and hear with their ears, and should understand with their heart."* We have to understand the teachings with our heart. Our heart is to be filled with love and devotion for the Father. That is the real understanding of the soul, or of the heart.

> *...and should be converted...* (13:15)

Why are they so worried? Because they are afraid of losing faith in their own traditions and are afraid of accepting some other teachings.

> *...and I should heal them.* (13:15)

His healing here does not refer to physical healing at all. He says, they are frightened that I might heal them—that I might spiritually heal them, spiritually make them clean and pure, make them whole. That is the healing of mystics and saints, and for which Christ also came to the world. Otherwise who would not like to be healed? A sick person would like to be healed by anybody. So he says, these people are frightened of coming to me. Their eyes are always closed, their ears dulled and their heart dirty. They are always worried that I might heal them, that I might convert them to my way of thinking.

> *But blessed are your eyes, for they see: and your ears, for they hear.* (13:16)

He says, you are the few selected chosen fortunate people—those blessed by the Father—because you have eyes to see me outside, to understand me, and you have also opened your inner eye to see that light and to see me within yourself. You have outside ears also, to understand my teaching, and you have also opened your inner ear to hear the spirit of God.

> *For verily I say unto you, That many prophets and righteous men have desired to see those things which ye see, and have not seen them; and to hear those things which ye hear, and have not heard them.* (13:17)

He says, do not think that you are ordinary people. You are the most fortunate people in the world because, having taken this birth, you are in the company of a great saint and mystic. There has been no dearth of prophets in the world, no dearth of righteous and noble people, those of very high character who always tried to be loving and good to people and to humanity, yet they were devoid of the realization of the Holy Spirit. They were not destined to understand what I am telling you. They have desired to know the Lord, but he has deprived them of that privilege and kept the secret of that spiritual truth from them.

By 'prophet' here he does not mean saint. I have read in many places, the word 'prophet' has been used very loosely by people. Sometimes 'prophet' refers to a saint, sometimes to the incarnation of the negative power or just to good high souls. And sometimes it is used for religious leaders—those who are blind to the reality and only give themselves to rituals and ceremonies. So to follow the path and to be attached to the Shabd and Nam is something very different from being a prophet or a righteous man.

As Kabir has pointed out in one of his poems, even the angels are yearning to take human birth and follow some mystic's teaching. That is what Christ is also saying, that you are far superior even to the prophets and righteous people because you have opened your eyes and your ears and are seeing that light and hearing the voice of God within yourself, which those people never had the opportunity to hear at all during their life.

*Hear ye therefore the parable of the sower.* (13:18)

Now he explains that parable of the sower, after explaining to them that you are the few selected chosen souls whom my Father has marked for me, and through me you understand my parables and teachings. Why have you been marked? The Father knows best. You must have done some good karmas in your past births, Christ says, so that my Father has marked you for me, to understand this reality and the need of spirituality.

> *When any one heareth the word of the kingdom, and understandeth it not, then cometh the wicked one, and catcheth away that which was sown in his heart. This is he which received seed by the way side.*
> (13:19)

Who are the people where the seed has fallen by the wayside? *"When any one heareth the word of the kingdom, and understandeth it not."* The 'word of the kingdom' means that voice of the Lord within everyone. Through the grace or blessing of the Lord, they have been brought into touch with the Word of the kingdom of God, the Sound or Shabd within themselves. But *"understandeth it not"*—they do not appreciate what the saint has done for them. They do not understand the greatness of the light and sound, nor the importance of initiation.

*"Then cometh the wicked one, and catcheth away that which was sown in his heart."* Then the moment they go away from the company of the saint, they go back to their old habits and to the company of bad people. And whatever they have learned from the saint, they absolutely forget. They are initiated, but they never think about the saint or try to practise meditation again in that lifetime. They just forget what they have received from him. *"This is he which received seed by the way side."*

> *But he that received the seed into stony places, the same is he that heareth the word, and anon with joy receiveth it.* (13:20)

The second kind of person is he that hears the Word, is in touch with the voice of God, is giving some time to meditation, and is very happy in his meditation but does not fully do what he is expected to do.

*Yet hath he not root in himself, but dureth for a while: for when tribulation or persecution ariseth because of the word, by and by he is offended.* (13:21)

But he says that he does not have any deep roots, any firm foundation, so during that lifetime he does not last very long on the path. He is not very eager to go back to the Father, though he is in touch with the light and sound within and is enjoying meditation. But since he does not have much love and devotion for the Father, he is easily deflected. When he thinks that he will have to leave his friends and family, or have to detach himself from sensual pleasures or from the unnecessary worldly obligations and duties which he has taken on his shoulders, he cannot face all this because his whole heart and mind are in the world. If members of his family taunt him, he just leaves meditation. If his friends ridicule him or try to take him away from the path, he also goes astray. This is the second class of people, where the seed has fallen on stony ground.

*He also that received seed among the thorns is he that heareth the word; and the care of this world, and the deceitfulness of riches, choke the word, and he becometh unfruitful.* (13:22)

The third kind is *"he that heareth the word"*—he is in touch with and enjoys the divine melody within and also sees the light within himself, but he is also full of the cares of the world. No doubt he is attending to meditation and also gets some results in it, but he is very anxious to collect worldly wealth and is ambitious to rise in the world, to achieve something high and great. He wants his name to be left in this world so that people should know that so-and-so has come. Hence, his ego is in his way. Although he is very sincere and wants to go back to the Father, and he is faithful to me, lives on the diet and practises every day, his worldly ambitions are choking his progress. He is deceived by material things, so his progress is blocked because of the desires he has created in himself to have material objects and comforts surrounding him.

*"And he becometh unfruitful."* It means that in this life, such people do not achieve much and do not bear fruit. No doubt they are good disciples, but they cannot get rid of their worldly ambitions and desires, so their spiritual progress is very poor. They are still attached to the world, and certain desires have made a deep groove on their mind. They have to come back to fulfil those desires; but definitely they get the advantage of their meditation. They will be born with better facilities and in a more conducive atmosphere to meditate and make further spiritual progress.

> *But he that received seed into the good ground is he that heareth the word, and understandeth it; which also beareth fruit, and bringeth forth, some an hundredfold, some sixty, some thirty.* (13:23)

And the fourth class is where the ground is fertile. He has love and devotion for the Father, he is attached to the Holy Spirit by the saint, he is hearing and enjoying the divine sound and has no attachments with this world at all. His only attachment is to the light and sound within. He has become absolutely blind to the world—he is living in this world only for the Lord. He is the person whose result is a hundred percent. It means that he may be able to progress enough to enable him to reach the Father in this very life; or he may be able to cover sixty or thirty percent of the distance. But he will definitely get fruit or results in this life.

Even if you get thirty percent result, you are at least saved from birth and death. But if you are fortunate enough and are able to get a hundred percent, then in this very life you will go back to the Father. And if sixty percent, you can go to the second or third stage. And thirty percent—at least you save yourself from birth and death and you can be kept in the inside stages, and from there practise, make spiritual progress, and slowly and slowly go back to the Father.

Christ said: "In my Father's house are many mansions" (*John 14:2*). So you may be taken to those regions, and each individual soul will be allotted a place in those spiritual regions—some in the first, some in the second or third regions, and some will be able to go back to the Father straightaway. But they are all fertile ground, all receptive to the teachings. And they always live in the will of the Father. But the fruits of their efforts differ from one another.

I will just explain further. Christ has given a very beautiful example or parable about this.

> *Another parable put he forth unto them, saying, The kingdom of heaven is likened unto a man which sowed good seed in his field.* (13:24)

He says 'good seed', meaning the seed and the field should be of the right type. If the ground is not fertile but the seed is good, or if the seed is not good though the ground be fertile, the result cannot be a hundred percent. The seed must be very good and the ground very fertile.

*But while men slept, his enemy came and sowed tares among the wheat, and went his way.* (13:25)

He says, a farmer went to a field. The field was all right, it was fertile—the man was receptive to the teachings of the Father, of the mystic. And the seed was all right—the Master was also of the right type and had properly initiated the disciple. The seed was sown, *"but while men slept"*, when the disciple was not watchful and cautious, *"his enemy came."* He was allured by the mind, by the negative power, by Kal. And what did the enemy do? He *"sowed tares among the wheat"*. It means that the mind started tempting him. Mind also became active, because Satan does not want any soul to escape from birth and death, to leave his domain and go back to the Father. He fights to retain each and every individual soul in this world. So he says, Kal or Satan also became active the moment the soul was initiated and deceived him with the riches of the world or with worldly love or material things. Satan also played his hand and played tricks on the person. So the disciple was progressing in meditation but at the same time tempted by worldly pleasures. His mind was still in the world too.

Therefore, he gives the example that tares were also sown in the field where the wheat was sown. The ground was fertile, and whatever fertile seed you sow in good ground will grow. So Satan also took the opportunity to sow bad seed in the fertile ground.

*But when the blade was sprung up, and brought forth fruit, then appeared the tares also.* (13:26)

In the beginning the farmer does not realize what has happened. He thinks: The ground is very fertile, I have sown good seed, so my crop should be very good. But when the seed sprouts, he finds that weeds are also coming up. So he is surprised and wonders who has sown them.

> *So the servants of the householder came and said unto him, Sir, didst not thou sow good seed in thy field? from whence then hath it tares?* (13:27)

Naturally, the other disciples come to the Master. They take pity on that disciple: He was so loving, so good, so faithful a disciple, and attended to meditation. And yet he has become a victim of weaknesses and cannot leave the sensual pleasures. How is it that the ground and the seed were all right, yet he has given himself to sensual pleasures and weaknesses?

> *He said unto them, An enemy hath done this.* (13:28)

The Master says: I have, of course, sown good seed in the field, but Satan was also very active and has induced him to indulge in worldly passions and sensual pleasures, and has also sown some worldly desires in his mind.

> *The servants said unto him, Wilt thou then that we go and gather them up?* (13:28)

The other disciples say: If you permit us, we will go to this disciple and explain to him that he should abstain from sensual pleasures, remain strictly on the diet, live the life of the teachings, have faith in you and attend to meditation again.

And what does the Master advise?

> *But he said, Nay; lest while ye gather up the tares, ye root up also the wheat with them.* (13:29)

He says do not do that. If you try to uproot the weeds from the field, you are also likely to shake or uproot the real crop, because they are both growing together. No doubt your intentions are good, but my only fear is that while you are trying to explain all that to him, you may uproot or shake the seed which I have sown in him. You may even offend him, and he may give up meditation and the path completely and have to come back to this world again. So that may not be in his interest.

Now he thinks that his weaknesses are not known to anybody; under the cover of darkness he can do anything. He thinks he can even deceive his Master and his Lord. If you go and admonish him that you know about his weaknesses and that you want to help him to rise above them, he may become so conscious of them, thinking 'Everybody knows that I am given to bad influences, bad weaknesses', that he may become shy to be in your presence and shy to come to me, and may leave the company of the Master. But now, at any rate, he has not turned against the Holy Ghost or against the Master.

*Let both grow together until the harvest.* (13:30)

He says to let him continue what he is doing, as long as he is also giving his time to meditation. I will wait till 'the harvest'—meaning the end of his life.

> *And in the time of harvest I will say to the reapers, Gather ye together first the tares, and bind them in bundles to burn them: but gather the wheat into my barn.* (13:30)

At the time of harvest, all the weeds which have been sown in the field will be gathered first. They will be picked out one by one and burned, because then the crop will have become ripe and will not be affected. It means that at the time of death, all the wicked and bad karmas which a disciple has done during the span of his life will be collected together on one side. And all the good things which he has done—the time which he has given to meditation, the service he has done in the name of the Father, and all the life he has lived in love and devotion for the Father—that will be collected together on the other side.

So he says let them both grow together. At the time of his death I will see what meditation he has accumulated. With the help of that meditation, I will help him to burn all the sins which he has committed, and whatever is in the balance will be to his credit. Why deprive him at least of that?

> *Another parable put he forth unto them, saying, The kingdom of heaven is like to a grain of mustard seed, which a man took, and sowed in his field.* (13:31)

Christ says, do not take this initiation as a very minor thing. It is just like a grain of mustard seed which, to look at, is a very small thing, but when it grows and becomes a plant, the yield is great. The seed of initiation which a Master sows seems, to begin with, to be a very minor thing. But when you build up and grow up with the meditation, then it becomes very big like a tree and yields a lot of good fruit. It means that it burns all your bad karmas, not only of this birth, but even of previous births, and makes you one with the Father. So do not take your initiation lightly. Similarly, he says:

> *Which indeed is the least of all seeds: but when it is grown, it is the greatest among herbs, and becometh*

> *a tree, so that birds of the air come and lodge in the branches thereof.* (13:32)

But when that seed grows, when the disciple spiritually becomes high, many people benefit by his spiritual development. Not only does the tree yield good fruit, but it also gives shelter to other creatures. Other people are also influenced by that seed and enjoy the shade of that tree. Other seekers also are helped to come onto the path through that initiate.

So if the seed is there, do not worry. As long as the seed of meditation is there, it will grow. It will become a big tree and the disciple will be able to wash away all the sins with the help of the Holy Ghost, with the help of that seed.

Now he gives another parable:

> *The kingdom of heaven is like unto leaven, which a woman took, and hid in three measures of meal, till the whole was leavened.* (13:33)

Here he gives us an idea of the greatness of the saints. You know that leaven causes bread dough to rise, and very little is required to make a large batch of bread. And so it is with the grace showered on us by the saints. Only by their grace and mercy can we even think of going back to the Father. Only with the grace of the Master are we able to catch hold of the Shabd, the divine melody, and rise up to our true home. And only a spark of this divine melody is sufficient to burn our karmas and clear that veil of darkness between us and the Father —such is the greatness of the saints and their gift of Nam or Shabd.

Then he explains to them what he means by the parable of the tares:

> *And his disciples came unto him, saying, Declare unto us the parable of the tares of the field.* (13:36)

And Christ explains:

> *He that soweth the good seed is the Son of man.* (13:37)

Who has sown the seed? Who has done the initiating? The son of man, the mystic, the Master. Why is Christ known as the son of man? Sometimes he is referred to as the son of God, sometimes as the son of man. A son of God is of no use to us unless he becomes a son of man. Unless he takes birth in a human form and becomes like us at our level in order to initiate us, we cannot make any use of his spiritual heights or of his guidance at all. He cannot initiate us if he is only a son of God, if he is only with God. So he says: *"He that soweth the good seed is the Son of man."* He must be a 'son of man', and he must initiate you. That is the number one priority.

> *The field is the world.* (13:38)

This world is the field where the seed has to be sown. It can only be sown in the heart of the initiate when he is in the world.

> *The good seed are the children of the kingdom; but the tares are the children of the wicked one.* (13:38)

The 'good seed' means the initiation, which entitles you to become *"the children of the kingdom"* of heaven. Whatever time you are devoting to the light and sound within, you are nourishing the good seeds; and whatever time you are giving to sensual pleasures, you are nourishing 'the tares of the wicked one'.

*The enemy that sowed them is the devil.* (13:39)

The devil is the enemy—the negative power or Kal, who has sown the seeds of tares.

*The harvest is the end of the world.* (13:39)

'The end of the world' means that moment when a person dies. For him the world comes to an end. It does not mean the resurrection, as is generally understood. For us, the end of the world comes when we leave this body. As long as we are in the body and we are living, the whole world exists for us.

*And the reapers are the angels.* (13:39)

It means the angel of death, or Dharam Rai as we call it in our Indian language. At the time of death the balance is seen.

*As therefore the tares are gathered and burned in the fire; so shall it be in the end of this world.*
*The Son of man shall send forth his angels, and they shall gather out of his kingdom all things that offend, and them which do iniquity;*
*And shall cast them into a furnace of fire: there shall be wailing and gnashing of teeth.* (13:40–42)

'Wailing and gnashing of teeth' means that at the time of one's death, the karmic account will be adjusted. "Whatsoever a man soweth, that shall he also reap" *(Galatians 6:7).* At the time of your death, whatever bad deeds you have done will force you to the *"furnace of fire"*—hell. The wicked ones will wail in agony. Or you will get the result of whatever good deeds you have done, in that after death you may go to heaven.

> *Then shall the righteous shine forth as the sun in the kingdom of their Father.* (13:43)

If in the balance a lot of credit is in your favour, then your soul will shine like the sun. Similarly he says, do not worry unnecessarily about the bad deeds which you have been tempted to commit. There are no failures after initiation. Because as long as you are attending to your meditation, all bad deeds will be taken care of by attaching yourself to the voice of God, the light and sound within, and then your soul will shine just as the sun in this world. So don't worry about the darkness. Light the candle.

A diamond never loses its value, but its lustre is gone when it is thrown into the mud. The moment you wash that mud from the diamond, it shines with the same lustre. Christ says that the soul is always shining like the sun; the soul is bright and pure, because it is a drop of that divine ocean. But having taken the company of the mind, which itself is in the sway of the senses, there is so heavy a covering of sin on the soul that we do not see its brightness. But when all those coverings are removed by meditation, then the soul will again shine like the sun.

> *Who hath ears to hear, let him hear.* (13:43)

He says, whoever has understanding, let him try to understand my teachings.

*Again, the kingdom of heaven is like unto treasure hid in a field; the which when a man hath found, he hideth, and for joy thereof goeth and selleth all that he hath, and buyeth that field.*
*Again, the kingdom of heaven is like unto a merchant man, seeking goodly pearls:*
*Who, when he had found one pearl of great price, went and sold all that he had, and bought it.* (13:44–46)

Here Christ explains in parable form the value of the wealth of the light and sound within, of that treasure within. He likens it first to a great treasure hidden in a field. When a man learns of such a treasure, he doesn't broadcast that fact for everyone to hear, but rather keeps that knowledge to himself and does not pass it on to anyone. Then, realizing the great value of that treasure, he sells all that he possesses in exchange for that field, knowing that what lies in it, that buried treasure, is far greater than anything he is giving up to get it. The same is the case with the example of the merchant, who having found a pearl of great value, gives up all else to purchase it.

And so too must we, to get our treasure within this living temple of the human body. No sacrifice is too great to make in exchange for that treasure. Nor do we lay that treasure open for others to deplete by telling anyone about it. As Kabir says, the price of the love of the Father, of the Master's grace, is your 'head', your ego, all that you possess as yours. And at that price, it is a bargain. So he says, don't delay. Be prepared to sacrifice everything to obtain that treasure within. We must want only the Father, only our Master.

*Again, the kingdom of heaven is like unto a net, that was cast into the sea, and gathered of every kind:*

> *Which, when it was full, they drew to shore, and sat down, and gathered the good into vessels, but cast the bad away.*
> *So shall it be at the end of the world: the angels shall come forth, and sever the wicked from among the just,*
> *And shall cast them into the furnace of fire: there shall be wailing and gnashing of teeth.* (13:47–50)

By 'end of the world' he refers to the day of judgement of each individual at the time of his death. At that time our karmic account is checked and our actions weighed, the good against the bad. Then, depending upon the resulting balance, we are sent into that field where we can best satisfy our unfulfilled desires and reap what we have sown. If we have wasted this human opportunity in worldly and sensual pursuits and have not found a living perfect Master and have not turned our attention towards realizing the Father within, then we are again sent into the wheel of transmigration, of birth and death, where there is much *"wailing and gnashing of teeth"*, where there is much pain and suffering.

Then he talks further about the mystics or saints:

> *A prophet is not without honour, save in his own country, and in his own house.* (13:57)

He says, generally people always recognize a mystic or a saint, except those of his own household and surroundings and his own country. They have been so familiar with his life and doings from childhood onward that this intimacy does not permit them to realize and appreciate his greatness now. They always see him in the perspective of their own relationship, never as a saint. So he says that every saint is honoured, *"save in his own country"*. Otherwise, they are always honoured everywhere else.

## Questions and Answers

### *The parable of the sower (13:3–8, 18–23)*

Q. Do we ourselves have any control over where the seed falls or has that all been planned out beforehand because of our karmas?

A. It is all planned out, we are just puppets. We feel that we have found the path and the teachings and have love and desire to go back to the Father, but the pull always comes from within. It is the Father who is pulling us towards the path and who is creating the environment in which we will be able to follow it.

Q. Maharaj Ji, last night you were speaking about the four sowings of the seed. Does every soul have to go through the sowing on barren ground and then…?

A. No, it is not essential. It does not mean that you always start on barren, then go to rocky, then to marshy and then to fertile ground. What he means to say is that when a sower goes to sow, seeds do fall here and there. Undeserving people do come onto the path, so to say. Undeserving in the sense that they are not fully ready to go back to the Father. But they become deserving when they come to the saints and keep their company, and they go on becoming more and more deserving. That is what he meant to say.

But this parable continues on a very long way. Further on *(20:1–16)* he says that a householder engaged some people to work in his vineyard. Some worked for ten hours and some for six hours, but everybody was paid the same wages. And the employer said to the first ones: Why are you jealous of the others, when whatever was settled with you has been given to you? It is my wealth. I may give to a person even if he has not worked. You should only be concerned with what I have settled with you—and that has been paid to you. Whether this man gets paid with or without work is no concern of yours.

So what he means to say is that saints promise to take every soul back to the Father. But looked at outwardly, some seem to get more grace, some less; some have to work more, some less. But that is no reason for other people to be jealous or to complain. As long as they get their due, that is the main thing. That is why he said that the first may be the last, and the last may be the first *(19:30)*.

Actually there are so many things missing from the Bible. Whatever anybody could not understand, he just eliminated or probably gave his own interpretation in translations. But still, there is a lot to understand.

Q. Maharaj Ji, coming back to the four seeds and "many that are first shall be last": Assuming everyone in this audience here has come to the path for the first time and never approached Sant Mat except in this life, does this still apply—that progress will not be the same and is determined by past karmas?

A. It is determined by past karmas also. Even if everybody were on the path for the first time, the individual karmas are different. Everybody is not carrying the same load. Some people have to their credit certain good karmas from the past, so they have been able to get more of the grace of the Lord. Some people have committed very serious sins, but due to certain circumstances or certain good acts, they have also come onto the path for the first time. So everybody's load is different, and their individual progress will be different, even if they have all come onto the path at the same time, in the same life. Fire burns all the wood. Some heaps are too big, so naturally that takes more time. Some heaps are very small and they are consumed in no time.

> Q. Maharaj Ji, you just mentioned in what you read tonight that with the fertile ground, some bear a hundredfold, which means they go straight up, and others sixty percent, which means they do not have to come back. Is it not quicker to come back than to progress from the regions?

A. If it is in the interest of the disciple. That is for the Master to decide, not for us. What he means to say is that their ground is fertile, the seed is good and the ground is good. They have put in all possible effort, but they could not get a hundred percent result in that life. Some got a hundred, some sixty, some only thirty.

So it means that in any case they will not come back to this world. They will be in those mansions and will go back to the Father slowly and slowly. It is as good for them as being with the Father, because eventually they will find their place with the Father.

Q. What I meant to ask, Maharaj Ji, was if there is a sixty percent one that does not have to come back, and one with a smaller percentage that does come back, is it not possible for the one who comes back to get home sooner than the one who is waiting in the regions?

A. It depends upon the individuals. We definitely make better progress when we are here. But if we are sent back here to make better progress, there is also a chance of our being engrossed in worldly things again and collecting more karma, more debris. So the Master sees which souls will not collect a lot more debris in this creation and will be able to put in the effort to enable them to go back to the Father, and he will send them here. Where he finds any chance or risk that a soul may be lost in worldly pleasures again if he sends it to the creation, he may not send it at all. That is for the Master to decide.

Q. Master, what is the significance or how is it determined that we take a maximum of four lives, once the soul is initiated, to return home? Why four instead of three or five?

A. Well, that is the divine law. Tomorrow you may say, why Shabd, why Master, why not straight to the Father? That is the divine law. That is the maximum, they say, that you will take to clear the karma. The Masters know how much time we need to clear all the dirt which we have been collecting and they know we don't need to take more than that. That is the maximum the soul will take. So they have fixed the maximum time.

Christ says the same thing in this parable of the sower. He also talks about four things: seed falling on barren ground, seed falling on rocky ground, seed falling on marshy ground, and seed falling on fertile ground. So when the seed falls on the fertile ground, he says, then you get a hundred percent result, or sixty, or thirty percent result. He also talks about the number four, but in a very indirect way.

Q. Master, is it possible to turn from rocky to completely fertile in one life?

A. He knows best. He knows best. He can do anything. He can take you right from the barren ground to his own level. The Lord can make a king of anyone, but the general rule is what they say. That is what we have to discuss.

Q. If a seed drops into a thorny bush, is it possible that it will ever be washed down into fertile ground?

A. Christ has given a very beautiful parable. I will just discuss it with you.

He says, the seed falls into marshy ground where there are also tares. And naturally the growth of the seed is hindered by the growth of the tares—the weeds, reeds and all kinds of marsh plants which grow up along with the crop. He says, if you try to pull up the tares now, you are likely to uproot or shake the roots of the crop also. So what the farmer does is he lets them both grow together, and when the crop is ripe, he cuts down the tares and burns them, and then harvests the crop.

Similarly, Christ says that the soul is initiated, but when it goes away from the Master it is influenced by bad company and starts doing the wrong type of actions: meditating sometimes, but also given to sensual pleasures or to bad actions.

Thus, saints do not shake such people so much that they become very conscious of their weaknesses, despair and leave the path altogether. They let them carry on. But at the time of harvest, it means at the time of death, the crop and the tares will be balanced. If the balance is favourable to meditation, that will burn the tares; and whatever is left will be to his credit, and that will make the soul shine to that extent.

### *The parable of the tares (13:24–30)*

> Q. Master, some satsangis seem to apparently go off the path. Is this necessary for their spiritual progress? They seem to go off the path, but some people say: 'Oh well, how do you know they are really off the path? Maybe they have to go through that particular karma.'

A. It is very difficult to say that it is good for their progress to be off the path. That is why Christ gave that very beautiful parable about the tares, that if you try to remove them, you might shake the very roots of the main crop. So the Master knows that the disciple is off the path, has given himself to bad company, and is not absolutely straight on the path. But sometimes he does not pull him up and expose his weaknesses so much that he may even leave the path and go away from the Master—he may become so shy of his brothers and of the Master that he does not go to them, and slowly and slowly he veers away from the path for the remainder of his life. But it does not mean that he will not have to pay for it. He will definitely have to pay for it. Rather, the Master's punishment may sometimes be more severe than Kal's punishment.

If a child does anything wrong, the mother never gives him up to the police. She may spank the child, may not even give him food, may cut down his allowances, may use all sorts of ways to set him right. But behind all that is love to make the child a good and well-behaved boy. She does not hate him, but she does not want him to misbehave.

Similarly, Masters will not send us to hell or back to the world unless our karmas are very, very heavy. But all the same, the Master will spank us. He will set us right. If a child is dirty, the mother does not lift him up. First she cleans the child. So if we become dirty, however much we may dislike it, by cold water or hot water we have to be washed clean. So even if we sometimes stray away from the path, we are brought back again. The seed is not wasted, nor does it die. It must sprout. Sometimes it remains dormant under the earth, but when the rain comes, it starts to grow.

> Q. Maharaj Ji, if we have friends who have seemingly gone away from the path, and we are here at the Dera, so happy with the Master, should we write to them and explain this to them and say that we are happy here and—?

A. There is absolutely no harm in that, but what Christ means to say is something very different. He says that if a devotee has fallen victim to sensual pleasures and has gone a little astray from the path, if you make him too conscious of his weaknesses, he may carry such a feeling of guilt in himself that he may not be able to come back to the path again—so you have not done him any good at all. So try to reach him with love and affection, and try to explain the teachings to him. Try to build his love and devotion, to strengthen his faith, but do not expose his weaknesses to others.

## ⇉ SEVEN ⇇

# Discourse on Matthew 14–18

Christ has described an interesting incident or personal experience about faith. You know when he walked on the water, Peter also wanted to do the same.

> *But straightway Jesus spake unto them, saying, Be of good cheer; it is I; be not afraid.* (14:27)

He said this because the people were surprised that anybody could walk on water and were all amazed.

> *And Peter answered him and said, Lord, if it be thou, bid me come unto thee on the water.* (14:28)

If it is you, let me walk on the water also.

> *And he said, Come. And when Peter was come down out of the ship, he walked on the water, to go to Jesus.*
> *But when he saw the wind boisterous, he was afraid; and beginning to sink, he cried, saying, Lord, save me.* (14:29–30)

He could not walk and started to sink.

> *And immediately Jesus stretched forth his hand, and caught him, and said unto him, O thou of little faith, wherefore didst thou doubt? (14:31)*

When I said 'Come and walk', you were worried about the rushing of the wind and that you would drown in the water. And though you obeyed me, you had no faith in me. So naturally you could not walk on the water. If you had just had full faith in me, that I had told you to walk and you had faith in yourself that you would be able to walk on water, then you would not have sunk. But because there was not much depth in your faith yet, that was why you could not walk on the water.

These little incidents are mentioned only to impress upon us how much faith we have to build in order to follow the Master. It hardly makes any difference whether anybody can walk on the water or not, but these small things are just to remind us of the value of faith.

In a previous chapter Christ discussed fasting, when somebody had pointed out that his disciples did not fast, and he said: 'Why should they fast when I am here with them? They will also start indulging in rituals and ceremonies when I am not with them' *(9:14–15).* Now here he talks about a similar thing when the Pharisees raised another such frivolous objection of his followers not washing their hands before eating:

> *Then came to Jesus scribes and Pharisees, which were of Jerusalem, saying,*
> *Why do thy disciples transgress the tradition of the elders? for they wash not their hands when they eat bread.*
> *But he answered and said unto them, Why do ye*

> *also transgress the commandment of God by your tradition?*
> *For God commanded, saying, Honour thy father and mother: and, He that curseth father or mother, let him die the death.*
> *But ye say, Whosoever shall say to his father or his mother, It is a gift, by whatsoever thou mightest be profited by me;*
> *And honour not his father or his mother, he shall be free. Thus have ye made the commandment of God of none effect by your tradition.* (15:1–6)

Of course we should keep clean, but this refers to a ceremony. And Christ says that these traditions are man-made, but God's commandments are not only binding on my disciples, they are also binding on you. You have forgotten many commandments; for example, giving respect to your father and mother, obeying the elders, and such things, while adhering to futile worldly traditions and taking them to have spiritual value.

> *This people draweth nigh unto me with their mouth, and honoureth me with their lips; but their heart is far from me.* (15:8)

He says that people come to the mystics or the Masters but do not have real faith in them. They honour the Master with their lips only, not from their heart. Their heart feels one thing and their tongue says something different.

> *But in vain they do worship me, teaching for doctrines the commandments of men.* (15:9)

He says that there is no use in worshipping me like that. Worship must come from the heart. They do not have to tell me that they have faith in me, that they abide by my teachings. It must be impressed on their heart that this is the teaching for them and that they have to follow me. It is their heart that matters to me, not their tongue or their lips.

> *And he called the multitude, and said unto them, Hear, and understand:*
> *Not that which goeth into the mouth defileth a man; but that which cometh out of the mouth, this defileth a man.* (15:10–11)

He says, we are very fussy about these worldly things, that the body, our clothes and house and everything should be scrupulously clean. But the thing which needs cleansing, the heart—that we never try to clean at all. What difference does your wearing a beautiful suit make if your heart is evil—if bad, adulterous and murderous thoughts are coming from it? So he says, all these wicked deeds and sins that you commit are all coming from within you. What you put into the stomach will go out as roughage into the world. But what comes out of the mouth, 'that defiles a man'. You are not giving any attention to what comes out of you—to your thoughts, words and deeds—but are so particular in giving attention to what goes into your stomach to satisfy your appetites.

So he says, what difference does it make whether you eat food with washed hands or not? It is not so important. There is nothing spiritual in these things. Whether you wear beautiful and expensive clothes or simple and cheap clothes, it hardly makes any difference. Your human values are the same. You do not become a better person by putting on a better suit or by putting on luxurious clothes. No doubt the body should be kept clean, but that clean body is useless if the heart is not clean. So try to improve your human qualities, try to purify your heart. That is the main thing. Do not worry so much about your body or about these traditions and rituals.

> *But he answered and said, Every plant, which my heavenly Father hath not planted, shall be rooted up.* (15:13)

From where does the heavenly Father plant? From heaven. It means that those souls which have not been selected by the Father who is in heaven will be *"rooted up"*. Those plants will not bear any fruit. The planting is done in the world here, but the seed comes from heaven. The Father plants from heaven. When we are initiated here on the earth, we are planted in heaven. The more we spiritually advance within ourselves, the plant is growing in heaven. And when it ripens and bears fruit, then we are in heaven and have no roots on the ground at all. So what Christ means to say is that whosoever is initiated here by the grace of the Father, only he goes back to him.

> *Let them alone: they be blind leaders of the blind. And if the blind lead the blind, both shall fall into the ditch.* (15:14)

He says, if anybody in this world tries to 'plant' without his consent, without the Father's marking, they are just the blind leading the blind. Do not worry about them. They will never be able to go back to the Father, nor bear any fruit. The marking or allotment has to be done by the Father who is in heaven. And only his son, the living Master of the time, does the planting.

> *Then answered Peter and said unto him, Declare unto us this parable.*
> *And Jesus said, Are ye also yet without understanding?* (15:15–16)

Peter, as you know, was the foremost disciple of Christ; he even succeeded him. And Christ says to him, Even you do not understand these things—you who are so advanced spiritually within yourself?

> *Do not ye yet understand, that whatsoever entereth in at the mouth goeth into the belly, and is cast out into the draught?* (15:17)

Whatever you put into the stomach, whether you use washed or unclean hands, ultimately it just goes out from the stomach into the draught.

> *But those things which proceed out of the mouth come forth from the heart; and they defile the man.* (15:18)

Whatever comes out of the mouth, actually it is the heart which is speaking. Unless the heart feels emotions, good or bad, the mouth never speaks. When the heart is full with love, loving words always come from the mouth. When there is anger in the heart, angry words always come from the mouth. Only that comes out from the heart which is in it. The mouth is only expressing what is in the heart.

> *For out of the heart proceed evil thoughts, murders,*

> *adulteries, fornications, thefts, false witness, blasphemies.* (15:19)

If our heart is noble, we always share noble thoughts with others. We always try to do good to them, to console them and help them, to talk sweetly with them, and try to help them to get out of their trouble and misery. But if our heart is wicked, is crooked or bad, we always like to hurt and injure them, give false witness against them, think bad things about them, try to steal their property or transgress against their rights.

> *These are the things which defile a man: but to eat with unwashen hands defileth not a man.* (15:20)

He says that it does not defile a man if he eats with washed or unwashed hands; but what definitely defiles a man, degrades him, and even takes him to the lower species, is what comes out of his heart. So care more about your heart. Try to purify it and make it a temple in which the Lord can dwell, and do not worry so much about whether it is traditional or not to eat your food with washed or unwashed hands. If your hands are otherwise clean, there is no ceremony that you have to wash them. These are very minor things. Do not give so much importance to them. They are all ways of living in this world. These have nothing to do with spirituality. Spirituality comes from the heart. So try to attach your heart to the Shabd and Nam and make it pure.

Now Christ explains to us that the teachings of the saints and their initiation is not meant for everyone, but only for their allotted sheep. You know the incident of the woman from Canaan who came to Christ crying out to have him heal her daughter:

*But he answered her not a word.* (15:23)

Even though she begged for mercy, he didn't answer her. Then his disciples 'besought him to send her away'.

*But he answered and said, I am not sent but unto the lost sheep of the house of Israel.* (15:24)

He says that the mystics and saints are only sent to take back to the Father those *"lost sheep"* allotted to them. The Father sends his beloved sons to find and collect these 'sheep' who are lost and attached to the rituals, ceremonies and sensual pleasures of the world. And once the Master has found them, he attaches them to the Shabd within. And this attachment automatically detaches them from the world.

So Christ says: *"I am not sent but unto the lost sheep of the house of Israel."* He was sent only for his marked souls, for his lost sheep. And the area he was sent to find them was, at that time, around Israel. However, Israel also means 'God's chosen people' or all those who are marked by the Father—not only those living in Israel. At that, the woman again came to Jesus asking for his help.

*But he answered and said, It is not meet to take the children's bread, and to cast it to dogs.* (15:26)

He makes his point very clear. He says that the teachings of the mystics and saints are not meant for everybody. They bring 'bread', that is, their grace, their gift of Nam, for only those who are marked to receive it, only for their 'children'. And this precious gift is not squandered on those not ready to appreciate its value and beauty. He explained the same thing before by saying: "Give not that which is holy unto the dogs, neither cast ye your pearls before swine" *(7:6)*.

The Father showers his grace on us only when we are marked to receive it. And the Master teaches us to become receptive to that grace. He guides us at every step of the path back to the Father, and through meditation he gives us the spiritual wealth within. So Christ says, that grace and that treasure are meant only for those destined by the Father to go back to him, not for everybody.

> *And she said, Truth, Lord: yet the dogs eat of the crumbs which fall from their masters' table.*
> *Then Jesus answered and said unto her, O woman, great is thy faith: be it unto thee even as thou wilt.*
> *(15:27–28)*

But the woman said that she understood the truth of Christ's statement and she did not want that grace meant for his disciples. But her faith in the Lord was deep, and she relied upon the soft-heartedness of the mystics and saints, saying: *"Yet the dogs eat of the crumbs which fall from their master's table."* She meant that she did not want to take away any share from his children's treasure, but only the 'crumbs' which fall from the table. She begged only for such 'crumbs' of his grace. She knew the value of the grace of the saints.

The woman had such appreciation for the saints and such faith in Christ that he was moved to grant her wish and he healed her daughter. The saints are nothing but an ocean of mercy and compassion. And when the heart of a saint is moved, no law stands in the way of the love that he showers.

Then, you know the two incidents of the feeding of the multitudes:

*Do ye not yet understand, neither remember the five loaves of the five thousand, and how many baskets ye took up?*
*Neither the seven loaves of the four thousand, and how many baskets ye took up?*
*How is it that ye do not understand that I spake it not to you concerning bread, that ye should beware of the leaven of the Pharisees and of the Sadducees?*
*Then understood they how that he bade them not beware of the leaven of bread, but of the doctrine of the Pharisees and of the Sadducees.* (16:9–12)

He says, don't you understand that the bread given to feed the multitudes, which when collected in the end was more than that with which they began, even after everyone was fed, was the 'bread of life', of spiritual life. The multitudes hungered for the grace of the Father, for his teachings which gave them peace. And the Master fed them that 'bread' in abundance. His grace was bountiful and filled those hungry for it to overflowing.

The bread of spiritual life is that audible life stream within. Its source is infinite and boundless. And when you get a taste of that nectar, you just want more. Everything else becomes insipid and tasteless. Nothing attracts you in the world any more. You become completely attached to that sound and light, and by the grace of the Master you become whole, you become pure.

So Christ spoke about that bread which satisfies our hunger for the Lord. And he continued by comparing it to the *"leaven of the Pharisees and of the Sadducees"*. He told his disciples to 'beware of their leaven', of their teachings, of their dogmas and doctrines. For you who fall into such a mire become further enmeshed in the illusions of the world and only tie your fetters and attachments here with stronger chains. Those doctrines only serve to satisfy your ego and build a greater treasure on this earth, which you will have to return to collect. So he says, *"Beware."* Don't be misled by the doctrines of men. Rather seek the company of the saints and become receptive to their 'bread', to their grace.

Then Christ asked his disciples:

> *Whom do men say that I the Son of man am?*
> *And they said, Some say that thou art John the Baptist:*
> *some, Elias; and others, Jeremias, or one of the prophets.* (16:13–14)

Some say that you are John the Baptist; others, an incarnation of some other past saint or prophet for whom they were probably waiting.

> *He saith unto them, But whom say ye that I am?* (16:15)

He asked Peter directly, who do you think I am?

> *And Simon Peter answered and said, Thou art the Christ, the Son of the living God.* (16:16)

Peter said, for me you are the son of the living God. Why does he say "*living God*"? God never dies. He meant that now, through you, my God is always living for me. And when I had not come into contact with you, had not met you, I never knew anything about God. I had never seen him. Whether or not he existed, he was of no use to me. So Peter says, you are *"the Son of the living God"* because now I live with my God. Now I see God through you. For me, God is living here on earth, and that is what you are to me—my Lord, my God on earth.

> *And Jesus answered and said unto him, Blessed art thou, Simon Bar-jona: for flesh and blood hath not revealed it unto thee, but my Father which is in heaven.* (16:17)

He refers to the body as 'flesh and blood' because it consists of that. He said, you have really recognized me. But do not think that you have obtained this recognition through your intellect, or just by having come into the human body, or that finding me is *your* discovery. It is just the grace of my Father. He has given you that vision, that understanding, that faith, so that you now realize that I am the son of the living God.

> *And I say also unto thee, That thou art Peter, and upon this rock I will build my church; and the gates of hell shall not prevail against it.* (16:18)

He says, since you now realize me, you know what I am, I appoint you as my successor because your faith is unshakeable like a rock. You have built your meditation, or your understanding of the teachings, on a rock, on deep faith. Nobody can shake you. So I appoint you in this world to carry my teachings to the people.

> *And I will give unto thee the keys of the kingdom of heaven: and whatsoever thou shalt bind on earth shall be bound in heaven.* (16:19)

There is something very deep in this. If your house is locked, unless you have a key you can never unlock it and get into the house. So nobody can go back to the Father unless they have a key to the lock: 'And that key I give to you,' he says to Peter. 'Only he to whom you deliver it, will be able to unlock the gate and go back to the Father.' And that key is initiation. Guru Nanak also refers to initiation as a key of the house.

How to unlock the gate? He says: *"And whatsoever thou shalt bind on earth shall be bound in heaven."* This is very essential. It means that both the Master and the disciple must be present on earth. And the disciple has to be bound on earth before he can gain access to heaven, where the Father lives. He must come across a living Master, go to his company, physically, and get initiated.* Then only is he bound in heaven and is entitled to go back to the Father.

> *And whatsoever thou shalt loose on earth shall be loosed in heaven.* (16:19)

And whom you do not initiate while he is living on the earth will not have access at all to the Father. We must be initiated while both we and our Master are physically living. Otherwise, if we just have faith in those past Masters who left us long, long ages ago, we cannot be bound on earth. And that is what Christ tells Peter, that you will be able to bind people on earth as long as both you and they are on earth.

'Binding' means initiating, attaching someone to yourself. It means binding your heart, attaching another person to your-

* While the need is to be initiated during the lifetime of both disciple and Master, the Master may designate another person to explain the meditation technique on his behalf.

self. We are all bound to one another by our attachments. Wherever your hearts are, it is there that you will go. If you are attached to the Master, you will go to the Master. If you are attached to the world, you will come back to the world. And if the Master binds the disciple to himself, it means that that bond can never be broken and it will ultimately take the soul back to the Father.

Actually, the binding has to be done by the Father through the living Master, not by the disciple. 'Whosoever *you* bind on earth'—he does not say whosoever binds himself to you. The Master is to bind the disciple to himself, then only is the soul entitled to go back to the Father. That is what he is trying to explain.

> *If any man will come after me, let him deny himself, and take up his cross, and follow me.* (16:24)

Let him deny himself the pleasures of the world, this worldly merrymaking, *"and take up his cross"* and live in the teachings, take them seriously, bring his consciousness here to the eye centre. Our forehead is like a cross. [The Master gestured, showing how the intersection of the 'cross' is at the eye centre.] So whosoever comes *here* is the one who takes up his cross.

He says: *"And follow me."* Have faith in me and meditate and try to follow my teachings. He says that only they will *"come after me"*—go where I go. After death the Master merges back into the Father. So he says, wherever I go, they will also follow and go to the same place.

> *For whosoever will save his life shall lose it: and whosoever will lose his life for my sake shall find it.* (16:25)

He says, those who do not want to make any sacrifice *"for my sake"* will lose this opportunity of going back to the Father. And whosoever is prepared to face hardships and abstain from sensual pleasures *"for my sake"* will find his life worthwhile. He will be able to go back to the Father.

To achieve God-realization one has to make many sacrifices, face many hardships, break away from worldly attachments of countless lives, turn away from many comforts and pleasures of the world. The attraction of wealth, worldly possessions, power and position, love for the family, society and country—all such desires and ambitions have to be curbed, and only the urge to go back to the Lord takes precedence—over all else.

Christ says that those who are always anxious about their material life and its comforts will lose the precious opportunity of finding the Lord in this human birth. But those who are prepared to forego all these ambitions, pleasures and attachments, and do not care much about the attractions of this life—they are only eager to follow the instructions of their Master and live for him—will find eternal life. In other words, if we think more of the comforts of this life, we lose the precious opportunity of finding eternal life in this human birth; but if we are prepared to sacrifice the attractions of this life, we gain eternal life.

> *For what is a man profited, if he shall gain the whole world, and lose his own soul?* (16:26)

Then he says, what difference does it make even if you become the ruler of this whole world, so that everything is under your command, that whatever comes out of your mouth becomes law? Ultimately you will lose the body and will go into the cycle of birth and death. What type of a bargain are you making? You are losing your soul and winning this world—which is perishable, which is only for sixty, seventy or eighty years. What is the use of becoming a ruler in this world if you are to take birth in some lower species after this human birth?

> *Or what shall a man give in exchange for his soul?*
> *(16:26)*

He says that no price is too high, no sacrifice too great to save your soul. You should be prepared to face any type of hardship or sacrifice to save your soul.

> *For the Son of man shall come in the glory of his Father with his angels; and then he shall reward every man according to his works. (16:27)*

Christ says that the son of man, our Master, will reward every one of us at the time of death according to the meditation that we have put in and our way of life, according to our individual good deeds and our good karmas.

> *Verily I say unto you, There be some standing here, which shall not taste of death, till they see the Son of man coming in his kingdom. (16:28)*

Now this is something very mystical, because all those disciples to whom Christ was referring ultimately died. He says, many of you here, whom I have initiated and who are following me and have faith in me, will not taste death until I come in my Radiant Form to receive you and take you back to the Father. But he says, 'many of you', not every one of you.

Only those will I receive who are living in my teachings and denying themselves the pleasures and attachments of the world. He says: *"Till they see the Son of man coming in his kingdom."* Until they see their Master coming from the Father and receiving them, they will not die, the soul will not leave the body.

So he assures them that if you follow and live my teachings, then I will receive you and reward you at the time of death. Not only will I reward you, but I will come in my Radiant Form to receive your soul, and you will not have to go alone to the Father.

> *While he yet spake, behold, a bright cloud overshadowed them: and behold a voice out of the cloud, which said, This is my beloved Son, in whom I am well pleased; hear ye him.* (17:5)

All this refers to inner experience and does not refer to any outer natural phenomenon.

> *And when the disciples heard it, they fell on their face, and were sore afraid.* (17:6)

They were frightened. When a disciple in the beginning sees something within himself—supposing he sits in meditation and suddenly a light appears or he suddenly hears a voice like that from a thundercloud within himself—many who are not prepared, not concentrated enough for the experience, become bewildered. He just gets puzzled at what has happened to him and feels frightened.

> *And Jesus came and touched them, and said, Arise, and be not afraid.*

*And when they had lifted up their eyes, they saw no man, save Jesus only.* (17:7–8)

When they lifted up their eyes, they saw their own Master standing before them.

*And as they came down from the mountain, Jesus charged them, saying, Tell the vision to no man, until the Son of man be risen again from the dead.* (17:9)

He says, for as long as I am in the body, do not tell this experience or this vision to anybody in the world, because if people think that I am performing miracles, they will unnecessarily follow and run after me.

*And his disciples asked him, saying, Why then say the scribes that Elias must first come?*
*And Jesus answered and said unto them, Elias truly shall first come, and restore all things.*
*But I say unto you, That Elias is come already, and they knew him not, but have done unto him whatsoever they listed. Likewise shall also the Son of man suffer of them.* (17:10–12)

He says that people of every religion always think that their saint, the founder of their religion, will come again. The Sikhs think that Guru Nanak, the Christians that Christ, and the Jews that Moses will come again. Similarly, people also thought that Elias would come again. And Christ says, how do they know that Elias has not come already? It means that saints have always been coming to this world, one after another, and there is no difference between one saint and another.

*"And they knew him not."* He has already come, but they never knew him. *"And have done unto him whatsoever they listed."* They have even caused him hardship, scorned or abused him, even killed him—he whose coming they are anxiously awaiting. He did come and they treated him very cruelly. He says: "*Likewise shall also the Son of man suffer of them.*" Similarly will they also treat me. In like manner, people are waiting for a Messiah to come, and all the while I am here in their presence. I am telling them that I have come—but they have no faith in me. They are still waiting for some mystic of old to come and guide them. He says, do not wait for him. If you want to go back to the Father, you must follow me, you must live my teachings.

What he means to say is that mystics are all waves of the same ocean. We are waiting for a particular wave, thinking that perhaps that wave will come again. A wave comes, does its job and merges back into the same sea. Do not think that that particular saint will come in the same body, environment and dress, and present himself to you. That which is a saint is the 'Word made flesh'. The Word is the saint, and the Word may come in any body.

> *Then the disciples understood that he spake unto them of John the Baptist.*
> *And when they were come to the multitude, there came to him a certain man, kneeling down to him.*
> *(17:13–14)*

This is about miracles. Somebody asked him:

> *Lord, have mercy on my son: for he is a lunatick, and sore vexed: for ofttimes he falleth into the fire, and oft into the water.*

*And I brought him to thy disciples, and they could not cure him.*
*Then Jesus answered and said, O faithless and perverse generation, how long shall I be with you? how long shall I suffer you? bring him hither to me.*
*(17:15–17)*

What he means to say is, I have not come to cure those who are lunatics, who are diseased or are lepers. How long will I be in the body to go on curing them? When I am not here, what will you do after that? Then also you will adopt some means of getting yourself cured and of getting worldly possessions and riches. I have come to take you out of this world, back to the Father, but you are a *"faithless and perverse generation"*, you want nothing but miracles from me. That is your only object in life for running to me. He says, what is the use of such faithless creatures? I have not come for that purpose. You should have faith. Develop faith in my being able to take you back to the Father, and for this make use of my being in the body. Live in my teachings, detach yourself from the world and go back to him.

So he says: *"How long shall I be with you? how long shall I suffer you? bring him hither to me."* Saints are always kind-hearted, so they sometimes do what people insist and beg for. But that is not their purpose in life. That is what he is trying to impress upon them. Then naturally he cured that child by casting out the devil.

*Then came the disciples to Jesus apart, and said, Why could not we cast him out?*
*And Jesus said unto them, Because of your unbelief: for verily I say unto you, If ye have faith as a grain*

> *of mustard seed, ye shall say unto this mountain, Remove hence to yonder place; and it shall remove; and nothing shall be impossible unto you.*
>
> (17:19–20)

A disciple asked, why could we not cure him? Why could we not help this person? He said, because you had no faith—neither in me, nor in the Father. You pray to him every day without having the least faith that he is hearing you or will grant you your wish. So he says: *"If ye have faith as a grain of mustard seed"*, if you can develop that little faith in the Master like that of a mustard seed, you will get so much power within yourself that you can remove mountains from one place to another. It means that you too can then do anything in this world.

> *At the same time came the disciples unto Jesus, saying, Who is the greatest in the kingdom of heaven?*
> *And Jesus called a little child unto him, and set him in the midst of them,*
> *And said, Verily I say unto you, Except ye be converted, and become as little children, ye shall not enter into the kingdom of heaven.* (18:1–3)

Somebody asked him, *"Who is the greatest in the kingdom of heaven?"* Who is entitled to go back to the Father? And he said: *"Except ye be converted"*—which means that your whole outlook on life should be changed. Now the tendency of your mind is outwards. But you have to withdraw your mind inwards to the eye centre and turn it upwards; that is conversion. You change from one way of living to another. And conversion comes by initiation and meditation. So he says unless you be 'converted'—initiated, and do your meditation, and become as little children—you will not be able to eliminate ego from yourself and become as innocent as a child, and *"ye shall not enter into the kingdom of heaven."* Then he explains:

> *Whosoever therefore shall humble himself as this little child, the same is greatest in the kingdom of heaven.* (18:4)

A child is always simple and innocent. He has no malice or ill will against anybody. His mind is still pure, unsullied by the evils of the world. So he says, unless you become like him, you cannot go back to the Father.

> *And whoso shall receive one such little child in my name receiveth me.* (18:5)

He says, if anybody is fortunate enough to live in or go to the company of such a high, evolved soul—someone who has eliminated ego from himself and become very simple and innocent—actually he has come into my company, because that man has nothing else in his mind but me, nothing else except the Master. He always talks about me, he is filled with my love and devotion, and whosoever goes to him, he also fills him with love and devotion for the Father. So he says if you happen to find any such company, actually you have also found me.

> *But whoso shall offend one of these little ones which believe in me, it were better for him that a millstone were hanged about his neck, and that he were drowned in the depth of the sea.* (18:6)

If anybody offends or hurts such good, loving souls who have nothing else within them except the Father, except their Master, and are only living for him, with no ambition of their own in this world, it would be better for them not to have come to this world or to drown in the sea rather than to exist, because they are very evil and wicked persons. They are just like any lower species.

> *Woe unto the world because of offences! for it must needs be that offences come; but woe to that man by whom the offence cometh!* (18:7)

He says there is no use in going to the company of *manmukhs* or worldly people.

> *Wherefore if thy hand or thy foot offend thee, cut them off, and cast them from thee: it is better for thee to enter into life halt or maimed, rather than having two hands or two feet to be cast into everlasting fire.* (18:8)

Then he explains that if you do any bad deeds in this world by going to the company of wicked people, you will have to pay for those karmas. But if you have already done such karmas, it is better to clear them now while you are in the body, while you are on the way to the Father. Otherwise you will not get the chance again. You will have to go to hell or back into *chaurasi* again. This verse has nothing to do with mutilating or disfiguring the body.

> *Take heed that ye despise not one of these little ones; for I say unto you, That in heaven their angels do*

> *always behold the face of my Father which is in heaven.* (18:10)

He says, do not hate such noble and good people who just live for our good, because they always have access to the Father. They always see the shining face of their Father within themselves. Make best use of their company. Do not hurt them or cause them hardship.

> *For the Son of man is come to save that which was lost.* (18:11)

'Which was lost' are those marked souls in this world who are lost in ritual and ceremony, or in worldly pursuits and worldly love. Those sheep have already been marked by the Father; but the son of man, the mystics, are sent because they are lost, to put them on the path and take them back to him. Then he gives a good example:

> *If a man have an hundred sheep, and one of them be gone astray, doth he not leave the ninety and nine, and goeth into the mountains, and seeketh that which is gone astray?* (18:12)

If a shepherd has a flock of a hundred sheep, and one goes astray, he leaves the ninety-nine and runs after that one sheep and brings it back to the fold. And if that sheep cannot walk, is lame, he even lifts it on his shoulders, because he loves all the hundred sheep, even the one which has gone astray. And he probably has to give more attention to that one than to the other ninety-nine. So if they complain and think: 'Our shepherd has left us. We were good and disciplined sheep. He has not cared for us, but has run after that one', they are not justified in thinking like that. He loves all the hundred sheep. He is responsible to the Father for all the marked and allotted souls.

If a sheep doesn't go astray from the fold, it pleases the shepherd, but the shepherd won't ignore the sheep which has gone astray. He will bring it back and may even carry it, but sometimes he scolds the sheep and even spanks it. Definitely he's displeased with the sheep which has gone astray and he's happier with those sheep that have remained within the fold. So naturally the Master is pleased if the souls are within the fold, remain within the disciplined way of life and are attending to their meditation.

So what Christ is trying to explain to us is that the Master loves all the disciples. Some disciples need more, perhaps, personal attention. But he is to take every soul back to the Father, so the question of loving one disciple and not another does not arise with the Master.

> *And if so be that he find it, verily I say unto you, he rejoiceth more of that sheep, than of the ninety and nine which went not astray.* (18:13)

If a gardener plants a hundred plants, and one plant starts withering while all the others give fruit, the gardener directs all his attention and energy towards that weak plant. And when he is able to put life into it again and it starts yielding fruit like the others, he becomes very happy. He loves and has to take care of all the plants, but that particular plant needed more of his personal attention, because he does not want a single plant of those entrusted to him to wither away. Similarly, Christ says:

*Even so it is not the will of your Father which is in heaven, that one of these little ones should perish.*
*(18:14)*

My Father has allotted me all these hundred sheep, all these marked ones. And he does not want me to lose even one sheep in this world. So if any sheep goes astray, I must go and search for it, and even physically lift it onto my shoulders and bring it back to the fold, because I am responsible to my God, to my Father, to deliver all the hundred sheep to him at his court. Then he gives beautiful advice to us:

*Moreover if thy brother shall trespass against thee, go and tell him his fault between thee and him alone: if he shall hear thee, thou hast gained thy brother.*
*(18:15)*

He says, we are all travellers on the same path. We are all struggling souls, full of weaknesses. We slip here and there. And if we really feel that some brother is slipping and is going astray from the path, and we really have love for him, then we should quietly go alone and approach him and explain to him lovingly: You are going astray and forgetting the real teachings, brother. Try to live in the teachings and help yourself.

But he says, go to him alone. Do not try to let his weakness be known to other people. Do not expose him or let him down before other people. He says: *"If he shall hear thee, thou hast gained thy brother."* So he remains your brother if you are able to save him by thus helping him, by explaining things to him, and in this way bringing him back to the path.

*But if he will not hear thee, then take with thee one*

> *or two more, that in the mouth of two or three witnesses every word may be established.* (18:16)

If he still does not listen to you, take another couple of fellow devotees to him. He may be impressed by two or three or four people, and in their presence may be able to give up his weaknesses and get back his faith again.

> *And if he shall neglect to hear them, tell it unto the church: but if he neglect to hear the church, let him be unto thee as an heathen man and a publican.* (18:17)

If he still does not listen to you, then all of you who are devotees and lovers of the Father, try to explain to him, try to bring him back to satsang and to hearing the discourses. And if he still does not care about all this, then leave him alone. Do not worry about him.

> *Verily I say unto you, Whatsoever ye shall bind on earth shall be bound in heaven.* (18:18)

Christ is explaining all this to Peter, because he is briefing him as to how he is to conduct himself as his successor after his departure, how he is to keep the torch burning. So he says, whomsoever you initiate during your lifetime on this earth will automatically be *"bound in heaven"*.

> *And whatsoever ye shall loose on earth shall be loosed in heaven.*
> *Again I say unto you, That if two of you shall agree on earth as touching anything that they shall ask, it*

> *shall be done for them of my Father which is in heaven.* (18:18–19)

He says, if two of you or if many of you ask me anything, for any favour, collectively, I will always be there. I will always hear you and take care of you. Do not feel that since I have appointed you as my successor to give the teachings, I am leaving you as an orphan. Whenever you remember me, alone or in a gathering, I will always be there to help you. I am always with my disciples, wherever I am talked about or thought about. Do not think that I am not there.

Jesus is saying this because he knew that he would have to leave his physical body and leave his 'sheep' after some time, so he is trying to instruct his disciples, and Peter particularly, as to how they are to carry on after him.

> *For where two or three are gathered together in my name, there am I in the midst of them.* (18:20)

He says, wherever people meet in my name, I am always there with them. Then they are all thinking about me and of nothing else. Therefore they should never think that I am not there.

> *Then came Peter to him, and said, Lord, how oft shall my brother sin against me, and I forgive him? till seven times?*
> *Jesus saith unto him, I say not unto thee, Until seven times: but, Until seventy times seven.* (18:21–22)

It does not mean exactly seventy times seven. It means many times—again and again. If a man does not forgive you, you have to go on asking for forgiveness until he does. There is no particular number of times that you have to ask forgiveness. Then he gives a parable to explain all this:

> *Therefore is the kingdom of heaven likened unto a certain king, which would take account of his servants.*
> *And when he had begun to reckon, one was brought unto him, which owed him ten thousand talents.*
> *But forasmuch as he had not to pay, his lord commanded him to be sold, and his wife, and children, and all that he had, and payment to be made.*
>
> (18:23–25)

In olden times, if a person owed money or had any debt, his property could be sold, and the man and his family sent to prison against the debt. So he says, there was a servant who owed a lot of money to the king, and the king demanded it many times from him, but he did not pay. So the king said that he and his wife and children, and all that he had, should be sold.

> *The servant therefore fell down, and worshipped him, saying, Lord, have patience with me, and I will pay thee all.*
> *Then the lord of that servant was moved with compassion, and loosed him, and forgave him the debt.*
>
> (18:26–27)

Naturally he asked for more time in which to pay his debt. He pleaded: 'I am sorry, I could not save the money to pay you. But just give me more time—you are the king, you are my lord.' So the king was moved with compassion and forgave the servant his debt.

*But the same servant went out, and found one of his fellowservants, which owed him an hundred pence: and he laid hands on him, and took him by the throat, saying, Pay me that thou owest.* (18:28)

By chance the same servant was also the creditor of a certain fellow-servant, for a very small sum of money. Forgetting that his king had forgiven him such a big debt, he was not prepared to forgive a fellow-servant even so small an amount. So he got hold of him and said: 'You must pay me, otherwise I will have you put in prison.'

*And his fellowservant fell down at his feet, and besought him, saying, Have patience with me, and I will pay thee all.* (18:29)

He said: 'I cannot pay you your money yet, because my harvest is not completely gathered in. I will need a little more time to pay.' So he asked him to have patience and he would eventually pay what he owed him.

*And he would not: but went and cast him into prison, till he should pay the debt.* (18:30)

But he was so heartless that he never paid any heed to his fellow-servant's request, or to his begging. He just had him put in prison.

*So when his fellowservants saw what was done, they were very sorry, and came and told unto their lord all that was done.* (18:31)

The fellow-servants reported all this to the lord, that another servant had been put in prison by your servant because he also owed him some money.

> *Then his lord, after that he had called him, said unto him, O thou wicked servant, I forgave thee all that debt, because thou desiredst me.* (18:32)

The lord was very angry and said, I have forgiven you so much money because you begged me for it and I was moved with compassion.

> *Shouldest not thou also have had compassion on thy fellowservant, even as I had pity on thee?* (18:33)

But you were not moved with compassion when your fellow-servant asked you for forgiveness and patience. Every day we pray to the Lord to forgive us for our sins and for our misbehaviour towards other people. But we are not prepared to forgive even the little faults of others. We are so heartless and cruel that we do not want to forgive our fellow beings. That is what Christ is trying to impress upon us. He says, how can you be forgiven when you have no compassion for your own brothers? First you should learn to forgive others, then ask for the Father's forgiveness.

> *And his lord was wroth, and delivered him to the tormentors, till he should pay all that was due unto him. So likewise shall my heavenly Father do also unto you, if ye from your hearts forgive not every one his brother their trespasses.* (18:34–35)

So Christ draws the conclusion, advising us that if we do not forgive our brothers in this world, how can we expect our Father, the Lord, to forgive us our sins? We first have to forgive them, then we are entitled to ask for forgiveness from the Father.

## Questions and Answers

***"How oft shall my brother sin against me, and I forgive him?"* (18:21)**

Q. Maharaj Ji, if you have hurt someone or offended someone either wilfully or out of ignorance and you ask them for forgiveness and they do not forgive you, how can you—?

A. Christ has referred to that point—should we ask seven times for forgiveness or seventy times seven? You should always continue asking for forgiveness until the person forgives you. There is no question of thinking 'I have done my duty and gone to him once. I asked for his forgiveness and he did not forgive me. Why should I worry now?' There is ego in that. He says: 'I do not say for seven, but for seventy times seven.' It means many times. If you really feel that you owe an apology to the other person, you should not hesitate to seek his forgiveness.

But if you are really sincere in your asking for forgiveness and if the other person still does not forgive you, then the Lord will forgive you. Then you have not to worry about the other person because from your heart you have given an apology. The humility with which you approach him, the repentance which you have in your heart in thinking 'I am really sorry for offending or hurting this person'—that is then what actually forgives you.

So you have done your duty when you have asked for forgiveness from another person. But mere asking for forgiveness is not sufficient to get you out of a karma or clear a karmic relationship. Forgiveness is something that goes a long way to clear that karmic action. But only this is not enough. We still have to meditate, and attachment to Shabd will forgive and permanently clear all karmas.

If you have some grievance or anger in your heart and you sit in meditation, your mind will never be still. You will always be thinking of that grievance or thinking ill of the other person, and you can never even concentrate or be in touch with the Shabd nor enjoy the bliss within. But if your heart is relaxed, is free of all ill will, and you do not have any malice or grievance against anybody, then your meditation is easy because then you are receptive to the grace of the Father. Otherwise you are closed to his grace.

So in order to be receptive to his grace, if anybody asks for forgiveness, we should always readily forgive. And if somebody expects us to ask for forgiveness, we should never hesitate. That is what Christ tries to explain in this incident.

Q. Well, you could slander somebody, perhaps; the person would not know that you had done it, yet you have done him a wrong.

A. You mean, you have done something behind his back?

Q. Yes, so if you go to him and ask his forgiveness, you are hurting him more by letting him know that.

A. If you have been backbiting in someone's absence, you can pray to the Father to forgive you, and by your actions you can praise him. And with whomsoever it was that you slandered that person, you can tell them you were wrong, you are sorry for making such statements. You owe an apology to them, not to that person about whom you have talked.

Q. In a situation like that, how do we know that we are not paying back a karma that was done to us in our previous life?

A. If we think in that way we will never behave rightly. How do you know what the other person did to you in one of the previous births, for which you think you are paying him back now? How do you know that he did it to you? If you have reached that level of consciousness where you know, then it is all right to say that. But then, at that high level, you will never do such things.

We should not worry about the other person's karma, we should only worry about our karma—the part we have played in offending him. We have only to clear that part. We have to clear our conscience, to make our mind clean.

Q. I have heard that at the time of initiation the Master takes four-fifths of our karmas upon himself. That he takes all the karmas that we have accumulated in this life.

A. Well, brother, there is absolutely no ratio or proportion as to how much he takes and how much we have to share.

These are all justifications for our not doing anything. As I gave an example, when you are going to a forest where there are lions, your friend may give you a gun or a sword to protect yourself. But when a lion comes, you do not call your friend also to fire your gun. You have to face the animal with the arms with which you have been equipped. So the Master equips us with Shabd and Nam. And then he helps us also and teaches us how to use those arms and is always there with us to guide us. But we have to do our own shooting—our meditation. That does not mean that we should throw ourselves absolutely on the Master. We have to account for our own karmas.

Everyone has an individual load of karmas, and the Master knows what a particular person will be able to go through in this birth, or in two or three or four births. He knows how much he is able to go through. So individually he is helped at that level to go through his load of karmas. You cannot set a particular time limit—that it has to be cleared in this life, and that this much the Master will take and this much I have to go through. That is a wrong way of calculating.

Q. Is this an altering of the karmas by the Master in getting us straight? Is it a conditional thing?

A. That is what I said. The Master sets us right.

In the Bible, when people accused a lady of adultery, Christ said to her: "Neither do I condemn thee: go, and sin no more" *(John 8:11).* It means that he attached her to the Holy Spirit within. So whatever we have done, if we are sincere and devoted in our meditation, it will be cleared by the Shabd and Nam provided that we "sin no more", that we do not collect more karmas, more dross—then we will be forgiven. If on the other hand we collect more dross every day and expect that whatever we do, both the past and the future, will be forgiven, that is just self-deception. That is why we are asked to remain steady on the principles of Sant Mat, so that we do not collect more dross.

## ⇶ EIGHT ⇷

# DISCOURSE ON MATTHEW 19–20

> *For there are some eunuchs, which were so born from their mother's womb: and there are some eunuchs, which were made eunuchs of men: and there be eunuchs, which have made themselves eunuchs for the kingdom of heaven's sake. He that is able to receive it, let him receive it.* (19:12)

It means that there are some people who are born as eunuchs and others who abstain from lust and sensual pleasures just in order to go back to the Father. He says that they are the real people. So we have to abstain from lustful desires. Only then are we able to go back to the Father. Otherwise our heart does not become pure enough to receive his grace.

> *And, behold, one came and said unto him, Good Master, what good thing shall I do, that I may have eternal life?* (19:16)

'What should we do in this world to seek the blessings of the Father? What type of life should we lead so that we may be able to go back to him?' asks one. And Christ replies to him:

> *Why callest thou me good? there is none good but one, that is, God: but if thou wilt enter into life, keep the commandments.* (19:17)

He is saying all this out of humility. He says, why are you calling me good? We are all struggling souls. There is no question of there being any good or perfect man in this world. There is only one, namely God, who is perfect. But since you have faith in me, you have asked me what can take us back to the Father, so I will tell you:

> *If thou wilt enter into life, keep the commandments. He saith unto him, Which? Jesus said, Thou shalt do no murder.* (19:17–18)

Murder does not just mean the murder of humans; it means that you should not take the life of any creature.

> *Thou shalt not commit adultery.* (19:18)

You should not look at any woman with a lustful eye.

> *Thou shalt not steal, Thou shalt not bear false witness, Honour thy father and thy mother: and, Thou shalt love thy neighbour as thyself.* (19:18–19)

He says that these are the simple things which every man should know. We must respect our parents, must do our duty towards our mother and father and must be good to our neighbours. We are all children of the same Father, so everybody is our neighbour and we must love everybody. The One who has created this universe permeates this creation. We must see and love that Creator in everybody in this world.

> *The young man saith unto him, All these things have I kept from my youth up: what lack I yet?* (19:20)

The young man said, I am doing all these things. I do not kill anybody, I do not commit adultery, I do not give any false witness, and I am also loving and kind and good to everybody. What do I lack? I have still not seen the Father.

> *Jesus said unto him, If thou wilt be perfect, go and sell that thou hast, and give to the poor, and thou shalt have treasure in heaven: and come and follow me.* (19:21)

Christ says, these things will make your heart clean, but your vessel is still empty—you have to fill it with something. Not just leading a neat, clean life in this world will entitle you to go back to the Father. That will only remove all the dirt and make your cup clean. And with what do you have to fill it? He says, go and sell whatever you possess in this world. It means that you should take your mind out of all these things, detach yourself from the possessions of the world, and then *"come and follow me."* Then live in my teachings, have faith in me, and follow the path which I will explain to you.

Unless you detach yourself from the creation, from worldly possessions, you are not capable of following me. It is self-deception if you say that you are doing so. If you want to follow me, you must leave everything to which you are attached in this world. Only I should be in your mind, and nothing else. Then you can go back to the Perfect One.

> *But when the young man heard that saying, he went away sorrowful: for he had great possessions.* (19:22)

Now this man was a multimillionaire, a very rich person. So it was very difficult for him to leave all those things, or at least to take his mind out of everything.

*Then said Jesus unto his disciples, Verily I say unto you, That a rich man shall hardly enter into the kingdom of heaven.* (19:23)

A rich man is one who is attached to the riches of the world. It does not mean one who has riches. Those who are possessed by their possessions, be they great or small, and are day and night obsessed by worldly riches, can never go back to the Father, howsoever pure, neat and clean a life they may lead, because they have built their treasure in the world. Unless they build their treasure in heaven, they cannot go back to heaven. They go where their heart is. That is the teaching which Christ gave us previously *(6:21).*

So he tells us that since this young man has a lot of property and wealth and his heart is also attached to it, it will be very difficult for such a man to go back to the Father.

*And again I say unto you, It is easier for a camel to go through the eye of a needle, than for a rich man to enter into the kingdom of God.* (19:24)

Christ means that it is as impossible for a person to go back to the Father while he is attached to the riches of the world as it is for a camel to go through the eye of a needle. And unless we attach ourself to the audible life stream within, it is impossible for us to detach ourselves from worldly things.

*When his disciples heard it, they were exceedingly amazed, saying, Who then can be saved?* (19:25)

Then naturally the disciples asked, How can anybody ever go back to the Father? Everybody has the instinct of possession, everybody has property, everybody is being possessed by these things.

*But Jesus beheld them, and said unto them, With men this is impossible; but with God all things are possible.* (19:26)

He says that it is impossible for human beings to detach themselves from the world on their own or by themselves, but with the grace of the Father it is not impossible. When we are receptive to his grace and blessings, when the Father wants us to merge back into the Perfect One and he pulls us from inside, then he can detach us in a second from the world. So he says, do not worry. The blessings of the Father are always upon you. With his grace it is possible to detach yourself from the world. How does God make this possible? When he wants to pull us from the creation to his level, he puts us in the company of a living Master and, through him, attaches us to the Spirit or Holy Ghost within. That attachment to the Spirit detaches us from all the riches of the world and from the creation.

*Then answered Peter and said unto him, Behold, we have forsaken all, and followed thee; what shall we have therefore?* (19:27)

Peter said, we have left everything. We have no kith and kin. We have left our children, our property and all the wealth that we had in this world, and we just follow you and live in your teachings. What will be our fate?

*And Jesus said unto them, Verily I say unto you, That ye which have followed me, in the regeneration when the Son of man shall sit in the throne of his glory, ye also shall sit upon twelve thrones, judging the twelve tribes of Israel.* (19:28)

He says, you people who have left so much of the world to follow me and live in my teachings will be honoured by sitting by my side. It means, you will always be with me.

*And every one that hath forsaken houses, or brethren, or sisters, or father, or mother, or wife, or children, or lands, for my name's sake, shall receive an hundredfold, and shall inherit everlasting life.* (19:29)

He says, whosoever detaches himself for my sake, for my love, to live in my teachings, to become one with me, and forsakes houses, property, wealth, sister, father, mother, children, wife—it means everything in the world that we are possessed of—he will have a hundredfold. In this very life, he will go straight back to the Father *"and shall inherit everlasting life"*—he will go to that place from where he will never have to take birth again.

*But many that are first shall be last; and the last shall be first.* (19:30)

This has a very deep meaning in it. Do not think that if you are able to follow the path right from childhood, you are entitled to attain your goal first, and another person who started to follow the path when he had become quite aged will be the last to reach the Father. He says: *"Many that are first shall be last; and the last shall be first."* There is no seniority on the path in this world. Everybody has individual karmas to clear. Then he gives another parable also, to explain how the first can be last and the last first:

> *For the kingdom of heaven is like unto a man that is an householder, which went out early in the morning to hire labourers into his vineyard.* (20:1)

He says that a landlord goes out and engages some labourers for his vineyard.

> *And when he had agreed with the labourers for a penny a day, he sent them into his vineyard.* (20:2)

He fixes a daily wage and puts them to work in his vineyard.

> *And he went out about the third hour, and saw others standing idle in the marketplace.* (20:3)

And when he has put the first batch to work, he again goes out and finds some people sitting idle on the roadside. He asks them if they also want some work and engages them.

> *And said unto them; Go ye also into the vineyard, and whatsoever is right I will give you. And they went their way.*
> *Again he went out about the sixth and ninth hour, and did likewise.* (20:4–5)

And though it was a couple of hours later that this new batch was hired, he also agreed to pay them for the day and put them to work. Then, even after six or nine hours, he finds some more people sitting idle and he also engages them for the day and puts them to work, saying, you will get what is right.

> *And about the eleventh hour he went out, and found others standing idle, and saith unto them, Why stand ye here all the day idle?*
> *They say unto him, Because no man hath hired us.*
> *He saith unto them, Go ye also into the vineyard; and whatsoever is right, that shall ye receive.*
> *So when even was come, the lord of the vineyard saith unto his steward, Call the labourers, and give them their hire, beginning from the last unto the first.* (20:6–8)

So when the day's work is over, he calls all the labourers. He assembles those who have worked for twelve hours, and those who have worked for only ten, nine, six or even two hours or one hour. Then he instructs his clerk to pay them all, whosoever worked in the field that day.

> *And when they came that were hired about the eleventh hour, they received every man a penny.* (20:9)

Even those who were engaged at the last hour, who had only worked for an hour or so, were paid the same wages as those engaged in the first hour of the day.

> *But when the first came, they supposed that they should have received more; and they likewise received every man a penny.* (20:10)

So naturally the first batch started grumbling, saying they had worked for twelve hours throughout the day and these people for only one hour. The landlord is very unfair. He has paid us one penny and has paid the same wages to the others also.

> *And when they had received it, they murmured against the goodman of the house,*
> *Saying, These last have wrought but one hour, and thou hast made them equal unto us, which have borne the burden and heat of the day.*
> *But he answered one of them, and said, Friend, I do thee no wrong: didst not thou agree with me for a penny?* (20:11–13)

The landlord says, I have done you no harm. I have not kept your wages back. I have paid you all that was agreed upon between us. So why are you jealous of the other people, if I have also paid them the same? There is no reason for your murmuring and grumbling and protesting about it.

> *Take that thine is, and go thy way: I will give unto this last, even as unto thee.* (20:14)

He says, it is my wealth and my sweet will. I can give to these people whatever I feel like giving. You have no right to be envious of others as long as you have received the wages agreed upon for your labours. It is my wealth and I am free to give it to anyone.

> *Is it not lawful for me to do what I will with mine own?* (20:15)

He says, it is my property, my wealth, and I have full rights to do with it as I like. I can distribute it as I wish. You have no business to discuss or even to question or ask me why I so favour these people without their doing any work.

> *Is thine eye evil, because I am good?* (20:15)

He asks, are you evil and jealous because I am good, because I am noble and compassionate, full of kindness for these people? It is just your evil eye, just jealousy, nothing else. You should not grumble as long as you are getting your wages.

> *So the last shall be first, and the first last: for many be called, but few chosen.* (20:16)

He will explain this point again, further on. He says, you people do not know why I have paid them an equal amount. So as long as your wages are being paid, you should not worry.

What he means to say is that when saints come to this world, many people are initiated by them but few are chosen to go back to the Father in that very life. The others will also go, but by their turn, perhaps not in that very life. Some people come early and work the whole of their life for spiritual progress. Some people come quite late in their life and they also work the remainder of their life for spiritual progress, but equal wages are paid to everybody, whosoever is initiated. What are the wages of an initiate? That he ultimately must go back to the Father. That is the wages which a saint will pay to every labourer, to every initiate in this world.

So he says that you have no business to be jealous because you were the first to come to the path and laboured a longer time to go back to the Father than another man who worked very little and attained his goal though he came to the path very late in life. It is the saints' own treasure. They can give whatever they feel like to anybody. We have no business to ask them why more grace is bestowed on this person and less grace on that soul, why this one is favoured and that one not. We should only feel concerned about ourself: 'As long as I am initiated, I am on the path and being taken to the Father, I am happy. It is not my concern whether the other soul is taken in one or two or three births, or whether he is getting more or less than I. That is not my concern at all. That is Master's job. The Master knows his duty.'

Then Christ explains to them:

> *Ye know that the princes of the Gentiles exercise dominion over them, and they that are great exercise authority upon them.*
> *But it shall not be so among you: but whosoever will be great among you, let him be your minister.*
> *(20:25–26)*

He says, whosoever is a high soul, is spiritually advanced, let him try to guide the others.

> *And whosoever will be chief among you, let him be your servant. (20:27)*

If anybody is spiritually advanced and is trying to give strength and faith to other disciples, he should feel that he is their servant and has been given that seva and opportunity by the Master, and he should be happy to be their servant. So whosoever is given the duty of being a leader or generally is given some seva, he should be more humble and meek. Then only can he be perfect in his seva and do his duty. If he begins to think that he is above others, is superior to others, then the ego comes in and he loses all the opportunity of that seva. That is what Christ is trying to tell us.

> *Even as the Son of man came not to be ministered unto, but to minister, and to give his life a ransom for many.* (20:28)

He says, I am the son of the Father. I have stood as a ransom for the disciples. The ransom is that I have stood as a surety to Kal for all the disciples—that all the sheep belong to me and whatever they owe to you, I will owe to you on their behalf. I will take their sins, stand for their karmas, and see that they pay every little thing that they owe you in this world.

Whether by going through physical ailments, by going through them in the body or by meditation or by the grace of the Master—whatever it may be—but whatever is due to Kal must be paid to Kal before the soul can go back to the Father. So saints always stand as a ransom or surety for all their disciples, whomsoever they initiate. But still they always are an example of humility, and behave and live in such a way as if they are the servants of the disciples.

Actually, Christ is trying to brief Peter by giving him parables and other advice, because he has asked him to keep the torch burning, to keep people on the path.

## QUESTIONS AND ANSWERS

***"So the last shall be first, and the first last: for many be called, but few chosen" (20:16)***

Q. Master, at the end of the parable of the vineyard and the workers, Christ said: "Many be called, but few chosen." Can you explain that?

A. What he means to say is that saints come and they initiate thousands of people in the world, but few are the fortunate ones who go back to the Father in that very lifetime.

Actually, it is a continuation of the parable of the sower taking seed to a field. Some seeds fall on the wayside, some on rocky, some on marshy and some on fertile ground. It is actually the same parable that he is explaining all along, and he takes other points from it and explains them further.

Q. Master, it is rather difficult to believe that anyone could be jealous of somebody else reaching the Father.

A. Why should they mind it if anyone else reaches the Father? Generally, fellow students do become envious of one another in a class. You know that a professor may love all the students in a class, but you will find a lot of envy among them, thinking: 'The professor is good to that boy and does not bother about me. He favours him and not me.' So actually he is referring to the Master, because they have not reached the Father at all.

He also gives the same example of the hundred sheep. The shepherd loves all the sheep, but if one goes astray he has to run after it and even lift it up and carry it back to the fold. So the others have no business to be envious of that one sheep, because he loves them all, equally.

It is the same thing that he is saying here, that we should not be envious of one another. If we have been given our reward by the Master, we have been promised that we will reach the Father and our initiation and efforts are being accepted, then if another man gets the same reward from the Master without even putting in any effort, we have no business to be envious at all. He knows best to whom it is due. We do not know how much that man worked in his last birth—or his previous three births. We only know about this present life. Since we do not know the facts, we cannot complain about it. Actually Christ has explained the two parables, this one and the one about the hundred sheep, in sequence, to illustrate the same point.

## NINE

# Discourse on Matthew 21–22

*And Jesus went into the temple of God, and cast out all them that sold and bought in the temple, and overthrew the tables of the moneychangers, and the seats of them that sold doves.* (21:12)

When Jesus went to the Temple, he found that people were selling charms and other things, just to make money. The people in such places are more interested in making money than in your soul. They were trying to commercialize the teachings. And he went in and upset their tables and threw down their wares, and explained to them:

*It is written, My house shall be called the house of prayer; but ye have made it a den of thieves.* (21:13)

All these houses of prayer—these temples, synagogues, churches and gurdwaras—should be places in which to worship and pray to the Father. There should be peace and solitude. The atmosphere should be spiritual all around you and there should be no commerce, no business, no other activity in such places. Christ says: *"But ye have made it a den of thieves."* The aim of a thief is to rob you of your wealth. So he says, you are priests, you should help people to pray to the Lord, but you are trying to rob them of their wealth, so you are misusing these temples.

There is another meaning also. *"My house shall be called the house of prayer."* By 'house' is meant the body, where the soul and the Lord live. And this body is given to us for praying to the Lord. This is the place where we have to worship and pray to him within, but we have made it a den of thieves. These five passions* and senses are thieves and are looting us day and night. We are possessed by them and are always a slave to them. So he says that instead of using your body to pray to the Lord, to seek him within, you have made it a place of pleasure, you have become a victim of the senses. You are not rightly using your body for the purpose for which the Lord gave it to you.

Then he tells us about how much faith we should have. You know about the fig tree which bore no fruit and which became withered when Christ verbally condemned it:

> *I say unto you, If ye have faith, and doubt not, ye shall not only do this which is done to the fig tree, but also if ye shall say unto this mountain, Be thou removed, and be thou cast into the sea; it shall be done.* (21:21)

He says, if you can develop faith even as little as a mustard seed, even a little faith in the Father, you will get so much power within yourself that if you want to move a mountain from one place to another, you can easily do so.

> *And all things, whatsoever ye shall ask in prayer, believing, ye shall receive.* (21:22)

*"Believing"*—having faith in the Father that he is hearing you and is capable of giving you what you are asking for. We

* Lust, anger, greed, attachment and egotism.

generally pray because our mind wants to pray for fulfilment of worldly ambitions and desires. But we do not really believe in him. Just out of habit, we pray to him. He says that kind of prayer is useless. First you must develop faith in the Father. You must know that he exists, that he is hearing you and that he does not need vain repetition or any set prayer, because your heart and soul can reach him. If you have faith in him that he will give you only what is best for you and then you pray to him, he will grant your prayer.

> *And when he was come into the temple, the chief priests and the elders of the people came unto him as he was teaching, and said, By what authority doest thou these things? and who gave thee this authority?*
>
> (21:23)

Then the priests asked Jesus, has anybody given you authority to give such teachings to the masses? Have you been appointed Master by someone?

Because Christ's teachings were very simple, very convincing, and full of love and devotion for the Father, naturally people were greatly impressed by him. But the hierarchy of organized religions can never tolerate people following the saints and mystics and not coming to the churches or the synagogues. So they started questioning Christ, asking: 'Who has given you authority to give this teaching?' One must be chosen by somebody. As Christ says, one must be marked and stamped by the Father to give the teachings.

> *And Jesus answered and said unto them, I also will ask you one thing, which if ye tell me, I in like wise will tell you by what authority I do these things.*

*The baptism of John, whence was it? from heaven, or of men?* (21:24–25)

He answered them saying, first you must answer my question. Was John sent by the Father and did he have access to him, or was it only that the people selected him as a Master? Do you believe that he was sent by the Father and was his son? Or do you believe that he was just a noble man and people came together and chose him as a leader of the community? What do you think: was his baptism from men or the Father?

*And they reasoned with themselves, saying, If we shall say, From heaven; he will say unto us, Why did ye not then believe him?* (21:25)

This question was a very clever one, a catch. If they answered that John was from the Father, he had access to him, was sent to us as his son, then the next question would be: if so, why didn't you put your faith in him and believe in him? And since he has baptized me and appointed me as his successor, why ask now who I am and who has given me the authority to teach?

*But if we shall say, Of men; we fear the people; for all hold John as a prophet.* (21:26)

Because John the Baptist was well known and had a lot of followers, naturally the priests were frightened of the masses, of the multitudes, since the people would resent it if they said he was just an ordinary man, a good and righteous person, and elected or given honour by them only, and not sent by the Father.

> *And they answered Jesus, and said, We cannot tell.*
> *And he said unto them, Neither tell I you by what authority I do these things.* (21:27)

Actually, he tried to hint to them that John the Baptist had access to the Father and came from him to teach you. And now that he is not here, he has asked me to teach you. So John the Baptist has given me authority to teach you, to fill you with love and devotion for the Father. And if you have faith that John the Baptist had access to the Father and had authority to teach, then you should also have faith in me that I also have authority to teach, because he has appointed me as his successor. I was baptized by him, initiated by him, and have access to him. So my teachings are being given to you because my Father wants me to do so. He instructed John the Baptist to select me, so I derive my authority from the Father, through John the Baptist.

Then he gives a parable:

> *But what think ye? A certain man had two sons; and he came to the first, and said, Son, go work to-day in my vineyard.*
> *He answered and said, I will not: but afterward he repented, and went.* (21:28–29)

A man had two sons. To one of them he said: 'Go and work in my vineyard today', and the son refused him. But then he realized his mistake, so he repented, went to the vineyard and started working.

> *And he came to the second, and said likewise. And he answered and said, I go, sir: and went not.* (21:30)

The other just said: 'Yes, yes, I will go to the vineyard', but he never went there. Christ says, you people are like that. You were very quick to recognize John the Baptist as having come from the Father, that he was a great saint. Though you heard him, yet you do not understand his real teachings, nor follow them, nor try to meditate and live the life that he wanted you to live. You are like the second son.

However, other people refused to listen to him at first because they were victims of the intellect. But once their intellect was satisfied, they repented for their mistake, they realized their folly, and came to think: 'He really is a saint and it is not right to refuse to accept his teachings.' Then they heard and followed and lived his teachings.

*Whether of them twain did the will of his father?*
*(21:31)*

Which will please his father, the first one or the second?

*They say unto him, The first. Jesus saith unto them, Verily I say unto you, That the publicans and the harlots go into the kingdom of God before you.*
*(21:31)*

He says that you people are only giving lip-sympathy to John the Baptist. You call him a saint, but it is only in name. Actually you have no faith in him and do not follow his teachings. However, the other people—who at first did not listen to him, but once having become convinced about his teachings now follow them—are the real disciples of John the Baptist.

What Christ implies is that I and my disciples are living in the teachings of John the Baptist, so we are his real disciples.

You may give your allegiance or loyalty to him and say that he is your Master, but that is in name only. You are not his real disciples.

> *For John came unto you in the way of righteousness, and ye believed him not: but the publicans and the harlots believed him: and ye, when ye had seen it, repented not afterward, that ye might believe him.* (21:32)

He says, the others may not have listened to him at first, but once they were convinced, now they believe and have faith in him and are trying to follow his teachings. But you still do not believe.

> *Hear another parable: There was a certain householder, which planted a vineyard, and hedged it round about, and digged a winepress in it, and built a tower, and let it out to husbandmen, and went into a far country.* (21:33)

Christ always tries to give us spiritual truths by stories, by parables. This has been the practice of most saints, especially in the Middle East.

> *And when the time of the fruit drew near, he sent his servants to the husbandmen, that they might receive the fruits of it.*
> *And the husbandmen took his servants, and beat one, and killed another, and stoned another.* (21:34–35)

The vineyard was given to husbandmen to take care of. And when the landlord sent his servants to collect the crop, to get the lease money and so on, whosoever was sent, they attacked and killed them.

> *Again, he sent other servants more than the first: and they did unto them likewise.* (21:36)

The others were also assaulted and murdered.

> *But last of all he sent unto them his son, saying, They will reverence my son.* (21:37)

Then the landlord sent his son, thinking that at least they will recognize my son and give what is due to me.

> *But when the husbandmen saw the son, they said among themselves, This is the heir; come, let us kill him, and let us seize on his inheritance.* (21:38)

Because they were evil-minded, they said that after the landlord dies, the son is going to inherit this entire property, so let us tie up the son and murder him, and we will be the owners of this farm.

> *And they caught him, and cast him out of the vineyard, and slew him.*
> *When the lord therefore of the vineyard cometh, what will he do unto those husbandmen?* (21:39–40)

Actually, this parable means that the Lord has sent us into this world for the purpose of meditation, for finding our path back to the Father. But if anybody in this world talks to us about the Father, we always become hostile towards him. We even go to the length of killing them, of getting rid of those people who always talk about the Lord and about devotion. And then, when the Lord himself sends his son, when he comes himself in the garb of a saint, even on those saints we always inflict hardship. We crucify them or put them on hot plates or torture them in other ways. We place all sorts of difficulties in the path of the sons of the Father—and what for? Their 'fault' is just that they tell us what our purpose is of living in this world. They do not collect any money from us, nor create any religion here, nor set one person against another. They only try to fill us with love and devotion for the Father. And because we cannot tolerate anybody talking to us about the Lord, we crucify them.

> *They say unto him, He will miserably destroy those wicked men, and will let out his vineyard unto other husbandmen, which shall render him the fruits in their seasons.* (21:41)

So what is the result? What does the Lord do? He gives the human opportunity to other more deserving souls. And those who do not make use of this human birth, he sends into hell or into *chaurasi,* and there they suffer for their misdeeds. So in this parable he is trying to explain to us the purpose of our life.

> *Did ye never read in the scriptures, The stone which the builders rejected, the same is become the head of the corner: this is the Lord's doing, and it is marvellous in our eyes?* (21:42)

He says, you do not know the karma of any individual. When a builder erects a building, he may pick up a stone to put on the wall, but throw it away because it is the wrong shape or size. And he just picks up another and uses it, and the wall gets built. But when he reaches the top, he finds that the same stone which he threw away at the bottom fits better in the arch. So it is in the hands of the 'builder' and because of the karma of a person as to where he will ultimately find his place. Similarly, Christ says that many types of people come to the saints, and you never know which one will reach the top and which will just be used in the foundation.

> *Therefore say I unto you, The kingdom of God shall be taken from you, and given to a nation bringing forth the fruits thereof.* (21:43)

By 'nation' he is not referring to any particular nation, whether Jewish or Christian or any other. 'Nation' in this context means those people who will seek more earnestly and are really honest in their desire to go back to the Father.

Then Christ gives another parable about a king and a feast. You must have heard and read a lot about it:

> *And Jesus answered and spake unto them again by parables, and said,*
> *The kingdom of heaven is like unto a certain king, which made a marriage for his son,*
> *And sent forth his servants to call them that were bidden to the wedding: and they would not come.*
> (22:1–3)

He says, a certain king wanted to arrange a marriage for his son, and he invited a great many people to the feast, to the banquet. But they were so haughty that they never came.

*Again, he sent forth other servants, saying, Tell them which are bidden, Behold, I have prepared my dinner: my oxen and my fatlings are killed, and all things are ready: come unto the marriage.*
*But they made light of it, and went their ways, one to his farm, another to his merchandise:*
*And the remnant took his servants, and entreated them spitefully, and slew them.* (22:4–6)

The king found that the servants who went to invite those people to the feast of his son's marriage were manhandled or even murdered.

*But when the king heard thereof, he was wroth: and he sent forth his armies, and destroyed those murderers, and burned up their city.*
*Then saith he to his servants, The wedding is ready, but they which were bidden were not worthy.*
*Go ye therefore into the highways, and as many as ye shall find, bid to the marriage.* (22:7–9)

He then tells other servants to go to the streets, to the roadside, and give an open invitation to anybody, saying that the king's son is going to marry, the banquet is spread, all the dishes are prepared, just come and take part in the wedding.

*So those servants went out into the highways, and gathered together all as many as they found, both bad and good: and the wedding was furnished with guests.* (22:10)

Because they could not discriminate who were good or bad or wicked people, they gave an open invitation. So naturally all types of people came, just to have a feast with the king.

> *And when the king came in to see the guests, he saw there a man which had not on a wedding garment: And he saith unto him, Friend, how camest thou in hither not having a wedding garment? And he was speechless.*
> *Then said the king to the servants, Bind him hand and foot, and take him away, and cast him into outer darkness; there shall be weeping and gnashing of teeth.*
> *For many are called, but few are chosen.* (22:11–14)

Christ has only given the parable to explain this point: *"Many are called, but few are chosen."* Actually, this parable has a very, very deep mystical meaning behind it. He says that the Lord invites the souls back to himself, and he sends his sons, the devotees, to the world to awaken the sleeping souls and to fill them with love for him. And those people are victims of the senses, of their riches and of their attachments, and do not listen to those saints, nor bother about their talk of the Father. They have given themselves to merrymaking and to enjoyment. And the Lord says, do not worry about these people, they are condemned now, they will never hear you. Go to the poor, the real people, who are innocent and simple, always thinking about me.

So when they were invited by the saint, naturally they were all attracted to him. But when they all came to the satsang, heard the discourses and meditated, one came without a wedding garment. The 'wedding garment' of a soul is its cleanliness and perfection, being full with love and devotion, having cleared all its karmas and paid all that was due to Kal. So it means that at the time of death, all the other souls had become ready by practising meditation and living in the teachings of the mystics, but one soul was not yet ready to meet the Father.

What is meant is that when saints come, they initiate all types of people. But only that soul can go back to the Father who has a 'wedding garment', who is properly 'dressed'. But some half-baked souls are also attracted by the saints. They are the people who have not been able to abstain from sensual pleasures, though initiated, and are still attached to the world. They will not be able to go back to the Father, but will be sent back again to this world to account for their karmas. They will be taken within their next two or three births, at the most, but in this life they were not able to make themselves pure. They could not get the 'wedding garment' which is necessary for returning to the Father.

So this whole parable means that many are called by the saints, but few are chosen to go back to the Father in that very lifetime; though ultimately every soul will be taken back to him. But you see, naturally, everybody is not prepared in one life.

It is again a continuation of the parable of the sower who went to a field. He says, just as the farmer has a lot of seeds and throws them about here and there, similarly saints come into this world, but not every soul that comes to them is deserving. There are many half-baked souls who come and are not ready to go back to the Father, but circumstances bring them into the company of the mystic and they are initiated. So they will have to come back to clear their karmic accounts with the world. When they have been able to clear all that with the help of meditation, in their second or third or fourth birth they will get a 'wedding garment' and then they will also be honoured in the court of the Father.

> *Then one of them, which was a lawyer, asked him a question, tempting him, and saying,*
> *Master, which is the great commandment in the law?* (22:35–36)

He said: Tell us in a nutshell the teachings of the mystics and saints. Which is the greatest of the commandments which are given to us by every mystic?

> *Jesus said unto him, Thou shalt love the Lord thy God with all thy heart, and with all thy soul, and with all thy mind.* (22:37)

Christ says, my first piece of advice to you is: *"Thou shalt love the Lord thy God."* Love only the Father. Everything that we have in this world is perishable, so nothing here is worthy of our love.

To love God 'with all your heart' means with all your emotions, with all your feelings, with all your devotion, because love for the Father must start from the heart. Unless we feel the separation, unless we have a desire and longing to go back to the Father, we can never worship him, can never feel the necessity to become one with him.

To love God 'with all your mind' can only be done when the mind is cleared of all the filth it is carrying. A dirty, unclean mind can never love God. As long as the mind is full of pride, lust, anger, greed, attachment, ill will, jealousy, backbiting, hatred and so forth, it is not fit to love the Lord. It has countless desires and ambitions for worldly attainments, it is all the time lost in the sense pleasures of the world, so it has become absolutely unfit to think of or worship the Lord. Hence, loving the Lord with all your mind will only be possible when it is cleared of all this rubbish, becomes clean and is ready to turn towards the Lord. The mind cannot love both the world and the Lord at the same time.

This cleansing of the mind takes place through simran and by attending satsang meetings. Then it becomes fit to attach itself to the Spirit within, will happily return to its home and thus release its hold on the soul.

The inclination of the soul is always towards its own home, its origin—the Father himself. When the soul is released from the mind in the second spiritual stage, it sheds all coverings—the three bodies, the five elements, three attributes, mind and maya. From the second stage onward the naked or unencumbered soul shines in all its glory. Then, ever conscious of the company and guidance of the Radiant Form of the Master within, it swiftly and joyfully moves on the current of light and sound towards its own home—that ocean of eternal peace and bliss, of which it is a drop. That is worshipping the Lord with the soul.

So the first thing is, you must miss the Father and feel the separation from him. Only the Father should exist for you. Do not forget your goal or your destination. Always keep the Lord in front of you, in whatever situation you may be. Never forget him at all. That is the first commandment.

*This is the first and great commandment.* (22:38)

He says, once you are able to achieve and live up to this commandment, then what will the second commandment be?

*And the second is like unto it, Thou shalt love thy neighbour as thyself.* (22:39)

After the first commandment, when we love the Lord with all our heart, mind and soul, then we naturally realize and see him within ourselves. When this happens, then we are able to see him outside in all his creation. Only when we see him within ourselves first are we able to see him outside. Guru Nanak also says: 'When we realize that the body is the temple of the Lord—and this we only do when we see him within our body—then the entire world becomes the temple of the Lord for us. Then no living being is a stranger for us here because we see him in everyone.' Kabir also says that 'From one light the entire creation has come into being and the same light is shining in everyone. Then who is high and who is low?' When this realization comes, then we see him everywhere, and not only all human beings become our neighbours, but also all living creatures—the animals, birds and beasts.

Therefore 'loving thy neighbour' means to love the One who is in everyone. 'Loving' means to have a kind and gentle nature, to be helpful and generous towards others. Then there is no place in our heart for any ill will, hatred, jealousy, envy or any such vicious thoughts. Then we are at peace within ourselves and with the whole world.

This commandment follows after the realization of the first. So Christ says, always remember two commandments in life. First, love the Lord with all thy heart, with all thy mind, with all thy soul. And when you are able to practise this commandment, then you will be in love with every human and every creature in the whole world, because you will not see anything else in this creation except the Father. He says that is the second commandment.

*On these two commandments hang all the law and the prophets.* (22:40)

If you search through any of the scriptures of the world, whether of Buddha, or Krishna, or Christ, or Nanak, or of any other mystic, you will find that all their sayings and teachings are based on these two commandments.

## QUESTIONS AND ANSWERS

***"The stone which the builders rejected, the same is become the head of the corner"*** **(21:42)**

Q. Master, could you please explain this saying from the New Testament: "The stone which the builders rejected, the same is become the head of the corner."

A. You must have seen buildings being constructed, and generally when a mason is working, he just picks up a brick for the foundation and says 'It does not fit in here', and he throws it away. But ultimately the same brick may find a place in the roof, at the top. You often see masons working like that. Similarly, he says that those people who have been rejected by the world might find themselves at the top. They may be accepted by the Father, by the saints or mystics—when their time comes. They are rejected in the beginning and accepted in the end.

So we try to search for the Father right from our birth but we do not succeed. Only when our time comes are we accepted. When the time of that brick comes, it finds its place not just on the ground, but even at the top. So when the time of the disciple comes, he follows the Master and is attached to the Shabd and Nam. When the time has not come, he is put aside. The saint may even be living as his next-door neighbour, but he will not hear him. He will have no faith in him. However, when his time comes, then that very soul may find its place at the highest point on the path.

### *Parables as teaching stories*

> Q. There is the parable of the prodigal son that Christ gave. Now, that son was with the father in the beginning, and he took all of his inheritance and left the father and found himself eating swill with the pigs. Then he said: 'I will return unto the father.' That is why I thought that since we were sons in the beginning with the Father, we became disobedient and left the light of God like the prodigal son. So then we return on our journey back.

A. These are just parables to explain certain spiritual truths to us. You cannot analyse these stories too much. We have just read about the parable of the king and his feast *(22:1–14).* He said that oxen were killed, and this and that. But that does not justify our eating meat. It was just a parable that there was a grand feast and people were invited to it. We have only to consider that part of the story which is relevant to the subject in hand. Christ is only trying to give us a story, that one person came without a wedding dress. That is the main point that he is impressing upon us, that unless you have a wedding dress you cannot enter the king's chamber. Unless the soul is ready it cannot go back to the Father. This whole story, as a story, is of little value.

So we should not try to analyse these parables. We are all disobedient sons of the Father. And when we become obedient sons, we go back to the Father. As long as we do not go back to him, we are all disobedient.

⇶ TEN ⇷

# Discourse on Matthew 24–25

Then Christ talks about the coming of mystics to this world:

> *For as the lightning cometh out of the east, and shineth even unto the west; so shall also the coming of the Son of man be.* (24:27)

Christ says that when the son of the Father comes to this world, he shines just like the sun which rises in the east and travels to the west, shining upon the whole world.

And how are people attracted towards the mystics? Though this example is not very pleasant, still saints have to explain to people according to their way of life, by those examples with which they are familiar and that can explain the real truth to them. Christ says:

> *For wheresoever the carcase is, there will the eagles be gathered together.* (24:28)

Wherever the carcass or dead body of an animal is, nobody goes to call the eagles or vultures—they automatically fly to that place. Similarly, Christ says that wherever the son of man is, wherever the mystics or saints come, disciples or seekers automatically gather around them. Saints do not have to go to find the seekers or call them. They are automatically drawn to the Master because the pull is from within. And just as the light shines from the sun, similarly their light also attracts the seekers, automatically.

Then he talks about the coming of the mystics or saints at the time of our departure from this world:

> *Immediately after the tribulation of those days shall the sun be darkened, and the moon shall not give her light, and the stars shall fall from heaven, and the powers of the heavens shall be shaken:*
> *And then shall appear the sign of the Son of man in heaven: and then shall all the tribes of the earth mourn, and they shall see the Son of man coming in the clouds of heaven with power and great glory.*
> *And he shall send his angels with a great sound of a trumpet, and they shall gather together his elect from the four winds, from one end of heaven to the other.*
> *(24:29–31)*

This is entirely a mystical experience, an inner experience, for the disciple of a perfect Master. He refers to the *"sign of the Son of man in heaven"*—which is the coming of the inner Radiant Form of the Master to meet his disciples at the time of their death, to guide them at every step within, back to the Father.

So Christ first tells us about the process of dying, which his disciples do daily through meditation, by withdrawing their consciousness back to the eye centre and contacting their real Master, the Shabd, within. Then he gives us a glimpse of the majesty and bliss that the Master showers, through his grace, on these blessed ones who mourn and yearn for the Father, who struggle and sacrifice everything of this world to die the living death to go and meet him within. In this way, Christ gives us an idea of the absolute importance of meditation preparing the disciple for his ultimate death in this world while building his treasure within and invoking the grace of the Lord to take him back into his lap. For he says:

> *But of that day and hour knoweth no man, no, not the angels of heaven, but my Father only.* (24:36)

This statement is significant. He says, you don't know when your time will come when you will have to leave this world, which you now take so seriously. It is all completely perishable, just an illusion, yet you waste your time in useless pursuits, dancing to the tune of the mind and the senses, never for a moment considering when the inevitable time will come to leave all this. So he reminds us that the hour will come when we must die, but only the Father knows when. Therefore he tells us to make adequate preparation for that day, through our meditation and strictly adhering to the teachings of the Master, through obedience to the Master and living a Sant Mat way of life. Then, with the grace of the Master, we make our way back with him to our eternal home.

Then Christ continues to impress this point, that if we say we are truly desirous of going home and we say we will follow the Master, then we should make the very best use of this opportunity while in the human form.

Then he follows with three parables in succession that emphasize the absolute necessity to make the wisest use of this human body if we want to go back to the Father. He begins with the example of the faithful and wise servant:

> *Watch therefore: for ye know not what hour your Lord doth come.* (24:42)

This is really the gist of this particular parable. Christ warns, be ever mindful—*"watch"*—keep your heart ready to receive the Lord, because we don't know at what time or in what circumstance we may be when he comes for us.

> *But know this, that if the goodman of the house had known in what watch the thief would come, he would have watched, and would not have suffered his house to be broken up.*
> *Therefore be ye also ready: for in such an hour as ye think not the Son of man cometh.* (24:43–44)

He tells us, if a man knew at what time a thief would be entering his house, he would be watchful for him at that time. But who is the 'thief' and what is the 'house'? The thief is our own mind, and the house is our own body. We never know when or how the mind will distract our attention and take us headlong into the sensual pursuits, towards our destruction, and thus waste this life in futility. The mind is a formidable thief which is so crafty and clever that it can rob us without our even being aware that we are being robbed. Hence Christ warns us to be wary all the time. We must hold fast our attention at the eye centre, never let it fall under the sway of the mind and the senses. Rather, with firm determination and with love and devotion, keep our attention always receptive to his grace. Then he continues:

> *Who then is a faithful and wise servant, whom his lord hath made ruler over his household, to give them meat in due season?*
> *Blessed is that servant, whom his lord when he cometh shall find so doing.*

*Verily I say unto you, That he shall make him ruler over all his goods.* (24:45–47)

Now he tells us who are the blessed ones of the Lord and what their reward is. He says the *"faithful and wise servant"* is that disciple who is always steeped in love and devotion of his Master. This disciple is completely obedient to the Master, does only what he says and seeks only to please him. He has no other thought in his mind than that of his Master and keeps his beloved before him in whatever circumstance he may be. His faith is firm and unshakeable, and nothing else exists for him in the creation save his Master, his Lord. So Christ says: *"Blessed is that servant."* That disciple is the blessed one. And what is his reward? He says: *"He shall make him ruler over all his goods."* His reward is the Creator himself. Everything the Creator has created are 'his goods', and the creation is handed over to such a disciple. The Master has made the disciple fit to merge into himself, thus making him one with the Creator, one with the Father. And when you have the Creator, you automatically have the creation.

*But and if that evil servant shall say in his heart, My lord delayeth his coming;*
*And shall begin to smite his fellow-servants, and to eat and drink with the drunken;*
*The lord of that servant shall come in a day when he looketh not for him, and in an hour that he is not aware of,*
*And shall cut him asunder, and appoint him his portion with the hypocrites: there shall be weeping and gnashing of teeth.* (24:48–51)

Then we are told of the consequences of following the dictates of the mind. If our mind gets the upper hand and begins to create doubts in us saying: 'When is that Lord going to come? I have been waiting here so long in utter darkness. What is keeping him? Why has he not yet taken me into his lap?' In such a way the mind causes our faith to falter, puts us further under the spell of illusion and causes us to lose heart. We may even return to a worldly way of life and live a sinful existence. And what is our punishment from the Father? He comes with his grace and finds us not receptive to it, but instead lost in the creation, completely forgetting the Lord. The penalty may even be to be cast again into the cycle of birth and death, to reap the seeds we have sown, and to continue experiencing the pain and suffering of this world. So he says, do not be swayed this way. Be always attentive and obedient to your Master. Become deserving and receptive to his grace, and become pure and strong enough to be worthy of his reward.

Christ then gives the second parable which also tells us what use we should make of this human life if we do not want to waste it in vain. It is the parable of the ten virgins:

> *Then shall the kingdom of heaven be likened unto ten virgins, which took their lamps, and went forth to meet the bridegroom.*
> *And five of them were wise, and five were foolish.*
> *They that were foolish took their lamps, and took no oil with them:*
> *But the wise took oil in their vessels with their lamps.*
> *While the bridegroom tarried, they all slumbered and slept.* (25:1–5)

He gives an example to explain to us how we should prepare ourselves in order to make the best use of this life. He says there were ten virgins who waited for their bridegroom to come for them. Five of them were foolish and five were wise. The foolish virgins made no preparations to meet their beloved and only left everything to the last minute, whereas the five wise virgins made all the proper arrangements in advance for their bridegroom's coming.

> *And at midnight there was a cry made, Behold, the bridegroom cometh; go ye out to meet him.*
> *Then all those virgins arose, and trimmed their lamps.*
> *And the foolish said unto the wise, Give us of your oil; for our lamps are gone out.*
> *But the wise answered, saying, Not so; lest there be not enough for us and you: but go ye rather to them that sell, and buy for yourselves.*
> *And while they went to buy, the bridegroom came; and they that were ready went in with him to the marriage: and the door was shut.* (25:6–10)

Then at midnight, the call came that the bridegroom was on his way. But only the five wise virgins who kept enough oil to light their lamps could see him. The five foolish virgins, who did not have any oil, at that moment begged for some oil from the wise ones so they too could see the bridegroom and be taken by him. But the wise ones feared that if they shared their oil they would also suffer since they had only enough for themselves. So they told the five foolish virgins to go out and purchase oil for themselves. The bridegroom arrived in the meantime and received only the five wise virgins who could see him and were ready for him. They went with him, and the door was shut to all others behind them.

> *Afterward came also the other virgins, saying, Lord, Lord, open to us.*
> *But he answered and said, Verily I say unto you, I know you not.*
> *Watch therefore, for ye know neither the day nor the hour wherein the Son of man cometh.* (25:11–13)

When the five foolish virgins returned, they begged their lord to let them also enter. But he said that he did not know them. They were not keeping constant vigil for him, so he could not accept them. Thus, Christ is telling us how we should be waiting for the Lord. The soul is the virgin, waiting to be carried back home by her Master, her Lord. How should we wait? With enough oil in our lamps, with enough meditation to our credit, to be fit to meet the Lord.

Spiritual experiences are individual and not to be shared with others. We must do our meditation with one-pointed attention, fully concentrated at the eye centre. And the Master waits for that effort, which invokes his love and devotion that he gives us. It is all a gift from the Master, but we must be ready for it, we must be receptive to it. There is no dearth of his grace—it is always being showered in abundance. But we must put in our effort. We must show him we are truly grateful, that we have faith that he really is there within to give it to us, so when he appears to us in his inner Radiant Form we are ready to go back with him.

In this third parable, Christ stresses the essential necessity for giving full time to our meditation, to 'living' in meditation if we truly want to go back to the Father. That, he says, is making the very best use of this human opportunity. Because it is only in this form that we can find a perfect living Master to show us the way and take us back to him. So he explains in the parable of the talents:

> *For the kingdom of heaven is as a man travelling into a far country, who called his own servants, and delivered unto them his goods.*
> *And unto one he gave five talents, to another two, and to another one; to every man according to his several ability; and straightway took his journey.*
> *(25:14–15)*

He says a landlord, who was about to travel into a far-off country, called his servants and gave each of them some of his wealth, according to what each deserved.

> *Then he that had received the five talents went and traded with the same, and made them other five talents.*
> *And likewise he that had received two, he also gained other two.*
> *But he that had received one went and digged in the earth, and hid his lord's money.* (25:16–18)

Then each servant took that with which he was entrusted and did with it what he felt he could. The servants given each five and two talents doubled theirs, whereas the servant given one talent buried his. So the Lord gives us what we deserve of his wealth of Nam when we are initiated. Then we, as his disciples, can either make use of this rare and precious opportunity to go on multiplying this wealth through our meditation, or we can just bury it and waste this human opportunity. Then he continues:

> *After a long time the lord of those servants cometh, and reckoneth with them.*
> *And so he that had received five talents came and brought other five talents, saying, Lord, thou deliverest unto me five talents: behold, I have gained beside them five talents more.*
> *His lord said unto him, Well done, thou good and faithful servant: thou hast been faithful over a few things, I will make thee ruler over many things: enter thou into the joy of thy lord.* (25:19–21)

After a long time the lord of these servants returned to see what his servants had done with what he had given them. The servant who had been given five talents had doubled them, and this pleased his lord. The lord saw that his servant had used this wealth wisely, so he was now deserving of much more. So his lord, who was extremely wealthy and could give him a vast amount, took his faithful servant in with him to enjoy his wealth.

> *He also that had received two talents came and said, Lord, thou deliveredst unto me two talents: behold, I have gained two other talents beside them.*
> *His lord said unto him, Well done, good and faithful servant; thou hast been faithful over a few things, I will make thee ruler over many things: enter thou into the joy of thy lord.* (25:22–23)

The same thing happened with the second servant, who also pleased his lord by doubling his share, and therefore was also taken in to enjoy the wealth of the lord.

> *Then he which had received the one talent came and said, Lord, I knew thee that thou art an hard man, reaping where thou hast not sown, and gathering where thou hast not strawed:*
> *And I was afraid, and went and hid thy talent in the earth: lo, there thou hast that is thine.*
> *His lord answered and said unto him, Thou wicked and slothful servant, thou knewest that I reap where I sowed not, and gather where I have not strawed:*
> *Thou oughtest therefore to have put my money to the exchangers, and then at my coming I should have received mine own with usury.*
> *Take therefore the talent from him, and give it unto him which hath ten talents.* (25:24–28)

But when the third servant was questioned, he said that he feared his lord, who was a hard task master, and the vast wealth he had gathered by means of his tremendous power. So instead of investing the one talent given to him, fearing its loss and the consequent anger of his lord, he buried it in the earth. This displeased the landlord, who expected on his return to find his wealth increased. So he took back what he had given to this faithless servant and gave it to the one who most valued it and could make best use of it.

Christ says that the Lord gives every human being in this world a capital amount, the number of breaths which are allotted, and expects us to make proper use of this in our life. He expects us not only to make use of these breaths merely to live in this world but to add to this capital by doing something else. And that is to attempt to achieve the goal of God-realization, which is the purpose of human birth.

After our death the Lord enquires what we have done with the capital amount with which he sent us into the world. Those who made a 'profit' please the Lord and he takes them unto himself. Others who did not make the right use of the breaths he gave them, did not make any profit. They just ate, drank and enjoyed life in this world and died. Such people do not please the Lord and as a punishment he not only takes away from them the privilege of the human birth he gave them, but throws them into the darkness of transmigration.

Christ means that we should be like the wise servants of the Lord and make the right use of the capital with which he sent us into this world. That is, to gather the spiritual wealth, clear all our burdens, live the teachings of the saints, follow them in obedience, and by so doing, attach ourselves to the divine melody within. Then we will be accepted by the Master and the Lord at the time of our death and go back to our real home. Now Christ concludes:

> *For unto every one that hath shall be given, and he shall have abundance: but from him that hath not shall be taken away even that which he hath.*
> *And cast ye the unprofitable servant into outer darkness: there shall be weeping and gnashing of teeth.*
>
> *(25:29–30)*

This is most important, and actually runs as a theme throughout these parables. He says: *"For unto every one that hath shall be given, and he shall have abundance."* The same statement was made in the parable of the sower *(13:12)*. 'Those who have' means those who have been given the gift of Nam by the Master. To them shall the Father give in abundance. Those who are attending to meditation, who have love and devotion for the Father, will be showered with his unending grace and love from within. *"But from him that hath not shall be taken away even that which he hath."* He says, 'those who have not'—have not been given this wealth by the Master—are not destined to go back to the Father. So from them will be taken away what they have, and that is this human opportunity to seek a perfect living Master. Those who don't make use of this opportunity will have it taken away and may again be cast into the lower species. Thus, make the best use of this opportunity. Attend to your meditation. Make spiritual progress. And on the wings of love and devotion, fly with him and become one with the Father within.

Now Christ refers to a person's time of death:

> *When the Son of man shall come in his glory, and all the holy angels with him, then shall he sit upon the throne of his glory.* (25:31)

There is no particular day when everybody's account will be examined. At their time of death, every disciple and every person will be judged. That is the resurrection as far as that soul is concerned. So for those who are initiated, naturally the Master, the son of man, will come and pass judgement according to their karma.

> *And before him shall be gathered all nations: and he shall separate them one from another, as a shepherd divideth his sheep from the goats.* (25:32)

'Sheep' means the marked ones who are initiated, or baptized, and on the path. 'Goats' means the *manmukhs,* those who are attached to the world. At the time of our death, it is immaterial to what nation or country we belong. We will be judged as to whether we are a goat or a sheep, whether we are initiated or not initiated, whether we are worldly minded or devoted to the Father.

> *And he shall set the sheep on his right hand, but the goats on the left.* (25:33)

The right hand, naturally, is the Father's side and the left is the negative, or Kal's side. The sheep will go back to the Father, and the goats will come back to the earth, to the creation again. All will be judged according to their karmas.

> *Then shall the King say unto them on his right hand, Come, ye blessed of my Father, inherit the kingdom prepared for you from the foundation of the world.* (25:34)

From the time of your birth, this path was prepared for your going back to the Father. By 'King' he means the son, the mystic or saint, or whatever you call the Master. So the soul will be collected at the time of death. And since it is initiated—it is a 'sheep'—the path is marked out for it to go back to the Father.

> *For I was an hungred, and ye gave me meat: I was thirsty, and ye gave me drink: I was a stranger, and ye took me in:*
> *Naked, and ye clothed me: I was sick, and ye visited me: I was in prison, and ye came unto me.* (25:35–36)

Here Christ explains to the 'sheep'—the good ones—why they will be placed on his right and why they will inherit the kingdom prepared for them. This naturally surprises the listeners and they ask:

> *Lord, when saw we thee an hungred, and fed thee?*
> *or thirsty, and gave thee drink?*
> *When saw we thee a stranger, and took thee in? or*
> *naked, and clothed thee?*
> *Or when saw we thee sick, or in prison, and came*
> *unto thee?* (25:37–39)

Then Christ replies:

> *And the King shall answer and say unto them, Verily I say unto you, Inasmuch as ye have done it unto one of the least of these my brethren, ye have done it unto me.* (25:40)

Christ reveals that whenever a hungry or thirsty person came to your door and you gave him food and drink, you gave it to me. Whenever you clothed a naked man or visited a poor man in prison, tended one who was sick, received a stranger as a guest, you did all this service to me.

This aspect of the teachings of the saints is a very important one: of being helpful to others, of supplying their needs, of being kind and good to others. It is very strongly emphasized by the saints and mystics, but is unfortunately ignored and overlooked by many of their followers.

Soami Ji says that if you desire to make a search into spirituality, to start in this direction— first you must have a very tender and kind heart, a heart which bleeds at the suffering of others. You should, even at personal sacrifice and inconvenience, go to the help of the needy and the poor. If this compassion and tenderness is not in you, you are not fit to follow this path. 'Do unto others as you want others to do unto you' is a very important and well-known truth. It also has a practical side too. If we do not go to the help of others, how can we expect anyone to come to our aid in time of need. However, we should not render help to others with the idea of any reward.

Christ means that you served me in everyone when you came across these needy persons and did not hesitate to help them and meet their needs, even those of the most lowly and humble. You made no distinction between man and man when it was a question of mitigating their suffering. The saints themselves come from those regions of bliss to this world because their heart is moved by compassion for the misery and suffering of the souls here in this world. The saints then suffer even here for the sake of these souls, to help them and take them out of the realm of the negative power.

By acts of compassion our heart becomes gentle and kind, and that has a purifying effect on the mind. A hard-hearted person who has no feeling for others is not fit to go back to the Lord. The Lord himself is an ocean of love, compassion and mercy. He is called a 'benefactor'. So unless we also inculcate in us these qualities, we cannot merge back into him.

He is just comparing those people who love his creation and those who do not. Because the Father is in his creation, and those people who do not see him in his creation, they ignore the Father, have no love for him, so they will suffer; and others will merit going back to the Father. That is what he is trying to explain to them.

# Questions and Answers

### *"From him that hath not shall be taken away" (25:29)*

Q. In the parable of the talents, why was it said: "From him that hath not shall be taken away"?

A. Because he did not make the right use of the opportunity, therefore he did not deserve it. The human birth is given to us to increase our wealth, to make spiritual progress, and those who are doing this by building up meditation to their credit will get the advantage and benefit from it. Those who are wasting this human opportunity, just burying that money and not putting it to proper use, will be cast out.

### *Love the Creator in the creation*

Q. Maharaj Ji, this passage *(25:31–45)* has got completely out of proportion in the understanding of the Church, because they are engaging themselves so much in social activities and so on. And they say: If we do this, then it will be sure that we will be saved.

A. We have to love the Creator in the creation, that is the point. And we love human beings because the Creator is in every human being. Actually, we love the Creator, we are not attached to anybody. To think that by loving the creation we will be able to love the Creator would be a negative approach.

You may be so much involved in the creation and its attachments that you may absolutely forget the Creator. And that concept has come in Christianity, and it comes in everybody—to serve humanity, yet eliminating the Lord. So social service is not bad, it is good; but only social service cannot take you back to the Father.

To serve humanity is a good cause—you are cleaning a vessel. But my approach is that if you love the Lord, all good qualities rise in you like cream on milk. You develop all the human qualities if you love the Lord. If you just go on cleaning a vessel every day, it will become dirty again. But if you fill it after cleaning it, the purpose is fulfilled. So we have to be helpful to others, we should be good, kind and loving to others. That is just to clean our vessel. Then we have to fill it with that nectar, with that Holy Ghost, that Spirit.

Christ says: "Now ye are clean through the word which I have spoken unto you" *(John 15:3).* Only the Word, the Spirit, can make you clean, nothing else. 'Clean' means clean from all karmas, from all coverings. And all the coverings will be removed from the soul only by attaching ourself to that Spirit or Holy Ghost within. All other things are a means to that end—social service and being good, noble, kind, loving and helpful—but you must not ignore the end. These other things should prompt you to attach yourself to that Spirit within.

⇶ ELEVEN ⇷

# Questions and Answers on Matthew 26–28

### *The Last Supper (26:26–28)*

Q. Could you explain when at the last supper, Jesus took bread, broke it, and said to his disciples: "This is my body"?

A. What he meant was that the real body, or blood or flesh of the living Master, is the Shabd and Nam, because he is the Word incarnate, the Word made flesh. Your Master is always with you, but the physical body of your Master cannot always remain with you. So the real Master is the Shabd and Nam which is in that body, and that is the real blood. It is described as blood and flesh in the sense that without blood and flesh this body cannot exist.

In *Saint John* he said that unless you eat my flesh and drink my blood, you cannot dwell in me and I in you *(John 6:56)*. 'Drinking the blood' and 'eating the flesh' of a Master is to abide by his teachings. Thus you attach yourself to the spirit of God. You merge into the Word, the real Master within yourself. It is not eating his physical body, nor drinking his blood. So it is only a way of explaining it, because the Word or Shabd cannot be easily explained. You cannot see it, nor feel it. You can only experience it or realize it within yourself. That is what he means.

'Dwell in me' means that you merge into the Sound, the Shabd and Nam—his real self. When we merge into the

Shabd, we automatically become part and parcel of that Shabd, which is the real or Radiant Form of the Master within. In one of Guru Nanak's shabds, there was this sentence: You have to merge into your Master, to become one with him, to lose your own identity and become someone else, become the Master—then you will go back to the Father. As Christ says, I will come unto you, and you will come unto me, and we will both become one, and since I have become one with the Father, you will also become one with him *(John 14:20).* It is the same idea which lies at the back of it.

Q. You know, Maharaj Ji, you mentioned once that if we belong to a particular religion, then we should more or less become a better person with those people. And I was thinking that in Christianity, those who take communion, mostly what they give us is some bread and even wine. But that means that when somebody becomes a satsangi, he could not partake of it any more because they use alcohol.

A. But where is the necessity of taking all that? Who is a Christian? A Christian is one who follows the teachings of Christ. A Christian is not one who becomes a member of an organized religion.

Q. Well, that is one of the very main tenets of the whole religion.

A. That is right, because in every religion, only rituals and ceremonies are left. The reality is lost. Christ makes it very clear what his blood and flesh are. He says: "The flesh profiteth nothing" *(John 6:63).* Everybody has to leave the flesh. The real blood and flesh is the Shabd, the Spirit, the Truth. If you can get the communion of *that* blood and *that* flesh, then it is real communion. Otherwise it is only a ritual and ceremony. But why do they substitute his blood with wine? Why not with water?

Q. Master, wine is mentioned many times in the Bible. Is that due to the writers?

A. It may be grape juice—fruit of the v-i-n-e, not w-i-n-e.

Q. Well, like at the last supper, they made mention of wine, and at the wedding feast that Christ attended, they referred to wine.

A. Because people are fond of wine, they probably have started writing or thinking of it as wine! Unless they put it in Christ's mouth, how can they justify their drinking it? It is the same in the Sikh religion. All the Sikh Gurus were strict vegetarians, but I think that now Sikhs are great meat eaters; and they have also put it in the Gurus' mouths now, in stories. So they are very happy when they take meat, which is absolutely wrong. The saints' life histories must tally with their teachings. If they are contradictory to the teachings, then there is something wrong with the history.

### *Christ's betrayal and Judas's repentance (26:14–50, 27:3–5)*

Q. If someone speaks against the Master, denies him or even betrays him, as Judas did to Christ, what will the consequence be? What is the punishment?

A. He sinned against Christ, but sincerely repented later. As Christ was nothing but grace and an ocean of mercy, so he is just in the lap of Christ. This is very clear from the Sant Mat teachings. When Judas betrayed Christ, he was still his disciple and so he would go wherever Christ was. It is not that he would not be punished for that. There is punishment for every karma. But then, after punishment, where else would he go? He was Christ's own disciple, his own initiate, he had been baptized by him personally; and if his own initiate could not go to him, then who else could?

Every father does not have all his children obedient and loving, but he loves every child, even those who are disobedient to him or even turn their back on him. The father does not turn his back on any child. So how could Christ have turned his back on Judas? A father loves all his children, so the question of his going anywhere else does not arise.

And as far as punishment is concerned, we are punished only if Master turns his back on us. If a child disobeys the father, is rude to the father or hurts the father, the father never punishes the child in anger. A loving father will discipline the child to set him right. He wants to make him a good child, a loving, obedient son, but he will not give the child to the police—he will never send him to jail. The father loves the child. He will punish him, but not in anger. So Master doesn't condemn us. It is our own karmas that punish us, that condemn us. Our own weaknesses are making us miserable in this world.

Christ said: I have not come to condemn you; I have come to save you *(John 3:17).* Masters come only to save us; they don't come to condemn us. If *they* start condemning us, then where else can we go?

Q. Judas might have repented also.

A. Naturally, he must have been given an opportunity to pay for all that and then ultimately he would have gone back to Christ.

***"My God, my God, why hast thou forsaken me?" (27:46)***

Q. Master, why did Jesus Christ, when he was on the cross, say: "My God, My God, why hast thou forsaken me"?

A. This statement is quite baffling when taken literally, as it is translated. However, when we read *The Gospel According to Saint John,* we find that Christ had said previously that the Father would 'glorify' him. And later he prayed, "Father, the hour is come; glorify thy Son", and mentions words to the same effect in other places *(John 17:1, 5).*

There could have been a mistake, also, in translation from one language to another. Some Bible scholars say that the word 'glorify' has been wrongly translated as 'forsaken' because the words are similar in the Aramaic language, spoken by Christ at that time. This seems most likely, as to a non-initiate it would be difficult to believe that Christ was being glorified when he was tortured, crucified and dying on the cross. But when you read where Christ said 'I and the Father are one' *(John 10:30),* how could the Father forsake him? At the time when Christ uttered these words, his attention was no doubt withdrawn from his body and he was completely absorbed in the Father within, where he was conscious in all his glory—the same as in deep meditation one is unconscious of the body but fully conscious within. Only those who understand the teachings of the saints can comprehend this possibility.

When Christ was praying to the Father earlier, when he knew his end was coming, he told his disciples: After a little while you will not see me and after a little while you will again see me *(John 16:16)*. Then he prayed to the Father: I have finished my allotted task and now, Father, glorify me and take me back to the same place from where I have come *(John 17:4, 6)*. He was just praying to the Father in that context.

But there are many possible explanations for that saying. He may have been reciting something in love and praise of the Father. Because I know about the Great Master, in his last days when he was not well, he used to recite Soami Ji Maharaj's hymns a lot, from memory. He remembered most of the verses. He was especially fond of reciting: "O soul, let us go back to our home, why stay in a foreign land?" He was very fond of reciting it early in the morning. This I remember because we were always in attendance on him then. Now a person who was not an initiate, or did not know that hymn, may have thought that the Master was probably saying those words as from himself. But actually, that hymn belongs to Soami Ji, and in love of Soami Ji or of his own Master, he used to recite it quite often.

Sometimes, in the bath, I have heard him chanting Guru Nanak's hymns. And sometimes he used to tie a very long turban—it would take him about fifteen or twenty minutes—and I have heard him standing near my doorway reciting a poem while he was tying it. It would be one of Kabir's, or Guru Nanak's, or Soami Ji's, or somebody else's. So they were not his own words. Guru Nanak himself says: "O Lord, save me from falling. Come and help me." He was saying it or praying to the Father from the disciples' point of view.

So you see, it is very difficult to interpret every word after two thousand years. We can only take Christ's general teachings from the Bible, and about that I have also told you that

Christ himself did not write anything, nor did he dictate it, nor was it written down in his lifetime. It was written down much later on. And it has passed through so many translations, and so many deletions and additions have been made. Many times the language has been 'straightened'.

Even now, under our eyes, in this modern Bible they say that they have straightened the language. But after another thousand years, people will think that Christ probably said all these straight prose words in English. But he just gave general teachings, and they were written down according to his disciples, and somebody collected them into one book form as the New Testament.

Q. I think I read in Dr Johnson's book, *The Path of the Masters,* that he said that at that moment, God had forsaken him. And the reason, said Dr Johnson, was that he had done so many miracles and taken so much karma on himself. But that cannot be, for you told us that a Master has no karma.

A. That is the writer's own approach and opinion—I do not agree with him. Dr Johnson, fortunately or unfortunately, was a missionary, and he was so embittered at what he had gone through, and was so happy when he came out of it and with what he got then, that he could not forgive them for wasting his life. And so he was embittered here and there, and I do not agree with his approach on many points. But since the author is no more, we cannot touch his writing. We do not want to add anything at all or eliminate anything from his writing. I accept the facts that he gives, but do not agree with his approach. He himself said: "My approach is like a surgeon, and a surgeon always knows how to use a knife."

### *"He is risen from the dead" (28:1-18)*

Q. Maharaj Ji, in your interpretation of *Saint John,* Christ said that when he died, the Shabd would leave his body; that then his flesh would no longer be the Shabd, but just flesh. But how about the resurrection and the ascension? Didn't Christ take his flesh up to heaven?

A. There is not going to be a general resurrection at all. That is a wrong concept—that everybody will rise on one particular day and be accounted for then. Resurrection is individual, with every disciple, with every person who is living. When I die, my resurrection is on that day. On that day, my Master comes and raises me up. It is a wrong concept of resurrection that I will stay somewhere until one particular day when the Master will come.

Q. I mean the resurrection and ascension of Jesus Christ. It is said that on the third day, Christ rose from the grave and went up into the sky.

A. No, it is not physical at all.

Q. Well, after the crucifixion, Christ was said to have returned to the physical body.

A. I do not think he came back to the body at all after the crucifixion. Why should he first leave the body and then come back into it after three days? Where was the necessity? He could have kept his body here, if he had wanted.

Q. You see, all the Christians believe this.

A. Christians believe many things, brother.

Q. There is a part in the Bible, Master, where it says that Christ was taken out and cremated.

A. Maybe. After the crucifixion, when the body had been given to his disciples, they may have cremated him. All these stories generally arise just so that the disciples can give greatness to the mystic or saint. Actually, it has no foundation at all. Even about Guru Nanak, it is said that when the disciples came, they removed the sheet that covered him and his body was not there.

Q. Similarly with Kabir, Maharaj Ji?

A. With Kabir also. Such stories do spring up after mystics have gone, but there is no reality in them at all.

Q. Well, there are some people that have what they think to be the shroud of Christ.

A. How can you consider it? I wonder what type of cloth there used to be in those days—two thousand years ago? These are far-fetched imaginings. And these things do not make mystics great at all. Their teachings and their way of life make them great—that even today we are trying to follow them—not their being able to come back to the body.

Q. Yes, but you see, many satsangis who were Christians think that Christ gave the esoteric teachings or gave the simran and the Shabd, the initiation, to his apostles after his death, after the resurrection, during those forty days.

A. I do not think so. I will discuss it from the Bible; he will make it a little clearer. Christ said: "As long as I am in the world, I am the light of the world" *(John 9:5)*. But he himself indicated that when he left the body he would no longer be the light of the world. Why should he at all come back to the same flesh, to become the light?

Q. Don't you think he was in the flesh for those forty days, between the resurrection and the ascension?

A. I do not know about the history of it at all, but—

Q. He came in the flesh on Easter Sunday, then he stayed in the flesh until the fortieth day after Easter Sunday.

A. But my point is why should he leave the body at all if he wanted to take it up again? Where was the necessity of getting himself nailed on the cross, and then taking that nailed body again? What for?

Q. Oh, so this is all just a myth that Christ came back for forty days?

A. It is possible that his disciples saw him. Those experiences were visions of the astral form of Christ. We are discussing whether he came back into the physical body, which is not so.

Q. Oh, it was just his astral body?

A. His disciples saw him and they may have seen him inside and outside many times, but that would not have been his physical body with which they came into contact, but his astral body, his spiritual body. He may have come, may have been guiding and meeting and advising them, but not with that physical body. And because people do not understand this philosophy, they think that he came to them physically.

Q. Master, in the writings of Paul in the New Testament, he says somewhere that he has had an experience where he could not tell whether it was in the body or out of the body.*

A. Actually, when you have such visions, such experiences, you cannot say whether you are having them outside or inside. These visions become so much part and parcel of you that you do not know whether you are seeing the Master within or outside. The same thing happens to every disciple even now. We often say: 'I saw the Master here, I saw the Master there.' Actually, it is all inside. It is the astral form of the Master, not the physical form. But people do not understand this spiritual philosophy, so they try to explain to us that he appeared in the physical body. But I do not think he would take up that physical body again after he had left it. He must have been so happy to have left it.

I will discuss it with you from *Saint John*. He prayed to the Father: Father, I looked after these sheep as long as I was with them. Since I am leaving them, take care of them now.† Why should he pray to the Father like that if he knew that he would come back to them again? That shows that he never came back to the flesh and that he had no intention of doing so. Why should he? Where was the necessity for it, when he could guide them spiritually from within?

* *2 Corinthians* 12:2–6.

† *John* 17:6–26.

Q. So then, there is the story of doubting Thomas, when the apostle Thomas put his hand into the sword wounds of Christ, and that was after the resurrection. So that would just be a myth?

A. It may be, or he may have had a vision of him. That is what I am trying to explain. When you see the astral form of the Master, actually he looks as if he is physically moving about.

Q. Oh, but you could actually have felt it—possibly?

A. You would feel that you had been talking to him, had kissed him, had met him, but actually you would have done nothing. It would all have been the manifestation of the Shabd.

Q. But Jesus said: Bring your hand and put it in the wound.

A. It may have been inside. After all, nobody took down every word that Christ said.

Q. Is it possible, Maharaj Ji, for a Master to guide or take care of the disciple from the astral world? Supposing the Master has left the mortal frame, can he continue to guide the destinies of the disciples from the astral plane?

A. He will definitely guide those whom he has initiated. Even if he has left the physical body, he will be guiding them from within, just as he had been guiding them from outside. But actually that would be in his astral form. And it would only be for those disciples whom he had initiated, who had come into contact with him. Those who had never seen him, never been initiated by him, had never come into contact with him, he would not do anything for those persons.

Q. Then where is the necessity of passing on responsibility to the successor of the Master? Is that so that he can inculcate the disciple's looking for the astral guidance?

A. The successor does nothing for those initiated souls. It is not the duty of the successors to take care of the souls at all. They can only give the initiates their outside guidance, or help them by creating love and faith in the disciples for their Master. They do not want to transfer their love from that Master—to uproot them and try to change that love to be for themselves. But you see, the successors automatically become one with their predecessors.

Q. So why is it that we cannot have initiation of disciples after he has died?

A. He will not initiate anybody after he has left the physical body.

Q. No initiation from the astral body?

A. No, that is what Christ said, that those who have seen me and those who believe in me, I will only raise those people on the last day *(John 6:40)*. He mentioned those two fundamental things. So the word 'seeing' is very important. 'Seeing' means physically present in this universe, in this world at the same time—the opportunity to see.

Q. Do you think there is any spiritual significance in the gospel stories of the disciples meeting Christ after he was supposed to have risen from the dead? Or do you think that is just a — ?

A. I think they must have had some visions of him after his death. You see, those writers could not understand how the disciples had met Christ after his crucifixion, because the gospels were not written by the people who had seen him. His direct disciples saw Christ after the crucifixion, and they must have seen the spiritual body of Christ within or even outside—not the physical body. That had been crucified. The body which Christ is referring to is that body of which, unless you eat its flesh and drink its blood, you cannot be part of me and I cannot be part of you.* That is the spiritual body.

So they must have had a vision of Christ after his death. And disciples definitely have visions, spiritual experiences about the Master, after his death, because they are so unbalanced at that time, so shaken by the physical departure of their Master, that they do not find anything to hold on to, because they are so much attached to the physical form. So just to relax them and keep them straight on the path, the Master does shower that grace and they do see the Master within sometimes, in his spiritual body. I think that is what those disciples were trying to tell of, when they said we have seen Christ after his crucifixion *(28:9–11)*.

But the writers who wrote about it so many years after the experience of the disciples, misunderstood what was meant. They probably understood that the disciples had seen the physical form of Christ. Because by that time, the teachings

* *John* 6:51–59.

had degenerated and were not experienced. Experience finished along with the direct disciples of Christ. Only the stories were circulated, and they just wrote down the stories. If those people had written who had actually had spiritual experiences, or had seen the spiritual form of Christ, they would have rightly described it. But not when it had been circulated from mouth to mouth, from generation to generation, would they have been able to understand all that truth. So that is why there is such a misunderstanding.

Q. Maharaj Ji, once I read in *Spiritual Gems* that the Great Master told a Christian satsangi that he could meet his long-departed Master, namely Jesus Christ, when he was able to go to the higher lands, and that he could then even speak to him. And on the other hand, I also read, and you told us, that if a Master departs from this physical plane, his individual soul merges back suddenly into the ocean of the Father. But how can it be that a Master, say Jesus Christ, can be merged in the Father and also stay in his spiritual individuality in the realms between the earth and Sach Khand?

A. That form which you see of Christ, or of any other saint, is the Word personified, it is from the Word, the light and sound. But because you have the intention and desire to see him, so if at all you are to see him, it will be Shabd personified—it will be out of the Shabd. It is not that Christ will get up in the same physical body from somewhere in the world and come before you. The Word will take the form of Christ and you will see him as he was in the outside physical world. And you will be happy that you have seen him. Some people are so devoted to those past Masters that they are not satisfied unless they see them. So actually it is the Word which is presented before them in that form. And the Word is always one, whether it is merged into the Father or separate from him.

Q. Maharaj Ji, could you please tell us the gist of the teachings of Christ and all the saints?

A. The teachings contain the same subject matter—a little variation here and there, but always the same in principle. All mystics have the same teachings to share with us. Their approach and the words they use may be different, but the teachings are always the same. If the Lord is one, he is within every one of us, and we have to search for him within—naturally the path leading to him cannot be different for different people. It has got to be the same. Those who travel on that path within have to speak the same language—and that does not pertain to the language of this world. There is not much else to discuss.

First, there is the necessity for going back to the Father. Then to believe that he is one and he is everlasting, not subject to birth and death; and there is no question of caste, creed or religion attached to him. The Lord is within every one of us. You do not have to go to a forest or temple or search through books in order to find him. You have to search for him and find him within yourself.

The obstacle between us and the Father is our own ego, our mind. Unless we eliminate the ego, the soul can never shine and can never become one with the Being, one with the Father. How to eliminate ego? For that, we have to seek the company of mystics, the Masters, and they will show us the path or the technique of how to worship the Father within our body—how to search for the Father within our body and then how to eliminate that ego from within ourself.

What will the Master teach us? He will attach us to the sound and light within, to that Shabd, the divine melody within. And when we get a taste for that, automatically our mind will become detached from all the senses. Only attachment can create detachment within us. So when we are attached to that sound, to that divine melody within, we will automatically be detached from the senses. When, with the help of attachment to that divine melody, we come to Trikuti, our soul will get released from the mind. The mind will be happy in its home and the soul is then free to go back to its own home. That is when all coverings will be removed from the soul, and the soul shines and becomes whole. Then it becomes worthy to be one with the Father, as Christ has also indicated.

Whenever people worship the Father, whether they go to a synagogue, a temple or a church, they always give something. While worshipping, some people give money, some give just flowers, some give gold or silver or clothes, and in India there is a custom of giving coconuts. There is no necessity for giving anything for the worship of the Father. All this is nothing but exploitation by the priests. All we have to do is to surrender our self to the Father—unconditionally surrender to the will of the Father. In whatever way he keeps us, we should, with faith and devotion, remain attached to the sound and light within.

Unless we remain in the will of the Father, unless we worship the Father for the sake of the Father, we will never be able to become one with the Father. So we should not worship the Father to fulfil our worldly desires or to achieve worldly ambitions. That is not at all the purpose of worshipping the Father. If we worship with that idea, then we will have to come back to this creation again and again. So we must worship the Father for the Father's sake. We must have real love for the Father if we want to go back to the Father.

The method that is generally adopted in our endeavour to go back to the Father or to purify our mind is to go on pilgrimages to various holy places in this world—to holy rivers or tanks, to bathe in that holy water—and other outward practices. People think that probably all their sins, all their karma, will be washed away. That is absolutely wrong. Then they think that by reading the scriptures they will be able to go back to the Father. Some try to leave their kith and kin and run away to the forests, to hide themselves from the realities of life by living in the forests, mountains, caves or some secluded place. That is nothing but self-deception, because all that we need in this world we will also need even if we go to the forests. These needs are food, clothing, and shelter. And these three needs are such that no matter which corner of the world we may go to, they will always bother us and we will always have to fulfil these needs. So what is the sense in leaving our home and our kith and kin?

So all types of rituals and ceremonies are condemned. There is only one way to purify our mind and that is to attach ourself to the Holy Spirit, which is within every one of us irrespective of caste, creed, religion or country. There is no question of caste or creed arising here. The main emphasis is on devotion to his Name, to be one-pointed towards our spiritual practice. In order to succeed we should take our mind out of all rituals and ceremonies, as they are meaningless things. Another point to emphasize is that this body is the temple of the living God. Whatever we have to do, we have to do within our body under the guidance of a living Master. We do not have to search for anything at all outside.

All the mystics and saints have this same message to give. This is just a gist of the teachings. One can write many volumes to explain all this, or one can say it in a few words. Ultimately it is the same thing.

# Conclusion

I have been discussing with you Christ's teachings according to the *Gospel of Saint Matthew*. As I was trying to explain, the teachings of all the mystics and saints, wherever or whenever they may have come, are the same. No saint brings any new teachings or tries to give us any short cut. As Christ says: "My doctrine is not mine, but his that sent me" *(John 7:16)*. So they are as old as the creation and the Father himself. As I read to you, he says not a word can be added or eliminated from the teachings *(5:18)*. So the teachings of all mystics of all ages are always the same. They share the same experience, the same spiritual truths with us. But after a saint leaves the body, we forget the real teachings and we lose the essence of his teachings. We try to hang on to rituals and ceremonies, and forget the real spiritual truths. Then saints again come at some other place, at some other time, and try to revive in us the same old teachings.

So Christ was trying to tell us that the Lord is to be found nowhere outside; he is within every one of us. But we cannot see that Creator because we have to repent for the karmas or sins which we have collected during our past lives. Unless we are able to repent for them, though the Creator is within every one of us, we will not be able to realize him within.

And how should we repent? Christ told us: "If therefore thine eye be single, thy whole body shall be full of light" *(6:22)*. We have to withdraw our consciousness back to the eye centre, also called the single eye or third eye, and be in touch with the Holy Spirit, the divine melody within ourself, and see that light. With the help of the sound, we have to know the direction of our home within; and with the help of the light, we have to follow the path, and realize and reach our destination. Because all these sins, our karmas, are related to our mind, and the soul has taken association with the mind, so whatever the mind does, being the slave of the senses, the soul also has to bear the consequences. That is why we are always shifting from house to house, from body to body, from one form to another. So Christ is trying to impress upon us that unless we are able to clear all those karmas, wash off all those sins, shed all this load from the mind and soul, the soul will never be able to go back to the Father.

Christ says that when we are in touch with the Holy Spirit within, are one with the light within, then our mind becomes pure and goes back to its own source. And the moment it becomes pure, the soul gets release from it and can go back to the Father. Then only can we become whole and free.

Therefore every saint, every mystic, has the same spiritual truths to tell us. If we build our treasure in the world, then we come back to the world. If we build our treasure in heaven, we go back to heaven. And how do we build our treasure in the world? By our attachment to worldly faces, to our relations, and our love of worldly objects.

That is why he said: "A man's foes shall be they of his own household" *(10:36).* He says, who is your real friend? He who always thinks of your betterment. You consider these friends and relations the be-all and end-all of everything in this world, but Christ says that they are actually your enemies, your foes, because they involve you so much in their own love and attachment that you forget the real object of your having this human form. You forget your destination and you never try to tread that spiritual path. Day and night you are attached to them and are either running about for them or they for you. And this attachment has made you blind to the Creator who is within you.

That is why he says these relations are not our real friends—actually they are our foes, they are responsible for pulling us down to their level all the time. We have to stay with them to discharge our duties and responsibilities; we must respect our mother and father and do our worldly duty in whatever situation the Lord has placed us; but while doing so, we are not to be so much involved in them that we forget the spiritual path and our destination and have absolutely no time to go back to the Father or to realize the Lord within ourself. Because, as he said, a tree is judged by its fruit *(3:10, 7:20).* So, after having had this human form, we will be judged by our fruit, or the meditation which builds that treasure in heaven. And for that, we have to attach ourselves to the Holy Spirit, and be one with the light and sound.

So he said: "I have not come to create peace in this world. I have come with a sword" *(10:34).* You are so much attached to one another that these attachments are always pulling you to each other's level. So he says, I have come so that with the help of that Holy Spirit, you should be detached from one another, for otherwise you will never be able to go back to the Father.

And how do we detach ourselves? First we have to contact a living Master who will baptize or initiate us into the method, the technique of how to withdraw our soul current up to the eye centre and attach ourselves to the Holy Spirit within. And that attachment will automatically help us in detaching ourselves from everything in this world. Then we are building our treasure in heaven. We go where our heart is. If it is with the treasure which we have built in heaven, we go to heaven; if it is with the treasure which we have built in the world, we come back to the world. Therefore, he says, we must detach ourself from everybody and attach ourself to the Holy Spirit within ourself. That alone will take us back to the Father.

# Glossary

**chaurasi** Eighty-four; refers to the eighty-four lakh (8,400,000) categories of life-forms the soul may assume in the cycle of transmigration.

**Dharam Rai** The judge *(rai)* of righteousness *(dharam)*, a name for Kal, the lord of death, who metes out perfect justice by the law of karma.

**dhyan** Contemplation; part of the spiritual practice taught by the saints, *dhyan* holds the attention within.

**haumaiŋ** I, me, I-ness; ego, which is the great barrier of mind between the soul and the Lord.

**Kal** The universal mind, the negative power (in contrast to Dayal, the positive power), Kal is the ruler of the three impermanent realms—the physical, astral and causal worlds. Kal is dependent for all power on the Supreme Being.

**karma** Action; the law of action and reaction, cause and effect, reaping what one sows. Karma is of three types: *pralabdh,* the fate or destiny one experiences in the present life; *kriyaman,* the debits and credits one creates in the present life, to be settled in future lives; *sinchit,* the store of unremitted karma. Until all three are fully settled, the soul cannot return to its source, the Lord.

**manmukh** One whose face *(mukh)* is turned towards the mind *(man)*, the world; a lover of the world, a self-willed person dominated by ego.

**maya** That which comes and goes; impermanent, transient; illusion; the physical, astral and causal worlds.

**Nam** *(naam)*, the Name, also known as the Word *(shabd)*; the dynamic power of God that creates, enlivens and sustains the universe, and through which the soul returns to its source. It manifests within each being as sound and light.

**Sach Khand** True and eternal *(sach)* realm or region *(khand)*, the realm of pure spirit, the true home of the soul, the final stage on the inner journey of the soul.

**Sant Mat** The teachings or path *(mat)* of the saints *(sant)*.

**satsang** The company *(sang)* of the true (*sat*); a saint's company or discourses.

**satsangi** An associate *(sangi)* of the true *(sat)*; a disciple.

**seva** Selfless service, service rendered with no desire for acknowledgment or reward.

**Shabd** Word, also known as the Name *(naam)*; the dynamic power of God that creates, enlivens and sustains the universe, and through which the soul returns to its source. It manifests within each being as sound and light.

**simran** Repetition, remembrance; part of the spiritual practice taught by the saints, simran is the process by which the attention is concentrated at the eye centre.

**Soami Ji** Seth Shiv Dayal Singh of Agra, a nineteenth-century saint who taught the path of Shabd or Word; he summed up his teachings in *Sar Bachan Prose* and *Sar Bachan Poetry*. His disciple and successor, Baba Jaimal Singh, was the first Master to settle at the place now known as Dera Baba Jaimal Singh, the Radha Soami colony near Beas, Punjab.

**Trikuti** The causal region, the second stage on the inner journey described by the saints.

# Subject Index

# Index of Verses From the Bible

(page numbers refer to commentary on the verses)

## From St. Matthew

## OTHER VERSES FROM THE BIBLE

# Addresses for Information and Books

## INDIAN SUB-CONTINENT

*INDIA*
The Secretary
Radha Soami Satsang Beas
Dera Baba Jaimal Singh
Punjab 143204

*NEPAL*
Mr Dal Bahadur Shreshta
Radha Soami Satsang Beas
P. O. Box 1646, Sundarighat,
Kirtipuri, Kathmandu

*PAKISTAN*
Dr Bhagwandas M. Pathai
Resham Gali, Larkana, Sindh

*SRI LANKA*
Mr D. H. Jiwat
c/o Geekay Ltd.
33 Bankshall Street, Colombo 11

## SOUTHEAST ASIA

*Representative for other countries of Far East Asia:*

Mrs Cami Moss
Radha Soami Satsang Beas, Hostel 6
Dera Baba Jaimal Singh
Punjab 143204, India

*MALAYSIA*
Mr Selvarajoo Pragasam
No. 15 Jalan SL 10/4,
Bandar Sg. Long,
43000 Kajang

*THAILAND*
Mr Harmahinder Singh Sethi
58/32 Rachdapitsek Road, Soi 16
Thapra, Bangkok Yai 10600

*INDONESIA*
Mr Ramesh Sadarangani
Jalan Pasir Putih IV/25, Block E 4
Ancol Timur, Jakarta Utara 14430

*PHILIPPINES*
Mr Kay Sham
Radha Soami Satsang Beas
#1268 General Luna Street
Paco, Manila

*SINGAPORE*
Mrs Asha Melwani
Radha Soami Satsang Beas
19 Amber Road
Singapore 439868

## ASIA PACIFIC

*AUSTRALIA*
Mr Pradeep Raniga
6 Westminster Avenue
Bulleen, Victoria 3105

*NEW ZEALAND*
Mr Tony Waddicor
Science of the Soul Study Centre
P. O. Box 5331, Auckland

*GUAM*
Mrs Hoori M. Sadhwani
115 Alupang Cove
241 Condo Lane,
Tamuning 96911

*HONG KONG*
Mr Manoj Sabnani
T.S.T., P.O. Box 90745
Kowloon

*JAPAN*
Mr Jani G. Mohinani
Radha Soami Satsang Beas
1-2-18 Nakajimadori
Aotani, Chuo-Ku
Kobe 651-0052

*SOUTH KOREA*
Dr Moon Jin Hee
#2011 Jung San 4RI Buron-Myun
Won Ju-City
Gang Won Do
Korea 220-814

*TAIWAN, R.O.C.*
Mr Larry Teckchand Nanwani
P. O. Box 68-1414
Taipei

## NORTH AMERICA

*CANADA*
Mr John Abel
#701-1012 Beach Avenue
Vancouver, B.C. V6E 1T7

Mrs Meena Khanna
149 Elton Park Road
Oakville, Ontario L6J 4C2

*UNITED STATES*
Dr Eugene Ivash
4701 Shadow Lane
Austin, TX 78731-5334

Dr Vincent P. Savarese
3507 Saint Elizabeth Road
Glendale, CA 91206-1227

Dr John Templer
114 Verdier Road
Beaufort, SC 29902-5440

Dr Frank E. Vogel
71 Old Farm Road
Concord, MA 01742

Science of the Soul Study Center
2415 Washington Street
Petaluma, CA 94954

Science of the Soul Study Center
4115 Gillespie Street
Fayetteville, NC 28306-9053

## CARIBBEAN

*Representative for the Caribbean, Suriname and Guyana:*

Mr Sean Finnigan
P. O. Box 2314
Port-au-Prince, Haiti, W. I.

*BARBADOS*
Mr Deepak Nebhani
Radha Soami Satsang Beas
Lot No. 10, 5th Avenue
Belleville, St. Michael
Barbados, W. I.

*CURACAO*
Mrs Komal Lachman Vasandani
P. O. Box 426, Curacao, N. A.

*GUYANA*
Mrs Rajni B. Manglani
A-80 Eping Avenue,
Bel Air Park,
Georgetown, Guyana

*JAMAICA*
Mrs Shammi Khiani
P. O. Box 22
Montego Bay, Jamaica, W. I.

*ST. MAARTEN*
Mrs Kanchan Mahbubani
Court of Jewels, 47 Front Street
P. O. Box 512
Phillipsburg, St. Maarten, N. A.

*SURINAME*
Mr Murli J. Thani
Hoekstrastraat #30
P. O. Box 8309
Paramaribo, Suriname

*TRINIDAD*
Mrs Anganie Chatlani
8A Saddle Road, Maraval
Trinidad, W. I.

## CENTRAL AMERICA

*BELIZE*
Mrs Chand Babani
5789 Goldson Avenue, Belize City

*MEXICO*
Mr Jorge Angel Santana
Jacarandas #30
FTO. Azaleas Recidencial
Zapopan 45090

*PANAMA*
Mr Pritam Tewaney
RSSB - Panama
P. O. Box 6-8318
El Dorado, Panama City

## SOUTH AMERICA

*Representative for other countries of South America (Argentina, Brazil, Chile):*

Mr Hiro W. Balani
P.O. Box 486,
Malaga 29012, Spain

*COLOMBIA*
Mrs Emma Orozco
P. O. Box 49744, Medellin

*ECUADOR*
Dr Fernando Flores Villalva
Calle de la Grulla, lote 11
Urbanizacion Valle 3 - Cumbaya
Quito

*PERU*
Mr Carlos Fitts
P. O. Box 18-06-58, Lima 18

*VENEZUELA*
Mr José Antonio Peñaherrera
Radha Soami Satsang Beas
Apartado Postal 63-436, Chacaito,
Caracas Miranda 1016

## EUROPE

*AUSTRIA*
Mr Hansjorg Hammerer
Sezenweingasse 10
Salzburg A-5020

*BELGIUM*
Mr Piet J. E. Vosters
Lindekensstraat 39 Box 4
Turnhout 2300

*BULGARIA*
Mr Emilio Saev
Radha Soami Satsang Beas
P. O. Box 39, Bourgas

*CYPRUS*
Mr Heraclis Achilleos
P. O. Box 29077
Nicosia 1035

*CZECH REPUBLIC*
Mr Vladimir Skalsky
Maratkova 916
142 00 Prague 412

*DENMARK*
Mr Tony Sharma
Sven Dalsgaardsvej 33
DK-7430 Ikast

*FINLAND*
Ms. Ritta Anneli Wingfield
Hansinkatu 12 C 33
01400 Vantaa near Helsinki

*FRANCE*
Ct. Pierre de Proyart
7 Quai Voltaire, Paris 75007

*GERMANY*
Mr Rudolf Walberg
P. O. Box 1544
D-65800 Bad Soden / Taunus

*GIBRALTAR*
Mr Sunder Mahtani
Radha Soami Satsang Beas
Flat 401 Ocean Heights, 4th Floor
Queensway

*GREECE*
Mrs Eleftheria Tsolaki
14-20 Korizi St.
Alimos 17455, Athens

*ITALY*
Mrs Wilma Salvatori Torri
Via Bacchiglione 3
00199 Rome

*THE NETHERLANDS (HOLLAND)*
Mr Henk Keuning
Kleizuwe 2
Vreeland 3633 AE

*NORWAY*
Mr Sohan Singh Mercy
St. Halvardsgt. 6
N-3015 Drammen

*POLAND*
Mr Vinod Sharma
UL. 1go Sierpien 36 B M-100
PL-02-134, Warsaw

*PORTUGAL*
Mrs Sharda Lodhia
Rua Quinta Das Palmeiras, Lote 68
11° andar C, Oeiras 2780-145

*ROMANIA*
Mrs Carmen Cismas
Str. Hipodrom
BL. A10, Apt.25
Braila-6100 RO

*SLOVENIA*
Mr Marko Bedina
Brezje pri Trzicu 68
4290 Trzic

*SPAIN*
Mr J. W. Balani
Calle Panorama no. 15
Cerrado de Calderon
Malaga 29018

*SWEDEN*
Mr Lennart Zachen
Norra Sonnarpsvägen 29
S-286 72 Asljunga

*SWITZERLAND*
Mr Sebastian Zust-Bischof
Weissenrainstrasse 48
CH 8707 Uetikon am See (ZH)

*UNITED KINGDOM*
Mr Narinder Singh Johal
Haynes Park Estate
Haynes, Bedford MK45 3BL

Mrs Flora E. Wood
Haynes Park Estate
Haynes, Bedford MK45 3BL

## AFRICA

*BENIN*
Mr Jaikumar T. Vaswani
01 Boite Postale 951,
Recette Principale, Cotonou

*BOTSWANA*
Dr Krishan Lal Bhateja
P. O. Box 402539
Gaborone

*GHANA*
Mr Murli Chatani
Radha Soami Satsang Beas
P. O. Box 3976, Accra

*IVORY COAST*
Mr Konan N'Dri
08 Boite Postale 569
Abidjan 08

*KENYA*
Mr Surinder Singh Ghir
P. O. Box 15134,
Langata 00509, Nairobi

*LESOTHO*
Mr Sello Wilson Moseme
P. O. Box 750
Leribe 300

*LIBYA (G.S.P.L.A.J.)*
Mr Roshan Lal
P.O. Box 38930
Bani Walid

*MAURITIUS*
Mrs Doolaree Nuckcheddy
17 Avenue Le Conte De Lisle
Quatre Bornes

*NAMIBIA*
Mrs Jennifer Mary Carvill
P. O. Box 1258
Swakopmund 9000

*NIGERIA*
Mr Nanik N. Balani
P.O. Box 10407, Lagos

*RÉUNION*
Ms Danielle Hoareau
23 Rue Juiliette Dodu
97400 St. Denis

*SIERRA LEONE*
Mr Kishore S. Mahboobani
P. O. Box 369, Freetown

*SOUTH AFRICA*
Radha Soami Satsang Beas
14-16 Hope Street
Gardens Cape Town
Waterfront 8002

Mr Gordon Clive Wilson
P. O. Box 47182
Greyville 4023

Mr Sam Busa
P. O. Box 41355, Craighall 2024

*SWAZILAND*
Mr Peter Dunseith
P. O. Box 423, Mbabane

*TANZANIA*
Mr Surinder Singh Oshan
P.O. Box 6984
Dar-Es-Salaam

*UGANDA*
Mr Sylvester Kakooza
Radha Soami Satsang Beas
P. O. Box 31381
Kampala

*ZAMBIA*
Mr Chrispin Lwali
P. O. Box 12094
Nchanga, North Township
Chingola, Lusaka

*ZIMBABWE*
Mrs Dorothy Roodt
P. O. Box 7095
Harare

## MIDDLE EAST

*BAHRAIN*
Mr Mangat Rai Rudra
Flat No. 12 Building No. 1694
Road No. 627, Block 306
Manama

*ISRAEL*
Mr Michael Yaniv
Moshav Sde Nitzan 59, I1
D.N. Hanegev 85470

*KUWAIT*
Mr Vijay Kumar
P. O. Box 1913
13020 Safat

*U.A.E.*
Mr Mohanlal Badlani
R.S.S.B., P.O. Box 32049
Dubai

# Books on this Science

**SOAMI JI MAHARAJ**

*Sar Bachan Prose*
*Sar Bachan Poetry (Selections)*

**BABA JAIMAL SINGH**

*Spiritual Letters* (to Hazur Maharaj Sawan Singh: 1896-1903)

**MAHARAJ SAWAN SINGH**

*The Dawn of Light* (letters to Western disciples: 1911-1934)
*Discourses on Sant Mat*
*My Submission* (introduction to *Philosophy of the Masters*)
*Philosophy of the Masters* (*Gurmat Sidhant*), in 5 volumes
(an encyclopedia on the teachings of the Saints)
*Spiritual Gems* (letters to Western disciples: 1919-1948)
*Tales of the Mystic East* (as narrated in satsangs)

**MAHARAJ JAGAT SINGH**

*The Science of the Soul* (discourses and letters: 1948-1951)

**MAHARAJ CHARAN SINGH**

*Die to Live* (answers to questions on meditation)
*Divine Light* (discourses and letters: 1959-1964)
*Light on Saint John*
*Light on Saint Matthew*
*Light on Sant Mat* (discourses and letters: 1952-1958)
*The Master Answers* (to audiences in America: 1964)
*The Path* (first part of *Divine Light*)
*Quest for Light* (letters: 1965-1971)
*Spiritual Discourses,* in 2 volumes
*Spiritual Heritage* (from tape-recorded talks)
*Thus Saith the Master* (to audiences in America: 1970)

**BOOKS ABOUT THE MASTERS**

*Call of the Great Master*—Diwan Daryai Lal Kapur
*Heaven on Earth*—Diwan Daryai Lal Kapur
*Treasure Beyond Measure*—Shanti Sethi
*With a Great Master in India*—Julian P. Johnson
*With the Three Masters,* in 3 volumes—from the diary of Rai Sahib Munshi Ram

**BOOKS ON SANT MAT IN GENERAL**

*A Spiritual Primer*—Hector Esponda
*The Holy Name: Mysticism in Judaism*—Miriam Caravella
*Honest Living: A Means to an End*—M. F. Singh
*In Search of the Way*—Flora E. Wood
*The Inner Voice*—Colonel C. W. Sanders
*Liberation of the Soul*—J. Stanley White
*Life is Fair: The Law of Cause and Effect*—Brian Hines
*Message Divine*—Shanti Sethi
*The Mystic Philosophy of Sant Mat*—Peter Fripp
*Mysticism, The Spiritual Path,* in 2 volumes—Lekh Raj Puri
*The Path of the Masters*—Julian P. Johnson
*Radha Soami Teachings*—Lekh Raj Puri
*A Soul's Safari*—Netta Pfeifer
*Yoga and the Bible*—Joseph Leeming

**MYSTICS OF THE EAST SERIES**

*Bulleh Shah*—J. R. Puri and T.R. Shangari
*Dadu, The Compassionate Mystic*—K. N. Upadhyaya
*Dariya Sahib, Saint of Bihar*—K. N. Upadhyaya
*Guru Nanak, His Mystic Teachings*—J. R. Puri
*Guru Ravidas, Life and Teachings*—K. N. Upadhyaya
*Kabir, The Great Mystic*—Isaac A. Ezekiel
*Kabir, The Weaver of God's Name*—V. K. Sethi
*Mira, The Divine Lover*—V. K. Sethi
*Saint Namdev*—J. R. Puri and V. K. Sethi
*Saint Paltu*—Isaac A. Ezekiel
*Sarmad, Jewish Saint of India*—Isaac A. Ezekiel
*Sultan Bahu*—J. R. Puri and K. S. Khak
*Tukaram, Saint of Maharashtra*—C. Rajwade
*Tulsi Sahib, Saint of Hathras*—J. R. Puri and V. K. Sethi